IRON ROAD

Some other books by P. J. G. Ransom

Railways Revived: an account of preserved steam railways

The Archaeology of Railways

Your Book of Steam Railway Preservation

The Archaeology of the Transport Revolution 1750–1850

Scottish Steam Today

The Victorian Railway and How it Evolved

Narrow Gauge Steam: Its origins and world-wide development

The Mont Cenis Fell Railway

Locomotion: Two Centuries of Train Travel (anthology)

Snow, Flood and Tempest: Railways and Natural Disasters

Loch Lomond and The Trossachs in History and Legend

The Golden Age: North British Atlantic no. 872 *Auld Reekie*, one of the first batch of these locomotives built in 1906, heads over the Forth Bridge with an express from Edinburgh to Aberdeen. Rail transport was as yet unchallenged by road or air.
(photograph by Valentine & Sons Ltd, Dundee, from the series *Bonnie Scotland*, published by John Leng & Co. Ltd, Dundee & London, 1907)

IRON ROAD

THE RAILWAY IN SCOTLAND

P. J. G. RANSOM

BIRLINN

This edition published in 2007 by
Birlinn Limited
West Newington House
10 Newington Road
Edinburgh EH9 1QS

www.birlinn.co.uk

Hardback
ISBN13: 978 1 84158 366 2
ISBN10: 1 84158 366 9

Paperback
ISBN 13: 978 1 84158 728 8
ISBN 10: 1 84158 728 1

British Library Cataloguing-in-Publication Data
A Catalogue record for this book is available from the British Library

Typeset by Maria Streiter
Printed and bound in Slovenia

CONTENTS

The Golden Age: Caledonian Railway 4-6-0 *Cardean* prepares to leave Glasgow Central with the 2 p.m. 'Corridor' for London, one day in 1908. Locomotive, station and train were alike famous. (National Railway Museum / Science & Society Picture Library)

ACKNOWLEDGEMENTS

I am most grateful for assistance rendered by: Paul Adair (Perth Museum and Art Gallery); Philip Atkins (National Railway Museum); Gwydion Ball; John Burnie; Elizabeth Culver (The Royal Mail Archive); Robert Forsythe; Niall Ferguson; Kevin Groves (Network Rail); Susie Haywood (Network Rail); John Litten (Science Museum); Allan McLean (Virgin Trains); Pamela McTaggart (SPT); Don Martin; Colin Mountford; Bill Roberton; Keith Verden Anderson; Russell Wear; Michael Wrottesley; John Yellowlees (First ScotRail); and the staffs of: Dundee Central Library; National Archives of Scotland; National Galleries of Scotland; National Library of Scotland; National Railway Museum; Scottish Poetry Library; William Patrick Library, Kirkintilloch (East Dunbartonshire Council).

My wife Elisabeth, my sons Robert and Hugh, and my agent Duncan McAra have been as supportive as ever. I have a particular debt of gratitude to my publishers for their patience in awaiting delivery of a manuscript much delayed.

Every effort has been made to trace copyright holders of pictures reproduced and material quoted. Apologies are offered to any who may have been missed.

The modern railway: ScotRail Turbostar from Inverness to Glasgow passes English, Welsh & Scottish class 66 with freight from Mossend to Laurencekirk, near Blackford between Stirling and Perth. (Bill Roberton)

PROLOGUE

A nation's railways reflect national characteristics. Verve and dash and efficiency in France, solidness and efficiency in Germany, respect for an *ancien régime* in India where British practices still hold good. In England, perhaps, the relevant characteristics are muddling through, or else letting others do better what one first thought of oneself!

Scotland is a country of contrasts in a small space. The contrasts are both natural and cultural. Consider Lowland and Highland. Consider Edinburgh and Glasgow. And Cockburnspath is as different from Kyle of Lochalsh as Kent from Connemara. Contrasts too are the principal characteristic of its railways.

In some parts of Scotland, such as the Borders, railways are largely things of the past. They disappeared in father's or grandfather's day and are now represented mostly by disused viaducts and station buildings adapted to other purposes. One may – and the author recently did – descend the flight of steps through the handsomely restored station building at Melrose during the dog's pre-breakfast walk, and imagine oneself just arrived by Pullman sleeping car, overnight from St Pancras: but in reality all that lies beyond the deserted platform at the top of the steps is a new main road with motor cars rushing by.

In other parts of Scotland, however, railways are very much things of the present. Stand among the crowds on the platform at Partick in the evening rush hour: every couple of minutes modern electric trains, clean and comfortable and full of homegoing Glasgow commuters, swish to a halt. Passengers alight, more passengers board, and the train heads onward to be replaced soon after by the next. This, as much as the main road at Melrose, is reality. In the region extending from Ayr to Airdrie, and from Lanark to Balloch, (within the confines, that is, of what was until recently Strathclyde Passenger Transport Executive), the railway system is the apotheosis of a modern, efficient, big-city suburban network. It carries around 50 million passengers a year,[1] and is said to be the busiest such system in Britain outside London.

Yet further down the line from Partick, on their way to Balloch or Helensburgh, some of those trains will be using tracks that are used also, during the course of its journey, by the train that makes the most remarkable, perhaps the most romantic, of all British train journeys: the Fort William sleeper. Setting out in the evening from Euston, one of the busiest and most famous of London termini, before it reaches its destination the following morning it will have travelled through the wildest and most mountainous country traversed by any railway in Britain. In the middle of that wild country it calls (by request) at what is famously the highest station on the main

British railway network – Corrour, 1,327 feet above sea level[2] – and probably also the most isolated, for no public road comes within seven miles of it.

Yet paradoxically that isolation is far from meaning that Corrour is little used – rather, in an era when access to open country is valued as never before, it is a popular destination providing among other things the most practicable approach to half a dozen Munros – hills, that is, over 3,000 feet high. Indeed in my experience travelling thither by the ordinary train service, the train took on something of the character of a ski train in Switzerland: at each of the little stations along the way – Tyndrum, Bridge of Orchy, Rannoch – more and more hardened hillwalkers piled in, only to pile out again at Corrour when the train could take them no higher. And on a sunny evening in June 2005, while waiting for the 18.28, which was the last train out southbound on a Saturday, I counted forty-five passengers, plus two dogs and a bicycle, all waiting to join the two-car diesel train, which, when it came in, was already well filled.

There have not always been such contrasts. For seventy or eighty years in the late nineteenth and early twentieth centuries, the whole trade and commerce of mainland Scotland was dependent upon a nationwide railway system. Towards the end of the period, few people can have remembered a time when it was not so: railways must then have seemed permanent. Trains were a familiar part of the daily scene in Castle Douglas and Hawick and Colinton and Fraserburgh and Craigellachie, just as they continue to be today in Dumfries and Linlithgow and Milngavie and Thurso and Crianlarich. In those days railways operated with an aura of confident prosperity. They were interwoven with daily life to an extent now forgotten. For example, in Ballater in 1914, people wanting the latest news

The railway in the city: Glasgow Central, Low Level. (Bill Roberton)

The railway in the hills: Corrour. (Author)

The railway in the country: Kingskettle, Fife. (Bill Roberton)

from the Front headed for the station to meet the train bringing the evening papers from Aberdeen; likewise, in Fort William, they met the afternoon train from Glasgow. Broadcasting by radio and television lay in the future. Passengers arriving in Glasgow from the Western Isles, and perhaps a little hesitant in English, found a notice on Queen Street Station written reassuringly in Gaelic to direct them to the enquiry office. Over a long period, the local train became a friend, familiar to those who used it – and to those who ran it too. The locomotive which for many years regularly hauled the trains on the branch line from Inverurie to Old Meldrum was, properly speaking, Great North of Scotland Railway locomotive no. 45A, a 4-4-0 built in 1866. To the staff still running her in the 1920s she was known as *Meldrum Meg*.

As recently as the early 1960s, people still congregated at Fort William station to meet the train. Elsewhere things had not changed much either. Alasdair Morgan MSP recalled, when addressing the Heritage Railway

Association at Boat of Garten in 2003, that he had as a young man worked in an Aberfeldy hotel. When fish was needed, the proprietor telephoned the fish merchant in Aberdeen in the morning. In the afternoon, Morgan drove to the station to collect the box of fish off the train. He pondered the reaction of a present-day courier company asked to provide a comparable service.

The fish box was presumably consigned as a 'to be called for' parcel, which staff would dispatch on the first available train from Aberdeen, and again at junctions where change of train was necessary – Perth and Ballinluig. Such a service was dependent on a widespread network of passenger trains, which then also carried quantities of parcels. Once the passengers deserted rail for road, the parcels service was scarcely viable – its final flowering was the Red Star service. By the mid-1960s the Aberfeldy branch train often comprised a new diesel locomotive, representing a substantial investment, hauling a single coach. It

The railway in the suburbs: Shettleson.
(Bill Roberton)

can scarcely have been economic, and the branch soon went the way of many others. Indeed the whole railway system might have seemed to be in terminal decline in the late 1960s, when a huge part of it was closed. But subsequently it has seen no closures since the 1980s, and latterly has been enjoying a period of modest and increasing expansion. In the financial year 2004–5 passenger journeys originating in Scotland approached 73 million, the highest figure since 1964[3] when the system was far more extensive.

In 2001 the main Scottish railway network extended to some 1,675 miles (2,696 km) out of a UK total of 10,187 miles (16,397 km); by way of comparison the Irish Republic had 1,006 miles (1,619 km) of railways, Denmark 1,272 miles (2,047 km) and Belgium 2,146 miles (3,454 km).[4] At the time of writing (early 2007) the main Scottish railway system has 1,700 miles of route (2,736 km) with 344 passenger stations.[5] Of these the most westerly is at Arisaig, the most northerly at Thurso. It includes five of the seven highest summits on the British railway system: Druimuachdar (1,484 ft), Corrour (1,350 ft) and Slochd (1,315 ft) are all higher than the highest summit south of the border, Ais Gill (1,167 ft), and those three, together with Tyndrum or County March (1,024 ft) and Beattock (1,015 ft), are all higher than Shap (915 ft). With a tendency evident for Scottish railways to go up and over mountain ranges, rather than tunnelling through them, it is less of a surprise than it might be to find that the longest tunnel in Scotland, without intermediate stations, burrows not beneath the hills but beneath the urban area between

The railway of the past: throughout mainland Scotland there are grass-grown roadbeds to show where once there was a railway. This was the Wanlockhead branch. (Bill Roberton)

Greenock West and Fort Matilda – Newton Street tunnel, 1 mile 350 yd.[6]

The Scottish railway system includes the longest bridge on the British network, the Tay Bridge at 2 miles 364 yd, and the highest, Ballochmyle where the track is 164 ft above the Water of Ayr. The Forth Bridge comes in with the longest spans, for two of its spans are 1,710 ft long.[7] Curiosities among bridges are at Paisley where Blackhall bridge has long since carried trains but was built as long ago as c.1810 as an aqueduct for the Paisley Canal, and at Struan between Perth and Inverness. Here a masonry viaduct was built with its central span carrying the single-track railway obliquely over a road, which is itself crossing the River Garry at this point by a stone bridge. The arrangement satisfied the demand of the Duke of Atholl of the day that a favourite view of falls in the river should not be spoilt.[8] The unusual effect is heightened further by the contrasting presence, alongside the masonry viaduct, of a separate girder bridge built later to carry the southbound track when the line was doubled.

So the contrasts characteristic of the railway system in Scotland extend both to place and to time. Contrasting topography of different localities is matched by the contrasting ups-and-downs of the fortunes of railways throughout their history. Technical developments, on the railway and elsewhere, have influenced, and perhaps even more been influenced by, developing notions of how the country and its railways should best be run. To find out how things have come to be the way they are it is necessary to begin, as one always should, at the beginning.

A waggonway formerly passed beneath one of the main streets of Alloa through this tunnel, its height and width notably restricted compared with later railway tunnels. (Author)

WAGGONWAYS: THE EARLIEST RAILWAYS IN SCOTLAND

The first, simple, railway in Scotland of which we have definite knowledge was built in 1722 between Tranent and Cockenzie harbour, on the Forth. This was long before steam powered transport became practicable: waggons of coal ran down to Cockenzie by gravity over wooden rails, and horses hauled the empties back up again. It may not have been the first such waggonway: there are tantalizingly obscure earlier references. As early as 1606 Thomas Tulloch was granted a patent by the Privy Council of Scotland of an 'ingyne' for 'commodious and aisie transporting of coillis', which may quite possibly have been some sort of railway.[1] Likewise, in 1646, James Allan of Stakis proposed 'ingynes for … transporting of coals to the sea', but what such 'ingynes' were, and whether any were built, remain uncertain.[2]

Railways with rails of wood, which both carried and guided the waggons that ran along them, had been known in the mines of central Europe since mediaeval times, and in England, on the surface, since about 1604 – first in Nottinghamshire, then more extensively on Tyneside and in Shropshire. But 1722 remains the first certain date for a railway in Scotland, and for it we are indebted to the York Buildings Company – that remarkable undertaking which, incorporated by Act of Parliament for the purpose of supplying London with water from the Thames, was exploited by financiers as a vehicle for speculation in Scottish estates forfeited by their owners in the aftermath of the 1715 rising. To the company's proprietors the limitation of liability provided by incorporation was the important feature. Limited liability companies, of the type that remain familiar, first appeared much later following legislation of the 1860s – so that promotion, construction and initial operation of the bulk of the railway system were achieved without their benefit.

In 1719 the York Buildings Company purchased the forfeited estate of the Earl of Winton. This included coal pits at Tranent and, a couple of miles to the north, salt pans at Preston and the harbour of Port Seaton (Cockenzie). These the company set about modernising: they installed one of the first atmospheric steam pumping engines in Scotland to drain the pits, and built the waggonway to carry the coal down to salt pans and harbour.[3]

Coal had then been dug in Scotland, in a small way, since the thirteenth century. Usually outcrops near the coast were exploited, so that ships could carry the coal away. Even in the early eighteenth century, there was little alternative for bulk materials such as coal. People in Scotland still travelled in the manner that they had always done, and transported their goods likewise. That meant by ship or boat wherever there was navigable water – coast, firths, sea lochs and inland lochs. On land, travel was usually on foot: most people went on their own feet; the wealthy rode on horseback. Goods were carried in creels by men, and women, and on pack horses – as late as the 1890s, pack horses were used to carry materials for construction of parts of the West Highland Railway where there was no road access.[4]

In the early eighteenth century, people and horses travelled along narrow horse roads – the beaten track. Horsedrawn sledges, two-wheeled carts and even four-wheeled waggons were all known, but their use was restricted by the inadequacy of the roads. The condition of roads has ever lagged behind the aspirations of users.

Attempts to remedy the situation had been made in the seventeenth century when Parliament gave powers to Justices of the Peace, and to Commissioners of Supply, to order roads to be repaired by local inhabitants: an Act of 1669 even specified details such as a road width of twenty feet. But these were powers, not duties; they had some limited effect in the Lowlands, virtually none in the Highlands. Real progress was only made with establishment, from the first half of the eighteenth century onwards, of turnpike trusts. These trusts, established by Act of Parliament with responsibility for main roads, were entitled to borrow funds for improvement and maintenance against the security of revenue from tolls paid by users. Such organisations were proof against neither misuse of funds or inadequacy of maintenance techniques: J. L. McAdam in the early nineteenth century did much to reform the trusts financially and improve their techniques physically; Thomas Telford did still more to improve the technology of road building. (Although as long as wheels had tyres of iron, road surfaces continued to be 'Macadamised',

that is, composed of water-bound loose material: 'tarmac' surfaces, bound by tar, came in only a century later to counteract the pothole-making tendencies of the pneumatic tyre.)

In the meantime, communications in the Highlands, where it was considered there would be insufficient traffic for turnpike trusts to be viable, had been much improved in the mid-eighteenth century by construction of military roads by Wade and Caulfield, and then even more in the early nineteenth century by the roads built by the Commissioners for Highland Roads and Bridges – Thomas Telford, engineer.

Hand-in-hand with these road improvements went increasing use of coaches – private coaches owned by the wealthy, and public coaches too. By the second decade of the nineteenth century highly efficient networks of stage coaches and mail coaches operated throughout the Lowlands, and extended into the Highlands too. As roads were improved, so coaches were accelerated: it was at this period that the quest for speed began.

Improved roads facilitated use of wheeled carts and waggons, but for the heaviest freight a development of greater importance was construction of canals. The Forth & Clyde Canal, built between 1768 and 1791, enabled coasting ships to reach Glasgow from the east coast, and indeed to cross from one coast to the other. The Monkland Canal, opened in part in 1772 and completely in 1793, carried Monklands coal into Glasgow, and the Edinburgh & Glasgow Union Canal, completed only in 1822 between Edinburgh and the Forth & Clyde Canal above Falkirk, placed the capital in direct waterway communication with the West. Meanwhile the Crinan Canal had provided west coast shipping with a short cut avoiding the Mull of Kintyre, and the Caledonian Canal through the

The course of the Tranent-Cockenzie waggonway heads towards Cockenzie over the battlefield of Prestonpans. In the distance, far left, is part of the installations of Cockenzie power station, destination in a later age of some of the earliest merry-go-round block coal trains. (Author)

Great Glen enabled some of the largest ships of the day to pass from the Atlantic to the North Sea while avoiding the dangerous passage round the north of Scotland.

The canals became important not just for carriage of goods, but also as a means of travel by passengers. Swift boats were pulled by galloping horses, and early steamships on the Caledonian Canal provided Inverness with mechanised transport at a period when inland travel throughout most of Britain was still horsedrawn.

Against this background, it would be pleasant to record that the York Buildings Company's activities had been an instant success, but this does not seem to have been the case: the company had invested heavily, but more heavily than was justified by eventual profits. Technically, however, the waggonway does seem to have been successful. It was based on Shropshire practice with narrow-gauge track and waggons hauled in trains, rather than that of Tyneside where gauges of about 5 ft were used, and waggons hauled singly. It had its moment of history in 1745, when Sir John

Cope positioned his artillery along it and the brief and bloody Battle of Prestonpans was fought over its course. It is perhaps an indication of the peaceable nature of Great Britain subsequently that Prestonpans remains the only occasion when a railway has been directly involved in land warfare.

The Tranent–Cockenzie waggonway became a lasting feature of its district, outliving its original owner.[5] It went without imitator, however, until the second half of the century when, over several decades, a dozen or so wooden-railed waggonways were built in Scotland. Some of them, with branches, developed into small systems.[6] One of the first was built underground in 1754 in a coal pit at Bo'ness, where it replaced carriage of coal in creels on the backs of women. The three partners who established the Carron Company in 1759, John Roebuck, Samuel Garbett and William Cadell, all had close links with Prestonpans and Cockenzie, and the first two were also well informed of ironmaking as practised at Coalbrookdale, Shropshire, where waggonways had been in use for many years. It is no surprise, therefore, to find that contemporaneously with construction of the Carron works in 1760 came construction of a waggonway to carry coal to the works from Kinnaird colliery one and a half miles away.[7]

At Alloa, coals were carried from pit to shore by carts until a waggonway was made in 1768. This seems to have been of the Shropshire pattern, but other lines built further down the north shore of the Forth were modelled on those of Tyneside. The earls of Elgin had a complex of coalpits, limekilns and harbours in the Dunfermline area. Thomas Pennant noted 'a variety of rail roads', i.e., waggonways, at work there in 1772[8] and some at least of these are likely to have been of the Tyneside pattern, for advice had been taken from

Tyneside experts on how best to construct them. An extension to the new port of Charlestown was built in 1799. The waggonway built about 1770 from coal pits at Fordell, east of Dunfermline, to the harbour of St Davids was built to 4 ft 4 in. gauge; its waggons held 48 cwt of coal; such waggons needed two horses to pull them, even though the down gradients were mostly with the load. Running largely parallel to the Fordell waggonway was the similar Halbeath waggonway built about ten years later to carry coal to Inverkeithing harbour.

In the West, there was a waggonway extending northwards from Ayr harbour to coal pits by the early 1770s;[9] initially only about 800 yd long, it was subsequently much extended and improved by owners Taylor and Sons. Running down to the Clyde at Yoker, a two-and-a-half-mile waggonway may have been built as early as the 1750s; on the south bank of the river, a waggonway from Govan colliery was running by 1778. Even away in the far North, a colliery at Brora may have been linked to the nearby harbour by a waggonway by the mid-1770s.[10]

Wood, as a material for rails carrying heavy loads, is unsatisfactory: it quickly becomes worn. An early improvement was to make the rails in two halves, one above the other: this not merely strengthened them but meant that the upper rail, when worn, could easily be replaced. A further refinement was to make the upper rail of harder wood. The waggonways at Alloa went through these three stages – initially the rails were of Scotch fir, then of upper and lower rails of the same timber, then with the upper rails of beech.[11]

Carron, in 1767, laid upper rails of cast iron on lower rails of wood – pioneering work, for the technique originated at Coalbrookdale that same year.[12] Alloa attempted the same, but found that as soon as the

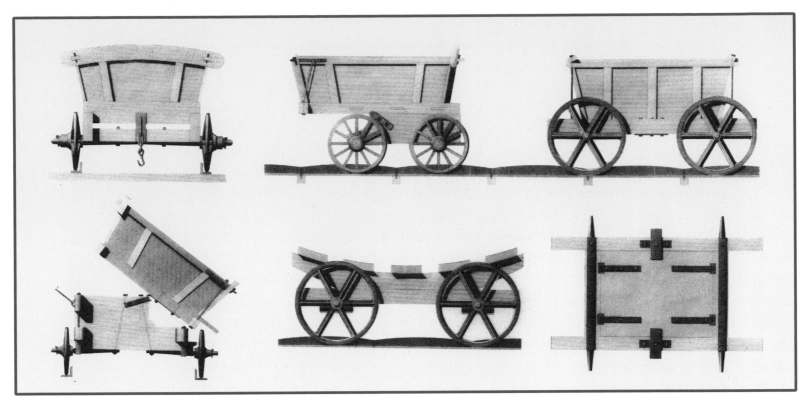

Waggons employed on the temporary tramroads during construction of the Caledonian Canal. In the top row are, left to right, side-tipping, end-tipping and bottom-door waggons; central in the second row is a stone waggon. (Trustees of the National Library of Scotland, *Life of Thomas Telford*)

wood gave way, the cast iron broke: they went for malleable iron plates instead, with good results.[13] Malleable or wrought iron plates had been used in this way on Tyneside for many years but to a limited extent, and were also possibly used at Carron.

In the early 1790s, 'edge rails' wholly of cast iron came into use in Leicestershire and in South Wales. On these rails, as with wooden rails, wheels guided by their flanges ran along the top edge. It is necessary to make the point, because at the same period an alternative pattern of wheel and rail appeared: cast iron plate rails of L-section, with the horizontal part of the L forming the running surface for flangeless wheels guided by the upright flange on the rail. To match, perhaps, their hard-wearing qualities, these

rails were generally laid on stone blocks instead of wooden sleepers.

Largely because of the promotional activites of Benjamin Outram and William Jessop – engineers and partners in the Butterley ironworks, Derbyshire – plateways of this construction became popular in central England, and in South Wales where they largely replaced edge railways. They were much less popular on Tyneside and in Scotland. Here it seems the only plateways of importance were the extensive temporary lines used in building the Caledonian Canal, and the Kilmarnock & Troon Railway. For both of these undertakings, Jessop was engineer; the Kilmarnock & Troon will be described in the next chapter. Construction of the Caledonian Canal started in 1804 and many temporary plateways, ranging in length from a few yards to a mile and a half or more, were used to move earth, spoil and building stone. At Fort Augustus, for instance, a plateway linked the site of the locks with the quarry from which stone was obtained; at Banavie, where the flight of locks that became known as Neptune's Staircase was to be built, stone was brought to Corpach by sea, and carried to Banavie by a plateway laid upon an embankment which eventually became the south bank of the canal.[14] The gauge of these plateways was 3 ft 10 in., and in this instance wooden sleepers were employed, to facilitate removal and reuse of the track materials.

In 1797 for the first time on Tyneside, a wooden waggonway was reconstructed with iron edge rails, after which began a steady process of converting other wooden waggonways in that region. There was a similar process in Scotland. Iron edge rails may have been in use on the Earl of Elgin's railways as early as 1794, and at Carron in 1795. They were certainly brought into use at Brora and at Ayr early in the next century, and around 1810–15 iron edge rails replaced wood at Charlestown, Halbeath, Alloa and Tranent. This list is not exhaustive. In many cases, wooden sleepers were also replaced by stone blocks. The Fordell Waggonway was still using wooden rails as late as the early 1830s.

Among the varied terminology of this and earlier periods, the term 'iron railway' or 'railway' came increasingly to be applied to lines with iron rails, and it is as 'railways' that we can now refer to them, although they were still powered by horses and on occasion gravity.

From this period too there survive clear descriptions of such lines, such as those contained in *Essays on Railroads, presented to the Highland Society*. These essays were prepared in 1818–21 in response to offers of prizes by the society: by that period people's minds were much exercised by wider possibilities for railways than as mere local adjuncts to mines and ironworks. They were eventually published in its transactions in 1824, edited by Robert Stevenson of the noted engineering family. Today they are of most interest for their summarising of the practice of the period. We learn for instance that the Tranent–Cockenzie line had become a 'cast-iron railway', 4,480 yd long, with the 'breadth of the horse-track'(i. e. the track gauge) 3 ft 3 in. Gross weight of loaded waggons was about two tons. 'A horse sometimes takes up 5 empty waggons, but the common number is 4, and these he generally drags three times a day'.[15]

New lines were built on the new principles, such as the iron edge railway built in 1810 by the Carron Company to link its works with the Forth & Clyde Canal at Bainsford. On the railways of the Earl of Elgin – by now the seventh Earl, collector of the Elgin marbles – changing patterns of traffic, and difficulties over wayleaves, resulted in construction of successive new sections, and disuse of earlier ones, between the 1790s and the 1830s: to the confusion of historians. Probably there was a lot of new building at the time of introduction of iron rails in 1810–12. A substantial three-arch stone viaduct which survives just west of Charlestown may date from this period. It carries the course of the railway over a sudden defile and can be found – at your own risk – apparently neglected, and concealed in a jungle of mature trees and lesser undergrowth.

Another new section, which had been planned in 1810, was built about 1821, and included two self-acting inclined planes. After a survey by Robert Stevenson, the supervising engineer was Charles Landale of Dundee. On self-acting inclined planes descending loaded waggons were connected by rope or chain, round a winding drum at the incline head, to the ascending empty waggons so that the former could haul up the latter. The technique was not new. Such an arrangement had been patented in 1750 by a Scot, Michael Meinzies, but it is not clear whether he exploited his patent before it expired in 1778.[16] Nevertheless self-acting inclined planes were in use in Shropshire by the 1770s and on Tyneside by 1784. They may have reached Charlestown by the late 1790s; otherwise, with one exception, to be mentioned shortly, there seems to have been none in Scotland before Landale's. But by the 1820s techniques of building and operating them were well established and Landale had evidently studied them. The longer of his two planes was about 511 yd in length, with a gradient of 1 in 20. On the short section between the two planes, where the ground was level, cutting and embanking were employed to produce not only a gentle down gradient for loaded waggons to run by gravity, but also a gentle reverse gradient on the line used by the empties so that they too could run by gravity from the head of one incline to the foot of the next. No horses were needed on this part of the railway. From 100 to 200 tons of coal were carried down these inclines daily.[17]

Opening celebrations on the Garnkirk & Glasgow Railway, 1831: locomotive *St Rollox* hauls an eastbound train carrying directors and friends, and passes a westbound train in Provan Mill cutting. Buildings on the right were temporary accommodation for navvies. (East Dunbartonshire Information & Archives)

PUBLIC RAILWAYS
AND THE COMING OF STEAM

All the waggonways and railways so far described were used solely by the traffic of their proprietors. The first public railway in Scotland, built by a railway company incorporated by Act of Parliament and intended for the use of the public, was the Kilmarnock & Troon Railway. This was incorporated in 1808 and opened in 1812. But there is, however, an earlier contender for the first public railway in Scotland, although a temporary one.

It formed part of the line of the Monkland Canal. As originally envisaged by James Watt, its engineer, this canal was to start at a point in the Monklands near Airdrie and run on one level, without locks, for some nine miles to Germiston, or Jermiston, located on high ground a mile north-east of Glasgow. Thence a waggonway, with a self-acting inclined plane, would carry coal down into Glasgow proper.[1] This layout was authorised by Act of Parliament in 1770 and Watt started to build the canal, working from east to west. By 1773 rather more than seven miles of canal were complete, but funds had been exhausted. When work started again in the early 1780s under a new set of proprietors, plans had altered. The existing canal was extended west a little way to Blackhill and, at a lower level, a canal was made thence into Glasgow to a basin at Castle Street which is now obliterated I believe beneath junction 15 of the M8 motorway.

Pending construction of a flight of locks to join the two levels of the canal, a waggonway was built. Into its waggons, coal was loaded from scows on the upper level of the canal, to be loaded again into scows on the lower level. This time-consuming and, for the coal, damaging process continued for about ten years, until 1793 when the locks were completed and use of the waggonway evidently ceased. It does appear that this was the earliest instance where a railway in Scotland was available for use by the public – even though there may well have been no more than two coal owners using the canal at this date, one of whom was one of its proprietors!

The *Old Statistical Account*[2] of 1793 refers to the works being completed except the locks 'which are in great forwardness' and then adds confusingly that 'a waggon road is also finished between the bason and Glasgow ...' At that period the term 'waggon road' was frequently used for 'waggonway', but once the western terminus of the canal had been altered to bring it into Glasgow, where by 1793 the Monkland Canal had already been joined to the Forth & Clyde, there can have been little point in building a waggonway there. I am inclined to suppose confusion between the waggonway proposed under the original plans but not built and that eventually built at Blackhill.

This waggonway appears to have been laid out as

an inclined plane – it was certainly so described by James Leslie, the engineer who in 1850 built the much better-known inclined plane at this location to transfer scows between the two levels of the canal in caissons running on rails.[3]

In the Kilmarnock area by the end of the eighteenth century, substantial tonnages of coal were being carted from mines to coast for shipment. A canal was proposed between Kilmarnock and Troon. In 1806 the Marquis of Titchfield – who became the Duke of Portland in 1809, and owned the largest estate in Ayrshire – proposed that a railway be built instead, being cheaper and causing less disturbance of land. He also proposed that it should be promoted jointly by all landowners on the route.[4] The outcome was an Act of Parliament of 1808 which incorporated 'The Company of Proprietors of the Kilmarnock & Troon Railway' with powers to raise the capital needed for construction and, eventually, to charge a rate of three pence per ton per mile 'for all Goods, Wares, Merchandize and other Things whatsosever' carried over its line. This process was comparable to contemporary establishment of canal companies and turnpike trusts, and had already been used to create railway companies in England since 1801. The Act did contain the unusual provision that if dividends exceeded 20 per cent over a period of time then two Justices of the Peace might order rates to be reduced, and vice versa. Titchfield eventually put up the great bulk of the funds needed to the extent of £37,000 and there were only three other shareholders who contributed £500 each.[5]

William Jessop had already built the pioneering Surrey Iron Railway during 1801–3 as a plateway, and a plateway was what he provided for the proprietors of the Kilmarnock & Troon, following what no doubt appeared to be the most advanced engineering

techniques of the time – techniques which would, however, very soon become outmoded. The railway was rather more than ten miles long, double track, laid with cast iron L-section rails 3 ft long and 4 ft apart, with a similar space between the two tracks. The rails were supported by stone blocks and laid, as was usual, with their flanges between the wheels; gravel between the rails was made level with the tops of their flanges to provide a path for horses. The railway crossed the River Irvine by a viaduct with four spans of 40 ft each, rising 25 ft above the river.[6] The line was opened in 1812 and the traffic was conveyed by carriers, whose horses could haul three waggons each with a one-ton load.

The form of construction did not prove satisfactory. The stone blocks settled, perhaps on account of the soft ground, and they were split by frost.[7] The Kilmarnock & Troon Railway did have two other claims to fame. It was the first railway in Scotland to carry passengers, and the first to use a steam locomotive. The first of these activities was more successful than the second. Passengers had first been carried by rail in 1807 on the Oystermouth Railway in South Wales, and seem to have been carried on the Kilmarnock & Troon since its earliest days. Famously, a French visitor described the *'diligences'* that were employed as resembling an enormous gypsy caravan, yet easily pulled by a single horse.[8] *'Diligence'*, in French, implies not only effort but also speed, and was the customary term for what we know as a stagecoach, pulled usually by four horses. A more prosaic description of the K & T vehicles was of yellow-painted vans or carriages with seats all round for passengers, some with seats on top. These coaches were operated by coach proprietors: the railway company, having no powers to charge passenger fares, charged the coach proprietors a toll

The Kilmarnock & Troon Railway crossed the River Irvine by Laigh Milton viaduct. When the line was eventually upgraded into a locomotive railway it was diverted; by the 1990s the viaduct, after a century and a half of disuse, appeared to be in a state of terminal dereliction. Happily it was instead restored, as seen here. (Author)

based on the estimated weight of passengers.[9] It placed them presumably in the category of 'other Things whatsoever'. The service continued into the 1830s and contributed to the growth of Troon as a resort.

The steam locomotive dates from 1804, when Richard Trevithick's first successful locomotive ran on rails on the Penydarren Tramroad, South Wales. Mechanically successful, that is: the weight of the locomotive imposed too great a load on the tramroad's brittle cast iron plate rails for it to be used regularly. Locomotives first entered regular service in 1812 on

the Middleton Railway, Leeds, as a consequence of the sharp rise in the price of horse fodder caused by the Napoleonic wars. The same rise prompted one of the Caledonian Canal contractors to try replacing the horses, used on his temporary waggonways, by oxen. On Tyneside, William Hedley built locomotives for the Wylam Waggonway in 1814, and George Stephenson did so for the Killingworth Waggonway very shortly afterwards. Middleton and Killingworth were edge railways, Wylam a plateway. As early as 1813 the Duke of Portland's agent was obtaining details of locomotives.

A locomotive was ordered from Stephenson – the first Stephenson locomotive built for an outside customer – and the locomotive was delivered in 1817[10] or, perhaps, the previous year.

It was brought to Kilmarnock by Robert Stephenson, George's younger brother, and placed on the railway. One of those who saw it, as a young man, was John Kelso Hunter, shoemaker and self-taught portrait painter who later exhibited regularly at the Royal Scottish Academy. Long afterwards he recalled:

> … *the first start was a grand sight. On the tram road near the auld toll on the Dundonald road sat the new power. As the steam got up the people stood farther back … A batch of women stood beside us, whose husbands had been deputed to assist in the start. They were to put their shoulder to the machine, to send it off without strain, … a wild shout was raised by [the women] when they saw their husbands left alone and unhurt. The engine was careering along the line … at a good horse trot pace.*[11]

Despite this promising start, the locomotive was not a success. The centre of the horse path between the rails was high in places (and in any case higher than the running surface of the rails by the 4 in. height of their flanges) and fouled the mechanism. Worse, however, was damage to the track: too many broken cast iron plate rails, as at Penydarren, and also at Wylam, where Hedley's locomotives, originally on four wheels, were being altered to run on eight to lighten the axle load. The locomotive saw little if any use.

The decade following construction of the Kilmarnock & Troon saw many proposals for public railways in Scotland, and much public debate about their possibilities, with little immediate effect. One proposal got as far as authorisation by Act of Parliament, only to fail to raise sufficient funds for construction –

a story that would be repeated time and time again over the ensuing century. In this case it was for a line from Berwick to Kelso; its Act of 1811 included for the first time provisions for carrying passengers. Of many other proposals, Robert Stevenson was associated with at least ten; for one of these, to run from Dalkeith to St Boswells, Sir Walter Scott was among the promoters. Scott was also connected with a proposal to revive the intended Berwick & Kelso line in the 1820s.[12] Stevenson was active south of the Border too: his advice was sought in 1818, and subsequently, by a group of County Durham businessmen attempting to promote a railway from Stockton-on-Tees to Darlington and the coalfield beyond. It would become the Stockton & Darlington Railway.[13]

However Robert Stevenson's greatest contribution probably lay in popularising use of edge rails made not of cast iron but of wrought or malleable iron. 'Regarding the description of materials to be used in the formation of railways, I have no hesitation in giving a decided preference to malleable iron, formed into bars of from 12 to 20 feet in length …' he wrote in his summing-up to *Essays on Railroads*.[14] One of the great advantages of malleable iron rails was that they could be rolled in such lengths, with the stability that resulted from track with joints every twelve feet or more instead of every three feet. In those days joints were made by butting the end of one rail up against the next in a chair common to both; a refinement was the half-lap joint. Another advantage was that malleable iron, unlike cast iron, was not brittle: weight for weight, rails of malleable iron were much stronger than those of cast iron. Their introduction was an essential preliminary to the general introduction of steam locomotives.

Although at this period engineers in the North of

England were making the running so far as railway development was concerned, it is clear that Scottish engineers were keeping a very close eye on what was happening and were quick to take up developments. Stevenson first mentioned malleable iron rails in a report about proposed railways from the Midlothian coalfield to Edinburgh and Leith: this was published in 1819 but appears to have been written during the previous year.[15] Three and a half miles of line with malleable iron rails had been in use for about eight years, wrote Stevenson, at Lord Carlisle's works at Tindal Fell in Cumberland, where there were also two miles of cast-iron rails. Not only were malleable iron rails cheaper in first cost than cast iron, but also 'much less liable to accident' – in other words, presumably, track of malleable iron rails with their joints every twelve ft kept its alignment much better than cast iron rails with joints every three feet or so. Elsewhere experiments had been made with malleable iron rails, he wrote, at Mr Taylor's works at Ayr, and Sir John Hope's at Pinkie. The short Pinkie Waggonway had been opened through Musselburgh in 1814.

Stevenson was also complimentary in this report about George Stephenson's locomotives – 'some of the most striking improvements in the system of railways'. He sent a copy of the report to George Stephenson, who in turn passed it on to Michael Longridge, owner of Bedlington Ironworks. Longridge decided to use malleable iron rails on a waggonway to bring coal into the works, but it was his principal agent (or, as we would now say, works manager), John Birkinshaw, who made the definitive improvement. Whereas the Tindall Fell rails were bars of cross-section one and a half inches square, Birkinshaw proposed, and in 1820 patented, rails rolled to a wedge shape.[16] This was developed into rails of T-section, to combine vertical strength and a broad running surface with lightness, and such rails were laid over most of the Stockton & Darlington Railway, in 1823–5.

Malleable iron edge rails were laid on the Monkland & Kirkintilloch Railway. This was authorised by Act of Parliament in 1824, to run from the Monklands Collieries north-west for ten miles or so to the Forth & Clyde Canal at Kirkintilloch. It would provide the coal owners with a route to Glasgow to compete with any monopolistic ambitions held by the proprietors of the Monkland Canal, and it also offered the potential to supply coal by canal to points east of Kirkintilloch, even to Edinburgh, whither the Union Canal had been opened two years before.[17] The Act of incorporation empowered 'the Company of Proprietors … to make and erect such and so many locomotive or moveable Engines as the said Company … shall from Time to Time think proper and expedient, and to use and employ the same in and upon the said Railway …' It appears to have been the first such Act to include such a provision: the Stockton & Darlington Railway, originally authorised in 1821, had obtained in 1823 an amending Act to allow locomotives.[18]

With the Monkland & Kirkintilloch there appear on the scene for the first time the names of two engineers who would soon seem to be almost synonymous with railway construction in Scotland: Thomas Grainger and John Miller. Grainger was the older: born in 1794, he had been practising in Edinburgh as an engineer and surveyor since 1816. He had worked largely on road improvements: the M & K seems to have been his first railway work – first preparing the plans, then supervising construction.[19] Miller, born in 1805, had originally intended to be a lawyer, but entered Grainger's office in 1823. In 1825 Grainger took him, still young, into partnership. He would eventually be responsible for building much of the main-line railway network of Scotland.[20]

The gauge chosen for the Monkland & Kirkintilloch was 4 ft 6 in. – a couple of inches narrower than Stephenson was using on the Stockton & Darlington, but there was as yet little concept of a national railway system. The 4 ft 6 in. gauge did become something of a local standard for further short railways which were built to connect with the M & K. The first of these was the Ballochney Railway, incorporated in 1826 to extend the Kipps branch of the M & K eastwards into the coalfield – its name derived from that of the colliery at its furthest extremity. Grainger was the engineer, and the route incorporated two successive self-acting inclined planes.

The Ballochney was one of four more Scottish railways authorised while the Monkland & Kirkintilloch was still being built. Their Acts of Parliament received the royal assent in May 1826:[21] the year 1825, when these lines were being promoted, was a year of much financial speculation, of which perhaps the most notorious effect was to bring about the financial ruin of Sir Walter Scott.

The other three railways were the Edinburgh & Dalkeith, the Dundee & Newtyle and the Garnkirk & Glasgow. The Edinburgh & Dalkeith was to bring coal into Edinburgh, running from Eskbank near Dalkeith for eight and a half miles to Edinburgh St Leonards, close by Arthur's Seat. Subsequent Acts authorised branches to Leith and Fisherrow (Musselburgh). St Leonards was approached by an inclined plane, sloping gently upwards at 1 in 30 for 1,160 yards through a 572-yard tunnel. Since the coal traffic was upwards, a stationary steam engine was installed to power the cable haulage:[22] such installations had been made on

plateways and railways in England, and particularly on Tyneside, since the first decade of the century.

With the Dundee & Newtyle we come for the first time in Scotland to a public railway that did not have transport of coal as its prime motivation. Intended to link the port of Dundee with its fertile hinterland of Strathmore, it was expected that traffic from Dundee would include lime, metal goods, manure, coal and flax products on their way to be bleached; returning would come grain, potatoes, stone and bleached flax goods.[23] The engineer was Charles Landale and on his recommendation the northern terminus was set at Newtyle, whence the line could easily be extended up and down Strathmore proper. There was at that date no village or town at Newtyle: Lord Wharncliffe, landowner and a promoter of the railway, took the opportunity to establish a village at the railway terminus after the line was open.[24]

The route meant crossing the Sidlaw Hills. Landale laid out a line in accordance with the best engineering practice of his day: three steep inclines, with gradients of 1 in 10, 1 in 25 and 1 in 13 to be worked by stationary engines and cable haulage, were interspersed with two comparatively long sections, near level but with sharp curves, to be worked by horses. At this period the locomotive had yet to prove itself, but stationary engines were well established. The route of the Stockton & Darlington Railway, opened in September 1825, surmounted a range of hills near its western extremity by the Brusselton cable-worked inclines with gradients of 1 in 33½. The Cromford & High Peak Railway, authorised a year before the Dundee & Newtyle, was even more ambitious, building a line that incorporated cable-worked inclines as steep as 1 in 8¼ and 1 in 7. It is worth mentioning this, because rapid advances in technology meant that Landale's

DRAGON

THE START.

This noble Animal the property of Mr Thomas Johnston of Langloan, hauled a train of fourteen Waggons weighing Fifty Tons from Gartsherry Colliery along the Monkland and Kirkintilloch Railway to its Northern termination, a distance of Six and three quarter Miles in One hour and forty one minutes.

Newspapers of the day

7th February 1828

On the Monkland & Kirkintilloch Railway a horse usually hauled four waggons at a time but, in response to a wager, the horse *Dragon* successfully hauled fourteen.
(McEwan Collection, East Dunbartonshire Information & Archives)

route soon became outdated, difficult and expensive to work, and as such it has been unjustifiably derided, from the 1840s to the present day.[25]

The Garnkirk & Glasgow Railway was a pioneer too, but in ways that were wholly different. For the first time in Scotland a railway was being planned that would compete directly with water transport, rather than feeding traffic to it. It was to run from a junction with the Monkland & Kirkintilloch into Glasgow, eliminating transfer of Glasgow-bound coal from rail to water, and so competing with both the Monkland Canal and the Forth & Clyde Canal – even

though its Glasgow terminus at St Rollox was placed adjacent to the Cut of Junction. An Act of Parliament was obtained in 1826, and a further Act in 1827 to enable the route to be altered. From the junction with the M & K at Gartsherrie the new line was to run as direct and as near level as possible for eight and a quarter miles to Glasgow: to achieve this the engineers, Grainger and Miller again, had to provide deep cuttings and high embankments, the biggest of the latter at Germiston where once the Monkland Canal had planned an inclined plane. Prominent among the promoters was Charles Tennant who,

29

No steam locomotives reached the Dundee & Newtyle station in Dundee. Trains leaving for Newtyle traversed a cable-worked incline up the hill in the background; tracks in the foreground were horse-worked and are the start of the extension to the harbour. The station, built c. 1830, survived little altered into the era of photography but was closed in 1861 after the Lochee deviation was opened. (Dundee City Council, Central Library)

starting out as a weaver, had moved into bleaching and then into manufacturing bleaching materials, so that by the 1830s he had established at St Rollox the largest chemical works in Europe. Tennant was on the management committee of the Monkland & Kirkintilloch Railway and had inspected the railways of north-east England; he was present at the opening ceremonies of the Stockton & Darlington Railway in 1825, and would attend the opening of the Liverpool & Manchester in 1830.[26] Malleable iron rails were used on the Garnkirk & Glasgow, as they had been on the

Ballochney, Edinburgh & Dalkeith and Dundee & Newtyle Railways also.

A sixth railway which can appropriately be considered in this group is the Ardrossan or Ardrossan & Johnstone Railway. It was intended to complete the route of an intended canal between Glasgow and Ardrossan, which had been opened from Glasgow through Paisley to Johnstone by 1811 but had gone no further. It became known as the Paisley Canal. An Act to complete its line to Ardrossan, by 4 ft 6 in. gauge railway rather than canal, was obtained in 1827.

By then the Monkland & Kirkintilloch Railway had already opened for traffic, by stages during 1826, and Monklands coal was on sale at the Union Canal's Edinburgh terminus, Port Hopetoun.[27] Despite use of locomotives to haul coal trains on the Stockton & Darlington since 1825, the M & K initially used horses rather than locomotives for motive power – as would, at first, all the railways in this group. On the M & K a horse usually pulled four waggons each loaded with three tons of coal, but just what a horse could do was demonstrated on 27 February 1828 when, following a wager, the horse *Dragon* hauled a load of fifty tons in fourteen waggons for six and three-quarter miles in 1 hour 45 minutes,[28] admittedly on a slight down gradient. Horses and waggons were both provided by users of the line.

The Ballochney Railway, feeder to the Monkland & Kirkintilloch, was opened during 1827–8. Over part of the line the gentle descent was sufficient for loaded trains to run by gravity, and at the rear of such trains was a dandy cart, or horse waggon, in which rode a horse resting from his labours prior to returning with another load of empties. Dandy carts had first been introduced onto the Stockton & Darlington Railway in June or July 1828: the idea had originated from George Stephenson.[29] Subsequently they would be used elsewhere, on for instance the Festiniog Railway.

With the Ballochney Railway open, a passenger coach service started from Leaend (*sic*), the terminus of its branch of this name near Airdrie, over the two railways to Kirkintilloch. Work on the Garnkirk & Glasgow was far enough advanced for horse-hauled trains to start in the spring of 1831, with a passenger coach starting on 1 June between Leaend and Glasgow over the Ballochney, M & K and G & G Railways (although the official opening ceremony of the Garnkirk & Glasgow, with steam locomotives, was deferred until late September and is mentioned below.) The Edinburgh & Dalkeith Railway was opened in July 1831, the Dundee & Newtyle by stages during 1831–2; both used horses, except on their steam-powered inclined planes. The short section of the Ardrossan Railway between Ardrossan and Kilwinning was also opened with horses in 1831; the rest remained unbuilt.

During the early and mid-1820s the development of the steam locomotive, mostly by George Stephenson and his associates, had been making measured progress, and the locomotives themselves were slow, lumbering monsters. But that was not the only attempt to apply steam power to land transport. The powered inclined plane evolved, in north-east England, into powered cable haulage of lines that were level or nearly so, with stationary engines at intervals hauling the trains. And on ordinary turnpike roads, during the 1820s and 1830s, innumerable inventors were attempting to design and build road steam carriages.

In 1827 Robert Stephenson, son of George, returned from an absence of several years in South America to Newcastle upon Tyne, to take charge of the works of Robert Stephenson & Co. The partners in this firm were George Stephenson, Robert Stephenson and Michael Longridge. Here Robert set about improving the steam locomotive, building a succession of locomotives each of supposedly improved design.

At this juncture the Liverpool & Manchester Railway was being built and approaching completion. Faced by a dilemma of how it was to be powered, by cable haulage or locomotives, its directors decided to hold a prize competition for 'an improved locomotive'. This became the famous Rainhill Trials of October 1829, which have often been described in print.[30] What an 'improved locomotive' was expected to do – and, conversely, how limited were the powers of existing locomotives – are shown by the conditions of the trials: if such a locomotive weighed 6 tons, the maximum permitted, it must be able to haul on the level a train weighing 20 tons (or less in proportion to its weight) at a speed of 10 mph. This it was to demonstrate by running up and down a completed section of the railway, at Rainhill, for a distance equivalent to the journey from Liverpool to Manchester and back.

The Rainhill Trials attracted the attention of every crackpot inventor in the land, but the eventual entry was whittled down to four steam locomotives, and one worked by a horse on a sort of treadmill. The four steam locomotives included *Perseverance,* entered by Timothy Burstall of Edinburgh. Burstall and his associate John Hill had built a steam road coach about 1825, in the form of a stagecoach of the period with engine and boiler mounted at the rear. This coach, though it incorporated many ingenious details including a pioneering form of optional four-wheel drive, was heavy and slow overall, and the boiler unsatisfactory. Burstall and Hill redesigned their vehicle with the boiler and furnace mounted on a two-wheeled trailer. *Perseverance* was probably of this type, and may have been intended for alternative road or rail use. Her boiler was vertical; hot gases escaped up the chimney above the fire with little opportunity for heat to be transferred to the water.[31]

It would be nice to be able to record that this first locomotive built in Scotland – the forerunner of a great industry – was an outstanding success, but unfortunately the opposite was the case. Although carrying the boiler separately had substantially reduced the weight of the coach, the speed remained too slow, and *Perseverance* had moreover been damaged

in transit. After repairs she ran at Rainhill but, her performance being inadequate, Burstall withdrew from the competition. An observer – admittedly one in the Stephenson camp – described her performance as 'full 6 miles an hour cranking away like an old Wickerwork pair of Panniers on a cantering Cuddy Ass'.[32]

The winner of the Rainhill Trials was, as every schoolboy knows, *Rocket. Rocket* had been built for the trials by Robert Stephenson and represented the latest stage reached by his development work. She was entered at Rainhill by a partnership of George and Robert Stephenson and Henry Booth. Another entry, Braithwaite & Ericsson's *Novelty*, was probably a better riding vehicle but was let down by, among other things, an inadequate boiler. Rocket's boiler, by contrast, was the secret of her success. In the boilers of most previous Stephenson locomotives, the fire was contained in a large cylindrical furnace tube passing through the water – an arrangement which limited the heating surface and in turn the production of steam and the performance of the locomotive. Robert Stephenson had been working on improved designs, but it was at the suggestion of Booth, who was the Liverpool & Manchester's treasurer but had a mechanical turn of mind, that the boiler of Rocket was made with a multiplicity of small diameter tubes to carry the burning gases through the boiler from firebox to chimney. Only this enabled transmission of sufficient heat to the water to generate the steam needed for a locomotive to run fast and far: the multi-tubular layout became the basic feature of all subsequent conventional locomotive boilers. *Rocket,* at Rainhill, was the only entrant to do all required of it, and indeed to exceed the requirements handsomely: with her load she ran up and down the course at a steady 14 mph or so, and then on her last run when she had already made a journey, in effect, of the unprecedented length – for a locomotive – of some sixty-six miles, George Stephenson opened her up to more than 24 mph. On other occasions she ran at 30 mph or more. Since the beginning of time, people had known no faster speed overland than a galloping horse could carry them: such speeds as these were revolutionary.

Robert Stephenson however continued his development work. Formerly, locomotive cylinders had been vertical and within the boiler. With Rocket he had moved them outside, and positioned them at 45 degrees to the horizontal. When he built *Planet* for the Liverpool & Manchester Railway in the autumn of 1830, he positioned the cylinders almost horizontal and low down at the front of the locomotive to produce a comparatively steady-riding vehicle. Here was the definitive layout for the steam locomotive, and it is from *Planet* that most subsequent designs are descended.

Timothy Burstall tried again too and was reported carrying out experiments on the Garnkirk & Glasgow Railway in September 1831, with a locomotive resembling *Novelty*, but 'quite different in its details'. Dendy Marshall illustrates a locomotive built by Burstall and answering to this description. It may be that this was the locomotive he took to Rainhill: contemporary descriptions are limited.[33] At any rate, Burstall seems subsequently to disappear from railway history.

The directors of the Monkland & Kirkintilloch Railway had not at first made use of their powers to employ steam locomotives. Perhaps the traffic did not warrant it. Opening of the Ballochney Railway brought more traffic, and by 1829 the M & K company was going to considerable expense to double its railway, which had been built as a single line.[34] Sometime in the early part of 1830 they did decide to introduce locomotives, and the Committee of Management 'after much consideration, devolved the whole form and plan for the constructing of these engines to MR GEORGE DODDS, the Superintendent'.[35]

George Dodds's origin lay in north-east England. As long before as 1808, according to Samuel Smiles,[36] George Stephenson 'with two other brakesmen, named Robert Wedderburn and George Dodds, took a small contract under the colliery lessees for braking the engines at the West Moor Pit'. West Moor Pit was at Killingworth; brakesmen were in charge of the winding engines, and the most critical part of their task was braking the engines to bring the cage gently and safely to a stop in the correct position at the top or bottom of the shaft: a task for trusted and reliable men. At that date, however, Stephenson had yet to make his name as an engineer. His big opportunity came in 1811 when he successfully modified a malfunctioning pumping engine, which had defeated all other attempts, and so enabled a new but flooded pit to be worked. The head viewer, or manager, Ralph Dodds, recognised his engineering talent and Stephenson's responsibilities were increased, leading eventually to construction of the Killingworth locomotives and the take-off of his railway engineering career.

Of the other two partners of 1808, Wedderburn, or Weatherburn, eventually moved to the Liverpool & Manchester Railway. George Dodds, who was probably related to Ralph Dodds, had by late 1822 been appointed superintendent of the Hetton Colliery Railway, in County Durham. This eight-and-a-half mile line was laid out by George Stephenson, but the resident engineer responsible for construction was his brother Robert. When opened that November it was the first railway designed so that no animal power need be used: it comprised a succession of powered and gravity-operated inclined planes interspersed with more easily graded lengths where locomotives of the Killingworth type were employed. It did not at first prove entirely satisfactory, and Robert Stephenson was dismissed late in 1823 or thereabouts. Dodds stayed, for the time being.[37]

George Dodds did move, however, to the Monkland & Kirkintilloch Railway while it was still being built. For this we have the authority of Thomas Summerside's *Anecdotes, Reminiscences and Conversations of and with the late George Stephenson …* Summerside had known Stephenson at Killingworth; he 'knew him when he was poor, served him when he was rich, and assisted to carry him to his final resting place' as he puts it on the title-page of his book. What he wrote is:

Mr [George] Stephenson was in Glasgow with Michael Longridge, Esq., of Bedlington, who was one of his earliest and best friends. He also knew George Dodds, who had been brakesman with him,(between whom and Slephenson [sic, but 'l' is clearly a misprint] an estrangement existed), and he looked upon the two men as unequalled in their ability for railway construction. Mr Longridge thought it was a thing very much to be desired that they should be reunited, as he knew their combined action and efforts would be universal good to the country. He, therefore, in order to bring about a reconciliation, sent for George Dodds from Gartsherrie, near Airdrie, for Dodds at that time was making and superintending the Ballockney and Kirkintillock [sic] Railway, to which message Dodds replied, 'Mr. Stephenson knows where I live; if he will come, I shall be glad to see him.' Mr. Longridge regretted his refusal to come and meet his old friend,

as he knew Dodds to be not only a mechanical genius, but also a man of considerable education.[38]

Remarkably, this occasion can be dated to within a few days. Michael Longridge described his travels to Edinburgh and Glasgow in company with George Stephenson in a long letter to Stephenson's son Robert, then in Colombia; the letter was written at intervals during the journey, and part of it is dated from Glasgow on 8 November 1825.[39]

It may reasonably be supposed that one of the objects of Longridge's and Stephenson's visit to Scotland was to drum up business for Bedlington Ironworks and for Robert Stephenson & Co. In that case a reconciliation between Stephenson and Dodds, as well as being for the good of the country, would have been very much in Longridge's commercial interest. But his effort was evidently unsuccessful, for Stephenson seems to have played no part in the affairs of the Monkland & Kirkintilloch and Ballochney Railways; likewise the cause of the estrangement can only be guessed at.

Once given the go-ahead for locomotives, Dodds evidently set to work with a will, for on 25 September 1830 the following advertisement appeared in the *Glasgow Courier:*

TO ENGINEERS
WANTED, *Offers or Estimates for Making and Furnishing* TWO LOCOMOTIVE ENGINES *for the Monkland and Kirkintilloch Railway.*
Plans and specifications of the work of these Engines will be seen at the Office of Messrs Mitchell, Grahame and Mitchell, 36 Miller Street, Glasgow, who will receive offers until the 30th September current.
Glasgow, 21st Sept., 1830.

Drawing of the first Monkland & Kirkintilloch locomotives in Hebert's *Engineer's and Mechanic's Encyclopedia* of 1849 shows that their layout closely followed that of earlier locomotives built by the Stephensons for Killingworth and for the Stockton & Darlington Railway. But the multi-tubular boiler required an external smokebox, shown as a rectangle at the base of the chimney. (Trustees of the National Library of Scotland)

within the same period. It was also contemporaneous with the design and construction of *Planet,* which was delivered to the L & MR on 4 October 1830. It is worth making these points because, so rapidly were the Stephensons then developing the steam locomotive that, by the time the M & K locomotives were delivered the following year, they already appeared old-fashioned and were stigmatised as such both then and in recent publications.

The locomotives were required to haul 60 tons at 4–5 mph and for this George Dodds adopted the Killingworth type with which he was familiar. Estranged from George Stephenson, he was evidently in any case in no position to know much of locomotive developments at Robert Stephenson & Co. He may have consulted his probable relative Isaac Dodds, who was much better placed: having been an apprentice at Robert Stephenson & Co., he had then established his own engineering business nearby, with work provided by Stephenson. Isaac Dodds has sometimes been credited with design of the Monkland & Kirkintilloch locomotives; this assertion, and other uncertainties about the origin of the locomotives and the Dodds family, are considered in the Appendix.

The order for two locomotives went to a local firm, Murdoch & Aitken, builders of stationary and marine engines in Glasgow. They are notable as the first locomotives built in that city. The first was delivered on 10 May 1831 and the second followed on 10 September.[41]

For all their well-tried layout, Dodds's locomotives did incorporate three notable innovations. One was that the coupling rods had ball-and-socket joints at each end, as the wheels were allowed sideplay to allow for sharp curves. A second innovation was that the pistons were made steamtight in the cylinders by,

A news item on the next page gave a glowing report of the performance of the 'steam carriages' on the Liverpool & Manchester Railway, which had just opened for business.[40] In other words, the decision to introduce locomotives on the M & KR had been taken after Rainhill had demonstrated what they could do, but before opening of the Liverpool & Manchester Railway had demonstrated them actually doing it. The design work on the locomotives had been done

The Garnkirk & Glasgow
Railway: locomotive
George Stephenson
hauls a train of coal
waggons towards
Glasgow.
(East Dunbartonshire
Information & Archives)

probably for the first time on a locomotive, metallic packing – in place of rope or tarred hemp which had to be replaced frequently. Third, and most important, at least one and possibly both of the locomotives were fitted with a multi-tubular boiler. It is often stated that both were, but an account published only the following year states that these locomotives were 'on the model of the old engines used in the north of England, and in the last one constructed, the recent improvement of air tubes in the boiler has been adopted'. Firetube boilers were also introduced at Killingworth at this period, on locomotives of otherwise traditional type, but whether the innovation was made first at Killingworth or on the M & K is not clear. Wood, in his *Practical Treatise on Railroads …*, was still advocating this type of locomotive, with firetube boiler, as late as 1838 in the third edition of his book.[42] Back in

1832 the directors of the M & K had reported to their shareholders that they were satisfied with the builder's performance, 'except as to the time taken by them in furnishing the second engine'.[43] That sounds very much as though Murdoch & Aitken had experienced problems in building a multi-tubular boiler, as well they might given the limited engineering expertise of the period. Robert Stephenson, in 1829, had had the greatest difficulties making the boiler for *Rocket*.[44]

The decision to use a well-tried design was shown to be justified once the locomotives were in traffic, for they did all that was asked of them and proved to be very light on maintenance.[45] They worked not only over the M & KR but also on to the Ballochney Railway as far as the foot of the inclines,[46] and they were maintained at the Ballochney Railway's Greenside Works, which served both railways.

Several more locomotives of similar type were later added to the fleet.

The opportunity to compare the old type of locomotive with the new quickly arose, for the Garnkirk & Glasgow Railway ordered two Planet-type locomotives from Robert Stephenson & Co. The first of these, called *St Rollox*, was delivered in June 1831 and ran its first trials on the twenty-fifth of that month.[47] This locomotive had the wheel arrangement 2-2-0, with but a single pair of driving wheels: the second, called *George Stephenson* and delivered by mid-September, had two pairs coupled together as a 0-4-0 and was the better suited for heavy trains of coal and goods. For the benefit of any readers who may be unfamiliar with the system, it is convenient to describe steam locomotives by their wheel arrangements (i.e., the totals of leading wheels, driving wheels and trailing wheels, in that order, with addition of a 'T' to indicate a tank locomotive) as these provide an indication of size and purpose.

With these two locomotives, the railway was opened ceremonially on 27 September 1831. Banners and flags flying, the *St Rollox* hauled a train carrying the directors, their friends and the Airdrie Instrumental Band from Glasgow to Gartsherrie. En route they passed the *George Stephenson*, hauling into Glasgow a train with thirty-two waggons of coal and goods, and three more waggons carrying passengers and another band. In charge on *St Rollox* was Thomas Grainger, and on *George Stephenson* was John Miller; later, when the directors returned to Glasgow – the *St Rollox* achieved 23 mph – they passed en route *George Stephenson* heading east again with a train of empty waggons carrying workmen employed on the railway.[48] Throughout the day, onlookers lined the tracks to cheer, and among the crowds was David Octavius

Hill, artist and – later – pioneer photographer, whose lithographs were to make the appearance of the event, and the railway, widely known. Regular steam-hauled passenger trains soon followed, and both railways increased their stock of locomotives. The era of the steam railway in Scotland was fairly launched – even though that of the horse railway was far from over. For a time, coaches which had been hauled by steam over the Garnkirk & Glasgow continued to be taken forward by horses over the M & K and Ballochney Railways.

The next railway to introduce steam locomotives was the Dundee & Newtyle. In 1833 it obtained two locomotives from J. & C. Carmichael of Dundee, who had already provided the stationary engines for the inclined planes on both the Dundee & Newtyle and Edinburgh & Dalkeith Railways. Their wheel arrangement was 0-2-4: the two rear pairs of wheels, unpowered, were mounted in a swivelling bogie so that the locomotive might better accommodate itself to the railway's sharp curves. Bogies had been used on Tyneside in the earliest days of steam locomotives, and were used in the USA, where railways were lightly laid and sharply curved, from 1832; Robert Stephenson built bogie 4-2-0 locomotives for export thither in 1833 and subsequently. Carmichael's design was therefore a pioneering one, but it saw little imitation. The Dundee & Newtyle's next locomotive was a 4-2-0 built by James Stirling & Co. of Dundee, in 1834,[49] but conventional British locomotives would have rigid wheelbases for the next three decades, while the railways upon which they ran were generally built without sharp curves. The Dundee & Newtyle locomotives took over haulage of passenger coaches – which had started in 1831 – on the near-level sections; passengers also had the noteworthy experience of

An everyday scene at the Glasgow depot of the Garnkirk & Glasgow Railway. Locomotive *St Rollox* prepares to leave with a train of empty waggons, some of which appear to have intending travellers aboard. Among the coal waggons on the sidings are two which are being tipped to empty their contents to the lower level; in the background is a gabbart or sailing barge on the canal, and further into the distance is Glasgow Cathedral. (Science Museum Pictorial / Science & Society Picture Library)

being raised and lowered by cable, up and down the steep inclined planes. An early traveller likened the experience to 'sudden movement … upwards like a flock of geese'.

Like other early railways of this period, the Edinburgh & Dalkeith was laid with malleable iron rails and had powers to use locomotives: but it did not see fit to exercise those powers. Rather, other than on its inclined plane, it stuck to horse and gravity

working, both for coal, and for passengers, of which it had plenty. Robert Chambers – prolific author and founder of the publishing house – left a description of it[50] which gives as vivid a picture as any of what travel on these horse railways was like. In the early 1840s he wrote:

While the railways in general are the scene of so many dreadful accidents, it is pleasant to know there is one which never breaks bones – namely the Edinburgh and Dalkeith Railway. A friend of ours calls it The Innocent Railway, as being so peculiar for its indestructive character, and also with some reference to the simplicity of its style of management ... On arrival at St Leonard's depot ... you are at once ushered into a great wooden carriage, where already perhaps two or three young families, under the care of their respective mammas, have taken up their quarters. But probably you prefer an outside seat ... and so you get mounted up beside the driver, or else upon a similar seat behind. Your companion is perhaps a farm-servant, or a sailor ... An open carriage, full of fishwomen from Fisherrow, is placed judiciously in the rear; and there they sit, smoking their pipes or counting their money ...

The coach is lowered by rope through the tunnel, and then a horse is attached: they trot briskly past Duddingston Loch – but scarcely have they started, than they stop at a crossroads to take up a lady with a parasol, and again a mile further on to let off a farmer. The journey continues, and eventually the coach runs by gravity down the branch to Fisherrow station, where:

The passengers land in a place like a farm-yard, where ducks and hens, and a lounging dog, and a cottager's children, are quietly going about their usual avocations ... And so ends the journey of exactly four miles and three quarters by the Innocent Railway. On consulting your watch, you find it has required exactly forty minutes.

Whishaw makes it clear that a train consisted of three passenger carriages – hence the number of passengers – which were lowered down the inclined plane together but otherwise had their own horses. Each guard, he also stated, carried a bugle-horn, which he sounded lustily as occasion required.[51]

The Edinburgh & Dalkeith was still being run in this informal manner in the early 1840s. The Paisley & Renfrew Railway, opened in 1837 with steam, found so little traffic that it reverted to horses in 1842. Haulage by horses as a general practice seems eventually to have died out in the 1850s, although it continued in certain specialised circumstances for many years. Use of horses to shunt wagons in goods yards also continued, on a large scale. Even as late as 1948 the newly nationalised British Railways inherited 238 shunting horses from the former companies,[52] although the statistics do not reveal, unfortunately, how many of these were based in Scotland. British Railways' last shunting horse of all was retired in the early 1960s.

Certainly in the 1830s the all-conquering nature of the steam railway was still not clear. Railways were still cooperating with canals: in 1835 the Forth & Clyde Canal introduced a 'waggon-boat' to carry laden waggons of coal from the Monkland & Kirkintilloch Railway to factories along its bank.[53] In 1839 experiments were made in the use of a locomotive to haul boats on the canal. A length of railway was laid upon the bank, and a towline from a locomotive attached to one of the passenger boats making its normal journey: a speed of 17 mph was achieved, compared with the boat's normal 8 or 9 mph behind a pair of galloping horses. The experiment was repeated with successive passenger boats, and also with other types of boat. At one stage the locomotive took two sloops and a large waggon boat in tow together, and hauled them at 2¾ mph.[54] The trials continued over a period, but there was no lasting outcome. The locomotive was the Monkland & Kirkintilloch Railway's *Victoria,* recently completed.

The Slamannan Railway, when opened in 1840 after five years in building, extended from the

Ballochney Railway to a basin on the Union Canal at Causewayend, west of Linlithgow, and provided a short route for coal from the Monklands to Edinburgh. Not only coal: passengers too, and through steam passenger trains were operated from Glasgow over the Garnkirk & Glasgow, Ballochney and Slamannan Railways to Causewayend where they connected with passenger boats on the canal.[55] But this service did not last long, for within a couple of years rail travel was possible throughout with opening of the Edinburgh & Glasgow Railway.

During the 1830s and early 1840s the Wishaw & Coltness Railway was built to extend the route of the Monkland & Kirkintilloch southwards, serving among other customers the newly established Coltness Iron Works. At this period all the railways in the Monklands benefited greatly from the expansion of the iron industry in the area. The Garnkirk & Glasgow Railway, for which some of the traffic originating on the Wishaw & Coltness was bound, then extended its own line southwards from Gartsherrie, running parallel to the M & K to its own station at Coatbridge and onward to its own junction with the Wishaw & Coltness. In 1844 the G & G changed its name to the Glasgow, Garnkirk & Coatbridge Railway.[56] The presence of these new lines, initially only of local significance, would become of national importance later in the decade.

The early railway companies had been established, by and large, on the principle that, like turnpike trusts and canal companies, they would provide a track that would be open to all comers on payment of tolls or 'tonnage'. Traders using the track would provide their own waggons, coaches and horses. But this principle had gradually been eroded. Sometimes traders were unwilling or unable to provide waggons, and the

A well-filled train of the Paisley & Renfrew Railway arrives at the Paisley depot in 1837; locomotive *Paisley* was one of the earliest tank locomotives so the absence of a tender is correct. Trains connected with the Clyde steamboats but busy scenes such as this did not apparently outlive opening of a direct railway between Glasgow and Paisley in 1840. (Ironbridge Gorge Museum Trust, Elton Collection)

company would hire waggons out to them. Where there were inclined planes with cable haulage, these could of necessity be operated only by the railway company itself. When railway companies introduced steam locomotives, they found themselves involved in haulage to a much greater extent, and making distinct charges for 'tonnage' and for 'haulage' as well as for wagon-hire. More problems arose when locomotive-hauled trains, which were fast by the standards of the time, mingled with those still hauled by horses: on the Garnkirk & Glasgow Railway, for instance, which was double track, it was arranged in 1840 that the slowest trains, that is, laden horse-hauled trains plodding west, had exclusive use of one track, while

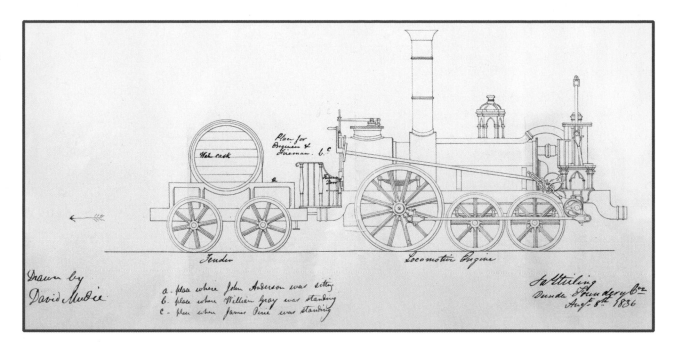

Remarkable appearance of this locomotive, built in 1834 for the Dundee & Newtyle Railway by James Stirling & Co. of Dundee, is known from this drawing. It survived among papers in connection with a legal case, held by the National Archives.
(National Archives of Scotland, Register Home Plans: 42535)

lighter horse-hauled trains heading east shared the other track with steam trains in both directions.[57] As the Monklands system expanded and became busier, the situation became more and more confused and dangerous, as more and more traders appeared, and companies sought to run their own locomotives over neighbouring companies' lines.

Inevitably, railway companies sought closer control of their lines, and to become carriers as well as providers of track. New railways authorised after 1836 did their own carrying,[58] and on the older lines independent carriage gradually died away. In this the Scottish railways reflected a much fiercer battle south of the border, where access by established carrying firms to the trunk railways built during the 1830s had been strongly contested between the carriers and the railway companies.[59] In Scotland, the appearance of trunk railways was delayed until the early 1840s.

On them and on the growing system that developed, railway companies in principle acted as carriers too – from a safety point of view, it would have been difficult as speeds increased for things to have been otherwise. There was, however, the continuing conspicuous exception of private-owner goods wagons provided by traders for their own goods, particularly coal, and the much less conspicuous exception where in a few localities locomotives from privately owned industrial lines were authorised to run on to company-owned tracks. There were also innumerable instances of arrangements, often complex, between the railway companies themselves – of joint ownership of lines for instance, of lines built by one company but operated by another, and of lines where trains of one company exercised running powers over the tracks of another. To these trunk railways we will now turn.

Extensive engineering works were needed on the Edinburgh & Glasgow Railway to achieve a line with no gradient steeper than 1 in 880 between Haymarket and Cowlairs. This is Avon viaduct, west of Linlithgow. (Author)

THE FIRST MAIN LINES

'An Edinburgh merchant could leave his house at seven, breakfast in Glasgow at nine (assuming that a railway is made), transact business there till two, and be home to his own dinner at four, at an expense of 7s. 6d., namely, 6s. for coach-hire [*sic*], and 1s. 6d. for breakfast. At present the journey, including subsistence and a night's lodging, would cost him seven times as much.' *The Scotsman*[1] pointed out this, and much more, to its readers in October 1829 in the aftermath of Rainhill. Charles MacLaren, editor for three decades from 1817, was using his position to do much to bring the potential of steam railways to the notice of the public. Nor would the effect of steam railways be limited to passenger travel. An Edinburgh dealer might post an order, he added, at 8 p.m. on a Monday evening to a manufacturer in Leeds or Manchester – who would receive it the following morning and be able to dispatch the goods in time to be in the dealer's shop when it opened on Wednesday.

The prospect was opening up of a transport system that would not only be much quicker but also much cheaper than anything then known. In these circumstances people started to think of railways not just as a means to carry coal to its point of embarkation, but as a means to link city with city, town with town. The corridor between Edinburgh and Glasgow attracted early attention. Robert Stevenson had looked at it as early as 1817, and from 1825 onwards there were successive proposals in greater or lesser detail. Even before the Garnkirk & Glasgow was complete, Grainger and Miller were putting forward an eastward extension to Edinburgh itself. But inevitably then and later there were varying time lags between early proposals for railways, successful authorisation and eventual opening – during which circumstances and the railway map might both change greatly. So the first town-to-town railways to be authorised in Scotland were the result of none of the Edinburgh–Glasgow proposals: they were to run from Dundee to Arbroath, and from Arboath to Forfar, and were authorised by Acts of Parliament in 1836. These were the first of six such railways authorised during the years 1836 to 1838.[2] Grainger and Miller were engineers for the Dundee & Arbroath, Grainger alone for the Arbroath & Forfar.

At this period the question of the best track gauge for railways was a matter of controversy. George Stephenson had used a gauge of 4 ft 8 in., familiar on waggonways in north-east England, for the Stockton & Darlington and Liverpool & Manchester Railways. Later an extra half-inch was added to ease the passage of locomotives round sharp curves. Most railways for which George or Robert Stephenson or their protégés were the engineers were being built to this 4 ft 8½ in.

gauge. But there was a considerable body of opinion in the engineering world that it was too narrow for speed, safety and convenient layout of locomotives.[3] Brunel, famously, was building the Great Western Railway to a gauge as broad as 7 ft 0¼ in. The Irish Railway Commissioners recommended 6 ft 2 in. in 1838. If 4 ft 8½ in. was too narrow, the 4 ft 6 in. gauge used by most railways in Scotland up to 1836 was evidently narrower still. For the two lines converging on Arbroath, Grainger and Miller selected a gauge of 5 ft 6 in. These lines were opened in 1838–9.

Construction of the third railway authorised in 1836 took much longer. This was the Edinburgh, Leith & Newhaven, a line which appeared to have good prospects, for its line to Newhaven would carry passengers heading for the North by ferry, and the Leith branch would carry into Edinburgh coal arriving by sea. There were problems. The southern terminus was to be situated near the east end of Princes Street, in Princes Street Gardens at a point from which, it was hoped, an Edinburgh-to-Glasgow railway would also originate. The proposal provoked strenuous opposition. There were engineering problems too. The railway would have to tunnel beneath the New Town for more than 1,000 yd, on a gradient of 1 in 27½ for which cable traction was planned. Then there were problems of finance: Edinburgh investors held back, and the company therefore looked to Lancashire and particularly Liverpool where investors – the 'Liverpool Party' – had no such qualms.[4] In Liverpool they were already accustomed to a railway that tunnelled beneath their city. But much would happen before this Edinburgh railway was open.

The Edinburgh, Leith & Newhaven was the first Scottish railway to seek investment from Liverpool on a large scale, but that city's railway investors were already looking to Scotland for another reason. At that time the Grand Junction Railway was being built to link the Liverpool & Manchester Railway with Birmingham, and the London & Birmingham Railway was being built to extend the route to London. This north–south spine could also be extended in the opposite direction. By the mid-1830s railways were being built northwards from the Liverpool & Manchester towards Preston, and in 1835 the Grand Junction board, almost two years before its own line was opened, instructed its engineer Joseph Locke to inspect the country north of Preston to see if a line to Glasgow was practicable.[5] Locke was a highly competent engineer who had trained under George Stephenson, but had fallen out with him over the Grand Junction, where the pupil seems to have excelled the master. What he found north of Carlisle were two possible routes, the shorter but more steeply graded route through Annandale via Beattock, and the longer but more easily graded route through Nithsdale via Dumfries and Kilmarnock. The choice between the two would soon become a matter of intense controversy, but for the moment Locke favoured Nithsdale.

At this stage, proposals for two railways to run south and west from Glasgow took shape. These were the Glasgow, Paisley, Kilmarnock & Ayr Railway, and the Glasgow, Paisley & Greenock. The former, often called simply the Ayrshire Railway, was to take a route from Glasgow to Ayr via the valley of the Garnock, with a branch from Dalry to Kilmarnock: not the most direct route but one which offered easy gradients and limited engineering works, and was endorsed by George Stephenson himself. Clearly it would eventually link with any railway built northwards from Carlisle via Nithsdale. It was promoted, mainly, by Glasgow merchants. The Glasgow, Paisley & Greenock by

During 1840 3,000 men and 200 horses were at work building the railway between Paisley and Greenock. The greatest obstacle was the ridge at Bishopton: to penetrate it meant excavation of two tunnels, and approach cuttings as much as 70 ft deep through the rock. But the result was a ruling gradient, at this location, no steeper than 1 in 289. Some of the temporary track appears to have rails of wood. (Ironbridge Gorge Museum Trust, Elton Collection)

contrast was promoted largely from Greenock with the intent that it should restore that locality's significance as a port for Glasgow trade, which it had lost as a combined consequence of improvements to the upper Clyde and introduction of steamboats.[6]

At first the engineer for the Glasgow, Paisley & Greenock was Thomas Grainger, for the Ayrshire Railway John Miller: although they were formally in partnership, they now worked on separate projects. Probably if left to themselves they would have built both lines, and indeed subsequent main lines in Scotland, to 5 ft 6 in. gauge.[7] But the Greenock promoters were looking to substantial investment from the South, and to encourage it they first had Grainger's plans checked by Joseph Locke, and then replaced Grainger by an initially reluctant Locke and his partner John Errington.[8] It was Locke who proposed that the two companies between them should build a single jointly owned railway between Glasgow and Paisley, a proposal which was accepted.[9] This was the first joint railway, a precedent for many more throughout Britain. It was Locke too who advised use of the 4 ft 8½ in. gauge for the Glasgow, Paisley & Greenock, foreseeing an eventual link with a main line from England. That almost inevitably meant that the GPKA had also to be built to 4 ft 8½ in. gauge, although the board did not formally approve this until July 1838 – a year after the line had been authorised by an Act of Parliament which conveniently omitted reference to track gauge.[10] The GPG had been authorised on the same day in 1837.

Needing a company secretary, the GPG Railway advertised and from sixty applicants chose to appoint Captain Mark Huish, lately a quartermaster in the East India Company's army.[11] It chose well, for Huish would in due course move to the Grand Junction and then, on its amalgamation with the London & Birmingham, the London & North Western Railway, to become one of the best-known and most influential of all early railway managers.

The mid-1830s had also seen revival of plans for a railway between Edinburgh and Glasgow – indeed there were personal links with the Ayrshire Railway, for one of the latter's promoters and in due course deputy chairman, John Leadbetter, became in due course chairman of the Edinburgh & Glasgow Railway. The company obtained its Act in 1838. Here again the engineer was John Miller who with some reluctance built the railway to 4 ft 8½ in. gauge.[12] The route selected lay via Falkirk, to the north of earlier proposals but closely parallel to the canals. This route enabled Miller to lay out a line very much in the manner of those built by George and Robert Stephenson who, when trunk railways were first proposed, considered that the steepest gradient for a line to be worked by locomotives should be 1 in 330. Miller improved on this, producing a railway with no gradient steeper than 1 in 880 between the Edinburgh terminus, at Haymarket, and Cowlairs on the northern edge of Glasgow. There were no sharp curves either, but to achieve this line, so well suited to fast running, meant excavating long, deep cuttings through rock and building viaducts that were both tall and long. Most notable was the half-mile-long Almond Viaduct with thirty-six arches between sixty and eighty feet high.

Beyond Cowlairs it was a different matter, and the railway plunged down a gradient of 1 in 45, through a tunnel beneath the Forth & Clyde Canal (a bridge over this canal for tall-masted vessels would have had to open, interrupting rail traffic) to reach the centre of the city at the terminus, which soon became known as Queen Street. Cowlairs bank was worked by cable

haulage. Trains were hauled up complete with their locomotives, and ran down by gravity in the charge of several brake wagons placed at the front. Cable haulage lasted – apart from two intervals in the 1840s when extra-powerful locomotives were tried without lasting success – well into the twentieth century.

Back in the late 1830s, techniques for building a railway such as this were developing. Responsible to the engineer were the contractors, of varying competence and honesty but still with limited financial resources. The E & GR's forty-six miles were divided into twenty-one contracts, of which two were for viaduct construction.[13] On later lines, as successful contractors flourished and enlarged their businesses, so larger contracts were let and fewer contractors needed for a given length of line – although they might pass on much of their task to subcontractors.

The actual work of excavating cuttings and tunnels, and forming embankments, to produce the trackbed was largely pick-and-shovel work for muscular labourers – navvies, so-called because their predecessors who built canal navigations had been called 'navigators' and the word had been abbreviated. To aid them in their work they had temporary railways with horsedrawn waggons to move the spoil. Where rock was encountered it was blasted with gunpowder. Many other trades were present: for example, for tunnels, bridges and viaducts there was a need for brickmakers, bricklayers and masons. Construction of the Edinburgh & Glasgow Railway employed 7,000 men and 700 horses, the Glasgow Paisley & Greenock 3,000 men and 200 horses.

Such men – and sometimes their women – were accommodated in temporary huts of notoriously poor quality, although those which appear in D. O. Hill's view of Provanmill Cutting do not look too bad by the standards of the time. At work, injuries were common and fatalities not infrequent. Navvies worked a sixty-hour week for wages of around three pence an hour, paid once a month or so. Pay day, naturally, was cause for celebration, when the natural boisterousness of men fuelled by drink, whose physical strength was their greatest asset, sometimes degenerated into pitched battles, particularly when Highlanders and Irishmen were present in the same vicinity. Navvies in general – the work they did, the lives they led, the dangers they faced – are well covered in Handley's *The Navvy in Scotland*.[14]

While these railways were being built much thought was also being given to a cross-border railway and many routes, practicable and impracticable, were considered.[15] The most important development, however, arose from discontent among the landowners of Annandale at being bypassed by Locke's proposal. Led by the most prominent among their number, J. J. Hope Johnstone MP, they persuaded Locke to return to the district in 1837. This time he found the gradients above Beattock likely to be less severe than supposed, and he may well have had a growing confidence in the powers of the locomotive, for railways which went up and over high ground, rather than round it, would soon become his trademark. At any rate, he now favoured the Annandale route, the more so because if, as then seemed likely, there was only going to be sufficient traffic for a single railway from the Border to central Scotland, then it was important to make one that not only went to Glasgow but also offered the possibility of a branch to Edinburgh. He suggested the government should appoint a commission to consider the problem. Such a commission was eventually appointed. It considered all the proposals of which it could obtain details, and when it reported endorsed

Locke's view – with the rider that, had two lines been considered practicable, it would have supported an east-coast line to Edinburgh and quite possibly a Nithsdale route to Glasgow. That was in 1841, and there matters rested for a while, for the times were not propitious for raising money for such ventures.[16]

What was happening, however, was that the railways under construction were being completed and coming into use. First in the field was the Glasgow, Paisley, Kilmarnock & Ayr Railway, which opened its section from Irvine to Ayr on 5 August 1839; further sections followed until the line was open throughout (including the joint line) from Glasgow to Ayr a year later.[17] That was for passenger traffic: unlike the earlier waggonways and coal railways, these new inter-urban railways found that their main appeal was the speed and economy they offered to travellers. Goods traffic followed, on the Ayrshire Railway from January 1841. At Ayr the Ayrshire Railway crossed Taylor's waggonway by a gated crossing[18] and near Barassie it crossed the Kilmarnock & Troon Railway, presumably on the level, which must have made for some interesting trackwork. At Kilwinning it formed a junction with the Ardrossan Railway, which had obtained powers to divorce itself from the Paisley Canal, rebuild its line to 4 ft 8½ in. gauge and introduce locomotives.[19] The Glasgow, Paisley & Greenock Railway was opened in 1841, and the Kilmarnock branch of the GPK & A in 1843. Thus was a small network of railways growing up south-west of Glasgow. Their Glasgow terminus was at Bridge Street, immediately south of Glasgow Bridge.

Of even greater significance was the opening in February 1842 of the Edinburgh & Glasgow Railway, which brought the steam-worked, main-line railway into the capital. 'Who can foresee, we say, the great, the wonderful revolution that will take place in the affairs of Scotland by the opening of this important line?' wrote Francis Whishaw.[20] Even Lord Cockburn, no lover of innovation, soon found it useful. In *Circuit Journeys* he wrote that, to avoid the 'horrors' of a Sunday in Glasgow in 1842:

I fell upon a better scheme. Because the Court having risen at six on the Saturday evening, I got into the seven o'clock train, and found myself here [on the edge of Edinburgh] ..., *at tea and an egg, before ten. On Monday morning at seven, the impatient engine, after grunting and hissing to get away, was set free; and at nine exactly I was back in Glasgow, and, after a leisurely breakfast, was in Court when it met at ten.*[21]

What did Lord Cockburn and other travellers find when they ventured on to these early main-line railways? Coming from the west end of Edinburgh's Princes Street, the eye was caught from half-a-mile away, according to Lizars's guidebook, by a 'splendid and imposing structure with a handsome colonnade'. It contained the booking office and waiting rooms of the Edinburgh & Glasgow Railway. Past these travellers descended stairs to the 'departure parade' within a 'beautiful and commodious shed'. The imposing structure is still there, serving its original purpose; the commodious shed is not, although part of it can be found at Bo'ness as will be mentioned in Chapter 11. Departing passengers were warned by a bell to take their seats; five minutes later another bell was rung for attaching the engine and, almost immediately afterwards, a third bell rang which was the signal to start. When trains arrived, remarked the guidebook, 'omnibuses are drawn up on the platform for all parts of the town and Leith' – a degree of coordination which would be welcome today.

The locomotive that Lord Cockburn observed 'grunting and hissing to get away' owed its layout to

Sometime in the mid-1840s, pioneer photographers D.O.Hill and Robert Adamson took a series of views of Linlithgow. This is one, and prominent in the foreground is the station of the Edinburgh & Glasgow Railway. The photograph is a strong contender for the earliest to include a railway in its composition. Some of the buildings can still be recognised. (Scottish National Portrait Gallery)

one or other of the two main schools of locomotive design at that date, that of the Stephensons, and that of Edward Bury.[22] The E & GR had prudently ordered ten of each type to start its services. Planet locomotives had been found to pitch badly, and Robert Stephenson & Co. had developed the design by adding an additional pair of wheels to the rear of the firebox to produce the 2-2-2 wheel arrangement. Bury, originally a Liverpool sawmill-owner, had been building locomotives since the late 1820s, his typical locomotive being a four-wheeler carried on frames of iron bar (where Stephenson used timber sandwiched between iron plates) and had a large firebox, resembling a large vertical cylinder at the rear of the boiler. Bury's type was popular on the London & Birmingham

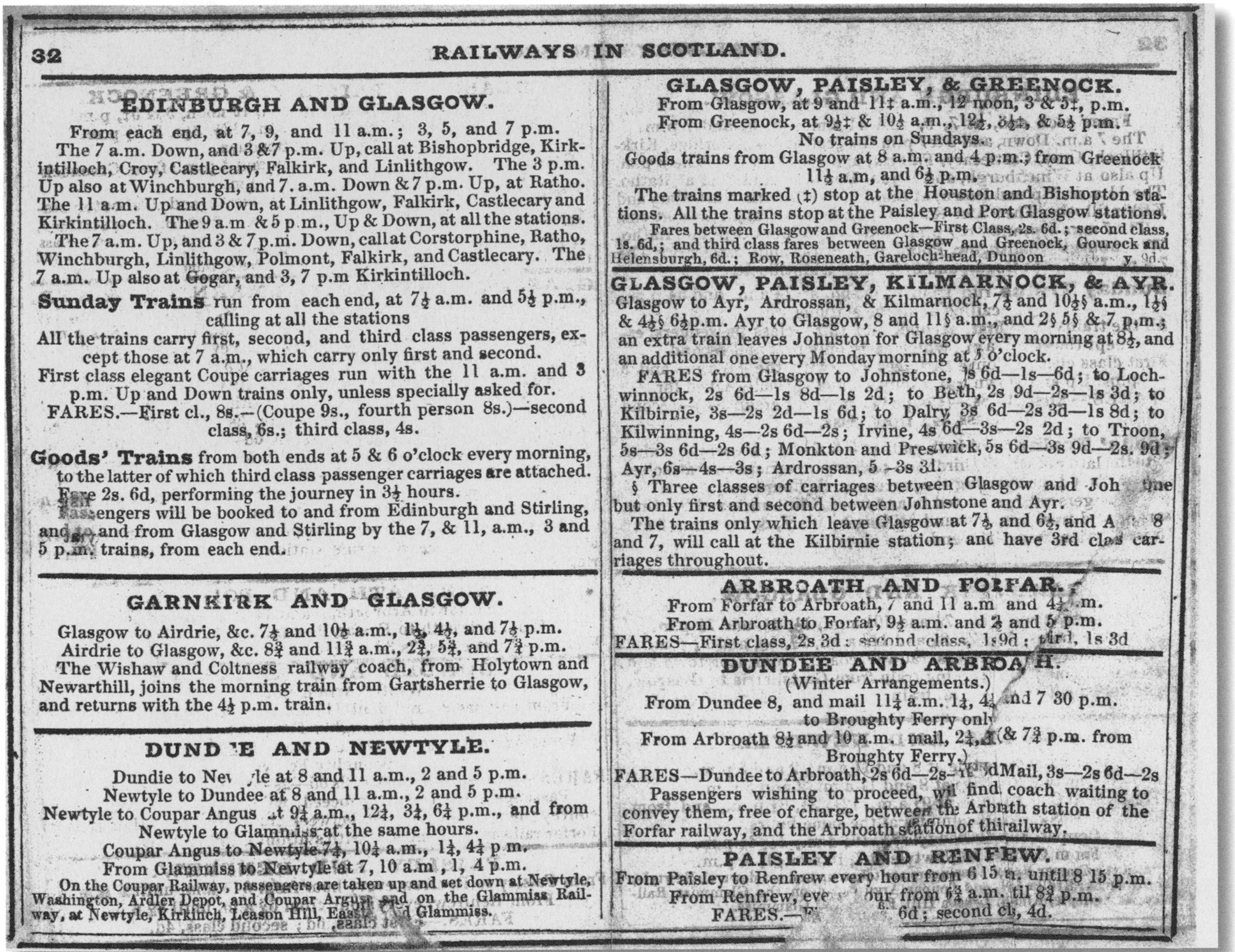

32 RAILWAYS IN SCOTLAND.

EDINBURGH AND GLASGOW.

From each end, at 7, 9, and 11 a.m.; 3, 5, and 7 p.m.

The 7 a.m. Down, and 3 &7 p.m. Up, call at Bishopbridge, Kirkintilloch, Croy, Castlecary, Falkirk, and Linlithgow. The 3 p.m. Up also at Winchburgh, and 7. a.m. Down & 7 p.m. Up, at Ratho. The 11 a.m. Up and Down, at Linlithgow, Falkirk, Castlecary and Kirkintilloch. The 9 a.m & 5 p.m., Up & Down, at all the stations.

The 7 a.m. Up, and 3 & 7 p.m. Down, call at Corstorphine, Ratho, Winchburgh, Linlithgow, Polmont, Falkirk, and Castlecary. The 7 a.m. Up also at Gogar, and 3, 7 p.m Kirkintilloch.

Sunday Trains run from each end, at 7½ a.m. and 5½ p.m., calling at all the stations

All the trains carry first, second, and third class passengers, except those at 7 a.m., which carry only first and second.

First class elegant Coupe carriages run with the 11 a.m. and 3 p.m. Up and Down trains only, unless specially asked for.

FARES.—First cl., 8s.—(Coupe 9s., fourth person 8s.)—second class, 6s.; third class, 4s.

Goods' Trains from both ends at 5 & 6 o'clock every morning, to the latter of which third class passenger carriages are attached. Fare 2s. 6d, performing the journey in 3½ hours.

Passengers will be booked to and from Edinburgh and Stirling, and to and from Glasgow and Stirling by the 7, & 11, a.m., 3 and 5 p.m. trains, from each end.

GARNKIRK AND GLASGOW.

Glasgow to Airdrie, &c. 7½ and 10½ a.m., 1½, 4½, and 7½ p.m.

Airdrie to Glasgow, &c. 8¾ and 11¾ a.m., 2¾, 5¾, and 7¾ p.m.

The Wishaw and Coltness railway coach, from Holytown and Newarthill, joins the morning train from Gartsherrie to Glasgow, and returns with the 4½ p.m. train.

DUND 'E AND NEWTYLE.

Dundie to Ne ,le at 8 and 11 a.m., 2 and 5 p.m.

Newtyle to Dundee at 8 and 11 a.m., 2 and 5 p.m.

Newtyle to Coupar Angus at 9¼ a.m., 12¼, 3¼, 6¼ p.m., and from Newtyle to Glammiss at the same hours.

Coupar Angus to Newtyle 7¼, 10¼ a.m., 1¼, 4¼ p.m.

From Glammiss to Newtyle at 7, 10 a.m , 1, 4 p.m.

On the Coupar Railway, passengers are taken up and set down at Newtyle, Washington, Ardler Depot, and Coupar Argus, and on the Glammiss Railway, at Newtyle, Kirkinch, Leason Hill, East d Glammiss.

GLASGOW, PAISLEY, & GREENOCK.

From Glasgow, at 9 and 11‡ a.m., 12 noon, 3 & 5‡, p.m.

From Greenock, at 9½‡ & 10½ a.m., 12½, 3½‡, & 5½ p.m.

No trains on Sundays.

Goods trains from Glasgow at 8 a.m. and 4 p.m.; from Greenock 11½ a.m, and 6½ p.m.

The trains marked (‡) stop at the Houston and Bishopton stations. All the trains stop at the Paisley and Port Glasgow stations.

Fares between Glasgow and Greenock—First Class, 2s. 6d.; second class, 1s. 6d,; and third class fares between Glasgow and Greenock, Gourock and Helensburgh, 6d.; Row, Roseneath, Gareloch-head, Dunoon y, 9d.

GLASGOW, PAISLEY, KILMARNOCK, & AYR.

Glasgow to Ayr, Ardrossan, & Kilmarnock, 7½ and 10½§ a.m., 1½§ & 4½§ 6½p.m. Ayr to Glasgow, 8 and 11§ a.m., and 2§ 5§ & 7 p.m.; an extra train leaves Johnston for Glasgow every morning at 8½, and an additional one every Monday morning at 5 o'clock.

FARES from Glasgow to Johnstone, 1s 6d—1s—6d; to Lochwinnock, 2s 6d—1s 8d—1s 2d; to Beith, 2s 9d—2s—1s 3d; to Kilbirnie, 3s—2s 2d—1s 6d; to Dalry, 3s 6d—2s 3d—1s 8d; to Kilwinning, 4s—2s 6d—2s; Irvine, 4s 6d—3s—2s 2d; to Troon, 5s—3s 6d—2s 6d; Monkton and Preswick, 5s 6d—3s 9d—2s. 9d; Ayr, 6s—4s—3s; Ardrossan, 5 -3s 3d.

§ Three classes of carriages between Glasgow and Joh ne but only first and second between Johnstone and Ayr.

The trains only which leave Glasgow at 7½, and 6½, and A 8 and 7, will call at the Kilbirnie station; and have 3rd clas carriages throughout.

ARBROATH AND FORFAR.

From Forfar to Arbroath, 7 and 11 a.m and 4½ .m.

From Arbroath to Forfar, 9½ a.m. and 2 and 5 p.m.

FARES—First class, 2s 3d; second class, 1s9d; third, 1s 3d

DUNDEE AND ARBROA H.

(Winter Arrangements.)

From Dundee 8, and mail 11¼ a.m. 1¼, 4¼ nd 7 30 p.m. to Broughty Ferry only

From Arbroath 8½ and 10 a.m. mail, 2¼, 4 (& 7¾ p.m. from Broughty Ferry.)

FARES—Dundee to Arbroath, 2s 6d—2s— dMail, 3s—2s 6d—2s

Passengers wishing to proceed, will find coach waiting to convey them, free of charge, between the Arbroath station of the Forfar railway, and the Arbroath station of this railway.

PAISLEY AND RENFEW.

From Paisley to Renfrew every hour from 6 15 a. until 8 15 p.m.

From Renfrew, eve our from 6¾ a.m. til 8¾ p.m.

FARES.—F s. 6d; second cl, 4d.

Bradshaw's Railway Companion for 1842 covered Scottish railways on a single page. The details repay study. (Author's collection)

Railway and elsewhere and was used in Scotland on the Ayrshire and Ardrossan Railways[23] as well as the E & G. But it could not easily be enlarged, and as trains grew heavier it was from the Stephenson type that larger and more powerful locomotives were developed.

Miller himself also specified a 2-2-2 design for the Ayrshire Railway and then, evidently for purposes of comparison, arranged for four locomotives to be built by each of three builders.[24]

Shortly after the E & GR was opened, the

attention of its directors was caught by an exhibition mounted in Edinburgh of apparatus powered by electromagnetic engines. These had been developed by Robert Davidson, an Aberdonian grocer turned chemist turned experimenter in electricity. Davidson had already produced a model electric locomotive powered by batteries: now he sought support for a full-size version. It was probably at the expense of the E & GR that Davidson was able to build one, and demonstrate it on the railway that autumn. This, the first electric locomotive, hauled six tons at 4 mph over one and a half miles. Despite that promising start, the railway company did not pursue the subject further: electric rail traction only became fully practicable in the 1880s after invention of the dynamo. Nevertheless Davidson's locomotive was destroyed by a Luddite element among the railway workforce.[25]

The earliest railway coaches intended for steam trains, those of the Liverpool & Manchester Railway, were each made by mounting three well-upholstered coach bodies, as used on road coaches of the period, upon a four-wheeled underframe. Such coaches were first-class; for passengers who preferred to travel 'outside' on stagecoaches the L & MR provided coaches with wooden bench seats, open to the elements although roofs were fitted, and for those whose preferences, or financial resources, were still more modest it provided open coaches without any seats or roofs at all. Subsequent railways followed this example, and from the pattern of the first-class coach there developed the compartment coach conventional on railways in Britain for over a century.[26]

The Garnkirk & Glasgow Railway had obtained two first-class carriages of Liverpool & Manchester pattern for its opening day, and after the custom of the period gave them names, *Royal William* and

At Haymarket, original terminus of the Edinburgh & Glasgow Railway, the station building backed onto the train shed; when the main line was extended to Waverley in 1846 it was diverted to the south, past the end of the building. Much of the train shed remained in situ, however, until 1982, latterly covering car-parking space; it was then demolished, and part of it re-erected at Bo'ness on the Bo'ness & Kinneil Railway. (East Dunbartonshire Information & Archives)

Royal Adelaide. But the railway's regular customers had less ambitious ideas: while the two first-class coaches languished in the shed, they flocked to travel in simpler coaches, which Whishaw[27] described as 'unsightly and uncomfortable old boxes' – and indeed on holidays also in open wagons normally used for coal and iron.[28] The two first-class coaches were eventually allocated to the Slamannan Railway for its through trains from Glasgow to Causewayend[29] where one hopes they came into their own, even if only for a limited period.

The Glasgow, Paisley, Kilmarnock & Ayr commenced operations in 1839 with first- and second-class carriages of the Liverpool & Manchester pattern and added some third-class within a few months. Then in 1840 the board decided that seats should be removed from the third-class, and future third-class coaches built without them.[30]

In this form Whishaw encountered them, referring to them as 'Stanhopes, or stand-ups'[31] – the name in both cases being pronounced, presumably, 'stan'up' as a pun on the Stanhope, at that period a well-known type of light two-wheeled horsedrawn carriage named after its inventor. Whishaw notes that the GPK & A 'Stanhopes' were similar to those on the Manchester & Leeds Railway, which were 17 ft long and 8 ft 8 in. wide with four entrances, and divided into four compartments by a wooden bar down the middle and another across it at right angles. 'The number of passengers it will contain' adds Whishaw 'depends on the bulk of the respective stanhopers'.[32]

Similar coaches ran on the Glasgow, Paisley & Greenock Railway, where the board was concerned to find them patronised by canny middle-class seaside-villa occupants en route for the city, in preference to more expensive accommodation,[33] while the honest working men for whom they were intended seem to have stuck with the Clyde steamboats.[34]

The GPG considered such vehicles to be fourth-class, and so did the Edinburgh & Glasgow when it introduced them soon after opening, although in this case they were larger vehicles on six wheels, with roofs. At opening the E & G had first-, second- and third-class coaches on all of its six daily passenger trains, except the 7.00 a.m. patronised by Lord Cockburn, which was first and second class only. Some of the first-class coaches were described as 'elegant Coupé carriages': probably they were similar to a type of coach popular with well-to-do travellers on the Grand

Junction Railway, in which an end compartment was laid out as a coupé with a single row of seats facing end windows. At the other extreme the E & G attached third-class coaches to two early morning slow goods trains, and charged extra low fares for them.[35] The same practice prevailed on some English railways: on roads at that period carriers generally carried a few passengers among the parcels on their waggons moving ponderously about the turnpike road network,

Rails were steadily becoming heavier, better able to withstand the pounding from heavy loads at speed. The Stockton & Darlington main line had been laid with rails of 28 lb/yd, and the Monkland & Kirkintilloch probably followed suit.[36] The two Arbroath lines were laid with 48 lb/yd rail, but the Ayrshire, the Glasgow, Paisley & Greenock and the Edinburgh & Glasgow Railways were all laid with rails weighing as much as 75 lb/yd. All these five railways still mounted much of their trackwork on stone blocks, but equally all to a greater or lesser extent also used wooden sleepers, particularly on embankments or elsewhere where the ground was soft. The GPK & A further had some 45 lb/yd rail of 'bridge' section laid on continuous longitudinal timbers, in a manner similar to that used by Brunel's Great Western Railway at that period.[37]

Horse railways had functioned on the principle that the driver would pull up if he saw an obstruction, and the earliest steam locomotives, moving at slow speed, meant little change. After Rainhill things were different, and the Liverpool & Manchester Railway stationed 'policemen' at intervals to indicate known obstructions to drivers – by flag signals in the daytime, lamps at night. The practice known as 'time interval' working grew up: one train was not allowed to follow another until an interval of five minutes or so had elapsed. The Grand Junction Railway used fixed signals – vertically pivoted boards mounted on top of posts – to warn drivers of obstructions. The Edinburgh & Glasgow Railway was equipped with fixed signals from the start: Lizars notes that on leaving Edinburgh the train passed first, on the right, the carriage and goods sheds, and then on the left, the first signal. This consisted of 'painted vanes' by day, and coloured glass by night. Further on a second signal was soon passed. The Edinburgh & Glasgow was also right up to date in having the newly invented electric telegraph installed,[38] although how extensive the installation was I do not know. Nor is it likely at this date to have been used specifically for signalling trains, but rather for general communication.

Few stagecoach services could long survive the opening of a parallel railway: their proprietors were reduced to operating in regions where there was as yet no railway, and to co-operating with the newcomer to the extent of running feeder coaches to and from railway stations. An early example was a coach between Kilmarnock and Irvine, where it connected with trains, prior to the opening of the Ayrshire Railway's Kilmarnock branch.[39]

Canals put up a stronger fight. For goods they remained in a strong position, particularly when speed was not critical or where traders had direct access to a canal wharf but not to a railway station. Canal passenger traffic was initially more problematical. It was highly developed: the Paisley Canal was carrying over 400,000 passengers a year prior to the railway, and when the railway was opened a period of cut-throat competition ensued with fare reductions leapfrogging one another. But trains were faster than even swift boats, and in 1843 the canal company agreed to give up carrying passengers in return for an annual payment from the railway.[40] Between Edinburgh &

Glasgow, through passenger boats struggled on for six years after the railway was opened but were then withdrawn;[41] local boats lasted for a while longer on the Forth & Clyde Canal section of the route, which was not paralleled so closely by the railway as was the Union Canal.

Competition from coastal steamboats was an even tougher nut for the railways to crack. Such vessels had been practicable since 1812, when Henry Bell put his pioneer paddle steamer *Comet* into service on the Clyde, and steamboat services flourished during the 1820s and '30s. In 1837, 692,000 passengers travelled over the Clyde between Glasgow, Greenock and beyond.[42] The promoters of the Glasgow, Paisley & Greenock Railway had hoped that steamboat owners would decide to start their boats from Greenock rather than Glasgow, a hope which proved false and the railway company was reduced to chartering steamboats to connect with its trains; some of its shareholders formed their own steamboat company for the same purpose, all of which attempts met with qualified success.

The Ayrshire Railway for some years participated in Anglo-Scottish traffic by connecting with a steamboat service started in 1840 between Liverpool – already reached by rail from London – and Ardrossan.[43] The southern port moved to Fleetwood when the railway system was extended thither. Thomas Cook used this route at midsummer 1846, to bring his first large party of tourists to Scotland. It was a great event: when they reached Glasgow, guns fired a salute as the train drew up, and a band played; his tourists continued later over the Edinburgh & Glasgow Railway to Edinburgh where a similar welcome awaited them.[44]

Local excursion traffic, however, was nothing new and had been contributing to railways' finances

TO BUILDERS.

The DIRECTORS of the EDINBURGH and GLASGOW RAILWAY COMPANY are prepared to grant

FREE TICKETS

TO PARTIES WHO MAY

BUILD VILLAS

within a Mile of any of the Stations on the Line, not being Town Stations, on the following terms :—

Certified Cost of Villa.		Free Ticket for Years.
£500		5
600		6
700		7
800		8
900		9
1000		10

and so on, an additional year for every additional £100 in the Cost of a Villa.

TICKETS TRANSFERABLE TO A YEARLY TENANT, IF THE HOUSE IS NOT OCCUPIED BY OWNER.

Further Information may be known on application at Company's Offices, George Square, Glasgow.

To encourage traffic, the Edinburgh & Glasgow Railway offered free tickets to those who built houses near its stations.
(East Dunbartonshire Information & Archives)

for years. But even everyday fares were cheap: on the Glasgow Paisley & Greenock the first-class fares were comparable to third-class in England, and even then 64 per cent of traffic was third-class, with a tendency for the percentage to increase.[45] Low fares undoubtedly encouraged traffic: Whishaw, visiting the Arboath & Forfar Railway, was surprised to find a party of reapers travelling by train rather than walk to work, and learned that such was not unusual. Unlike the main lines in England, which tended initially to cater primarily for first- and second-class passengers, third-class was important to the Scottish lines from the start.[46] Wherever railways were built, traffic tended to appear. Prior to construction of the Arbroath & Forfar, there had been no public conveyance at all between its termini.[47] To encourage this trend still further, the Edinburgh & Glasgow Railway offered a

supply of free tickets to those who built villas near its stations – an example followed by other railways in due course.

Only one cloud was appearing on the horizon: observance of the Sabbath. The first half of the nineteenth century, which saw the initial growth of the railway system, also saw the growth of Sabbatarianism and the theological dispute that accompanied it. Was work on the Sabbath to be banned totally, in accordance with the tenth commandment (Exodus chapter 20, verses 10–12), or were works of mercy or necessity to be exempted?[48] Sir Andrew Agnew MP, of Lochnaw, Wigtownshire, a noted Sabbatarian, inclined towards the former view, at least so far as travel on Sunday was concerned and, when the bill for the Glasgow, Paisley, Kilmarnock & Ayr Railway was before Parliament, attempted to have a clause inserted to prohibit Sunday travel on the line.[49] He was unsuccessful, but railways such as the Glasgow, Paisley & Greenock and the Arbroath & Forfar, in deference to local religious feelings, ran no trains on Sundays. Whishaw took this as a general prohibition throughout Scotland.[50] As the railway system expanded over ensuing decades, so would the controversy.

One of the consequences of low fares was that railwaymens' wages were low too, at least compared with England, although probably not by comparison with other occupations. Even so, although the railways found traffic higher than expected, so were costs, and railway companies, though they prospered, did not do so to the extent anticipated. But this in turn was due in part to the depressed state of the economy in the early 1840s; in 1842, so difficult was it to raise funds, the railway system of Britain was later considered to have been in a state of equilibrium. Things would soon change.

The Highland Railway reached the most northerly extremity of the British railway system, Thurso, in 1874. Locomotive no. 55 pre-dated this, having been built, as a 2-2-2, in 1864, and rebuilt as a 2-4-0 in 1874. The photograph could have been taken at almost any time between then and 1906 when the locomotive was withdrawn. (Author's collection)

HOW THE SYSTEM GREW

By 1844 the British economy was on the upturn, and there was capital lying idle awaiting profitable investment. The early trunk lines in England had been operating profitably for several years. It was to railway promotion that investors, and then speculators, now looked – and Parliament in its turn was looking at railways. Promoters of railways needed Parliamentary authorisation for two principal reasons: to be incorporated into a company and so to limit the financial liability of shareholders, and to obtain the powers they needed to build the railway, notably that of compulsory purchase of land.

The legislative process by which Parliament authorised railways had been based originally on that for turnpike trusts and, even more, on canals. Parliament took the opportunity to regulate formation of railway companies, in the public interest, through its procedure for considering private bills. Railway promoters had first to comply with Parliamentary standing orders, which became ever more elaborate, and then to justify themselves before the Parliamentary Committee that considered their bill. Standing orders required among much else the deposit, both in the Private Bill Office and in the localities concerned, of detailed maps, plans and sections of the proposed railway, estimates of the expense, lists of subscribers and lists of owners and occupiers of land. Before the Parliamentary Committee the promoters were represented by counsel who rapidly became well versed in terms of railway construction and endeavoured to show, by producing expert witness after expert witness, that the scheme was not merely in great demand by the public but also wholly practicable in financial and engineering terms: or not, as the case might be, for opponents of the scheme were also represented. Initially such opposition came from those who considered the scheme prejudicial or harmful to their interests, where they had not been bought off earlier by promise of compensation: but as the pace of railway promotion hotted up, opposition came more and more from rival promoters of railways to serve the same district. Originally the members of parliament who comprised these committees were drawn from those with local connections, so that the committee might have the benefit of local knowledge: from 1844, in the interests of the wider public benefit, they were not.[1] In that year, too, Gladstone as prime minister established an advisory board, under the chairmanship of Lord Dalhousie, to consider each scheme and report for or against it as a guide the committee concerned.

As it became increasingly clear that railway companies, once formed, were going to be in a powerful and monopolistic position in their dealings with the public, so Parliament through a succession of

Select Committees sought first to inform itself about railways in their various aspects, and then to regulate the activities of railway companies. The Regulation of Railways Act, 1840, and a further Act of 1842 gave the Board of Trade important powers over railways, and led to establishment of its Railway Inspectorate. The principal tasks of its inspecting officers were twofold: to inspect new railways and, if they considered them safe, to authorise their opening; and to hold enquiries into railway accidents in order to recommend measures to prevent recurrence. The Regulation of Railways Act 1844[2] – 'Gladstone's Act' – required, as probably the best known of its many provisions, all passenger railways incorporated subsequently to provide at least one train a day which called at all stations and carried third-class passengers for one penny a mile at 12 mph or more – the 'Parliamentary Train'. It also empowered the Government to, in effect, nationalise such railways after an interval of twenty-one years – powers which were never brought into play, although the possibility of doing so was seriously considered by a Royal Commission in 1865.[3] Indeed, since the 1840s the attitudes of successive governments towards railways have swung, pendulum-like, between unfettered *laissez faire* at one extreme and total state ownership at the other, with regulation and control in the middle. A further Act in 1846, the Gauge of Railways Act, established the 4 ft 8½ gauge as the standard gauge for new passenger railways in Britain.

In 1844–5 Parliament passed 48 railway bills out of 66 placed before it; in 1845–6, 270 were passed out of 560.[4] In 1845 railway promotion had moved from safe investment to financial speculation to speculative frenzy. This was the Railway Mania, a speculative bubble of which there was a pale shadow to be seen in the dotcom bubble, a few years back. And indeed

Crossing over the Forth & Clyde Canal required a swing bridge for sailing ships with masts, so early main lines passed below it wherever possible. Here the Scottish Central Railway burrowed beneath the canal between Larbert and Greenhill. (Author)

many Railway Mania proposals were no more than bubbles: share prices rocketed while the 'scrip', or shares in unincorporated railway companies, was negotiable and could be sold at a considerable profit by unscrupulous promoters. Such activities did not go unnoticed by satirists: for example, *Blackwood's Edinburgh Magazine* for October 1845 contained (anonymously) Professor W. B. Aytoun's 'How we got up the Glenmutchkin Railway, and how we got out of it'. Two hard-up young men see the way out of their difficulties as promoting such a line through the west Highlands. Their prospectus, prepared with the help of a cask of Oban whisky, listed a committee which included such imaginary worthies as The M'Closkie, and the Factor for Glentumblers; it also observed that in the twelve-mile line there were only four tunnels, adding 'the shortest of these does not exceed a mile and a half' – all of which gives some idea of the tenor of

Greenhill Lower, seen here in a recent view, has ever been one of the nodal points in the Scottish railway system. When opened in 1848 the Caledonian Railway, on the left, trailed into the Scottish Central Railway which descended from its junction with the Edinburgh & Glasgow, behind the photographer, and headed northwards for Perth. Caledonian and Scottish Central formed part of the West Coast route from Euston to Aberdeen. For some years it was uncertain whether the SCR would amalgamate with the E&G or the Caledonian, but eventually the Caledonian won. Container trains became a feature of the railway system in the late twentieth century; this one is en route from Grangemouth to Mossend. (Bill Roberton)

the whole. The proposal was a great success, of course, at least as far as the promoters were concerned. The Sabbatarians got a mention too, their money being as good as anyone else's.[5]

In setting his fictional proposal in the west Highlands, Aytoun was right on the mark: for there were as yet no main-line railways north of the Highland line and the field was wide open for speculative proposals. One such, backed by the Marquess of Breadalbane, would have run from Callander via Crianlarich to Oban, with branches to Killin, from Crianlarich through Glen Falloch to the head of Loch Lomond, and from Tyndrum to Dalwhinnie; in Glen Falloch the surveyors came to blows – in an echo of the clan warfare of earlier times – with the surveyors for a rival scheme backed by the Duke of Montrose. The steeply graded Glen Falloch line was to have been worked by atmospheric traction, that great Victorian blind alley diverging from the true path of technological progress. Noted engineers were tempted by it, Brunel in particular; John Miller was in good company, as engineer to the proposed Edinburgh & Leith Atmospheric Railway which promised a ten-minute interval service.[6]

None of these lines was built, at least at this period; nor were most of the 112 railways proposed in Scotland for which, according to the *Illustrated London News* (6 December 1845), the required details had been provided to the Board of Trade.[7] 'The country is an asylum of railway lunatics' commented Lord Cockburn,[8] crusty as ever. Regrettably, in that highly charged speculative atmosphere, the activities of the Dalhousie board came to seem unduly restrictive: it was wound up, and the development of the railway system left to chance and the will of Parliament considering individual proposals.

Financially, the bubble burst in mid-October 1845 –

Extension of the Edinburgh & Glasgow Railway through Princes Street Gardens was strongly opposed but eventually successful. Here it seems innocuous enough as the foreground to the lithograph *Edinburgh Castle from the Mound*. (Science Museum Pictorial / Science & Society Picture Library)

share prices collapsed and many who had thought themselves rich found themselves poor again. But in Parliament the process continued, for there were sound proposals amongst the froth, and this applied particularly to Scotland.

In this heady atmosphere of 1844–5 the concept of a single cross-border railway was rapidly disregarded if not forgotten. On the east side of England, the railway system was expanding northwards largely as a result of the entrepreneurial activities of George Hudson, 'the Railway King', whose star was then in the ascendant. It was with Hudson's support that an Act was obtained in 1844 for the North British Railway, to run from North Bridge, Edinburgh, to Berwick. John Learmonth, deputy chairman of the Edinburgh & Glasgow, was chairman; Miller was engineer. Within a year the NBR had purchased the Edinburgh & Dalkeith and obtained powers to build both a link to it and a long extension down to Hawick. The NBR's main line to Berwick was opened in 1846 – although, for the moment, road coaches carried southbound passengers onward – and the Edinburgh & Glasgow Railway, opposition overcome, was extended to meet it at what was then called the General station and later became Waverley. The Edinburgh & Dalkeith was rebuilt and regauged, and the line to Hawick opened by stages during 1847–9.

A branch from St Boswells to Kelso was opened in 1850; in 1849 the York, Newcastle & Berwick Railway, soon to be incorporated into the North Eastern, had opened a branch from Tweedmouth up the Tweed valley and over the Border to Sprouston. In 1851 the two branches were extended to meet one another in an end-on junction. The location of this gave the English company some three and a half miles of line, with two stations, north of the border: the only instance of an English railway operating a line in Scotland prior to the Grouping of 1923.

In 1846, despite continuing sharp controversy over routes northward from Carlisle, the Act of Parliament was passed for the Caledonian Railway, to link Carlisle with Glasgow and Edinburgh: nor did matters rest there, for other Acts the same session authorised the continuation northwards: Scottish Central Railway onward by Stirling to Perth, the Scottish Midland Junction to Forfar, and the Aberdeen Railway to the city of its name; while the Clydesdale Junction Railway was authorised to provide a link south of Glasgow

with the joint line to Paisley. The Glasgow, Paisley & Greenock Railway amalgamated with the Caledonian company in 1847.

It is evident that, as far as possible, the routes of earlier railways were incorporated into the new main lines. So although the Caledonian was to reach Edinburgh – the terminus was at Lothian Road – by its own branch from Carstairs, its main line was to run only to a junction with the Wishaw & Coltness Railway, whence there was access to Glasgow over the Glasgow, Garnkirk & Coatbridge. To go further north, its trains would diverge at Gartsherrie and run over the Monkland & Kirkintilloch Railway for five-eights of a mile before diverging again at Garnqueen on to a new line to be built by the Caledonian to Greenhill south of Larbert. The Scottish Central in turn was authorised to make junctions at Greenhill with both the Caledonian and the Edinburgh & Glasgow Railways. Further north through Strathmore the Scottish Midland Junction incorporated two short extensions of the Dundee & Newtyle Railway one of which, the Newtyle & Glammis (sic) had been so impoverished that it propelled its passenger coach by sail; beyond Forfar the Aberdeen Railway's route incorporated the first few miles of the Arbroath & Forfar Railway. To be incorporated into the new main lines, the earlier railways had to have their lines either widened in gauge or, in the case of the last mentioned, narrowed: the directors of the Arbroath & Forfar narrowed its gauge reluctantly, for they had at one time hoped that the 5 ft 6 in. gauge might be made the gauge for Scotland.[9]

For all these new lines except the Aberdeen Railway, Locke and Errington became the engineers, and Brassey, McKenzie & Stephenson the contractors; of all Victorian railway contractors, Thomas Brassey was

Perth station, as built, was given a long and imposing frontage. But later enlargement of the station isolated these buildings on an island platform, with railway tracks occupying the site of the road approach seen here. The effect of these alterations is shown in the illustration on page 84.
(Perth Museum and Art Gallery)

the greatest. By 1847 there were 20,000 men at work on the Caledonian alone. In the contractors' team was Isaac Dodds,[10] whose possible contribution to the design of the earliest Monkland & Kirkintilloch Railway locomotives was mentioned above. The route formed by successive railways northwards from Carlisle – with their English counterparts they became known as the West Coast route – was complete as far as Brechin and Montrose by the summer of 1848, and to Aberdeen in 1850. The Dundee & Perth Railway,

which absorbed the Dundee & Newtyle, was opened during 1847–9.

Noteworthy were the large stations, Carlisle Citadel and Perth General, provided for the joint use of the railways converging on those places. Carlisle Citadel, built at the joint expense of the Caledonian and Lancaster & Carlisle Railways, was provided by architect William Tite with an extensive and handsome Tudor-style station building; the same architect provided a similar building at Perth, built by the Scottish Central. Later, in the 1860s, joint committees would be formed for each of these stations, from representatives of the companies concerned, to regulate their use and operation.

In 1849 also the Clydesdale Junction Railway, already absorbed by the Caledonian company, was opened, including a short branch to a terminus at Glasgow, South Side; the same year the Caledonian reached what would for some years be its main terminus in central Glasgow, Buchanan Street, by means of a branch from the original Garnkirk & Glasgow line. From 1 March 1848, a daily through train left London at 9.00 a.m. for Glasgow, reached at 10 p.m., and vice versa. Completion of the Caledonian lines also meant that the CR started to operate its own train service between Edinburgh and Glasgow via Carstairs – a roundabout and slow route compared with the Edinburgh & Glasgow's direct line, but competitive with it nonetheless, provided the fares were kept low.

In 1848 the West Coast route had received an unexpected accolade when Queen Victoria, returning south from Balmoral and learning that the royal yacht was fogbound, travelled at short notice by train from Montrose to London Euston. That event, as much as any, may be taken as the moment when the railway became the normal means of long-distance travel in Britain.

The Caledonian did not have things all its own way between Carlisle and Glasgow. In 1845 the Ayrshire Railway was authorised by Act of Parliament to extend its Kilmarnock branch to a point near Cumnock, and in 1846 a further Act authorised the Glasgow, Dumfries & Carlisle Railway to continue the route as far as a junction with the Caledonian at Gretna, whence it would have running powers over the Caledonian into Carlisle. Miller was engineer for

both sections and near Mauchline built perhaps the greatest of all his engineering works, Ballochmyle Viaduct. Its semicircular central arch of 181 ft was the largest masonry span in the world, then and for five decades subsequently. As soon as the route was opened throughout – in 1850 – the two companies amalgamated in a prearranged merger to form the Glasgow & South Western Railway.

Meanwhile in 1846 the Ayrshire Railway had taken a lease of the pioneer Kilmarnock & Troon Railway, and rebuilt it as a standard-gauge locomotive-worked railway. The GSWR eventually bought it in 1899.[11]

Heading north from Edinburgh, the Edinburgh Leith & Newhaven Railway renamed itself the Edinburgh, Leith & Granton Railway to reflect a change in planned termini, but there were continuing problems. After seven men had been killed in four separate accidents during a period of fifteen months, the sheriff of Midlothian appointed an engineer to supervise construction – and his reports in turn gave so much concern that work was thrice suspended for a while.[12] The railway was open in part from 1842, but the tunnel – Scotland Street Tunnel – took so long to make that the railway was eventually completed between the three places of its new name only in 1847. Its Edinburgh terminus, Canal Street, did indeed adjoin the General station.

North of the Forth the Edinburgh & Northern Railway was authorised in 1845; it was opened in 1847–8 from Burntisland to Ferryport-on-Craig (Tayport), with a long branch from Ladybank to join the Scottish Central Railway south of Perth. In 1849 it amalgamated with the Edinburgh, Leith & Granton to form the Edinburgh, Perth & Dundee Railway.

The big problem faced by this company was of course the presence of the Firth of Forth and the

Firth of Tay, crossed by ferries between Granton and Burntisland, and between Tayport and Broughty Ferry. For passengers this was inconvenient and time-consuming. For goods and for livestock it was worse, for everything had to be trans-shipped between train and boat four times between Edinburgh and Dundee. Manager and engineer of the Edinburgh, Perth & Dundee at this time was Thomas Bouch, a native of Cumbria in his late twenties who had worked under Locke and Errington on construction of the Lancaster & Carlisle Railway. It was Bouch who designed for the EP & D what was then called a floating railway and later became known as a train ferry, together with the arrangements for loading and unloading. The first ferry, named *Leviathan*, was built by Robert Napier & Sons on the Clyde; for manoeuvrability she had rudders at both ends, and the paddle wheels were individually driven both as to speed and direction. Railway tracks were laid upon the deck.

There were precedents. Steam ferries were already carrying road coaches across the Firth of Tay, and the Forth & Clyde Canal had its waggon boats. Since 1843 a screw-steamer, the *Bedlington*, had been carrying chaldron waggons loaded with coal from the shallow harbour at Blyth, Northumberland, down the coast to the Tyne where the waggons were discharged into colliers.[13] Bouch must have been aware of some of this.

On the Forth he faced the problem of a tidal range of some twenty feet. This he solved in two stages. At each terminal a ramp was built, sloping down into the water and with two railway tracks laid upon it. Upon these ran a sixteen-wheeled cradle, moved up and down the ramp by cable from a steam winch, and on its level top were railway tracks; railway wagons could start down the ramp and run on to the cradle. At the

seaward end of the cradle the tracks continued on to a span of malleable iron girders which projected far enough for the squared-off bow of the ferry to butt up against it. This span was hinged so that its outer end, which was supported by chains from derricks, had enough vertical movement to align with the tracks on the deck of the ferry. Cables from the steam winch were used to transfer wagons on to and off the vessel. Usually only goods stock was ferried, although on a trial passage when the ferry came into use in 1850, directors and guests travelled in a passenger carriage which was put aboard at Burntisland and carried to Granton, after which they repaired to the Granton Hotel for a celebratory dinner.[14]

This ferry and others like her functioned well for more than four decades, until both firths had been crossed by bridges. Had Bouch not attempted to bridge the Tay with disastrous results in the 1870s, his memory would be highly respected as a pioneer of the train ferry, and indeed of the roll-on, roll-off ferry and the linkspan.

The 1840s, as well as being a period of much new construction of railways, were a period of complex negotiations for cooperation, even to the point of amalgamation, between existing railways, new railways, proposed railways and canals, as each concern sought to improve its competitive position relative to others. For a time in 1846 there was a conglomerate of railways and canals managed as a group, the railways being the Edinburgh & Glasgow, Monkland & Kirkintilloch, Wishaw & Coltness, Ballochney and Slamannan, and the canals the Forth & Clyde, Union and Monkland. This was intended as a preliminary to an amalgamation into which would also come the Scottish Central Railway, then being built. But the amalgamation did not come to fruition. Nor did

John Miller's masterpiece, Ballochmyle Viaduct, carried the main line of the Glasgow & South Western Railway high above the Water of Ayr near Mauchline.
(Author)

a proposal that the Scottish Central be leased by a consortium of three other companies: Caledonian, Lancaster & Carlisle, and London & North Western.

When the dust did eventually settle, the Wishaw & Coltness and the Glasgow, Garnkirk & Coatbridge Railways had been acquired by the Caledonian Railway; and the Monkland & Kirkintilloch, Ballochney and Slamannan Railways (all now standard gauge) had amalgamated together as the Monkland Railways; the Slamannan Railway had been extended to join the Edinburgh & Glasgow Railway, and the Monkland & Kirkintilloch linked to the E & G near Lenzie. On the canal side, the Monkland Canal had been taken over by the Forth & Clyde, and the Union Canal by the Edinburgh & Glasgow Railway.

Motive for the latter purchase, in 1848, remains unclear, since it must have been evident by then that the canal as such posed no long-term threat to the railway. This author has often wondered whether the E & GR bought the canal to pre-empt its purchase by another railway company for conversion into a competing railway line. Canals elsewhere were converted into railways, and for such purpose the Union Canal would have been attractive to both the Caledonian and the Scottish Central. But this possibility remains conjecture: despite a search through surviving E & GR records,[15] I have found nothing to confirm it, and from these the purchase of the canal appears to have been no more than the culmination of a rates war.

Groups of southern shareholders such as the 'Liverpool Party' showed their strength at this period too, achieving on separate occasions the resignation of the chairman and all or most of the boards of both the Edinburgh & Glasgow and Caledonian Railways. In the latter case, the board's talent for financial management of an operating railway had proved much inferior to its talent for promoting it and getting it built – leading to financial crisis in 1850.[16] In the former, among other concerns such as the proposed amalgamation – this was 1846 – there was a suspicion, not without foundation, that Scottish-based directors with numerous other business interests were more concerned to see freight rates kept low than dividends kept high. But the board was only ousted by what might be termed an unholy alliance, between English speculators and Scottish Sabbatarians.

On Sundays, under contract to the Post Office the company was obliged to run mail trains, and since opening, after much heart-searching by the board and against a constant background of dissent, it had provided two passenger trains each way on Sundays as well. For this, a reverend gentlemen advised most of the board that they were 'infidels, scoffers, men of unholy lives, the enemies of all righteousness, moral suicides, sinners against light, traitors to their country, robbers and murderers.' He was far from alone in holding such views. Sabbatarians bought shares and attended annual meetings. When the two groups with such divergent interests came together in 1846, the board was outvoted. The new board withdrew Sunday passenger trains: the mail trains continued to run, without passengers.[17] There was a similar prolonged controversy on the Edinburgh, Perth & Dundee Railway, without such dramatic results.

There had been temporary bridges over Tweed and Tyne, pending completion of permanent ones, since 1848.[18] These enabled trains from Edinburgh to London to go this way, travelling south of York over the Midland and London & Birmingham Railways to Euston. In 1850 the Royal Border Bridge – so called, although it is in fact in England – over the Tweed at Berwick was ceremonially opened by Queen Victoria. She was on her way north, and the Crampton-type locomotive provided by the North British Railway to haul her train onward to Edinburgh was painted – or perhaps draped – in Royal Stewart tartan.[19] With completion of the Great Northern Railway to London King's Cross in 1852, the East Coast route took the form which, with only a few alterations, remains familiar today.

The growth of train services was greatly influenced by the Post Office. Back in the 1830s the national transport system for passengers and mails had been the Post Office's mail coaches. But mail coach contractors were paid by the Post Office only for carriage of mails, and depended for their profits on passengers. Wherever railways were built, passengers transferred to the trains. Coach contractors gave notice to quit and, in the absence of formal arrangements between Post Office and railway companies, the postal system – on which government and commerce depended – faced the possibility of collapse. The situation was rectified in 1838 by Parliament with *An Act to provide for the Conveyance of the Mails by Railways*. This enabled the Postmaster General to require railways, against reasonable remuneration, to carry mails and Post Office staff at such hours as he might direct – hence the Edinburgh & Glasgow Railway's obligatory Sunday mail trains – and to provide carriages in which letters could be sorted.[20] As early as 1841 mails were being carried by train from Glasgow to Ayr, Greenock and Ardrossan, and from Arbroath to Forfar, and of course vice versa.

On the roads mail coaches had been held in high regard – they had right of way over all other traffic – and something of this rubbed off on mail trains. In 1845 the best train in Scotland was considered to be the day mail between Edinburgh and Glasgow, which covered the forty-six miles in one and a half hours with three intermediate stops. Mail trains originating in London were extended northwards over the West Coast route from Carlisle to Glasgow, Edinburgh and Aberdeen as the railways were opened; Glasgow had a sorting carriage or travelling post office (TPO) from the South from March 1848. The Aberdeen mail was originally routed via Dundee, but the Night Mail was diverted via Forfar in 1850 to give an earlier arrival. A general introduction of bag exchange apparatus, which enabled mail bags to be exchanged between moving trains and the ground apparatus, along the Caledonian and Scottish Central Railways in 1852–3 resulted in substantial accelerations, and in 1859 the Limited Mail from Euston was established, comprised mainly Post Office vehicles and with only limited accommodation for passengers – destinations included Glasgow, Edinburgh and Perth.[21]

Such a train of course ran overnight to provide morning deliveries of letters, and would scarcely have suited Thomas Cook: using the all-rail route from the South for the first time in 1853, he advertised that his special train would be detained at Gretna Green, if any ladies or gentlemen in the party wished to terminate their state of 'single blessedness' there.[22] Whether any took advantage of this offer, I do not know.

In October 1848 a meeting was held in Manchester with representatives present from the seven railway companies comprising the West Coast route and with Captain Huish in the chair. 'It was considered essential' they minuted ' … that arrangements should be made for a free and uninterrupted interchange of throughout [sic] traffic of every description, and that periodical meetings should be held …'[23] Thus was established the West Coast Conference, meeting monthly to consider everything: childrens' fares, excess luggage, passengers separated from their luggage, pilferage of salmon in transit, up to mail trains and revisions of timetables.

A comparable East Coast Conference was established in the early 1850s by the companies concerned, and during this decade also the East Coast and West Coast companies divided up the Anglo-Scottish traffic between them in a series of complex agreements largely masterminded by Huish.

After the boom of the Railway Mania came the inevitable slump. The year 1847 again saw many Acts of Parliament for railways in Scotland, but all these railways were short, and there were difficulties in completing those already authorised. The Caledonian & Dumbartonshire Junction Railway for instance was authorised in 1846 to link the railways east of Glasgow with the area north of the Firth of Clyde: but what the company succeeded in opening, in 1850, was a short line from Bowling on the Clyde to Balloch at the foot of Loch Lomond. Isolated from the main railway system, this provided a link between the steamers on the two waterways – and Burns & MacIvor, steamship owners, even received the contract to operate this little railway complete with its 4 locomotives, 11 carriages, 2 brake vans and 150 goods vehicles.[24] It was six years before the C & DJ obtained a rail connection to the outer world with the opening of the Forth & Clyde Junction Railway from

Stirling to Balloch, and two more before the original route was completed by a new company, the Glasgow, Dumbarton & Helensburgh Railway.

A short but important link opened in 1850 ran from Larbert on the Scottish Central, via Falkirk Grahamston to Polmont on the Edinburgh & Glasgow, which enabled trains coming south over the SCR to diverge towards Edinburgh over the E & GR. Promoted by a local company, the Stirlingshire Midland Junction Railway, it had been taken over by the E & GR before it opened. A branch led to the Carron Ironworks. The Monkland Railways, extending the Slamannan line, reached Bo'ness port in 1851. There was a connection to the Edinburgh & Glasgow Railway at Manuel. A branch from the E & GR at Ratho had reached Bathgate in 1849.

The 1850s saw similar progress in other parts of the Lowlands as branch lines were built to link existing main lines with country towns. Callander, Crieff, Dunkeld, St Andrews, Jedburgh and Peebles were among many towns reached in this manner. Generally such branch lines were built by a local company formed for the purpose, with some but not all of the necessary finance provided by an established railway which eventually operated the line.

It was a similar story further north. The Great north of Scotland Railway had been authorised in 1845 to run between Aberdeen and Inverness, but financial stringency meant that construction did not start until 1852, and even then only between Aberdeen and Keith. The contractor, impatient of further delays caused by legal reasons, prematurely drained the Aberdeenshire Canal, the course of which the railway was to adopt, and grounded several boats which were still at work. So the first railway actually to be opened in the North of Scotland, in 1852, was the five-and-

a-half-mile line of the Morayshire Railway between Lossiemouth and Elgin. Railways were customarily opened with ceremony, and even this little line was no exception: there were processions, triumphal arches, German bands parading, flags flying from every farmhouse and colours flying on every ship in Lossiemouth harbour.[25] The Deeside Railway was opened between Aberdeen and Banchory in 1853. Just over a month after opening, Queen Victoria and her family, en route south from Balmoral, joined the train at Banchory: the first of many occasions on which the reigning monarch would travel over the Deeside line. The Great North of Scotland Railway was eventually opened from Aberdeen as far as Huntly in 1854; Keith was reached two years later.

In the meantime, when it had become clear that the GNSR would not complete its line to Inverness within the time allowed by the original Act, the Inverness & Nairn Railway was promoted from the Inverness end, and opened between the places of its title in 1855. The gap between Nairn and Keith was filled – with financial assistance from the GNSR – by the Inverness & Aberdeen Junction Railway, with which the Inverness & Nairn soon amalgamated. It was opened in stages, Keith being reached in 1858.

The mails for Inverness, not just from Aberdeen but also from the south, were put on rail, with a sorting carriage between Aberdeen and Keith, soon after the line was complete. This seems to have given rise to one of the most extraordinary practices recorded of Scottish railways. The GNSR station at Aberdeen on Waterloo Quay was half a mile from the Guild Street station at which trains from the south arrived. Mails were transferred by mail cart, and passengers followed by omnibus. When the mail train from the south arrived punctually, there was ample time for the connection. When it was late, there was not. When it was so late that the mails reached Waterloo Quay after the scheduled departure time of the GNSR train, the latter waited only long enough for the mails to be put aboard and was then dispatched: as an aid to this, the station doors were locked at the departure time, and reopened only to admit the mail cart. Passengers from the south were locked out, to travel later. This gave rise to much bad feeling and hostility towards the company. On one occasion, it seems, one of the directors was in the crowd that was denied admittance to the station: incensed, he broke one of the windows and got in that way.[26] That incident may be apocryphal, but is not out of keeping. It is difficult to understand the motive for the GNSR's actions, unless it was meeting its responsibilities to the Post Office with zeal to excess. By acting as it did, the GNSR certainly encouraged construction of a more direct line south from Inverness. That however belongs to the next decade, and it is necessary first to look at what was happening elsewhere during the 1850s. With one small exception: the three-mile-long Findhorn Railway which diverged from the I & AJR at Kinloss: authorised by Act of Parliament in 1859, opened in 1860, and even in Victorian times so hopelessly uneconomic that it was closed in 1869 and eventually dismantled.

The traditional sea crossing from Scotland to Ireland of coaching days – it was used by Post Office mail packets – was from Portpatrick to Donaghadee. In 1849, however, in the absence of rail links at a time when the railway to Holyhead was almost complete, the Post Office withdrew from the route. There remained the possibility that it might return if rail links were built.[27] With Portpatrick as their ultimate goal, railways reached Castle Douglas from Dumfries in 1859 and Girvan from Ayr in 1860. Both lines were associated with the GSWR, and in due course taken over by it. Meanwhile in 1857 the Portpatrick Railway Company had been authorised to build from Castle Douglas to Portpatrick, with short branches to the harbours at both Stranraer (intended primarily for goods traffic) and Portpatrick; the Treasury undertook to finance improvements to Portpatrick harbour so that the mail packet service to Donaghadee could be reintroduced. The line from Castle Douglas as far as Stranraer was completed in 1861, but the GSWR had failed to provide all the financial support it had promised, and the local company, rather than have its line worked by the larger one for an excessive percentage of the gross takings, undertook to work it itself. The following year the line was completed to Portpatrick, to a terminus above the town. Also completed was the branch to Stranraer harbour whence a steamer started to ply to Larne; the steeply graded branch down to Portpatrick harbour was probably completed the following year.[28] The government, however, failed to complete the promised improvements at Portpatrick harbour. The mail packets did not reappear. What did appear, in 1863, was the Caledonian Railway branch from Lockerbie to Dumfries. The Portpatrick Railway, faced with excessive financial problems in the absence of through traffic, in 1864 entered into a twenty-one-year agreement with the Caledonian that the CR would work its line for about half what the GSWR had originally demanded.[29] The Portpatrick Railway did eventually receive some compensation from the government for its failure to complete the works at Portpatrick harbour, but the harbour branch lasted only until about 1870, after which Stranraer Harbour became the main line terminus and the line to Portpatrick a branch.

Extension of the Edinburgh–Hawick line to

Cast-iron columns carry the 193 spans of the Solway Viaduct away into the distance across the Solway Firth. The first of the great estuary crossings, it was also, in terms of traffic, the least successful.
(Micheal Wrottesley collection)

Carlisle had for long been the ambition of the North British Railway, an ambition which the Caledonian was equally anxious to thwart as competition for its own Edinburgh–Carlisle route. It was only after several competing schemes had been put forward by each company for a line from Hawick to Carlisle that the North British successfully obtained an Act of Parliament in 1859. This, the Border Union Railway, was to approach Carlisle by making a junction with the little Port Carlisle Railway which the North British leased for the purpose.

The Caledonian had been seeking to approach Hawick from the south, but was not the only company to do so. The Border Counties Railway was authorised in 1854 to run from Hexham, on the Newcastle & Carlisle Railway, up the valley of the North Tyne as far as Falstone, and sought powers to extend to Hawick. Eventually this extension, modified, was authorised in 1859 to join the Border Union Railway at the isolated spot, 850 ft up in the Border hills, which became known as Riccarton Junction – so isolated that, for the century or more of its existence, it famously had no access by road, despite the presence of a large resident community of railwaymen and their families. In 1860 the North British anticipated (correctly) that the Newcastle & Carlisle Railway would soon be amalgamated into the North Eastern. To prevent the Border Counties Railway going the same way, it itself absorbed the Border Counties. All these lines were opened in stages, but the whole system was complete between Hawick, Hexham and Carlisle by the summer of 1862.[30] The Port Carlisle Railway gave the North

British access to the harbour of Silloth, on the Solway, of which it was to make good use.

At the same time the North British acquired running powers over the North Eastern, from Hexham into Newcastle upon Tyne. The quid pro quo was running powers for the North Eastern over the North British from Berwick to Edinburgh. The North Eastern seems to have got the best of the bargain, and North Eastern locomotives hauling East Coast expresses into Edinburgh became a familiar sight until the Grouping. It was in 1862 that such a train first received a name: the 'Special Scotch Express', leaving King's Cross at 10.00 a.m. for Edinburgh and taking ten and a half hours for the journey.[31] It soon became known, at first unofficially, as the 'Flying Scotchman' or 'Flying Scotsman'. According to the timetable current as I write, the 'Flying Scotsman' continues to leave King's Cross at 10.00 every weekday, although the time for the journey has been much reduced, to 4 hr 26 min.

To revert to the new route which the North British had gained between Edinburgh and Carlisle: this passed through the Scott Country and came to be known, and promoted, as the Waverley Route. It was two miles shorter than the Caledonian route between Edinburgh and Carlisle, but steep gradients and sharp curves put it at a disadvantage. It included a short branch from Longtown to Gretna where it joined the Caledonian Railway: but the significance of this was that the junction was south of the point at which the Glasgow & South Western line joined the Caledonian, which it used to reach Carlisle. So the new link enabled traffic, both passenger and freight, to be exchanged between the NBR and the GSWR, without traversing the increasingly congested station and marshalling yards of Carlisle.

The Solway Junction Railway linked the railways of West Cumberland with those north of the Solway – in practice with the Caledonian Railway, which worked the line – and its object was to enable trains of Cumberland haematite ore to avoid congestion at Carlisle while travelling north to the blast furnaces of Lanarkshire. The company received its Act of Parliament in 1864; one of the principal promoters was ironmaster Alexander Brogden, and the engineer was the distinguished Scottish engineer James Brunlees who had worked under Locke on the Caledonian but most of whose career lay south of the Border or abroad. Readers of my *The Mont Cenis Fell Railway* will already have encountered Brogden and Brunlees occupying similar positions in the Mont Cenis Railway Co. Ltd, the astonishing British venture which at this period was building the first, although temporary, railway over the western Alps.

On the Solway Junction Railway the big problem faced by Brunlees lay by contrast at sea level, for the railway was to cross the Solway Firth where it was already more than a mile wide. For this he provided the first of the great estuary viaducts – a structure 1,940 yd long with 193 spans carried on cast-iron columns. It was completed, and the line opened, in 1869. Initially busy, the Solway Junction Railway sadly never realised its full potential, for traffic fell away with changes in the pattern of the iron trade. This did not, however, prevent the viaduct from being rebuilt and reopened – eventually – after floating ice demolished forty-five piers in January 1881.[32]

In the north, completion of the route from Aberdeen to Inverness was followed by extension northwards to Dingwall, reached in 1862 and to Invergordon the following year. Meanwhile in 1861 the Inverness & Perth Junction Railway had been authorised, to provide a route from Inverness to Perth without the detour via Aberdeen. It was to run from Forres, roughly midway between Inverness and Elgin, via Grantown-on-Spey and Pitlochry to Dunkeld, already reached by the Perth & Dunkeld Railway, which the larger venture took over; there were to be running powers from Stanley, where the Dunkeld line joined that from Aberdeen, into Perth itself.

The engineer of the I & PJR, as of the other lines radiating from Inverness, was the veteran Joseph Mitchell. Mitchell had trained under Telford, and had over several decades been Chief Inspector and Superintendent of the Highland Roads and Bridges. He knew the country. The country's titled owners knew him. The result was a 104-mile-long railway, which surmounted summits of 1,045 ft above sea level at Dava and 1,488 ft at Druimuachdar – to use the traditional railway spelling, although today's motorists know it as Drumochter – and yet which had no gradient steeper than 1 in 70 and only two tunnels, both of which were short and provided only to preserve the amenities of Dunkeld and Killiecrankie.[33] Highland rivers, however, did demand some substantial bridges and viaducts. The line was opened in 1863; the branch from Ballinluig to Aberfeldy, authorised in the same Act, followed a year later, and in 1865 the Inverness & Perth Junction Railway amalgamated with the Inverness & Aberdeen Junction to become the Highland Railway familiar in Scottish railway history.

For all the skill with which it had been laid out, the Highland Railway's main line from Perth to Inverness was no easy railway to work. Late connections from the South at Perth, long single-track sections, long ascents, severe weather – snow and floods[34] – all combined to cause delays and irregularities. Initially, too, the staff were of necessity inexperienced: a long delay on the opening day was caused by failure of the

electric telegraph system used to signal trains – failure itself said to have been the result of a wire's coming loose from its terminal, which no one knew how to fix.[35] But the mails were transferred to the railway in 1864, and a TPO introduced soon afterwards. And sheep and cattle, which had previously been driven south on the hoof on a journey taking a month or more, were soon being carried by train within a day. In 1867 Mitchell stated that over 21,000 sheep had been carried during a single week.[36]

In 1860, when construction of a direct line south from Forres was imminent, the directors of the Great North of Scotland Railway accepted an offer from the Inverness & Aberdeen Junction to buy out their interest in the latter company. The GNSR then concentrated on supporting the companies, nominally independent, which were being established to build branches from its existing line. In this manner Old Meldrum was reached in 1856, Banff and Alford in 1859, Peterhead in 1862 and Fraserburgh and Boat of Garten, with a junction with the Highland, in 1865. All these branch railways eventually amalgamated with the Great North, as did the Morayshire Railway which had been extended southwards to meet it at Craigellachie. In truth, as Acworth was later to put it, the Highland Railway was all main line, the Great North all branches.[37]

The Deeside Railway, however, was at this period by similar means independently pursuing its way westwards. It reached Aboyne in 1859 and Ballater in 1866. But it went no further for, to quote Acworth again, writing in 1890, 'It is an open secret, that but for the objection of an influential Aberdeenshire proprietor, who occupies Balmoral and Abergeldie Castles and a good deal of land in their vicinity, the railway would before now have been carried

RAILWAY MAP
OF
SCOTLAND

forward from Ballater at least as far as Braemar.'[38] And so indeed it proved, when the Deeside Railway Company's records eventually became available for public study, including an appropriate letter from Queen Victoria's private secretary.[39] Ballater was laid out as a through station, with the main road crossing over the incomplete extension by a substantial bridge, which remained in position long after the Deeside line proper eventually closed and probably still does.

Nothing in this prevented the Queen and the royal family from making regular use of the railway as far as Ballater; indeed the Prince and Princess of Wales used it almost a month before its opening to the public, and the queen herself the day before. Royal trains then became a regular feature to or from Ballater, often running direct to or from Windsor or Gosport (for Osborne, Isle of Wight). Another regular feature was the special trains provided for the benefit of Queen's Messengers bearing royal dispatches between Balmoral and London. The Messenger trains were available also to ordinary first-class passengers, with some third-class accommodation provided, initially, for their servants. These trains stopped only at Banchory and Aboyne – much to the displeasure of Sir Robert Burnett, owner of Crathes Castle, where land for the railway had been provided on condition that all trains stopped at Crathes station. The House of Lords eventually

The railways of Scotland, as depicted in a map published c. 1871. The backbone of the system is in place, but railways have yet to be completed north of Helmsdale, west of 'Killin' (in fact, Glenoglehead) and south of Girvan. Although described as a 'Railway Map of Scotland', the Caledonian and its allies – Highland and Great North of Scotland Railways in the North, Portpatrick Railway in the South – are shown in bold, while lines of the North British and Glasgow & South Western Railways get less prominence. (Author's collection.)

decided in Sir Robert's favour.[40]

The 1860s were a great period for amalgamations between railways previously independent. Such amalgamations required the sanction of a Parliament ever conscious of the dangers of monopoly in a particular region, often favourable to longitudinal combination, and open (in committee) to pleading by those affected, whether they were members of the public or other railways. So there were more amalgamations proposed than brought to fruition. Once things had settled down, however, there could be perceived the Scottish railway-company map which persisted in its entirety until the Grouping of 1923, and with little modification until nationalisation in 1948.

There had been a foretaste in 1856 when the Scottish North Eastern Railway was formed by amalgamation of the Scottish Midland Junction Railway with the Aberdeen Railway, which had already leased the Arbroath & Forfar, so that the line from Perth to Aberdeen came under a single management. In 1862 the North British Railway took over the Edinburgh, Perth and Dundee, and in 1863 the Scottish Central the Dundee, Perth & Aberdeen Railway Junction Co., as the Dundee & Perth had renamed itself.

At this period it appeared that the Caledonian Railway would amalgamate with both the Edinburgh & Glasgow and the enlarged Scottish Central. But after much negotiation, not to say intrigue, behind the scenes,[41] it was the North British which in 1865 took over the E & GR, which had itself the day previously acquired the Monkland Railways. The Caledonian Railway did acquire the Scottish Central at this time, and then in 1866 the Scottish North Eastern also, which gave it a main line extending from Carlisle to Aberdeen. In this there was an interruption,

in that the northern part of the line was still reached by running powers over five-eighths of a mile of the original Monkland & Kirkintilloch Railway between Gartsherrie and Garnqueen – a length now owned by the North British Railway. This anomaly, of a short length of the West Coast main line which required running powers over an East Coast company's rails, was to persist until nationalisation.

These running powers were, however, of very limited extent compared with what was happening further north. As a consequence in part of powers inherited from the former companies, and in part of new provisions in the amalgamation Acts, the Caledonian now had running powers over the North British, formerly Edinburgh & Glasgow, lines from Larbert to Edinburgh and from Greenhill to Glasgow – powers of which it made immediate and considerable use – while the North British had running powers for East Coast traffic over all or nearly all of the Caledonian lines from Larbert northwards to Aberdeen.[42] These it seems to have been in no immediate hurry to exercise, but in a few years' time they would prove of great significance.

With amalgamations south of the border also, the West Coast route from London Euston to Scotland was now operated by two railway companies only: the London & North Western as far as Carlisle, and the Caledonian thence to Glasgow, Edinburgh and Aberdeen. On the East Coast route from King's Cross there were three: the Great Northern to just north of Doncaster, the North Eastern thence to Berwick with running powers over the North British to Edinburgh, and the North British proper from Edinburgh to Glasgow, Larbert and (by ferries) Perth and Arbroath.

But for Anglo-Scottish traffic there was to be a third contender. In 1866 the Midland Railway obtained an

Act for the Settle & Carlisle Railway.[43] The Midland, with routes radiating from Derby, was then building its London extension; when this was completed, it would have a main line from London St Pancras as far as Settle, via Sheffield and Leeds. The Settle & Carlisle would enable it to exchange Glasgow traffic with the Glasgow & South Western at Carlisle. To further this end, the Act of 1866, which authorised amalgamation of the Caledonian and Scottish North Eastern Railways, had included also a provision to the effect that nothing should be done to obstruct the flow of Midland Railway traffic to and from Scotland.[44]

To further it still more, an Act to amalgamate the Midland and the GSW was sought in 1867. The GSW shareholders approved: but for Parliament this was an amalgamation too far, and it was not authorised. There were further attempts to amalgamate in 1872, and again in 1874, both equally unsuccessful.[45]

Shortly after the Act was passed for the Settle & Carlisle Railway came the stock market crash of 1866, which had itself been triggered by unsound methods of financing railways. Remarkably, it seems to have had little effect in Scotland, but construction of the Settle & Carlisle was delayed for some years.

At Aberdeen, after more than a decade of proposals and counter-proposals and mutual antagonism between GNS and SNE Railways, a connecting line between the two was opened in 1867, including the passenger station, joint between the Caledonian and the Great North. One consequence was that from 1869 to 1873 through coaches were run between Euston and Elgin, via Aberdeen and Craigellachie: the longest through coach working in Britain at the time, the 620-mile journey took 22 hours. The Deeside Railway, formerly more closely associated with the Scottish North Eastern, was leased by the Great North during

the 1860s; full amalgamation, of it and its extensions, with the GNS took place during 1875–6.

North of Inverness, successive companies backed by the Highland Railway were extending rail communication northwards, the HR operating each section once opened. In 1868 the Sutherland Railway, the most northerly of these concerns at that date, reached as far north as Golspie and there it stuck, from lack of funds to build further although authorised to do so as far as Brora. It was however approaching Dunrobin Castle, Highland residence of the dukes of Sutherland and hub of their 1,177,000-acre Sutherland estate.

George Granville William Sutherland-Leveson-Gower, Third Duke of Sutherland – he had inherited in 1861 – was one of the wealthiest men in Britain. But his fortune was in no way derived from the estate in Sutherland, or the questionable improvements of his forebears in facilitating the introduction of sheep-farming by clearing crofter tenants from their ancestral glens down to the supposedly fish-rich coast. It was rooted firmly in industrial England and, particularly, in transport. The foundation had been laid by his indirect ancestor the Duke of Bridgewater, who had initiated the canal era when he built the Bridgewater Canal to carry coal from his mines into Manchester. It had been consolidated and considerably augmented by his grandfather, the Marquess of Stafford, who had inherited the Bridgewater fortune and then subscribed one fifth of the entire capital needed to build the Liverpool & Manchester Railway. For this he acquired the right to appoint three directors to the company, a right which became transmuted, following amalgamations, into one director to the London & North Western. The marquess also, having married the Countess of Sutherland, took when elevated the title Duke of Sutherland.

The third duke, long before he inherited, had been appointed the family director of the LNWR in 1852 and held the post until he died forty years later. It was a felicitous appointment for he had, as was delightfully expressed in his eventual obituary in the *Proceedings of the Institution of Civil Engineers*, a 'taste for engineering … which in other circumstances might have acquired for him a high position as a professional man'.[46] He had worked under LNWR Locomotive Superintendent J. E. McConnell at Wolverton Works; he knew how locomotives were designed and built, and how to drive them. His influence would extend far and wide through the engineering world.

The duke was chairman of the Sutherland Railway and its largest shareholder. To extend the railway further north over his estate, however, he now decided to provide all the funding. The Act for the Duke of Sutherland's Railway, from Golspie by Dunrobin and Brora to Helmsdale, was passed in 1870, by which date construction had already started. Administratively, the railway seems to have been treated as one of the many activities of a large and progressive Highland estate. The duke purchased a 2-4-0 tank locomotive and a saloon coach, and borrowed more rolling stock from the Highland Railway. The length from Dunrobin almost to Helmsdale was ready first and this isolated section was given a ceremonial opening in the autumn of 1870. Locomotive and coach were garlanded with evergreens and the duke himself probably drove; he was certainly on the footplate. Coal came from Brora colliery. It seems likely that it was on this occasion that a navvy, standing by, was heard – allegedly – to observe: 'There, that's what I call a real dook! Why, there he is a-driving of his own engine on his own railroad, and a-burning of his own blessed coals!'[47]

The line was opened throughout the following year, and the Highland Railway, of which the duke was a director, took over operation. He continued to use his private locomotive and coach; they were also used, on occasion, on public trains. When the route northwards was continued to Wick and Thurso by the Sutherland & Caithness Railway, the duke once again was the largest shareholder. This line was opened in 1874. The route taken by the railways from Inverness to Wick was, and is, extremely circuitous – partly along the coast, partly by great loops inland, the distance by rail is 161 miles, compared with about 80 miles as the crow flies. This circumstance was derived partly from the need to avoid arms of the sea, and partly from the need to provide, so far as possible, railheads for places lying away to the north-west. Eventually the three northern railways – Sutherland, Duke of Sutherland's, Sutherland & Caithness – were amalgamated into the Highland Railway in 1884, the duke retaining the right to use his private locomotive and saloon.

The Dingwall & Skye Railway had been incorporated in 1865 to build from Dingwall to Kyle of Lochalsh. Financial difficulties eventually meant that when the line was opened in 1870, the western terminus was ten miles short of Kyle, at Strome Ferry. But that was still on the west coast, and steamers started to ply to Portree and Stornoway. Like the northern lines it was operated by the Highland Railway, and amalgamated with it in 1880. In the meantime traffic was light, requiring only two mixed trains each way daily, and sometimes only one. A remarkable traffic, which had been anticipated, when the line was building, was carriage of fishing boats between one coast and the other. Plans were prepared and cranes ordered, but then the scheme was allowed to lapse.[48] To this day, however, the tracks of the passing loop at

Building nineteenth-century railways was pick-and-shovel work for navvies. This group paused briefly for the photographer while excavating a cutting for the final section of the Callander & Oban Railway in the late 1870s, but the scene could have been anywhere in mainland Scotland from the 1830s to the 1890s.
(McEwan Collection, East Dunbartonshire Information & Archives)

Garve remain much farther apart than usual, to allow for this out-of-gauge traffic that never materialised. On Sundays at that period the only trains over most of the Highland Railway were the mail trains. On the Skye Railway there were no trains at all, and in 1883, when the railway attempted to have a fish special loaded at Strome Ferry on the Sabbath, there were riots.

The Dingwall & Skye Railway was, perhaps remarkably, the first railway to reach the western seaboard of the Highlands. The Callander & Oban Railway had been authorised the same year, 1865, with the benefit of an agreement with the Scottish Central Railway that it would provide a substantial subscription and work the line when opened. By 1870, however, the C & O had succeeded in opening only the first seventeen and a half miles, to a station called 'Killin' although it lay at the head of Glen Ogle, three and a half miles short of the village of that name, and 550 ft above it. What had happened was that even before the c & o Act was passed, the Scottish Central had been absorbed by the Caledonian: and to the Caledonian board, although it inherited scr obligations, to build a railway through the empty western Highlands seemed a much less attractive proposition than lines among the bustling collieries and ironworks of the Lowlands. In any case, after the 1866 crash funds everywhere were scarce. It was due largely to one remarkable man, John Anderson, who had been assistant to the general manager of the Edinburgh & Glasgow Railway until it amalgamated with the North British, and then became the c & o company secretary and sole direct employee, that funds were gathered in and the line built. It was a decade later before it, at last, reached Oban.

Other developments were improving the railway system of the Central Belt. On the NBR in Edinburgh a link from the main line at Abbeyhill, east of Waverley, curved round to the north to join the Edinburgh, Leith & Granton line. It avoided Scotland Street tunnel with its cable haulage, and after it was opened in 1868 the tunnel was no longer used. Twenty years later an entrepreneur formed the Edinburgh Mushroom Co. Ltd: he leased the tunnel, and used it as a place to grow mushrooms. The venture was a great success. Nor was this early example of reuse of redundant railway property carried out in isolation from the benefits of rail transport, as so often happens today. The tracks were still in position, mushroom spawn and manure for the mushroom beds went in by rail, and the mushrooms came out the same way.[49]

The Caledonian Railway terminus in Edinburgh had been a temporary structure adjoining Lothian Road since opening. In 1870 the line was extended slightly to a terminus at the west end of Princes Street, and here Princes Street Station was established although still, for the time being, with a temporary building. The previous year the opening of the Cleland & Midcalder line, via Shotts, had given the Caledonian a direct line between Edinburgh and Glasgow, some ten miles shorter than its route via Carstairs, and of comparable length to the North British, formerly Edinburgh & Glasgow line.

Yet a second North British route between the two cities was taking shape piecemeal. The E & GR's Bathgate branch has already been mentioned; as early as 1861–2 the Monkland Railways had opened a line which, although primarily intended for minerals, had in effect extended this to Airdrie and Coatbridge. A few years later the North British built a line from Coatbridge via Easterhouse into Glasgow, and in 1871 passenger trains started to run between Edinburgh, Bathgate, Airdrie and Glasgow College Station, later called High Street.

But this was not all. Prior to the 1860s there had been no railway bridge across the Clyde at Glasgow, and no connection there between the Glasgow & South Western Railway and the North British Railway. This link was provided by the City of Glasgow Union Railway, authorised in 1864 and owned jointly by the GSWR and the NBR. Viewed from the west, it diverged to the south of the Glasgow & Paisley Joint Line at Shields Road, a little short of the terminus at Bridge Street. It then swung north to cross the river, and veered off east to join the NBR's new line from Coatbridge, between Bellgrove and High Street. A later extension took it up to Springburn and the E & GR main line at Cowlairs. From the CGUR just north of the Clyde, a line diverged westwards to provide the Glasgow & South Western with its own Glasgow terminus in the city centre. Initially this was at a temporary station called Dunlop Street, but within a few years the line had been extended into St Enoch where a lavish new station was built.[50]

The first section of the CGUR was opened in 1870, when the GSWR diverted some of its trains from Bridge Street to Dunlop Street. The following year it started a local train service between Shields Road and Bellgrove, where there was interchange with trains on the new NBR line. To jump ahead, the lines into St Enoch were vested solely in the GSWR from 1883. The GSWR eventually stopped using Bridge Street Station in 1892, and in 1896 the City of Glasgow Union Railway was divided between the two companies which had owned it jointly: lines south of High Street passed to the GSWR and those to the north and east to the NBR, each company retaining running powers over the other's section.

From 1872 advantage was taken of the new connection to provide through coaches between Edinburgh Waverley and Ayrshire. By the 1880s they were running to Ayr, Ardrossan and Greenock, one of the latter connecting with the mail steamer for Belfast.[51] The Greenock trains used the GSWR's own line to Greenock Princes Pier, completed in 1869. Yet for reasons that remain obscure, all these through coaches had ceased by the turn of the century; perhaps trip-working the through coaches between Bellgrove and St Enoch or Shields Road was simply too complex and slow.

In the early 1860s the Glasgow & South Western Railway still suffered from the competitive disadvantage that its route from Glasgow to Carlisle was, at 125 miles, considerably longer than the Caledonian's 104-mile route. The GSW route could be shortened substantially by building a direct line to Kilmarnock,

and in 1865 powers were obtained to do so. But the Caledonian already had a branch to Barrhead and Neilston, halfway to Kilmarnock, and was authorised in the same year to extend it thither. Then the rival companies, remarkably, reached a compromise. Presumably financial stringency following the 1866 crash had something to do with it. Only the proposed Caledonian line would be built, they agreed, but the whole route from Glasgow to Kilmarnock would become a joint line, the Glasgow, Barrhead & Kilmarnock Joint Railway. This was authorised by Parliament in 1869, and when the line was opened in 1873, with a link from the City of Glasgow Union at Gorbals, the GSWR had its direct route of 115½ miles to Carlisle, and the South.

It is from the GSWR that we have definite knowledge of one remarkable individual among the anonymous hordes who by this date were working on railways in one capacity or another. Alexander Anderson was a surfaceman – one who maintains a road surface or railway track – on the Glasgow & South Western at Kirkconnel, but his fame did not rest on any particular skill with pick and shovel, although no doubt he possessed this. It rested, rather, in his talent as a poet. Anderson was a fine example of a self-taught man: he learned to read French, Italian and German fluently. His poetry was very much in the school of poems, chiefly in the Scottish dialect, which reached its zenith with Burns and its nadir with McGonagall, and was popular throughout much of the late eighteenth and nineteenth centuries. Anderson's best-loved poem was entitled 'The Bairnies Cuddle Doon at Nicht'.[52]

Some of his work, however, reflects his experiences as a railwayman. His 'What the Engine Says' is written from the point of view of the surfaceman who spies a train bearing down on him. Here it is, in part:

WHAT THE ENGINE SAYS

What does the mighty engine say
   Rolling along
   Swift and strong
Slow or fast as his driver may,
Hour by hour and day by day,
   His swarthy side
   Aglow with pride
And his muscles of sinewy steel ablaze?
This is what the engine says

First his breath gives a sudden snort
As if a spasm had cut it short
   Then with one wild note
   To clear his throat
He fumes and whistles – 'get out of my way,
What are you standing there for, – say?
   Fling shovel and pick
   Away from you, quick!
Ere my gleaming links with out reaching clutch
Draw you into your death with a single touch
For what care I for a puppet or two
A little over five feet like you? …

'Oh, well,' I said,
   And I shook my head
But all the while taking care to clear
The way, for the iron fellow so near,
'You carry things just a little too far
For great, and swarthy, and strong as you are,
With the strength of a hundred Titans within
Your seething breast with its fiery din
And your iron plates that serve you for skin
   With a single touch
   Of this crow-bar
I could make you welter within the ditch
As if Jove himself had open'd war
   So you see
You must pay a little respect to me
   I keep the rail
Tight and fine with chair and key
Fasten the joints as firm as may be
So that your pathway may not fail.
Why, if I twitched a rail from the chairs
Where would you be? At your smoky prayers …[53]

And so on, through as much again. But it grows on you. The irregular rhythm seems to reflect the sounds of a train, in the days when coaches were carried on four or six wheels rather than bogies.

Another of Anderson's poems, 'Nottman', relates the experience of a driver who suddenly sees, on the track ahead, a small child asleep with his head on the rail. Unable to stop in time, he scrambles to the front of the engine, balances with one foot in the coupling chain and with the other shifts the child clear – only to discover it is his own son. It sounds like pure Victorian melodrama – until you learn that it relates to a real incident and that Driver Nottman, whose little boy had wandered out to see Daddy's train go past, was a respected character on the GSWR.[54]

Anderson himself, in one of the most remarkable

career moves of all time, left Kirkconnel in 1880 to become Assistant Librarian at Edinburgh University. But there, although he wrote more poetry, his creative spark seems sadly to have dwindled.

At a period when the practice of smoking was on the increase, the Railway Regulation Act 1868 required railways to provide a smoking carriage on every train comprising more than one carriage of each class. Some railways, such as the Highland, interpreted this as meaning a single compartment. But other developments in passenger comfort were more important than this. Some railways in the north – the Deeside, Aberdeen, Great North of Scotland, Inverness & Aberdeen Junction and Inverness & Nairn Railways – appear to have provided only two classes of passenger accommodation, first and third class, from the start. With this as a precedent James Allport, general manager of the Midland Railway in England first arranged in 1872 for it to carry third-class passengers on all trains and then, in 1875, abolished second-class travel and merged it into third class; the Midland's new third-class carriages then became among the most comfortable of their kind, anywhere. From this date, although many companies might hesitate, the practice of having two classes only of passenger accommodation, then called first and third, spread inexorably through Britain.

The first sleeping car service in Britain began in 1873, when a car built by the North British Railway was put into service on the East Coast route, between Glasgow, Edinburgh and King's Cross. That was in the spring: in the autumn, sleeping cars built by the LNWR started to run between Glasgow and Euston. When the Midland Railway put its first sleeping car into service the following year, between London and Bradford, it was a Pullman car of typical North American pattern, very much more comfortable and spacious, and carried on bogies unlike contemporary British standard-gauge coaches. Allport had experienced Pullman cars in America, and had arranged for their originator, George Mortimer Pullman, to bring them to Britain. Soon they would reach Scotland.

Since the late 1860s, the Midland's contractors and their navvies had been toiling to build the Settle & Carlisle line, high among the Pennines. Late in 1875, it was opened for freight. On 1 May 1876 it was opened for passengers, and Midland trains started to run between St Pancras, Edinburgh and Glasgow. They were no ordinary trains for, aware that its Anglo-Scottish routes were longer and harder than either East or West Coast Routes, the Midland made its trains the most comfortable, not to say luxurious. The sleeping cars were Pullmans; many of the ordinary coaches ran on bogies. They included Pullman drawing-room cars by day. From Carlisle, the North British Railway took Midland trains onward over the Waverley Route by Hawick and Galashiels to Edinburgh Waverley. The Glasgow & South Western likewise took them forward by Dumfries and Kilmarnock to Glasgow. Although the direct line from Kilmarnock to Glasgow would not be ready until the following year, St Enoch station though incomplete came into use that same day. When the Prince and Princess of Wales made a formal visit to Glasgow later in 1876, it was at St Enoch that they chose to arrive, and the station was officially opened. Three years later St Enoch station became the first public building in Scotland to be lit by electricity. With these events, the formative years of the Scottish railway system ended, the bulk of it was complete and a golden age began.

A Glasgow St Enoch–London St Pancras express hauled by a GSWR 4-6-0 approaches Carlisle, exercising running powers over the Caledonian main line, which it has joined at Gretna. (National Railway Museum)

THE GOLDEN AGE

The Midland/North British expresses from St Pancras to Edinburgh were not only among the most luxurious trains in Britain: the manner in which they were worked over the Waverley Route was among the smartest to be found anywhere. NBR locomotive Superintendent Dugald Drummond provided new locomotives, bogie 4-4-0s, large by the standards of the time. By the early 1880s *Abbotsford* and her sisters – they were named after places on the route – were scheduled to take 2 hr 20 min. to haul the sleeper over the ninety-eight and a quarter sinuous and steeply graded miles between Carlisle and Edinburgh, including stops. In 1961, during the route's last sad declining years before closure, the equivalent train was timed to take 2 hr 46 min. Of the reasons for this decline, more later. Back in the expansive early days there were connections in the South to and from Birmingham and Bristol; and in the North, to and from Perth and Aberdeen. Sometimes a Pullman sleeping car worked through to Perth.

As for the ordinary carriages on the Midland Scottish routes, they were new, on bogies, and at first owned jointly by the three companies concerned; later they were divided up between Midland and North British jointly, on one hand, and Midland and GSW jointly on the other, for use on appropriate routes. Relations between the Midland and the GSWR continued close:

for a time from 1883 they shared the same chairman in M. W. Thompson. At this period also a Pullman sleeper, of a type less lavish than usual, was working through between St Pancras and Greenock.

Enterprise tends to be rewarded by competition, and during the 1880s Pullman sleeping cars were also operated between London, King's Cross and Edinburgh by the East Coast route. Two of these were of the less lavish type, but proved unpopular on this route: in 1885 they were transferred to the Highland Railway, renamed *Dunrobin* and *Balmoral* (Pullman cars traditionally carried names), and became for many years a regular feature of the night train from Inverness to Perth, and later to Glasgow.

All these Pullman cars belonged to the Pullman company; they were staffed by Pullman employees and were included in trains by agreement with the railway companies concerned. Their passengers paid a supplement. Railway managements tended to be equivocal toward such arrangements: once a demand had been established, they sometimes preferred to meet it in-house. So when the agreement between the Midland Railway and the Pullman company came to an end in 1888, it was not renewed and the cars were bought by the Midland. But they continued to run in the principal expresses to Glasgow and Edinburgh, and for many years thereafter the trains of which they formed part were known to railwaymen, particularly on the GSWR, as 'the Pullman'.

Although the bulk of the Scottish railway system was in place by 1876, there were still some notable gaps, and of these the most notable were provided by the Firth of Forth and the Firth of Tay, both still crossed by train ferries. The North British had obtained powers to bridge the Tay in 1870, and had added in 1871 powers to build its own line from Arbroath via Montrose to Kinnaber Junction, whence its trains could exercise running powers over the Caledonian to Aberdeen. By 1876 construction of the Tay Bridge was far advanced. The story of its construction, and more particularly of its subsequent collapse – probably the most infamous disaster in the history of British railways – is so well known that there is little new to add, but the sad story must be told.

The consulting engineer was Thomas Bouch. For this bridge, at 3,465 yd the longest anywhere at that time, he designed a structure of lattice girder spans supported on brick piers. For most of its length, the railway track was to run on top of the spans, but for thirteen spans in the centre of the bridge the railway ran through them – supporting these spans on higher piers provided the necessary clearance over the shipping channel in the firth. These spans became known as the 'high girders'.

In planning for brick piers it quickly became clear that Bouch had been misled by trial borings into the bed of the river, and that the rock required to support them was not present. He modified the design to incorporate piers of iron which would be much lighter. Each of them comprised six cast-iron columns, made in sections joined together one above the other, placed in hexagon formation on a masonry base, and braced together by wrought iron tiebars.

He had used comparable techniques before for speed and economy, notably on the Barnard Castle–Penrith line's Belah Viaduct which was 1,040 ft long with a maximum height of 196 ft. Gilkes, Wilson & Co. built it in the late 1850s and it lasted as long as the railway itself, being demolished in the 1960s after closure.[1] Contractors for the Tay Bridge, after a couple of false starts, were Gilkes, Wilson's successors Hopkins, Gilkes & Co.

But all did not go well with construction of the Tay Bridge. Supervision was inadequate at the foundry that made components, and defective castings were used with their faults concealed. Two of the high girder spans, after they had been raised but not positioned, were blown down into the firth by a gale: there was little knowledge of the effect of wind on such structures at that time. One of them could not be raised; the other was raised, straightened out and used, the southernmost of the high girders.

The bridge was eventually completed. The Board of Trade inspector, Major General Hutchinson, inspected, approved, recommended a 25 mph speed limit, and commented with sinister prescience that he would have wished to have an opportunity to observe the effect of a high wind when a train was running over it. The Tay Bridge was opened in 1878; Queen Victoria crossed it the following year and rewarded Bouch with a knighthood.

The night of the last Sunday in 1879 was more than usually dark and stormy. At about 7.00 p.m. the signalman at the south end of the Tay Bridge handed the single-line train staff to the driver of the mail from Burntisland to Dundee, and found the gale so strong he could return to his cabin only on all fours. From inside, he and a surfaceman watched the lights of the train dwindle. There was an exceptionally fierce

With the coming of daylight on a still-stormy Monday, 29 December 1879, horrified crowds gather on the north shore of the Firth of Tay to observe that the central part of the great Tay Bridge has disappeared. (Science Museum Library / Science & Society Picture Library)

gust, and they vanished altogether. By daylight it became clear that all the high girders had collapsed into the firth along with their supporting piers; a diver eventually found the train within the girders. All the seventy or so persons aboard had perished.

Girders, train and remains of piers were eventually raised and examined in detail. The piers had collapsed when the columns buckled at the joints: cast lugs holding the tiebars had given way and tiebars themselves were not strong enough. But the precise sequence of events that led to the collapse became and remains a matter of controversy. The locomotive showed surprisingly little damage, the leading coaches more damage, and the last coach and the brake van

a lot. Bouch contended that the gale had blown the last two vehicles off the track, and that they had then collided with the structure of the high girders initiating their collapse. He was overruled by the official Court of Inquiry, the members of which were H. C. Rothery, Commissioner of Wrecks, Col. Yolland, Chief Inspecting Officer of Railways and W.H. Barlow, President of the Institution of Civil Engineers. The collapse appeared to have started at the northern end, and after exhaustive enquiries the court found that the bridge was 'badly designed, badly constructed and badly maintained'. For this it considered Bouch mainly to blame. Bouch, who had had a continuing responsibility for maintenance of the bridge, was a

With traffic increasing, Perth station was much enlarged in the 1880s. New tracks on the right covered the former road approach, and the station buildings complete with watchtower illustrated in chapter 4 were now on an island platform. (Perth Museum and Art Gallery)

broken man. His health gave way: he died less than a year later.

The reports of the Court of Inquiry ran to more than 1,000 pages, and probably far more has been written on the subject since, in papers, articles and entire books. Much of these later writings casts doubts upon the findings of the court.[2] The recommended speed limit, if imposed, had been ignored, and the bridge structure had deteriorated in consequence. The court was in any case constrained by the knowledge of the day. In the light of subsequent accidents, in England and Ireland, in which trains have been overturned by gales,[3] it does seem that Bouch's views deserved greater respect. And internal NBR correspondence, then private but now in the National Archives of Scotland, makes clear that trains did sway slightly on entering the high girders from the south, probably from a misalignment in the track caused by remaining slight distortion of the span recovered from the river.[4] That dip, allied to the gale, might well have been enough to derail the last coach which, at only five tons, was the lightest in the train.

With the bridge debris blocking the channel, the NBR found itself receiving claims for compensation from owners of ships that had gone aground trying to avoid it, or were stranded up-river.[5] But apart from the high girders, most of the other spans of the bridge were undamaged. When the replacement Tay Bridge was built, alongside the old, during 1882–7,[6] they were moved across for reuse on more substantial piers. The stumps of the old piers remain to this day. Likewise the locomotive in the disaster was surprisingly so little damaged that she was repaired and went back into service. Nicknamed *The Diver*, for many years no driver could be found to take her across the Tay.

With reconstruction of the Tay Bridge planned, the Dundee & Arbroath Railway became a joint undertaking of the Caledonian and North British Railways in 1880, and the NBR opened its own line from Arbroath to Montrose and Kinnaber Junction in 1881–3.

Spurred on by the GSWR, the Caledonian had bridged the Clyde to reach its own city-centre terminus at Glasgow Central, opened in 1879. The North British, with access to Queen Street restricted by cable haulage on Cowlairs bank (as it would be until 1908), sponsored the Glasgow City and District Railway. Construction started in 1882. It was to run underground beneath the city, commencing at its secondary terminus at College, pass beneath Queen Street Station, and come to the surface near Finnieston. Thence it would continue past Partick and swing northwards to join the line to Helensburgh. With other railways already existing it offered the possibility of a circular service via Cowlairs.

Steam-worked underground railways of this type were already operating in London. Building them by 'cut and cover' was inevitably slow: houses had to be underpinned, sewers diverted and street traffic interrupted as little as possible, while successive short lengths of trench were excavated, the tunnel built, and the surface reinstated. Where the tunnel passed beneath Queen Street Station it was to be at right angles to the tracks on the surface: one after the other, each of these was closed while the tunnel was

advanced far enough for it to be reinstated before the next was tackled. Underground stations were built at Queen Street Low Level and Charing Cross, each with openings to the surface through which smoke and steam had some small chance to escape.

The line was opened in 1886; in the west a short branch led to a terminus at Hyndland (not the present Hyndland Station, but adjacent to Hyndland Road), and in the east a branch was added from College to Bridgeton Cross. Although there was a circular route, many trains instead ran from the east through the city to terminate at Hyndland, while many from the west ran through to Bridgeton. For many years, too, through trains ran between Edinburgh and Helensburgh and took this route, running fast up to the edge of Glasgow and then stopping at all stations through that city. In the 1880s and 1890s coaches lit after dark by gas were illuminated, when passing through the tunnel in daytime, by electricity supplied via a third rail between the running rails.[7]

The Caledonian Railway's comparable Glasgow Central Railway was built between 1888 and 1896, linking CR lines to the east and west and passing underground through the city centre, including the low-level station at Glasgow Central. The main terminus was enlarged in 1890, and enlarged very much more between 1899 and 1905 as described below. Such actions are indicative of booming traffic, there and elsewhere. When Perth Station was much enlarged in the 1880s the original handsome range of station buildings found itself on an island platform, with new tracks and additional platforms where the road approach had been.

After Parcel Post was introduced by the Post Office, an additional mail train had to be provided between Euston, Perth and Aberdeen in 1885: this, the 'Special

Mail', was run exclusively for the mails – the first such train – except between Perth and Aberdeen on the down journey only where four passenger carriages might be attached.

The Paisley Canal, which had been taken over by the GSWR in 1869, was closed in 1881 and its course used for a railway to act as a relief to existing lines,[8] with Paisley Canal station as a reminder of its origin. Such a route, though level, is sharply curved by railway standards, conditions that might well suit slow goods and mineral trains but were a different matter where expresses were concerned. D. L. Smith in *Tales of the Glasgow and South Western Railway* recalls how the 5.10 from St Enoch, non-stop to Ayr in 50 minutes, was routed that way until a group of directors travelled by it in the directors' saloon. This was attached to the rear of the train and round the curves it was (as Smith puts it) 'right out at the cow's tail and getting all the wag': directors were slid under the table more than once. When they found that the driver had actually *lost* a minute on the scheduled time to Paisley, the train was quickly rerouted to the straight main line.[9] Even today, when trains between Glasgow and Ayr are no slouches, the fastest are scheduled to take forty-six or forty-seven minutes, by the main line but with two stops.

Beyond Ayr, the Girvan & Portpatrick Railway (running to Challoch Junction with the Portpatrick Railway over which it had running powers for some seven miles to Stranraer) had been opened in 1877. But the bleak uplands through which it passed produced little local traffic, and through traffic between Stranraer and central Scotland had other routes available, so the Girvan & Portpatrick led a chequered existence, being closed, and reopened, and for a time worked independently, before final incorporation into the

GSWR in 1892.[10] On the Portpatrick Railway itself, long-distance traffic had eventually developed to the extent that, when the working agreement with the Caledonian expired in 1885, it was purchased by the London & North Western, Midland, Caledonian and Glasgow & South Western Railways acting in concert. Included in the deal was the Wigtownshire Railway which since the mid-1870s had been running southwards from Newton Stewart to Wigtown and Whithorn. This was being operated by Thomas Wheatley and his son – Wheatley senior, lately occupying the prestigious position of locomotive superintendent of the North British Railway, had parted company with it under a cloud. On the Wigtownshire he fulfilled the role elsewhere taken by an established railway company operating a local line: he provided the locomotives, ran the railway and took a percentage of the takings.[11] The new owners established a joint committee to operate the 'Portpatrick & Wigtownshire Joint Railways', using locomotives provided by both the CR and the GSWR.[12]

Cooperation between companies to this extent was unusual, and competition between them was still the greater characteristic of the age. This could be seen in microcosm in the continued attempts by the Great North of Scotland Railway to reach Inverness, and the equal concern of the Highland Railway to keep it out. The position seems to have been exacerbated because although the GNS portion of the Aberdeen–Inverness route, that is as far as Keith, was its main line, to the Highland Railway, viewed from Inverness, that part of the route from Forres to Keith was no more than a branch from its main line to the south. In 1886 the GNS completed a line from Portsoy – already reached by a branch – through Cullen, Portessie and Buckie to Elgin, including a vast viaduct over the Spey.

There were now three routes from Aberdeen as far as Elgin: the direct route, with interchange from GNS to Highland at Keith, and the two all-GNS routes via Buckie and via Craigellachie which, although indirect, served districts which were more populous. Yet the Highland naturally remained reluctant to interchange traffic at Elgin, for that meant losing traffic from its line between Elgin and Keith. Nor was that all. The Highland also had reached Buckie and Portessie by a branch from Elgin opened in 1884, and Parliament had additionally provided it with running powers over the GNS between Buckie and Portsoy – while the GNS was given reciprocal powers to run over the Highland from Elgin as far as Forres. Yet for the GNS this proved to be a dead letter. With the running powers came the proviso that both were to be exercised, or neither. The Highland chose not to run to Portsoy, so GNS was unable to run to Forres.[13]

By 1884 the GNS was on another tack: it promoted a line to extend its Speyside branch from near Boat of Garten via Carrbridge to Inverness. It was unable to obtain powers for this, and Parliament instead authorised the Highland Railway's direct line from Aviemore via Carrbridge to Inverness, which reduced the distance by rail between the two places to thirty-four and three-quarter miles, compared with sixty and a half miles via Forres. Yet the Highland was reluctant to build this route. It was forced on it by the threat of competition, not only from the GNS but even more by successive proposals for competitive main lines from Glasgow to Inverness via Fort William and the Great Glen. The Carrbridge line was expensive to build, with high viaducts over the River Findhorn and the River Nairn, and once completed it was expensive to work, with its 1,315-ft summit at Slochd. Despite the expense, revenues were reduced – in proportion to the reduction in distance. So although powers were obtained for the Carrbridge line in 1884, it was 1898 before it was eventually completed.[14]

The railway from Glasgow to Fort William eventually took shape, after many decades of proposals and counter-proposals,[15] as the West Highland Railway. This had the North British Railway behind it and got its Act in 1889. The route started at Craigendoran, one and a quarter miles short of Helensburgh on the line from Glasgow, and ran via Arrochar, Crianlarich and the Moor of Rannoch to Lochaber and an approach to Fort William from the north-east. By this date, railway builders had some mechanised equipment to supplement the muscles of men and horses: compressed air drills, which had originated on the Continent, and steam navvies, which had originated in North America. The latter, by substantially reducing the numbers of human navvies to be brought to site and accommodated, were particularly valuable in remote districts, and at least one was used in building the West Highland.[16] The line was opened throughout its entire length, almost 100 miles, in 1894 with the North British as operator. At Crianlarich it crossed above the Callander & Oban line, and a spur connected one line with the other: but when hoped-for North British running powers to Oban were not authorised, opening of the spur was delayed for three years, and even then it was used for many decades only for transfer of goods vehicles.[17]

A year after the West Highland opened, in 1895, a one-and-three-quarter-mile branch was added from Fort William to Banavie Pier, whence MacBrayne's steamers plied to Inverness over the Caledonian Canal. Both the North British and the Highland had promoted lines to link the West Highland at Fort William with the Highland at Inverness – and then reached agreement that neither should be built. In 1896 a local company, the Invergarry & Fort Augustus Railway, obtained powers to build from Spean Bridge on the West Highland up the Great Glen to Fort Augustus. This railway was opened, eventually, in 1903. It was to become notorious for the limited traffic generated, even at this period, and by its rural nature for a line equipped in the lavish manner appropriate to the first stage of a trunk route. The North British Railway was unwilling to operate the line on terms acceptable to the local company – and the line was worked instead for some years by the Highland Railway as an isolated appendage to its system.[18] The HR eventually withdrew in favour of the North British.

Once the West Highland had been authorised in 1889 it was evident that, whatever might happen in the Great Glen, there was every likelihood of its being extended to a port on the west coast that would offer a convenient route to the Hebrides and west-coast fisheries. This prompted the Highland Railway to obtain powers in 1893 to extend the Skye railway from Strome Ferry to the terminus originally planned at Kyle of Lochalsh which would be more competitive. The extension was opened in 1897 and the steamer services transferred to Kyle. Meanwhile powers had indeed been obtained in 1896 to extend the West Highland, and it was opened from Banavie through to Mallaig in 1901. Both these lines received financial support from the government, which was most unusual in Britain at that period.

While we have been taking this excursion round the periphery of the railway system, there had been other important developments closer to the centre. In cities, the Edinburgh Suburban & South Side Junction Railway, allowing a circular suburban service

So vast is the Forth Bridge that at track level one end can scarcely be seen from the other – the tracks within their framework of steel seem to stretch away to infinity. (Author)

The Forth Bridge, completed in 1890, is seen here illuminated for its centenary celebrations.
(Bill Roberton)

round the southern part of the city, was opened in 1884, and in Aberdeen the Great North introduced frequent inner suburban services over existing lines from 1887. Over the River Forth at Alloa, completion in 1887 of a 1,610-ft bridge, with a swing span and nineteen fixed spans, allowed the Caledonian Railway direct rail access into Alloa from Larbert and beyond.[19] But this was a small undertaking compared with what was happening further down the Forth.

A road bridge had been proposed over the Firth of Forth as early as 1818, and an Act of Parliament obtained for a railway bridge in 1865. It became a casualty, probably, of the financial collapse of 1866, and a second attempt in the 1870s for a bridge designed by Thomas Bouch became a casualty of the physical collapse of his Tay Bridge. Construction being too great a task for the North British Railway alone, it had joined with its southern partners, the North Eastern, the Great Northern and the Midland Railways, to form the Forth Bridge Railway Company. It was the Midland which then took the lead, persuading its partners to guarantee 4 per cent interest on the cost of the bridge and the cost of maintenance as well, and after a further Act had been obtained in 1882 the project went forward again.

The great depth of water in the firth – as much as 200 feet – precluded either a tunnel or a viaduct of many short spans. But between North and South Queensferry this depth is to be found in two channels which pass either side of a central island and its associated shallows. This enabled engineers Benjamin Baker and Sir John Fowler to design the bridge, the appearance of which remains familiar: three huge free-standing steel towers, each with vast cantilevers either side; two lattice girder spans between them, and approach viaducts of girder spans on masonry piers. The total length approaches one and five-eighths miles; the clear headroom for ships is 150 feet.

The workforce employed on building the bridge reached, at times, between 4,000 and 5,000; regrettably, 63 men lost their lives in accidents. Work went on day and night, for electric arc lights were now available for illumination. The sheer size of the bridge was well conveyed by W.M. Acworth who, arriving to see it under construction, wondered why no one was to be seen and work was apparently suspended: only, as he approached, to find men clustered like flies about the cantilevers, so small that they had earlier been invisible. More than 54,000 tons of steel were used in the bridge, and 6½ million rivets of which the last was inserted by the Prince of Wales on 4 March 1890 when the bridge was formally opened. Designed wholly for utilitarian purposes it has, as Hamilton Ellis put it, an unconscious beauty. Its image has become a symbol of Scottish railways, indeed of Scotland itself.[20] The cantilever principle was used again a few years later for a bridge over Loch Etive at the tidal Falls of Lora. It was intended from the start to carry a branch line of the Callander & Oban that was being built from Connel Ferry to Ballachulish, and which it seemed might form part of a main line from Oban to Inverness, and also a footway to replace, partially, the ancient ferry. The railway over the bridge was opened in 1903, but not the footway. Eleven years of disputes went by before the bridge was made available also to road traffic of all types, against payment of tolls.[21]

To return to the Forth Bridge: its construction implied also construction of new main lines to approach it, on both sides of the Forth. These were built largely at the cost of the North British alone. To bring traffic from the Edinburgh direction, a new line was built which diverges from the original Edinburgh & Glasgow line at Corstorphine; for traffic from the Glasgow direction, a new line diverges from it at Winchburgh. In the region to the north of the bridge, a complex system of local lines had grown up to link coal mines with coast, and Fife with the main railway system away to the west. The bridge's 150-foot headroom meant that the railway had to descend at 1 in 70 for two miles by rock cutting and viaduct to join existing railways at Inverkeithing. Beyond Inverkeithing there was more new construction, a main line running along the coast for seven miles to Burntisland ferry terminal. Ahead lay the main line to Aberdeen which the NBR had built up over the years. This also offered, via Ladybank, a route to Perth and the Highlands. However, a shorter route to Perth could be, and was, obtained from Inverkeithing via Dunfermline and Kinross. That meant upgrading existing lines and building new links, notably between

Mawcarse and Bridge of Earn, where the new line descended for six and a half miles at 1 in 74–75 through the narrow defile of Glenfarg.[22]

The effect of all this was to reverse totally the balance of advantage between West Coast and East Coast routes for travel from the South, both to Aberdeen and to Perth for the Highlands. The East Coast route, now unbroken by ferries, from King's Cross to Aberdeen became 523½ miles, compared with the West Coast from Euston at 540 miles; from King's Cross to Perth, 441 miles compared with West Coast at 450 miles. The Midland benefited too: the North British route from Carlisle to Perth via the Waverley Route and the Forth Bridge became shorter, at 146 miles, than the Caledonian at 151 miles; from Carlisle to Aberdeen the mileages were 229 and 240 respectively. Although the arduous nature of the Midland route from St Pancras to Edinburgh to some extent countered the advantage in distance, there was traffic to be gained from the industrial cities of Northern England. As for the East Coast route south of Edinburgh, in terms of gradients and curves it was already the easiest of the three, even though north of the bridge the piecemeal manner in which the routes had been built up left an uncomfortable legacy of curves and gradients.

Construction of the Forth Bridge took place against a background of rapid acceleration of Anglo-Scottish expresses: indeed the changes which its completion would bring about were in part the cause of this, as each of the three routes sought to gain a competitive advantage over the others. Not that train speeds early in the 1880s were fast by later standards: E. Foxwell and T. C. Farrer in *Express Trains English and Foreign* of 1889 took as their definition of 'express' a train that averaged 40 mph, including stops, for at least forty miles. Lest this speed appear modest, it is worth noting that they applied this figure only in Great Britain and the USA: for the rest of the world, they admitted trains travelling at speeds down to 29 mph.[23] (Despite its title, the book is divided into two parts, 'Express trains in Great Britain' and 'Foreign Express trains': the first includes Scottish and Welsh railways equally with English.)

There was, however, no lack of traffic. Anglo-Scottish traffic reached its peak each year early in August: this was 'the grouse fortnight' when the great and good, who had followed the example of their queen and purchased Highland estates, moved to them for the start of the shooting season. Inevitably they travelled by train: so did their families, and their guests, and their servants, and their dogs, and their horses and carriages too. The focal point for this traffic was Perth, where every morning there converged six or seven overnight trains, coming from the South by all three routes, and their vehicles were re-marshalled into two trains for Inverness, one for Aberdeen and one for Dundee. While this was going on, passengers could disembark: there were dressing rooms with hot baths in the station buildings, and breakfast of fresh Tay salmon; even dogs were provided with roomy kennels with fresh water and clean straw.[24] Many sleeping cars went no further, but some did, and so did family saloons: this was the era when the wealthy habitually hired family saloon coaches to make their entire journeys, handed over from train to train and railway to railway en route.

Foxwell and Farrer famously noted the composition of the 7.50 a.m. Perth to Inverness on 7 August 1888. At the front of the train was a medley of vehicles – saloons, sleeping car, ordinary coaches, horse boxes, luggage vans, carriage trucks, indiscriminately from West Coast joint stock and East Coast joint stock,

and London & North Western, Midland, Great
Northern, North Eastern and North British Railways,
even three horse boxes and a carriage van from the
London, Brighton & South Coast Railway and a
horsebox from as far afield as the London & South
Western. All these were coupled ahead of the eleven
vehicles of the Highland train proper. The grand total
was nine companies and thirty-six vehicles (many
of the vehicles, though, would have been on four
or six wheels and small by modern standards). This
astonishing train required two engines in front, and
another put on behind at Blair Atholl to bank it up
the hill to Druimuachdar.[25]

It was not, however, overnight first-class traffic,
but daytime third-class which prompted the start of
the series of leap-frog accelerations, by each Anglo-
Scottish route as it attempted to out-do the others,
which became known as the race to Edinburgh of
August 1888 – the first of the railway races to the
North. The previous November the Great Northern
Railway had announced that third-class passengers
would thenceforward be carried on the 10.00 a.m.
East Coast express from King's Cross to Scotland.
This train, which reached Edinburgh in 9 hours and
Glasgow in 10 hours 20 minutes, had previously been
first and second class only; the quickest daytime express
that carried third-class passengers had been taking
ten hours to Edinburgh and nearly twelve hours to

Every year, late in the summer the well-to-do, with their servants
and dogs, migrated North for the shooting season. George Earl's
Perth Station, coming South shows them on their return at the
season's end. At Perth, before the Forth Bridge was completed,
trains from Aberdeen, Inverness and Dundee were split up and
re-marshalled into trains for Glasgow, Edinburgh and the three
routes to London; while this was going on, passengers could
descend and renew old friendships.
(NMS Pictorial Collection/Science & Society Picture Library)

Glasgow. On the West Coast route, the fastest daytime expresses had been carrying third-class passengers for some years and took 10 hours or so from Euston to both Edinburgh and Glasgow. Consequently the West Coast companies found their third-class traffic, particularly to Edinburgh, ebbing away.

On 2 June 1888 the West Coast companies accelerated their 10.00 a.m. from Euston to a nine-hour schedule to both Edinburgh and Glasgow. The East Coast companies soon announced that from 1 July their trains would reach Edinburgh in 8½ hours and Glasgow in 9 hours 50 minutes. The Midland accelerated its fastest St Pancras–Glasgow train by one hour, to 9 hours 20 minutes, and for good measure knocked 25 minutes off its fastest Edinburgh train, although this still meant a 9¾-hour journey. The Midland then left it at that, but on East and West Coast routes the pace was only hotting up. On 27 July the London & North Western announced that the West Coast Edinburgh train also would take eight and a half hours from 1 August, no doubt anticipating that the East Coast companies would be unable to make, within three days, all the arrangements needed to accelerate their own train. If so, they were disappointed, for on 1 August the East Coast companies succeeded in reducing their schedule too – to eight hours.

Railwaymen were now on their mettle; such trains required skilled work on the footplate, smart work at stations and extra-careful work in signal boxes. The interest of the public was aroused too, and talk of the 'race to Edinburgh' had become common. Crowds gathered to see the trains come in. It is at this period that an amateur interest in railways and their operation first becomes apparent. One early enthusiast would see the East Coast train into Edinburgh Waverley, then have a hansom cab rush him along Princes Street

to the Caledonian station to see if the West Coast train had arrived.[26] On 1 August both trains arrived at their destination early. On 6 August the West Coast companies started to run their Edinburgh train in eight hours, like the East Coast. On 13 August the East Coast retaliated by reducing its schedule to seven and three-quarter hours. The train was late, because of a gale, but the West Coast train reached Edinburgh in 7 hours 38 minutes. The next day the East Coast train ran the journey in 7 hours 32 minutes. And then the companies seem to have decided that honours were even; they conferred, and decided that the schedules of seven and three-quarter hours and eight hours should remain for the rest of the month. This of course continued to require spirited performances from the train crews; as a 'farewell performance' on 31 August, the East Coast train drew into Waverley at 5.27 p.m., that is 7 hours 27 minutes from King's Cross, having achieved 76½ mph en route.[27]

The East Coast trains were, however, being worked by North Eastern Railway locomotives and men through to Edinburgh, in accordance with the arrangements then in force. Of greater interest from a Scottish viewpoint is the work done over the Caledonian Railway between Carlisle and Edinburgh. For this, one locomotive alone was employed, no. 123, which had been built by the noted Glasgow builder Neilson & Co. for display at the Edinburgh Industrial Exhibition of 1886. Neilson had the benefit of an arrangement that the Caledonian Railway would buy her afterwards. Also on display at the exhibition were the latest locomotives from the North British Railway and the Highland Railway, and examples of the latest rolling stock;[28] no. 123 was awarded a gold medal. This locomotive had the wheel arrangement 4-2-2, with, that is, a single pair of large-diameter driving wheels: a free-running arrangement popular in earlier years when trains were light, and in the 1880s enjoying a revival with the development of powered sanding gear to drive sand between driving wheels and rails, when needed to increase adhesion. No. 123's sanding gear used jets of compressed air, drawn from her Westinghouse air-braking system.[29] No doubt this enabled her to make some remarkably fast ascents of Beattock bank. Throughout August her average time for the journey from Carlisle to Edinburgh Princes Street was 107¾ minutes, which meant an average speed of 56 mph.[30]

With completion of the Forth Bridge the goal for competing East and West Coast expresses became Aberdeen. Over the next few years the overnight trains by each route were accelerated, but the principle that the West Coast should take fifteen minutes longer than the East was maintained. There were, however, two big changes from hitherto. Firstly, North British locomotives and men were now working the East Coast route expresses over their last lap, that is north of Edinburgh – and in those days between the North British and the Caledonian (and indeed also between the Glasgow & South Western and the Caledonian) what might have been considered in board rooms as free-market competition became, between railwaymen on the ground, outright fist-shaking rivalry. Secondly, unlike Edinburgh, Aberdeen had but one main station for which trains from both routes were bound. For the North British, that meant exercising running powers over the Caledonian from Kinnaber Junction – no station, but the point north of Montrose at which North British metals trailed into those of the Caledonian from Perth. In effect, Kinnaber Junction was the winning post: whichever train reached it first – indeed whichever was accepted first by the

Kinnaber signalman from adjoining boxes on each route from the south – would be first into Aberdeen. And although the East Coast route to Kinnaber was the shorter of the two, the West Coast, particularly in its final stages through Strathmore, was the better aligned for fast running.

During the spring of 1895 the 8.00 p.m. trains from King's Cross and Euston were due into Aberdeen at 7.35 a.m. and 7.50 a.m. respectively. On 1 June the West Coast train was retimed to arrive at 7.40, to allow passengers more time to connect with the 8.05 a.m. for Deeside. On 1 July the East Coast companies warily retimed their own train to arrive at 7.20. Then on 15 July the West Coast announced, with widespread publicity, that their train would be scheduled to arrive in Aberdeen at 7.00 a.m.: and that night it actually arrived at 6.47. The race was on. When the East Coast companies retaliated by accelerating their train on 22 July, to arrive at 6.45, the West Coast, while keeping the public time at 7.00, made the working time 6.35 and in fact got their train in at 6.39. A week later, the East Coast train was accelerated again to arrive at 6.25, and on its first night arrived at 6.23 – only to find that the West Coast train had arrived even earlier, at 6.06 am.[31]

By then the grouse fortnight was upon the railways, bringing the heaviest Anglo-Scottish traffic of the year, and further accelerations were for the time being impracticable, except that the West Coast advanced its working time of arrival to 6.20. But once again these racing trains had caught the public imagination: crowds gathered to see them go by, even in the middle of the night, and a small group of early railway enthusiasts was travelling, timing the trains and recording their speeds. Notable among them was Charles Rous-Marten, professional journalist. One morning he needed to return south as quickly as possible, and just as his overnight train from London pulled into Aberdeen he observed an early express setting off for Edinburgh. Leaping out, he rushed across the platform, tall hat, frock coat and all, to be bundled into it by the guard whose dry comment became famous: 'Ye'll no' be makin' a long stay in Aberdeen the mor-r-n'.[32]

Often there was a difference of no more than a few minutes in the times when the rival trains reached Kinnaber; on one noted occasion, early on 19 August, the Kinnaber signalman was offered both trains simultaneously.[33] Although a Caledonian man, he chivalrously accepted the East Coast train and let it through first.

Then, with the grouse fortnight out of the way, the East Coast companies announced that from that same evening their 8.00 p.m. train would be accelerated again, to reach Aberdeen at 5.40 a.m. This meant an average speed of 54 mph over the entire 523½-mile journey, and that, according to O. S. Nock, was a schedule far and away faster than anything previously tabled in Britain, or anywhere else in the world.[34] On board on 19 August were Rous-Marten, W. M. Acworth (whose *The Railways of Scotland* of 1889 has proved a fruitful source of material for the present book) and other timing enthusiasts. They landed in a confused heap on top of one another when the North Eastern driver took the curves at Portobello too fast: the train was still doing 64 mph when it burst out of Calton tunnel into Edinburgh Waverley. And even so the West Coast train beat the East Coast to Aberdeen by sixteen minutes.

By the night of 20 August the protagonists were planning to run as fast as possible, whatever the timetables might say. In the early dawn of the following morning, passengers in the 8.00 p.m. from King's Cross, as it approached Montrose, had the mortifying experience of seeing, far away in the distance across Montrose Basin, the smoke-trail of the 8.00 p.m. from Euston, running hard. It was through Kinnaber no more than a minute ahead of the East Coast train.

Changes of locomotives – several on each route – were reduced to a fine art. On the night of 21–22 August the West Coast train was into Carlisle at 12.53 a.m.; the North Western locomotive came off, the Caledonian one came on, and at 12.56 the train was away again to the cheers of the crowd, to run the next stage of 117.8 miles to Stirling in no more than 114 minutes. Meanwhile, on the East Coast at Berwick, where there was a 5 mph speed restriction, waiting onlookers had fled when they saw how fast the train was coming at them over the Royal Border Bridge. That night the East Coast route at last triumphed, through Kinnaber first and into Aberdeen at 4.40 a.m. The average speeds of both trains throughout their long journeys were both over 60 mph.[35]

The East Coast companies then decided to rest on their laurels and revert to a normal timetable: so ended what Nock describes as the greatest contest in speed that the world had then seen. But the following night West Coast companies made one last supreme effort and got their train into Aberdeen as early as 4.32 a.m. The crowds were waiting, even at that hour, and bore off driver John Soutar and his fireman shoulder-high to the refreshment room to celebrate.[36] As well they might: the record that had been set was to remain unbroken for over eighty years, until British Rail started to run High Speed Trains to Aberdeen.[37] Racing was past, but the overnight trains from London, by both routes, were retimed to reach Aberdeen by 6.30 a.m. In July 1896 a disastrous accident to the West Coast train at Preston, caused by excessive speed, effectively prevented any resumption of racing. The companies agreed that trains between London and Edinburgh, and London and Glasgow, should take at least eight and a quarter hours, whether by East Coast route or West Coast. That was for day trains; overnight trains were sometimes faster. Memories of the races remained, and for decades afterwards railway-race-to-the-North board games were familiar occupants of toy cupboards up and down the land.[38]

Prior to the 1880s train speeds in Britain had been held down by the measured development and application of the improved signalling methods and braking systems needed for safe operation at higher speeds. For years the Board of Trade had been exhorting railway companies to faster introduction of three important improvements to safety. Firstly, it wanted all railways (with a few exceptions) to be operated by the 'block system', allowing one train only upon each section of line at a time – so that trains would be separated by intervals of space, rather than of time. Secondly, it wanted signals interlocked with points, so that conflicting indications could not be given. Thirdly, it wanted all passenger trains to be fitted with continuous brakes, operated from the locomotive. All three were made compulsory by the Regulation of Railways Act, 1889.

The third of these requirements bore hard on the Highland Railway which customarily, and from motives of necessary economy, combined goods and passenger vehicles into the same trains, and put the goods wagons – sometimes thirty-five or more[39] – at the front where they could conveniently be attached and detached at stations. Continuous brakes on the passenger coaches meant putting these at the front instead, which in turn meant complicated shunting manoeuvres en route. Nevertheless, mixed trains

continued to run on Highland lines well into the twentieth century.

In the early 1890s hours of work were still very long. Signalmen worked twelve-hour shifts. A driver might leave Perth at 5.00 a.m. to arrive at Carlisle at 12.30 p.m. and return without a break to Perth by 8.30 p.m., fifteen and a half hours on duty for five or six days a week.[40] Such hours were not untypical. Even retirement from main-line duties to shunting, for reasons of health, brought little respite. Norman McKillop, later to be a famous locomotive man himself, found such a man in Andrew Manzie, driver of the yard pilot at Edinburgh Haymarket depot in 1910. This locomotive, a 'pug' saddle tank, lacked any form of cab: yet for ten hours every day, come rain, wind, sleet or snow, it shunted continuously up and down the yard. Nevertheless, Manzie was a good-natured man, pleased to welcome a youngster on to his footplate, and to pass on the knowledge accumulated by years of experience. In this and many other railway tasks, the satisfaction to be gained from the job was some compensation for arduous conditions. McKillop himself remarks of one of his earliest firing jobs, a couple of years later, that what really mattered to him was being *allowed* to handle a railway engine.[41]

In days when retirement was not enforced so rigorously as now, men who could stand the conditions at all could go on doing so far into old age. Driver Jimmy Nottman, mentioned earlier, was eventually persuaded to retire unwillingly from the footplate in the 1920s at the age of eighty-three – at which he was heard to comment that if he had kent the job wasna to be for life he would never have left the fishin'![42] And Robert Beattie, while not matching that record, joined the North British in 1884, fired in 1894 the first locomotive to work a construction train on the

West Highland Railway, became a driver in 1895 and eventually retired from the West Highland in 1931.[43]

During 1890, 84 railwaymen were killed in Scotland and 229 injured.[44] Working practices then, and for long afterwards, left much to be desired by later standards. At Falahill, the summit of the first steep bank south of Edinburgh on the Waverley route, the fireman of the banking engine, which had been helping a passenger train up the hill from the rear, would clamber forward along the footplating to uncouple from the train, all the while on the move.[45] In 1911 when a North British fast fish train ploughed disastrously into a gang of surfacemen working on the track near Kirkcaldy there was, as appears to have been normal in those days, no lookout man posted to protect them.[46] The everyday experience of a guard of a long train of loose-coupled goods wagons was ever uncomfortable, sometimes dangerous: when the train stopped and the wagons bunched up successively, the guard's van (unless the guard had his hand brake adjusted to a nicety) could be flung against the last wagon with great force – and starting was worse, for as the couplings tightened one by one the van at the end could be accelerated to 20 mph or more almost instantaneously by the snatch of the last coupling.

Excessive hours of work were a greater influence than low wages in the formation of railwaymens' trade unions. There had been attempts to form unions, mostly south of the border and short-lived, since the earliest days of railways; in 1866 the general managers of the North British, GSW and Caledonian Railways took these sufficiently seriously to put their names jointly to a circular to employees, warning them against combination, or joining any union 'for the avowed purpose of dictating to their employers', while reminding them that they and their officers

remained desirous of meeting employees' legitimate demands. Presumably the then existing practice of men putting their names to a memorial or petition against grievances seemed adequate. But trade unions gained legal status by Act of Parliament in 1871, and early in 1872 the Amalgamated Society of Railway Servants for Scotland was formed in Glasgow; there had already been formed, late in 1871, the Amalgamated Society of Railway Servants of England, Ireland, Scotland and Wales. These two, the 'Scotch Society' and the 'English Society' co-existed for some years, the English Society recruiting some members in Scotland although the Scotch Society's subscriptions were lower.[47]

Over the next couple of decades, a period when increasing concern over railway safety culminated in the Act of 1889, attempts by trade unions to have the working day reduced to ten hours or so gained much sympathy from the public. They were hampered, particularly where enginemen were concerned, by the growth of traffic, faster than the growth of facilities to handle it: this meant constant detention of freight trains in marshalling yards, while the position was made worse by the otherwise valuable practice of allocating each driver his own locomotive. During the 1870s and 1880s strikes broke out spasmodically with little lasting effect. Matters came to a head in 1890 following the opening of the Forth Bridge, when increased and altered flows of traffic seem to have been greater than the North British management anticipated, as mentioned below. It was also a period of industrial unrest – there were railway and dock strikes in the South that summer.

The Scotch society waited for the moment that seemed likely to have most effect: it brought its members on the North British, Caledonian and GSW Railways out on strike, without notice, on 22 December, and so

During the increasingly acrimonious strike of 1890-1, the Caledonian Railway started to evict striking employees from company-owned houses, to provide accommodation for strike-breaking labour it was bringing in. The consequence was riots, during the course of which the glass platform awning of Motherwell station as smashed by a barrage of flying stones. (Science Museum Library / Science & Society Picture Library)

striking at that time, railwaymen lost much public sympathy. But the strike itself became increasingly bitter. Early in January the Caledonian decided to evict some families from company-owned housing in Motherwell, to accommodate English labour it was bringing in. The evictions were accompanied by violence, despite the presence of a large force of police. On 5 January 20,000 people rioted and the Hussars were called out. Motherwell station lay in a cutting overlooked by a retaining wall: from this vantage point, rioters armed with stones let fly, smashing the extensive glazed canopy over the island platform, and the windows of the signal box too. The strike was to continue for almost six weeks. Two years later a Select Committee of the House of Commons found that 'Overwork on the railways of the United Kingdom is widespread and, in general, systematic, and not accidental or exceptional'.[48] Yet the outcome seems to have been equivocal.

In 1892 the Scotch Society and the English Society united as the Amalgamated Society of Railway Servants.[49] By then other unions were active: craft unions, the Associated Society of Locomotive Engineers and Firemen (ASLEF) formed in 1879, and the United Pointsmen's and Signalmen's Society of 1880, while the lowest-paid grades were catered for by the General Railway Workers' Union formed in 1889.[50] The Railway Clerks' Association originated in 1897; it would eventually become the Transport Salaried Staffs' Association (TSSA) in the early 1950s.[51]

Recognition of trade unions was slow in coming. In 1906 a national strike – that is, throughout the whole of Great Britain – by the Amalgamated Society and the General Railway Workers, acting together, was averted only by the intervention of Lloyd George as President of the Board of Trade. He persuaded

brought those railways almost to a standstill. People could not travel south for Christmas, nor north for Hogmanay. Coal could not be delivered. Poultry intended for festive ovens rotted in goods depots. By railway companies and unions to accept settlement of disputes, over pay and working conditions, through conciliation boards. But in 1911, a year of industrial unrest, a national strike broke out nonetheless. It was resolved only after the prime minister, Asquith, had brought representatives of the companies and the unions together, for the first time, to negotiate face to face. The eventual outcome was that the working of the conciliation boards would be reviewed by a Royal Commission – the work of this commission was, however, to be overtaken by outbreak of the the First World War. Meanwhile the Amalgamated Society, the General Railway Workers and the Pointsmen's and Signalmen's Society had united in 1913 to become the National Union of Railwaymen (NUR).[52]

Meanwhile, continuing growth of traffic had led to reconstruction of both the main stations in Edinburgh during the 1890s. The Caledonian Railway rebuilt its Princes Street terminus and at last provided a fine permanent building, in use from 1893. Alterations at the North British Waverley Station were far more fundamental. The principal feature of the old General Station, built for the Edinburgh & Glasgow and North British companies, was a large train shed with five tracks, linked by turnplates as was the practice of the time, but with only two platforms. The Edinburgh, Perth & Dundee, emerging from Scotland Street tunnel, had its own terminus at right angles. This must have crowded the main station towards the southern edge of their cramped location, in the dell between the Old and New Towns, which also accommodated both railways' goods depots. By the 1880s the EP & D station was closed and a couple of bay platforms had been added to the main station,[53] but it was still in essence the same. Foxwell and Farrer identified its shortcomings thus, in a passage which has often been quoted but bears repetition:

On the platforms of the Waverley station at Edinburgh may be witnessed every evening in summer a scene of confusion so chaotic that a sober description of it is incredible to those who have not themselves survived it. Trains of caravan length come in portentously late from Perth, so that each is mistaken for its successor; these have to be broken up and re-made on insufficient sidings, while bewildered crowds of tourists sway up and down amongst equally bewildered porters on the narrow village platform reserved for these most important expresses; the higher officials stand lost in subtle thought, returning now and then to repeated inquiries some masterpiece of reply couched in the cautious conditional, while the hands of the clock with a humorous air survey the abandoned sight, till at length, without any obvious reason and with sudden stealth, the shame-stricken driver hurries his packed passengers off into the dark.[54]

One among the crowds found yet another feature of the station to criticise: to William Morris the refreshment room coffee was 'ineffably bad'.[55]

Foxwell and Farrer were describing conditions *before* the Forth Bridge was opened: the extra trains which resulted in the summer of 1890 brought an already congested station almost to a standstill. Passenger trains, held up at signal after signal, took as much as one hour to cover the last three miles into Waverley. Goods trains were passed through when they could be – one reputedly was held up for twenty-four hours. The consequences of late-departing passenger trains were felt, in delays and missed connections, as far afield as Wick and Plymouth – or so *The Times* thundered, in a leading article entitled 'Waverley, or 'Tis Sixty Minutes Late'.[56] Readers no doubt saw in this the allusion to the full title of Scott's novel: *Waverley, or*

At Inverness, about 1906, the overnight train from the south has arrived, on the left: it has run past the station on the avoiding line, and backed into one of the northbound platforms. Passengers can change across the platform into the train on the right, which is bound for either the far north or Kyle of Lochalsh. Evidently there is no hurry, and passengers take their ease, although the little girl is holding tight onto mother and governess. Ten years on, everyone in a scene such as this will be in Naval uniform – see Chapter 6. (National Archives of Scotland, BR/HR/4/27 – Science and Society Picture Library)

'tis sixty years since. The extra hours which railwaymen had to work as a result of the delays, on top of hours that were already long, were, as has been mentioned, instrumental in provoking the strike that winter.

The eventual solution adopted by the North British, once the nettle had been grasped, was on a scale grandly commensurate with the problem. A second pair of tracks was provided at both the western and the eastern approaches to the station – that meant extra tunnels at Haymarket, the Mound and Calton Hill; it also meant, Heaven forbid, acquiring more land from Princes Street Gardens. The station itself was totally rebuilt between 1892 and 1900, the main part becoming a vast island platform, with each of its faces long enough to accommodate two full-length expresses (loops and crossovers enabled them to overtake one another), fifteen terminal platforms in between, and a central station building; a further island platform was added to serve the suburban line.[57] Once beneath the station's eleven and a half acres of glass roofs one was, as an enthusiast visiting in the 1920s wrote,[58] immune to the outside world – nothing could be seen of the Old Town, or the New. Exceeded in size only by London Waterloo, Edinburgh Waverley was and remains the second-largest station in Britain; it has become familiar to generations of travellers.

Even while the North British was still working on Waverley, the Caledonian was starting to rebuild Glasgow Central. Here the number of trains daily had increased from 173 in 1880 to 486 in 1897, the number of passengers using the station annually from 4¾ million to 15¾ million over the same period. The Caledonian planned to double the size of the station, and did so over six years from 1899. In a location hemmed in by city streets this could only be achieved by taking in a little land to the west of the station

and also extending the station back towards the River Clyde. The approach viaduct over the river already carried four tracks, and was not merely duplicated but *triplicated*, with a new viaduct alongside carrying as many as eight more tracks. The lozenge-shaped plan of the station site might have been awkward but was exploited to work well, the concourse widening from the main entrance to lead to the long, curving, main-line departure platforms on the left, shorter platforms for local trains in the centre, the long main-line arrival platforms on the right and beyond them two more platforms for Clyde Coast trains.[59] The whole was given a glazed roof in the spacious manner to which the Caledonian was by then accustomed, producing a light and airy structure which remains familiar and somehow seems more welcoming than Edinburgh Waverley – perhaps because you walk downwards into Waverley but upwards into Central! Between them the two stations, with Glasgow Queen Street, continue to provide Scotland's two principal cities with the vital feature of main-line stations in the city centres.

The joint station at Aberdeen was similarly located, and at the end of the nineteenth century was suffering similar problems of congestion. Likewise it was rebuilt, but gradually: with the intervention of the First World War, the work was not finally completed until 1920.[60] It too continues to provide a city-centre main-line station.

Amalgamation was on the cards again. In 1890 shareholders of the GSWR approved a bill, promoted by the North British, for amalgamation of the two companies; the Midland Railway supported them. At this point the Caledonian promoted its own bill to acquire the GSW. Both bills were heard by the same committee of the House of Commons. This committee rejected the Caledonian bill but approved the North

British – only for it to be rejected by the Lords. So the GSWR continued its separate way: the 'Good and Safe Wee Railway'.[61]

According to Acworth, the Great North of Scotland Railway was offering amalgamation to the Highland at the end of the 1880s.[62] Yet if that was so one can only suppose it a bargaining ploy in the long-running dispute between the two companies over Aberdeen–Inverness traffic. The GNS made several further attempts to build its own line into Inverness, or to obtain running powers over the Highland, with equal and constant lack of success. It improved the train services over its own lines, but found the Highland ever unwilling to improve arrangements for interchange of traffic, both in location, Keith or Elgin, and in type, through coaches or connections. On several occasions the two companies went to arbitration before commissioners appointed under the Railway and Canal Traffic Acts, which required railways to afford reasonable facilities, for receipt, carriage and delivery of traffic, to the public without undue preference between customers.[63] Eventually in 1897 arbitrators decided that Keith and Elgin should be the points of interchange for an equal number of train services in each direction.[64]

This eased the position and the two companies started to cooperate, so much so that in 1905 amalgamation was indeed proposed. Great North shareholders voted in favour and so too, in a meeting in 1906, did a majority of Highland shareholders: yet many other shareholders abstained or voted against. The Highland board felt that, in the absence of anything approaching near-unanimity, it should not proceed. By this narrow margin the amalgamation was lost, and the Aberdeen–Inverness route remained split between two companies for another forty-

one years until nationalisation.[65] But in 1908 it was arranged that some Aberdeen–Inverness trains should be worked throughout by locomotives of one company or other, and in the same year excursions from Aberdeen to Speyside were extended from Boat of Garten over the Highland Railway to Kingussie. Regrettably too few excursionists took advantage of this for the arrangement to be perpetuated, but the through-working of locomotives proved to be a lasting innovation.[66]

The excursionists to Speyside were provided with cold luncheons, but meals had first been both cooked and served on board a train in Britain as long before as 1878. The occasion was remarkable: a special train which ran from London St Pancras to Wick and back, taking in the Settle & Carlisle, Glasgow & South Western and Highland lines. The train comprised two Pullmans – one a sleeping car, the other a parlour car – and two vans, one of which was fitted up as a kitchen, the other as a bathroom.[67]

On scheduled trains, dining cars were introduced simultaneously in 1893 on all three Anglo-Scottish routes, and what was more for third-class passengers as well as first. On the Midland route, passengers reserved seats and travelled throughout their journeys in the dining car, as was then usual. East Coast and West Coast trains had a further novelty: corridors down the coaches, and corridor connections between them, so that all passengers had access to the dining car. The East Coast trains had separate kitchen cars, for the first time in Britain. The West Coast train, 2.00 p.m. from Euston to both Edinburgh and Glasgow, added at Preston sections from Liverpool for both destinations.[68] Railwaymen called this train 'The Corridor', and the name stuck; according to Jack Simmons, it was still in use in the 1950s, although the train's official name had

Highland Railway—Further North Express

The Highland Railway's 'Further North Express' heads for Wick and Thurso.
(Michael Wrottesley collection)

long since become 'The Mid-day Scot'.[69]

Better still was to come, with entire trains of luxurious new coaches for the 'Flying Scotsman' in 1900, and for 'The Corridor' itself in 1908. The latter stock, built at the London & North Western Railway's Wolverton Works, was comfortable, handsome, well decorated and plumbed and equipped with electric light: Hamilton Ellis considered that, for ordinary passengers who paid no supplement, there were no finer trains in Europe.[70] Nevertheless for internal trains the Caledonian Railway had already introduced its 'Grampian' stock in 1905. These coaches were 65 ft long or more, and on six-wheeled bogies, they must have appeared vastly impressive compared with ordinary bogie coaches of the day, around 50 ft long and on

four-wheeled bogies, and even more so compared with the many four- and six-wheeled coaches still running. Their outward appearance was elegant, their third-class accommodation comfortable, their first class luxurious.[71] They were used initially on trains from Glasgow and Edinburgh to Aberdeen, subsequently between Glasgow and Edinburgh, and Glasgow and the Clyde Coast. The North British quickly responded with some coaches for its Edinburgh/Glasgow–Aberdeen trains which were probably as comfortable although, being shorter, less impressive. With all this, one is forced to wonder whether trains in Scotland today are any better, so far as passenger comfort is concerned, than those of a century ago. The coaches of both companies had corridors, and both companies started to include dining cars in their trains.

Through sleeping cars between London and Inverness appear to have been introduced in the mid-1880s, and between London Euston and Oban in 1895. They started to run between London and Fort William in 1901. The Fort William cars for many years ran in summer only, and by the East Coast route to

---

Lines penned at Euston (by one who is not going)

Stranger with the pile of luggage proudly labelled for Portree,
How I wish this night of August I were you and you were me!
Think of all that lies before you as the train goes sliding forth
And the lines athwart the sunset lead you swiftly to the North.

Think of breakfast at Kingussie, think of high Druimuachdar Pass
Think of Highland breezes singing through the bracken and the grass
Scabious blue and yellow daisy, tender fern beside the train,
Rowdy Tummel falling, brawling seen and lost and glimpsed again

You will pass my golden roadway of the days of long ago.
Will you realise the magic of the names I used to know –
Clachnaharry, Achnashellach, Achnasheen and Duirinish?
Every moor alive with coveys, every burn aboil with fish.

Every well-remembered vista more exciting mile by mile
Till the wheeling gulls are screaming round the engine at the Kyle
Think of cloud on Ben na Cailleach, jagged Coolins soaring high
Scent of peat and all the glamour of the misty Isle of Skye!

Rod and guncase in the carriage, wise retriever in the van.
Go, and good luck go with you. Wish I'd half your luck, my man!

---

and from King's Cross.[72] The Inverness service was more equivocal: all three Anglo-Scottish routes fed into the Highland Railway at Perth, and in summer it was possible to see East Coast, West Coast and Midland sleeping cars from London all included in the same Highland train between Perth and Inverness. But the Highland Railway had no wish to haul three different sleeping cars to Inverness each night in winter when there was traffic only for one. In 1901 it suggested to the southern companies that they should share the traffic; eventually in winter the Midland sleeping cars to Inverness were withdrawn, and cars by East Coast and West Coast routes ran on alternate nights.[73] Nevertheless it was truly said that many of the Highland Railway's regular patrons never saw the inside of a Highland coach.[74]

Travellers from the south might well do so only if travelling beyond Inverness. The connection was aided by running the train from the south past the station on the avoiding line and then reversing it into one of the northern tracks, so that passengers had only to cross the platform to join the train for the far north. Inverness station is a terminus for both routes. The only passenger train regularly to bypass Inverness completely was the 'Strathpeffer Express' by which the HR, starting in 1911, encouraged custom at its new hotel in the spa town: connecting at Aviemore out of a train running from Perth to Inverness via Forres, it ran non-stop to Dingwall before continuing to Strathpeffer.

Just how much the annual journey North meant to those fortunate enough to make it can be gathered from the poem by A. M. Harbord 'Lines penned at Euston …'. Written, I believe, in the 1920s, it was clearly prompted by happy memories of earlier times and is reproduced on the left.

Kingussie was where breakfast baskets came aboard, in those days before restaurant cars. There is a little poetic licence in the order of events on the Highland main line, but the wayside stations beyond Inverness come through clear as a bell.

Harbord probably travelled first class by sleeping car – by the decade before the First World War sleeping cars had single- or double-berth compartments, wash basins, hot and cold water, electric light and electric fans. Overnight passengers in third class still had only ordinary compartments. R. B. Cunninghame Grahame describes such an overnight journey from Euston in his short story *Beattock for Moffat*, doing so evocatively even though compared with Harbord's verse the story lies at the opposite extreme of the spectrum of happiness. In this case an elderly Lowland Scot, consumptive and with death approaching, makes his last homeward journey from exile in London. For company he has his Cockney wife, and his Calvinistic brother reluctantly away from the family farm near Moffat. The fascination of the story lies in the contrasting attitudes and characters of these three, yet the journey and its landmarks provide a necessary backdrop. And though the compartment is not so well-upholstered as to render a supplementary air cushion unnecessary, and the 'half-candlepower electric light' is outshone by the moon despite the frost on the windows, yet there is no sense that physical discomfort is adding to the three travellers' problems, or hindering their converse. The train slips along smoothly, and successive landmarks seem to approach rather than be approached.[75]

Those were long-distance journeys. Something of the atmosphere of an everyday journey within Scotland can be gathered from Mary Campbell Smith's poem 'The Boy in the Train':

The Boy in the Train

Whit wey does the engine say 'Toot-toot'?
Is it feart to gang in the tunnel?
Whit wey is the furnace no pit oot
When the rain gangs doon the funnel?
What'll I hae for my tea the nicht?
A herrin', or maybe a haddie?
Has Gran'ma gotten electric licht?
Is the next stop Kirkcaddy?

There's a hoodie-craw on yon turnip-raw!
An' seagulls! – sax or seeven.
I'll no fa' oot o' the windae, Maw,
Its sneckit, as sure as I'm leevin'.
We're into the tunnel! We're a' in the dark!
But dinna be frichtit, Daddy,
We'll sune be comin' to Beveridge Park,
And the next stop's Kirkcaddy!

Is yon the mune I see in the sky?
It's awfu' wee an' curly,
See! There's a coo and a cauf ootbye,
An' a lassie pu'in a hurly!
He's chackit the tickets and gien them back,
Sae gie me my ain yin, Daddy.
Lift doon the bag frae the luggage rack,
For the next stop's Kirkcaddy!

There's a gey wheen boats at the harbour mou',
And eh! Dae ya see the cruisers?
The cinnamon drop I was sookin' the noo
Has tummelt an' stuck tae ma troosers …
I'll sune be ringin' ma Gran'ma's bell,
She'll cry, 'Come ben, my laddie',
For I ken mysel' by the queer-like smell
That the next stop's Kirkcaddy!

Caledonian expresses pass near Crieff Junction, later renamed Gleneagles, about 1909. The picture is from a painted photograph, the original artwork for a colour postcard of the period. (Michael Wrottesley collection)

Taken together, poems and story re-emphasize the disparate nature of Scotland, and the people who travel her railways – and, indeed, the extent to which railways have been interwoven with their lives.

Edwardian affluence was reflected in the train services provided by the three Anglo-Scottish routes. By around 1909 all their trains were formed of corridor bogie coaches on eight or twelve wheels; many included dining cars and/or sleeping cars as appropriate. By comparison with today, there was a greater range of through services and routes. This was achieved in part by attaching and detaching through coaches, of various origins and destinations, to and from trains during the course of their journeys; and in part because the presence of three distinct routes meant that, even though trains by all three originated in London and headed for similar destinations, intermediate towns on each route got the benefit of through services. On the other hand journey times were much longer – the London–Edinburgh daytime schedule was still at the agreed 8 hr 15 min. – and trains were less frequent. Train services tended to be built around departures from London after breakfast, in the early afternoon (the latest possible departure for a train to reach Edinburgh or Glasgow the same day), and in the evening for overnight travel. There were corresponding services from Scotland to London. Trains which in winter included coaches for several destinations often became transformed in summer into a series of trains leaving successively for each destination.

So in the summer of 1909 departures from London for Scotland were these (page 109):

iv APPROACHES.

"EAST COAST ROUTE," G.N., N.E., and N.B.
(via Forth Bridge). WEEK-DAYS.

M.		A a.m.	B a.m.	C a.m.	D a.m.	E a.m.	F p.m.	G p.m.	H p.m.	I p.m.	K p.m.
—	L'ndon (K's X) dep.	5.5	—	9.50	10.0	11.20	2.20	8.15	8.45	11.30	11.45
76	Peterborough ,,	6.36	—	10.33	10.37	12.16	3.29	8.17	10.20	12.33	12.33
—	Nottingham ... ,,	6.40	—	10.24	11.0	12.25	3.25	8.47	9.55	11.0	11.0
105½	Grantham ,,	7.21	—	11.14	12.5	1.2	4.26	10.19	11.5	1.34	1.49
156	Doncaster dep.	8.33	—	12.56	12.29	2.29	4.50	9.35	12.17	—	2.15
—	Hull ,,	8.30	—	9.53	12.5	12.55	5.5	8.40	11.25	—	—
—	Leeds ,,	9.5	9.40	11.55	1.3	2.20	5.20	10.50	—	—	2.40
188	York arr.	9.48	9.57	12.50	1.53	2.40	6.15	11.57	1.14	3.12	3.27
232	Darlington ,,	9.5	11.6	1.53	—	4.23	7.12	11.28	2.11	—	—
272	Newcastle dep.	11.17	12.12	3.21	3.39	5.15	8.8	1.33	3.6	4.48	5.3
338	Berwick ,,	—	2.5	4.46	—	6.38	9.31	—	4.37	—	—
395	Edinburgh arr.	1.35	3.30	6.5	6.15	8.5	10.45	4.0	5.55	7.15	7.30
—	Edinburgh dep.	2.5	4.0	6.30	6.30	8.15	p.m.	4.30	6.10	—	7.40
442	Glasgow arr.	3.25	5.7	7.35	7.35	9.33	—	5.35	7.23	—	9.5
—	Edinburgh dep.	2.5	4.0	6.30	6.30		—	4.30	6.10	—	7.40
464	Craigendoran arr.	4.29	5.42	9.9	9.9	*via Leeds and Harrogate*	—	7.27	8.33	—	10.19
485	Rothesay (St'r) ,,	5.55	—	—	—		—	—	—	—	11.42
554	Oban (St'r) ,,	—	—	—	—		—	4.50	—	—	—
564	Fort William ... ,,	9.21	9.21	—	—		—	9.42	11.48	—	2.12
566	Banavie ,,	—	—	—	—		—	9.56	12.1	—	5.16
606	Mallaig ,,	—	—	—	—		—	11.30	1.35	—	6.50
—	Edinburgh dep.	4.5	4.5	—	—	9.5	—	6.15	—	—	—
431	Stirling arr.	5.21	5.21	—	—	10.33	—	8.1	—	—	—
447	Callander ,,	6.7	6.7	—	—	12.35	—	8.46	—	—	—
518	Oban ,,	9.0	9.0	—	—	4.15	—	11.45	—	—	—
—	Edinburgh dep.	1.50	4.25	—	6.33	9.20	—	4.10	6.25	7.40	—
457	Dundee arr.	3.53	6.23	—	8.6	11.7	—	5.30	8.34	9.22	—
528	Aberdeen ,,	6.10	8.50	—	10.5	a.m.	—	7.22	—	11.30	—
—	Edinburgh dep.	2.15	4.30	—	6.38	9.5	—	3.55	—	7.30	10.10
438	Perth { arr.	3.32	6.26	—	7.51	10.36	—	5.0	—	8.55	11.21
	{ dep.	3.50	7.15	—	8.15	12.50	—	5.15	—	9.25	11.50
453	Dunkeld arr.	4.45	7.42	—	8.50	1.26	—	6.5	—	10.7	12.36
466	Pitlochry ,,	4.35	8.5	—	9.22	1.52	—	6.37	—	10.20	1.10
473	Blair Atholl ,,	4.52	8.20	—	9.40	2.8	—	6.10	—	10.54	1.25
509	Kingussie ,,	6.5	p.m.	—	p.m.	3.29	—	7.22	—	12.2	1.50
521	Aviemore Junc. ,,	6.40	—	—	—	3.52	—	7.48	—	12.35	2.15
534	Grantown ,,	7.25	—	—	—	4.25	—	8.55	—	1.9	2.45
556	Inverness ... ,,	7.42	—	—	—	5.10	—	9.8	—	1.50	4.20
—	Kyle of Lochalsh ,,	p.m.	—	—	—	11.42 noon	—	1.40 p.m.	—	6.30 p.m.	9.30 p.m.

A. Luncheon Cars, Newcastle to Edinburgh.
C. E. F. Dining-Cars to Edinburgh.
D. Luncheon and Dining-Cars to Aberdeen.
E. Via Harrogate.
G. Sundays also, but not Sats.
H. Sundays also.
I. Sundays also. (Sun. arr. Aberdeen, 11.25 a.m.; Inverness, 1.50 p.m.).
K. Sundays also.
Sleeping Cars by all night trains.
Highlands I.—Yellow Inset.

"MIDLAND ROUTE," MID., G.&S.W., N.B. v
(via Forth Bridge). WEEK-DAYS.

M.		A a.m.	B a.m.	C a.m.	D a.m.	E a.m.	F p.m.	G p.m.	H p.m.	I ngt.
—	London (St. Pancras) dep.	5.0	9.30	9.45	11.50	11.50	1.30	7.10	9.30	12.0
99	Leicester ,,	7.10	11.25	11.40	1.30	1.20	3.20	8.56	10.40	1.58
126	Nottingham ,,	7.25	10.48	10.48	1.0	12.55	2.43	8.25	12.0	2.0
—	Plymouth (MillBay) p.m.	8.20	—	—	7.0	—	8.30	1.48	3.50	—
53	Exeter ,,	10.8	—	—	7.0	7.0	10.15	3.12	5.28	—
128	Bristol a.m.	1.3	8.10	—	10.55	10.45	12.20	6.8	7.55	—
—	Bath dep.	11.0	8.0	—	10.33	10.32	11.55	4.35	7.35	—
165	Gloucester ,,	2.13	9.3	9.3	11.27	11.35	12.50	7.0	8.58	9.17
220	Birmingham ,,	4.8	10.23	10.24	12.53	12.50	2.23	8.15	10.23	11.25
262	Derby ,,	6.50	11.25	11.25	1.48	1.48	3.28	9.5	11.30	12.53
158	Sheffield ,,	8.57	12.12	12.12	2.0	1.57	4.48	10.20	12.33	1.58
196	Leeds ,,	10.0	1.33	1.45	3.28	3.28	5.33	11.12	1.50	4.8
—	Bradford ,,	9.42	12.53	12.53	2.52	2.52	5.5	10.5	1.15	2.5
219	Skipton ,,	10.38	1.13	1.13	3.35	3.34	5.43	—	1.51	—
—	Liverpool (Exch.) ,,	9.25	12.35	12.35	2.20	2.20	4.35	—	12.45	—
—	Manchester (Vic.) ,,	9.32	12.30	12.30	2.25	2.25	4.35	—	12.50	—
229	Hellifield ,,	11.5	2.24	2.35	4.21	4.40	6.27	—	2.40	—
308	Carlisle arr.	12.40	3.50	4.5	5.50	5.57	7.55	1.25	4.15	6.25
	Carlisle dep.	12.28	—	4.10	6.3	—	8.0	3.10	4.35	6.30
341	Dumfries ,,	1.8	—	4.50	6.44	—	8.38	3.50	5.14	7.10
423	Glasgow (St. Enoch) ,,	3.0	—	6.40	8.35	—	10.20	6.10	7.5	9.0
438	Greenock (Pr. Pier) arr.	4.28	—	7.58	9.53	—	12.5	7.43	8.38	10.26
454	Rothesay (steamer) ,,	5.50	—	9.25	—	—	—	—	10.0	11.55
528	Oban (steamer) ,,	—	—	—	—	—	—	4.50	—	—
	Carlisle dep.	12.45	3.55	p.m.	—	6.5	8.2	1.30	4.20	9.0
369	Melrose arr.	2.55	—	—	—	7.41	S.D.	—	6.34	11.4
406	Edinb'gh (Waverley) ,,	3.0	6.10	—	—	8.42	10.25	3.45	6.50	12.6
—	Edinburgh dep.	—	—	—	—	—	—	4.30	7.40	—
575	Fort William arr.	—	—	—	—	—	—	9.42	2.12	—
577	Banavie ,,	—	—	—	—	—	—	9.56	5.16	—
617	Mallaig ,,	—	—	—	—	—	—	11.30	*3.54	—
—	Edinburgh dep.	4.5	6.38	—	—	9.5	—	6.15	—	—
442	Stirling arr.	5.21	8.1	—	—	10.33	—	8.1	—	—
458	Callander ,,	6.7	—	—	—	12.35	—	8.46	—	—
529	Oban ,,	9.0	—	—	—	4.15	—	11.45	—	—
—	Edinburgh dep.	4.25	6.33	—	—	9.20	—	4.10	7.40	1.50
468	Dundee arr.	6.23	8.6	—	—	11.7	—	5.30	9.22	3.53
539	Aberdeen ,,	8.50	10.5	—	—	—	—	7.22	11.30	6.10
—	Edinburgh dep.	4.30	6.38	—	—	9.5	—	3.55	7.30	2.15
449	Perth { arr.	6.26	7.51	—	—	10.36	—	5.5	8.55	3.32
	{ dep.	7.15	8.15	—	—	12.50	—	5.15	9.25	3.50
464	Dunkeld arr.	7.42	8.50	—	—	1.26	—	6.5	10.7	4.45
477	Pitlochry ,,	8.5	9.22	—	—	1.52	—	6.38	10.20	4.35
484	Blair Atholl ,,	8.20	9.40	—	—	2.8	—	6.10	10.54	4.52
520	Kingussie ,,	p.m.	p.m.	—	—	3.29	—	7.22	12.2	6.15
532	Aviemore ,,	—	—	—	—	3.52	—	7.48	12.35	6.40
545	Grantown ,,	—	—	—	—	4.25	—	9.5	1.9	7.25
567	Inverness ,,	—	—	—	—	5.10	—	9.8	1.50	7.42
649	Kyle of Lochalsh ... ,,	—	—	—	—	11.42 noon	—	1.15 p.m.	6.30 p.m.	— p.m.

S.D.—Stops to set down from S. of Carlisle.

Extra:—St. Pancras, dep. 8.30 p.m.; Leeds, dep. 12.28; Carlisle, arr. 2.45; dep. 3.10; Glasgow, arr. 6.10 a.m. **Luncheon** and **Dining Cars** by day trains.
Sleeping Cars by night trains. For Sunday service north of Perth see opposite page. A, Passengers from Liverpool and Manchester arr. Carlisle, 12.40; dep. 12.45; arr. Dumfries, 1.29, Glasgow (St. Enoch), 3.20, and Greenock, 4.45 p.m. H, Begins on July 12. * Tu., Th., Sat.; other days, Mallaig arr., 6.50.
Highlands I.—Yellow Inset.

Some of the wide-ranging choices for Anglo-Scottish travel are shown by timetables for East Coast and Midland routes as inserted into a guidebook of 1912. More choices still were available in the West Coast timetable on another page of the guide book. (Author's collection)

FROM EUSTON (WEST COAST)

9.55 a.m.	Edinburgh
10.00 a.m.	Glasgow
10.05 a.m.	Perth, Dundee and Aberdeen
2.00 p.m.	Glasgow, Edinburgh, Aberdeen
7.45 p.m.	Perth and Inverness
8.00 p.m.	Aberdeen, Oban
8.10 p.m.	Stranraer (for North of Ireland)
8.50 p.m.	Glasgow, Gourock (for Clyde steamers), Edinburgh, Perth
11.35 p.m.	Edinburgh, Dundee
11.50 p.m.	Glasgow, Aberdeen

FROM ST PANCRAS (MIDLAND)

9.30 a.m.	Edinburgh, Perth, Aberdeen
9.45 a.m.	Glasgow
11.30 a.m.	Edinburgh (combined at Carlisle with Edinburgh coaches of 11.50 a.m.)
11.50 a.m.	Glasgow, Edinburgh (no public stops between St Pancras and Carlisle)
1.30 p.m.	Edinburgh, Glasgow
7.10 p.m.	Perth and Inverness, Aberdeen, Fort William
8.10 p.m.	Stranraer (for North of Ireland)
9.30 p.m.	Edinburgh, Glasgow
Midnight	Glasgow

FROM KING'S CROSS (EAST COAST)

5.05 a.m.	Leeds, with through coach to Edinburgh
9.50 a.m.	Edinburgh
10.00 a.m.	Edinburgh, Glasgow, Perth, Aberdeen
10.35 a.m.	Edinburgh semi-fast (17 stops en route), Glasgow
11.20 a.m.	(via Harrogate) Edinburgh, Perth, Dundee
2.20 p.m.	Edinburgh
7.55 p.m.	Inverness, Fort William
8.15 p.m.	Aberdeen
8.45 p.m.	Glasgow
11.30 p.m.	Edinburgh, Glasgow, Perth, Dundee
11.45 p.m.	Edinburgh

Clearly there was an element of duplication, indeed triplication. Yet with traffic enough for three routes, the public got the benefit of competition to keep fares down and facilities up.

Re-marshalling through coaches en route was a complex business. Fifty years on, a writer in *The Railway Magazine* recalled the scene at Edinburgh Waverley about 6.15 p.m. on a summer evening. The 9.50 a.m. from King's Cross was still standing at the front of the main down platform when the 10.00 a.m. 'Flying Scotsman' pulled in behind it. The 9.30 a.m. from St Pancras arrived in an adjoining bay. Then two pilot engines 'like well-trained sheepdogs … working in perfect harmony' went to work to collect the Aberdeen and Perth coaches from both the 'Flying Scotsman' and the Midland train, and distribute them between the 6.33 p.m. for Aberdeen and the 6.40 p.m. for Perth. These were standing in bay platforms at the west end of the station, so presumably a pilot engine at the east end of the station detached the through coaches and shunted them into one of the through roads, for a west-end pilot to collect in turn and attach to the appropriate departing trains: the sheepdog simile does indeed seem apt. And while all that was going on, the engine for the 6.30 p.m. train to Glasgow was collecting the Glasgow coaches off the 'Flying Scotsman' and attaching them to its own train.[76] The show was over within twenty-five minutes: no leader-writer for *The Times* could have found anything to criticise.

Internal Scottish train services continued to improve in both speed and scope. By the turn of the century the Caledonian Railway was already running trains at schedules which demanded a speed of 60 mph start-to-stop, the first such trains in Great Britain. The stretch of line concerned was the main line through Strathmore between Forfar and Perth, where the up 'West Coast Postal' was scheduled to cover the thirteen-two and a half miles in thirteen-two minutes.[77]

Fast running was usual on other parts of the Caledonian route to Aberdeen. By Stonehaven the line runs along the cliff top; one privileged passenger, riding on the footplate of a locomotive allowed to take a notoriously tight curve at full speed, was caught off balance and slid across the cab floor. Coated with coal dust he commented: 'Thought we were going over the cliffs, that time!' 'Och, ye get used tae it' came the driver's laconic reply. The passenger was a nineteen-year-old Englishman employed at the Caledonian Railway's office in Manchester. After several years' service he was sent north in 1901 with a free pass to spend a week familiarising himself with the lines of the company whose services he marketed. He lodged at Larbert, and every morning as he set out on his

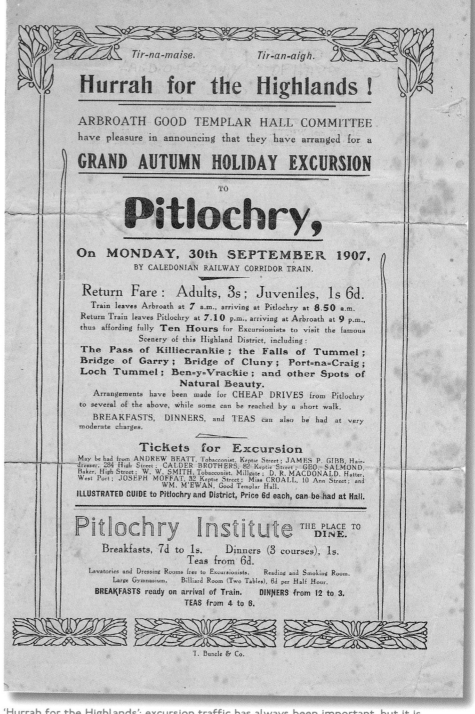

'Hurrah for the Highlands': excursion traffic has always been important, but it is noteworthy that the Caledonian had sufficient corridor carriages to spare for such an excursion as early as 1907. (R. Forsythe Collection)

Cover of North British timetable illustrated the principal places served – Edinburgh, Glasgow, Aberdeen and, for tourists, the Trossachs and Loch Katrine (which were in fact reached by connecting coach) but gave pride of place to the Forth Bridge.
(R. Forsythe Collection)

travels the stationmaster provided the important visitor with a buttonhole identical to the one that he himself was wearing.[78]

Through services were widespread: Edinburgh to Elgin, Edinburgh to Ayr, Glasgow to Moffat, to give but three examples. Even the severe winters of those days, despite the havoc they caused to train services, were not devoid of advantage. At Carsebreck, west of Blackford on the CR main line between Perth and Stirling, a curling pond was made beside the line; Aboyne Loch, beside the GNS Deeside line, was also popular with curlers. Platforms were built at both locations, and when the ice was bearing and an important curling match loomed, they became busy temporary stations. Trains stopped at Carsebreck on occasion between 1853 and 1935. Indeed, one of many incidental effects of the increasing ease of travel by rail was to change curling from a local game to a national sport.[79]

In summer a vast range of tours by interconnecting trains, steamers and coaches was offered to the visitor. The most famous was the Trossachs Tour: train from Glasgow to Balloch, Loch Lomond steamer to Inversnaid, coach to Stronachlachar, Loch Katrine steamer to Trossachs Pier, coach to Callander or Aberfoyle, train to Glasgow. The tour could equally be made in the opposite direction, or as a round tour from Edinburgh, or adapted to travel from Glasgow to Edinburgh or vice versa, or incorporated into tours further afield. One ticket with detachable coupons covered an entire tour.[80]

Much effort went into publicity. As early as 1881 W. Ferguson of Kinmundy, antiquary and chairman of the Great North of Scotland Railway, published a station-by-station guide to the line which related every imaginable piece of local history and folklore

Callander & Oban line train climbs away from Oban. Locomotive no. 54, built in 1905, was one of McIntosh's 55 class 4-6-0s designed specifically for this route.

(Michael Wrottesley collection)

connected with the district.[81] The North British in 1894 produced an entire illustrated book to publicise the brand new West Highland Railway: *Mountain, Moor and Loch*.[82] Later came a slimmer volume, also illustrated, *The Epistles of Peggy* ('Price 3d. Written from Scotland'). In this the eponymous young heroine describes, in letters to her nearest and dearest, her travels about scenic and historic Scotland in company with 'the Pater'. Always, of course, they travel by the North British, and somehow some very complimentary references to the company and its services are contrived to appear in each epistle. There were many comparable publications. The Caledonian Railway, equally conscious of the publicity value of young ladies, and also of the numerous golf courses

about its system, became famous for successive posters of 'The Golfing Girl'. On a different tack the Caledonian produced, through the agency of Bassett-Lowke & Co., some very fine, for the period, gauge O promotional models of its express locomotive *Cardean* and a West Coast Joint Stock coach, both representative of 'The Corridor'.[83]

The publicity value of the liveries – nothing so mundane as 'colour schemes' – for locomotives and coaches was well understood. Each company had its own, which rendered its passenger trains instantly recognisable. The most striking liveries were those of the Caledonian Railway – blue locomotives hauling carriages which were brownish lake below and white above. Other Scottish railways had green

locomotives, of distinctive shades. Glasgow & South Western locomotives were mid-green, carriages crimson lake. The North British had dark brownish-green locomotives, dark red coaches; North Eastern Railway locomotives working into Waverley were bright green. Further north, on the Great North of Scotland Railway bright green locomotives hauled trains of coaches which were dark red below, white above. On the Highland, locomotives and coaches were both olive green. On the three Anglo-Scottish routes, jointly owned coaches tended to follow the liveries of the southern companies: West Coast Joint Stock was chocolate below and white above, like the London & North Western; East Coast Joint Stock brown or varnished teak; Midland & North British, and Midland & GSW Joint Stock crimson lake.[84] All these colours were deep and lustrous: locomotives were clean. When the Glasgow & South Western Railway ran a rare Royal Train, in 1888, the locomotive was cleaned for a week beforehand.

Caledonian trains were distinctive also in another feature, the note of their locomotive whistles: a deep hoot based on the ships' sirens familiar to Clydeside residents.[85] No northbound sleeping-car passenger, however somnolent, could fail to note the passage of Carlisle, where the shrieking whistles of the North Western engines gave way to the foghorn of the Caledonian. What we would nowadays call a company house style extended even to distinctive patterns of signals and signalling equipment.

By the twentieth century railway companies were mature organisations using advanced techniques. Graphic design of the cover of *The Epistles of Peggy* ensures that it still catches the eye, and the message that you are to travel North British, though not over-emphasised, is unmistakable. (David Stirling collection)

Throughout Scotland, local trains served local communities. Here the 'wee train' for Lochearnhead, Comrie and Crieff prepares to leave Balquhidder. Yet even when the line was opened, the district was already popular with motorists.

(National Railway Museum)

Parcels and freight traffic were less in the public eye than passenger, yet worked with comparable efficiency, particularly where perishables and livestock were concerned. Acworth, writing of the late 1880s, noted an Aberdeen superintendent's concern to get a delayed fish special away ahead of the London express. He also noted the 1,016 head of cattle dispatched to London by the North British alone at Christmas time, and the salmon caught and the grouse shot on Monday in the furthest corner of Ross-shire which were delivered punctually on Wednesday morning to Leadenhall or Billingsgate market.[86] By the twentieth

century, Caledonian express parcels traffic was such that more than fifty horsedrawn delivery lorries might set out from Glasgow Central before 9.00 a.m.[87] On the Glasgow & South Western around 1910 fast freight trains, hauled by passenger locomotives, called only at New Cumnock, for water, between Glasgow and Carlisle.[88]

Railways in those days were among the most prosperous and progressive commercial organisations in the land, and could call on the services of remarkable men to run them. To give but three examples: Guy Calthrop was appointed general superintendent of the

Competition is emerging. An Argyll car, made in Alexandria, is posed alongside one of the Caledonian Railway's latest 4-6-0s, probably at Balloch.
(National Railway Museum)

Caledonian Railway in 1902 at no more than thirty-two years of age; William Whitelaw was the same age when he became chairman of the Highland Railway Company in 1901, and so successful was he that he was asked in 1912 to chair the North British, while continuing as deputy chairman of the Highland; William Jackson, general manager of the North British from 1899 to 1918, covered its entire system, nearly 1,300 miles, on foot.

The railway system flourished, yet there were straws in the wind suggestive of gales to come. The veneer of prosperity concealed declining profitability.

Throughout Britain, the railways' operating ratio – that is to say, operating costs stated as a percentage of revenue – had been at 51 per cent during 1870–4. By 1895–9 it was up to 57 per cent, and by 1900–4 up again to 62 per cent, and it remained at this level until 1914.[89] In Scotland, provision of railways and train services had been over-lavish. It was probably as early as the 1870s that Alexander Geikie, noted geologist, made his way to Dolphinton station, terminus of a North British branch, after a day in the Pentland Hills. He found the train waiting but the station 'solitary as a churchyard'. Having taken his seat, he heard the driver call to the guard: 'Weel, Jock, hae ye got your passenger in?' Yet Dolphinton, with a population of less than 300, had not one station but two, for the Caledonian also ran a branch thither from Carstairs, with its terminus across the road from the North British.[90]

The Invergarry & Fort Augustus Railway had its losses made good from the pockets of wealthy local proprietors, until 1911 when that source of funds dried up. The line closed. It took three years of delicate negotiations and a grant from Inverness-shire county council before the North British could be persuaded to reopen it and buy out the local company.[91] Even on the Waverley Route, during the 1900s operation of some of those impressive Anglo-Scottish expresses was being subsidised by the Midland Railway.[92]

About the turn of the century expansion of electric tramways on city streets was found to draw traffic away from inner suburban stations; stations were closed and train services withdrawn. This sudden outbreak of competition seems to have taken the railway companies by surprise, and some new lines which were being built were used eventually only for freight. On Caledonian lines built at this time in the vicinities of Paisley and Barrhead, passenger stations were completed at Ferguslie, Stanely, Glenfield, Barrhead New, Dykebar and Paisley East: but none of these was ever opened to regular passenger traffic.[93]

The first motor car to reach Scotland arrived at Leith Docks in 1895, and when in 1896 an Act of Parliament permitted such vehicles to travel faster than walking pace – and without being preceded by a man carrying a red flag – the way was open for far more. The Highlands in particular seem to have acted as an irresistible challenge to early motorists.[94] As early as 1902 William Whitelaw informed Highland Railway

shareholders that the previous year had seen first-class local journeys reduced by 1,000, and attributed this to 'the extraordinary development of motor cars'.[95] When, in 1904, the local newspaper reported opening of the Caledonian line from St Fillans to Lochearnhead, the same news item remarked on the new-found popularity of the district with 'automobilists'.[96]

There was as yet no sense that railways faced serious problems: the industry still rode the crest of the wave. This is well shown by the arrival of Pullman dining cars on the Caledonian Railway. By the early twentieth century most of the early Pullman sleeping car services had been bought out by the railways over which they operated: in Scotland the only Pullman sleeping-cars remaining were the two that worked over the Highland Railway. Then in 1907 Davison Dalziel, financier, bought the British Pullman Palace Car Company from the trustees of G.M. Pullman and energetically set about expanding its activities. The emphasis now was on luxury daytime travel, with meals and refreshments; Dalziel's early successes were with railways in the South of England, but in 1913 he achieved an agreement with the Caledonian Railway to provide all its dining cars, except those in through trains to and from England, for a twenty-year period commencing the following summer.

That spring ten new Pullman cars were built to run on the Caledonian. Nine of these were described variously as dining cars or buffet cars – authorities differ – but all had opulent interiors. There were inlaid and veneered panelling, velvet carpets, silk curtains and dining chairs upholstered in morocco leather, with each car decorated in its own individual style. Cars were named after heroines of Scottish history or folklore – *Flora MacDonald*, *Helen MacGregor* are good examples – although there was at least one curious choice upon which I have commented elsewhere.[97] All included kitchens; dining cars had first- and third-class accommodation, ran on long runs, and were accessible without supplement to those passengers who wanted a meal, but had seats elsewhere in the train: the first cars ran between Glasgow and Aberdeen. Buffet cars were first-class only, and employed on shorter runs where passengers occupied their seats throughout. The first cars went into service between Glasgow Central and Edinburgh Princes Street; Glasgow Central to Gourock soon followed. In later years the workings and function of the cars probably altered, and they became known generically as Pullman dining cars.

The tenth car was unique, the Pullman observation car *Maid of Morven*. One end was entirely glazed for passengers to admire the view; large windows occupied much of the sides. Within, movable armchairs enhanced the usual opulent decorations. A kitchen enabled meals to be served. The *Maid of Morven* was first-class only, one of the most luxurious coaches running in public trains anywhere in Britain. She was built to run at the end of trains between Glasgow Buchanan Street and Oban, and she started to do so on 3 August 1914.[98] On 4 August the First World War broke out.

A sad feature of the First World War was operation of immensely long ambulance trains to carry wounded servicemen from Channel ports to hospitals, many of which were located in Scotland. (National Railway Museum)

THE FIRST WORLD WAR AND THE GROUPING

The First World War and its demands were to transform the economy of Britain from one in which free-market competition was paramount to one that was closely regulated by the government. At its start the government commandeered the railway system. For over forty years the state had had powers to control the railways in time of war: they were put into effect on 4 August 1914. The companies placed their railways at the disposal of the government for wartime transport of men and materials free of charge; in return they were guaranteed an income, initially their net income for 1913. Railway charges and wages were to be settled by the government. Day-to-day management of the railway system was vested in the Railway Executive Committee, composed of railway general managers.[1]

A rapid rise in food prices led to a demand for a guaranteed level of wages for railwaymen and in turn, early in 1915, to negotiations between management and unions which led for the first time to agreed national rates of pay, that is, on an all-Britain basis.[2]

It was in the operation of goods wagons that there lay one of the most evident instances of scope for improving efficiency and economy. Although loaded wagons of any particular company might, and regularly did, leave that company's tracks to travel far and wide, once unloaded they had to be returned empty to the owning company. Introduction of 'common user'

arrangements, by which an empty wagon could simply be reloaded and dispatched elsewhere irrespective of ownership, would clearly greatly reduce empty wagon movements with their associated expense and track occupation. Such arrangements were introduced by stages from late in 1915; the first instance in Scotland came in June 1916 when the Caledonian, North British and Glasgow & South Western Railways agreed to use their wagons, with certain exceptions, in common. From 2 January 1917 most open wagons were in common use throughout Britain, and so advantageous did this prove that the process of establishing such arrangements became a continuing one long after the war's end.[3] Other economies, such as the general withdrawal of restaurant cars in 1916, were less constructive and, fortunately, less long-lasting.

At a detailed level, the coming of war brought innumerable changes. There was an immediate increase in traffic. During August 1914 alone the Caledonian Railway dealt with 342 naval and military trains.[4] On Sunday 16 August, no fewer than seventy special troop trains passed through Waverley station, Edinburgh.[5] Greatly increased traffic became a continuing feature of the war, including increased civilian traffic despite attempts to discourage it.

This increase in traffic, superimposed upon regrettably slack working, was to bring about a

With men away at the war, women filled many of their jobs at home. Here Highland Railway 4-4-0 no. 73 *Snaigow*, which was built in 1917 for the busy Far North line, is being cleaned by female engine cleaners at Inverness.
(National Archives of Scotland, BR/HR/5/10 – Science and Society Picture Library)

notorious disaster. In the early morning of 22 May 1915 the down overnight Scotch Express from Euston was running late, and a northbound local was allowed to leave Carlisle ahead of it with the intention that it should be shunted at Quintinshill, a couple of miles north of Gretna Junction, for the express to overtake. At Quintinshill were loops, and a signal box, but no station; the signalman on night duty was due to finish at 6.00 a.m., but when the local was due to stop his relief travelled out on it unofficially, so the night man was still working the box when it arrived. Because the down loop was already occupied by a freight train, he put the down local on to the up main line to stand there. This was acceptable provided that he sent a 'blocking back' telegraph message to the next box to the north, Kirkpatrick, to indicate that the up line was blocked, and placed collars on the levers of the signals controlling it so that they could not be cleared. He did neither. Shortly afterwards an up empty-wagon train arrived to be put into the up loop.

At that moment the daytime signalman then arrived in the box and took over. To indicate falsely that he had been present since 6.00 a.m., he started to copy out details of all these movements into the train register in his own handwriting, from the scrap of paper upon which the night man had recorded them. The night man remained in the box, studying the newly arrived newspapers and chatting to the brakesmen of the goods trains who were also there; the fireman of the local train came, properly, to remind the signalman of its presence, but failed to check whether lever collars were in position before he returned to it. The signalman cleared his signals for the down express. But with all these distractions, official and unofficial, he evidently forgot the presence of the local standing on the up line.

Kirkpatrick then offered an up special troop train. This was en route from Larbert to Liverpool, with the

Seventh Battalion the Royal Scots who were bound for Gallipoli. The signalman accepted it, offered it to Gretna Junction which in turn accepted, and cleared the signals for the up main line. Shortly afterwards the heavy troop train, composed of elderly gas-lit wooden coaches but travelling fast on a down gradient, came into head-on collision with great violence with the local. Shortly after that the down express, double-headed and composed of heavy bogie stock and sleeping cars – and despite the efforts of the guard of the local and the enginemen of the up empty-wagon train to stop it – was still travelling at speed when it ploughed into the wreckage, running down many survivors from the first accident. And then gas escaping from the shattered remains of the coaches of the troop train was ignited by the engine fires. The fire spread with appalling speed. Despite every attempt to extinguish it, it blazed for more than twenty-four hours; nineteen coaches, five goods wagons and all the supplies of coal in the engine tenders were destroyed. Of the civilians involved, twelve were killed and fifty-four injured; far worse affected were the Seventh Battalion the Royal Scots, who lost some 215 officers and men killed and 191 seriously injured.[6] In terms of casualties, Quintinshill remains the worst accident in the history of British railways.

Perhaps it acted as a 'wake-up call', for in general the safety record of railways during the First World War was good, despite loss of many skilled staff to the forces and replacement by men, and women, who were inexperienced at railway work.[7] Hours on duty became longer than ever. D. L. Smith recounts the tale of a pair of Glasgow & South Western enginemen who set out northwards from Carlisle in April 1916 with a trainload of South Wales coal destined for the Navy on the Clyde. With the effects of a Zeppelin

raid, and a breakaway, and numerous changes of plans and instructions, they found, when they got home to Carlisle, that they had been on duty for twenty-four hours.[8] A further addition to traffic, as the war continued, was provision of ambulance trains for wounded servicemen. R. D. Stephen recalled a June evening in 1916 spent watching the ambulance trains coming up the branch from Rosyth Dockyard to Inverkeithing. The Battle of Jutland had taken place a couple of days before. At Pitlochry, the station platforms were extended to accommodate long ambulance trains of wounded, who were en route for the hospitals into which the holiday hotels of the district had been converted.[9]

Direct involvement in warfare was rare, although two armoured trains were provided to defend the coasts of Berwickshire and Kincardineshire.[10] The railways of Britain however provided between them large quantities of locomotives and wagons for use in France and other allied countries in support of the armed forces.[11] Among the locomotives were twenty-five North British 0-6-0s which on their eventual return from Flanders were given appropriate names, of battles, generals and so on. It is one of these, *Maude*, named after the general of that name, which survives in the collection of the Scottish Railway Preservation Society. Nor were such things restricted to actual railway equipment: the entire Clyde passenger steamer fleets (see Chapter 7) of both Caledonian and Glasgow & South Western Railways were requisitioned, for use as minesweepers and troopships. To maintain services – so far as they could in the presence of a boom across the Clyde from Dunoon to the Cloch – the railway companies were obliged to charter ships from MacBrayne and other owners.[12]

'For the first six months of the war' wrote a Naval

lieutenant 'we in *Dreadnought* never saw a tree, a train or a woman.' The Grand Fleet – 96 ships and 70,000 men – had arrived at its new base in Scapa Flow.[13] A large repair base was also established at Invergordon. For the Highland Railway, the effect was as though a new city had materialised at its northernmost terminus. Although steam coal for the fleet came from South Wales by train to Grangemouth whence it was shipped north, and in due course many supplies were shipped from Aberdeen, men and mails and much else came and went by train via Thurso.

Naval personnel when going on leave, or returning, needed to make the long journey to and from the South in large numbers. The atmosphere of such travel can be gauged from the opening chapters of *The Long Trick*, a novel by 'Bartimeus' published in 1917. As he describes it, in the murky darkness of a foggy February evening at King's Cross, naval personnel of all ranks bid emotional farewells to their loved ones, half cheerful, half tearful, before boarding the 'Highland Express'. A Lieutenant–Commander and his young wife inspect his sleeping compartment with its 'shaded light, neat bunk and dark upholstery': the attendant, observing that the lady will not be travelling, tactfully closes the door on them while they make their farewells, with a promise to let them know when the train is due to start. If there are any civilians on the train, they are not mentioned.

Once on the move, the journey provides an opportunity for old friends and acquaintances, finding themselves travelling together, to catch up with one another: the talk alternates between young mens' banter, solemnity and shop. In the morning, when the express draws up at a station surrounded by snow-covered moorland, sailors stream forth in search of breakfast, and officers gather up breakfast baskets to take back to their compartments. More banter when, with the train about to start, the basket-girl complains shrilly that one of the gentlemen has not paid her: one of them hands half-a-crown out of the window, making out that he is really doing this on behalf of his friend inside who cannot apologise for himself because his mouth is full of bacon – only to be pulled suddenly backwards from the window as the train sets off. The girl, of course, has guessed which of them had really forgotten to pay.

The station was presumably Kingussie: once in the North, place-names are no longer given in this wartime publication. There can be no doubt that the 'junction' at which the express stops at noon was Inverness. Naval presence is already everywhere, and the travellers of all ranks, bound for fifty different ships, are mustered and fed, and then embarked on the train at the next platform, the 'Naval Special', which will carry them the rest of their journey. Compartment stock now, and as the train travels slowly northwards past deer forest and grouse moor of peacetime memory, there is time and scope for further animated discussion of naval experiences, so that the travellers, when they arrive at their destination, have scarcely noticed that night has already again fallen. From their long journey they emerge into the lamplit gloom of the platform, a flurry of snow and the tramp of sailors' boots through the slush.[14]

'Bartimeus' was Sir Lewis Anselm da Costa Ritchie, a naval officer who served on the staff of Admiral Sir John Jellicoe, commander-in-chief of the Grand Fleet until 1916.[15] So he was undoubtedly writing from personal experience.

From early in 1917 naval special trains started to run regularly between Thurso and London and vice versa. In addition to this extra passenger traffic over the

Highland Railway, timber traffic – timber baulks for defences going north, pit-props going south – reached ten times its peacetime level, and much civilian coal traffic, normally carried by sea, was diverted to rail. All this on a railway where goods traffic was normally light, and passenger traffic only heavy for a short period in summer, which meant that locomotives could be overhauled in winter. The Great North of Scotland helped by taking goods traffic via Aberdeen.

Inevitably the Highland Railway soon found itself short of locomotives, a shortage exacerbated when the first of a new class of powerful 4-6-0 locomotives, the River class intended to work the heaviest trains between Perth and Inverness, was discovered, on delivery in 1915, to be too heavy for track and structures, as described further in Chapter 9. The entire class of six locomotives was sold to the Caledonian.[16] The locomotive shortage on the Highland was alleviated when the Railway Executive Committee arranged for locomotives to be loaned by other railways, the North Eastern, the Caledonian and the London & North Western among them. Some forty-three borrowed locomotives worked on the HR between 1915 and 1919, and some of them stayed longer.[17] In 1918 work started on the Northern Barrage, a minefield to stretch from the North of Scotland to Norway: mine components made in the USA were landed at Kyle of Lochalsh and carried to the east coast in trains of wagons loaned by the South Eastern & Chatham Railway, hauled by locomotives loaned by the London & South Western. The Kyle line west of Dingwall was taken over by the Admiralty, and the HR allowed to run one train a day only, for passengers and mails.[18]

In 1918, at the end of the First World War, railways were physically in a bad state. While the level of traffic had been much higher than usual, the level of maintenance had been much lower: skilled men were away in the armed services; railway works were adapted to produce the needs of war. By the war's end British railways had 20 per cent of their locomotives, 5 per cent of their wagons and 10 per cent of their carriages awaiting repair.[19] There were comparable arrears of maintenance on the track. Although the Highland Railway was in a particularly bad way, the North British was not much better. Among much other additional traffic, the Naval specials from the South had been routed over the North British between Carlisle and Perth, so that they might en route serve Inverkeithing for Rosyth.

During the war arrangements had been made for the government to compensate the railway companies for increased wages, and for deferred maintenance and renewal of equipment. Government control of railways continued after the war, pending some final reorganisation. In 1919 the Ministry of Transport was formed with Sir Eric Geddes as minister. Formerly he had been deputy general manager of the North Eastern Railway, but was of Scottish descent.

Early in 1920 the North British claimed an instalment of compensation amounting to £616,194. The ministry decided that the claim required investigation, and provided only £186,194 pro tem. There then developed what Hamilton Ellis described as the biggest row there had ever been between railway company and government, as the NBR pursued its claim through the courts and the Treasury withheld further payments, while the other companies were concerned onlookers. It developed almost into a personal wrangle between Geddes and William Whitelaw, chairman of the NBR. By mid-1921 the NBR's claim, calculated in detail, had reached £10,681,243. The Treasury eventually paid £9,790,545. The NBR, in effect, had won.[20]

Meanwhile another battle had been taking place. The purchasing power of £1 in 1919 was less than half that of £1 in 1914. When the government, railway companies and trade unions attempted to standardise railwaymens' wages to incorporate wartime bonuses, the effect was that some grades were to have their wages cut. Only after a national strike that autumn did the government agree not to reduce wages.[21] Yet although this event demonstrated the power held by the railway trade unions, it also demonstrated new weaknesses in the railways themselves. The war had prompted great technical developments in the internal combustion engine and in the vehicles it powered, notably motor lorries and aircraft. Large numbers of war-surplus lorries were now on the roads, their owners only too happy to carry strike-bound goods that would otherwise have gone by rail. In the air, the General Post Office provided for the first time a temporary airmail service, to carry letters, with a hefty surcharge, between London, Glasgow and other centres. It was far from reliable, but it worked.[22]

Despite these portents for the future, it was not to the possibility of competition in the future that the government now addressed itself, but rather to redressing the inadequacies of the manner in which the railway system had been administered before the war. Certainly when the Rural Transport (Scotland) Committee, which had been appointed by the Secretary of State for Scotland, issued its report in 1919 it included many proposals for new and improved roads, as well as many new railways and steamer services. The former included an interesting proposal for equipping two roads in Aberdeenshire with concrete tracks for the wheels of motor vehicles, while its proposed railways, it considered, could be largely equipped from war surplus railway material then available in France. But

PUNCH, OR THE LONDON CHARIVARI.—OCTOBER 8, 1919.

THE DELIVERER.

LOCOMOTIVE (*stationary through strike*). "ONCE ABOARD THE LORRY AND THE GIRL IS MINE —NO MORE!"

the committee's work went largely without effect, for it had already been overtaken by the House of Commons Select Committee on Transport of 1918.

This considered it unquestionable that all other

As early as 1919, during the national rail strike of that autumn, *Punch* correctly foretold the eventual flight of freight from rail to road.

In the early 1920s, while railways awaited the reorganisation that became the grouping, little had changed on the ground. Here a double-headed Caledonian Railway express, probably Euston to Perth, is leaving Carlisle about 1921. The leading engine had been built the previous year.
(Michael Wrottesley collection)

forms of internal transport were subordinate and ancillary to the railway system. It noted the advantages derived from operation of the railways as a single national system during the war; it heard evidence from a member of the Railway Executive Committee that if management were unified and assets pooled, the public could be given better services at less cost to the railway system. In its report it came out in favour of single ownership and management – whether by a joint stock company or by the state. This view was widely shared. It was in the aftermath of the report that the Ministry of Transport was established.

The possibility of state ownership – nationalisation – had been considered at intervals down the years: in the 1840s, the 1860s and at the turn of the century. It was promoted by the Labour movement (it was railway trade union policy from 1894 onwards),[23] but it was also strongly supported by traders who foresaw benefits to themselves if railways functioned as public corporations rather than profit-making businesses.[24] By the end of the First World War it was even supported by Winston Churchill in a speech to Dundee Chamber of Commerce.[25] But the time for railway nationalisation was not yet.

Speaking in the House of Commons during one of the debates on the bill to establish the Ministry of Transport, Sir Eric Geddes said that it would be nothing short of criminal to continue the old system of competition between roads, railways and canals; he envisaged division of the country into non-competitive zones.[26] By May 1920 he was speaking in terms of transport being a 'regulated monopoly'.[27] By July his ministry was proposing that the railway companies should be grouped, or amalgamated, into seven much larger companies; six of these would be in England & Wales, and the seventh would incorporate the railway companies of Scotland. When the proposals appeared in the Railways Bill, published in the spring of 1921, the number of grouped companies had been reduced to six, but two of these were Scottish: a West Scottish Group comprising the Caledonian, Glasgow & South Western and Highland Railways together with lesser and local lines associated with them, and an East Scottish Group comprising the North British and Great North of Scotland Railways with lesser lines associated with the North British.

The bill contained other important provisions. One was that it provided for a settlement of outstanding compensation due to the companies for government control since 1914. Another was that railway wages, standardised throughout Britain, would be settled by a central board of railway officials and union representatives. But although rates and charges would be controlled by the government (through, eventually, a Railway Rates Tribunal), this would be done on a group basis, on the principle that each group would be enabled to earn a 'standard revenue' equivalent to the total net receipts of its constituent railways for 1913 (with certain adjustments such as an allowance for a return on subsequent capital expenditure). To the Scottish companies, these latter provisions appeared disastrous. Before the war their wages, costs and rates had all been lower than those of English railways.[28] Working costs of the five Scottish railways were said to

have increased, between 1913 and 1920, by 291 per cent; the equivalent figure for eight of the English railways was 227 per cent.[29] The proposals on rates would have the effect that prosperous companies (i.e., English) would charge lower rates than the less prosperous (i.e., Scottish) so that Clydeside traders for instance would lose business to Tyneside.[30] The proposals were opposed by Chambers of Commerce throughout Scotland.[31] The only solution appeared to be for the Scottish companies to be grouped longitudinally with the English companies with which they were already associated. This course of action had been advocated on their behalf by the Railway Companies Association (which had been representing the railway companies' interests since the mid-nineteenth century) as early as the autumn of 1920. Subsequently Scottish MPs of all parties conferred with representatives not only of the railways but also of the trading communities and the local authorities. When the bill was in committee, the Scottish position was put succinctly by Sir H. Mackinder, Unionist MP for Glasgow Camlachie. He said:

I am commissioned to state here to-night ... what we believe to be the Scottish view of the Bill. Roughly and simply put, Scotland does not like the Bill ... because it is doubly unjust. It is unjust where it puts Scotland apart and separates her interests from those of the remainder of the country, and it is unjust because, in regard to many matters, while thus separating Scotland, it maintains the central control. Before the War the Scottish railways were separate in every respect. They were separate in finance, in management, in rates, in wages, in hours and in conditions both of labour and of freight. During the War ... the Scottish railways were controlled by the Government, and were placed under the same control as the English railways;

First coach in the 7.35 a.m. Sunday train from Edinburgh to Aberdeen is the through coach from Penzance, a post-First World War development. The train, headed by North British Atlantic *Dunedin*, has made a special stop at Inverkeithing to allow the Earl of Elgin, a director of the company, to alight; the date is April 1922. (National Railway Museum)

and during that time the Government standardised the conditions of the railways to a considerable extent. That meant that the Scottish railways were compelled to standardise up to the standard of the richer neighbour, England. After the War, a Bill is introduced which, in the opinion of Scotland, gives us the worst of both worlds – the pre-War world and the War world. So far as finance is concerned, you separate the Scottish railways; but when it comes to fixing rates, when it comes to negotiation in regard to wages, you have central control and you establish a single rates tribunal, a single Wages Board …[32]

Another Scottish MP, Lt Col. A. Murray, Liberal MP for Kincardine & West Aberdeenshire, identified the nub of the problem thus:

Either the Scottish rates and fares will have to be raised above the level of English rates and fares, which will prejudice Scottish traders in competition with similar English traders, or if that does not happen, the attempt to increase rates in order to produce the standard revenue may not only not produce the standard revenue but actually decrease the revenue.

In either event the results to Scottish trade, Scottish railways and the Scottish community generally, must be very serious indeed, if not disastrous.[33]

Sir Eric Geddes demurred, contrasting the attitude of the Scottish railways in 1921 with that of 1908 when the North British general manager had spoken in favour of amalgamating the five Scottish railways into one.[34] (That was barbed: Col. Murray was a director of the North British.) Nevertheless, it was eventually agreed in committee (on 4 July 1921) that the West Scottish railways should be included in the same group as the London & North Western and Midland Railways, and (on 5 July) that the East Scottish railways should be included in the same group as the North Eastern and Great Northern Railways.[35] The Bill received the Royal Assent as the Railways Act, 1921, on 19 August.[36]

Its effect was that control of Scottish railways moved out of Scotland and into the hands of London-based companies. The circumstances have been considered here in some detail because so far from being something imposed on Scottish railways by a distant Whitehall – as one might have guessed in ignorance of the facts – the move was, remarkably, something which was in the circumstances demanded successfully by the Scottish railway companies, and by public opinion in Scotland, in the teeth of Whitehall opposition.

Whether they got it right is another matter. M. R. Bonavia, in his appendix 'The Scottish Experience' to *The Four Great Railways*, considers that, as things turned out, a single Scottish railway company would have been the better solution for Scotland.[37] But in 1921, no one knew what problems lay ahead over the next three decades.

On 15 August 1921, four days before the Railways Act received the Royal Assent, the government relinquished control of the railways and handed them back to the railway companies.[38] But under the Act, the companies allocated to each group were to agree terms for amalgamation before 1 January 1923; should any fail to agree, a tribunal would decide for them. The process was expected to be complete by 1 July 1923.[39]

While all this was going on the railways themselves were recovering from the war and indeed introducing improvements. Notable among these was introduction of through coaches between Aberdeen and Penzance, 794½ miles southbound via Bristol and 785 miles northbound via Westbury, in 21 hr 55 min. and 20 hr 40 min. respectively, and using the North British, North Eastern, Great Central and Great Western Railways. North British and Great Western coaches were used alternately. Northbound passengers could transfer to a sleeping car at York, where the through coach was attached to an overnight express from King's Cross.[40] R. D. Stephen recalled travelling from Nottingham to Edinburgh in it on an occasion when arrival at York was late and the connection missed: nevertheless the through coach was worked north as a special, with six horseboxes coupled to it.[41]

This, however, was but the most notable of many through services introduced or reintroduced at this period. At Edinburgh Waverley there were also to be seen not only coaches of the North British Railway, of the East Coast Joint Stock from King's Cross, and of the Midland & NB trains from St Pancras, but also Highland coaches from Inverness, Great North of Scotland from Elgin, Great Eastern from Harwich, and Great Central and Great Western from Southampton.[42] Through train services at a comparatively local level were the 'Lothian Coast Express' between Glasgow and Dunbar, North Berwick and Gullane, and the

'Fifeshire Coast Express' between Glasgow and Dundee via Anstruther, Crail and St Andrews.

Restaurant cars reappeared, as did the Pullman dining cars of the Caledonian. In 1922 one started to run on to the Highland as well, working between Glasgow and Aviemore in trains to and from Inverness. The Great North, having like the Highland no restaurant cars of its own, hired one from the North Eastern Railway in the same year to run in through trains between Aberdeen and Inverness.

There were other developments. Aberdeen Joint Station (Caledonian/Great North of Scotland, with running powers for the North British), construction of which had been suspended during the war, was eventually completed in 1920. Its total length of platform face was exceeded only by Waverley; steam heating apparatus was installed to warm the stationary coaches of trains awaiting their locomotives.[43]

There were negative aspects. The Highland Railway withdrew its Sunday trains in 1920, after the GPO suspended Sunday deliveries. The North British ceased to build new locomotives after passage of the Railways Act.[44] But in general, as the grouping approached, the railways of Scotland were recovering well. They still had friends in high places. There were eighty-two railway company directors in Parliament in 1922, thirty in the Commons and fifty-two in the Lords, and of these four and eleven respectively were directors of Scottish companies.[45] The Highland Railway alone numbered two dukes, two lords and a baronet among its fourteen directors. Although not so prosperous as formerly, all five companies were paying dividends.[46] And among their respective employees, there was a fine *esprit de corps*.

Railways in dock areas were often set into roadways and trains mingled with other traffic; in these circumstances locomotives were, for safety's sake, fitted with covers over wheels and motion. In Aberdeen the gasworks was reached by rail along cobbled quaysides and its locomotives were so fitted. Little changed down the years: locomotive no. 3 was built in 1926, but the photograph dates from as late as 1964. (Brian Dickson)

LESSER FRY, MIGHT-HAVE-BEENS, AND THE 'VAST MASS OF MISCELLANEOUS PROPERTY'

Before continuing the story of development of the main Scottish railway system, it is necessary to look at lesser developments which are nonetheless important. What, for instance, became of the waggonways of Chapter 1 while the main system was developing? Some of them, indeed, were rebuilt and incorporated into the main system. Others lingered on, little altered, until they died away as times and industries changed. Some of the waggonways that ran down to Ayr harbour, for instance, were closed during the 1860s as old coal pits closed, and GSWR branch lines were built into the district to serve new ones.[1]

Other waggonways, yet again, had their track upgraded by their owners, and locomotives introduced. They became privately owned industrial or mineral railways, carrying only their owners' goods. The pioneer Tranent–Cockenzie waggonway combined two elements. Although rebuilt with iron rails in 1815, it continued to use horses and gravity as motive power until the 1880s. Then its southern part was rebuilt as a standard gauge mineral railway worked by locomotives and linking the collieries with the North British main line, with which a junction was provided. The northern section of the waggonway was abandoned: Cockenzie harbour was small, and coastal shipping was replaced by rail as the means of onward transport for the coal.[2] The Fordell waggonway, which had been rebuilt with iron rails in the 1830s, was further rebuilt in 1867–9 using heavy rail (much of it was obtained from the North British Railway) but retaining the 4 ft 4 in. gauge. Locomotives were then introduced. In the 1890s the Fordell Railway, as it was evidently now called, was extended northwards to meet the North British Edinburgh–Dundee main line. Interchange sidings were of mixed gauge, which made for some interesting trackwork, and Fordell locomotives were fitted with two sets of buffers so that, when on mixed gauge track, they could shunt standard gauge wagons.[3]

At Brora, coal mining was intermittent, partly because of an alarming tendency of the coal to ignite spontaneously (caused, apparently, by a band of pyrites passing through the seams), and operation of waggonways was intermittent likewise. Mining was resumed under the third Duke of Sutherland in the 1870s and a long-disused waggonway from colliery to harbour reinstated as a 1 ft 8 in. gauge railway with a branch to the station of the Duke of Sutherland's Railway. Attempts to introduce locomotives on the narrow-gauge line were unsuccessful, however, and it continued to be operated by horses.[4]

In general during the second half of the nineteenth century, privately owned industrial railways worked by steam locomotives became increasingly common.

They became a normal part of the plant employed not only by collieries but also by ironworks (Dalmellington obtained its first locomotive as early as 1851[5]), gasworks, brickworks, quarries, paper mills, distilleries and many more. Often they provided a link between industry and nearby public railway; in some instances their locomotives were authorised to run for short distances over public railway tracks.

Some such lines were more adventurous than their public counterparts. Harbour and dock authorities often allowed trains to mingle with road traffic to a far greater extent than was usual, at least in Britain. Where industrial railways had no junction with the main network, there was no constraint as to track gauge. The Dalzell Steel Works at Motherwell used an internal railway – with three steam locomotives – with a gauge as broad as 10 ft 11 in. It operated between the 1880s and the 1920s.[6] Narrow gauges were more common. Skye Marble Ltd operated a four-mile-long locomotive-worked 3 ft gauge railway between Broadford and its quarry for a few years from 1910: one of few railways to have operated on a Hebridean island.

The British Aluminium Company's first works to produce aluminium from bauxite by use of hydroelectricity was established in the 1890s at Foyers beside Loch Ness, where the Caledonian Canal provided long-distance transport. Horsedrawn wagons initially provided internal transport between quay and works, but by 1915 production had increased sufficiently for a short 3 ft gauge railway to be built instead, and a steam locomotive was purchased to work it.[7] By then the company had already built a much larger works at Kinlochleven, completed in 1909 and here too a 3 ft gauge railway linked the quay, on Loch Leven, with the works almost a mile away.

This railway was double track and, appropriately in a scheme which incorporated what was then the largest hydroelectric installation in Britain, powered by electricity, which was supplied to the locomotives by overhead cables.[8] (The origins of successful electric traction for railways are described below.) Electrically operated railways, to the 2 ft 6 in. gauge, were also used extensively in the shale oil industry centred on Winchburgh, West Lothian.[9]

Some industrial railways were, and were intended to be, temporary – yet were soundly and substantially built. Noteworthy was the eight-and-a-half-mile standard gauge line built southwards from Broughton station on the Caledonian Symington-Peebles branch, and used for ten years or so from 1897 to carry materials for construction of Edinburgh Corporation's Talla reservoir.[10] During the latter part of the First World War many temporary railways were built to aid extraction of timber from the forests of the Highlands. One of these was standard gauge: a five-and-a-half-mile line running from Nethy Bridge down into Abernethy Forest. Most were 3 ft gauge; one ran east from Aviemore to the vicinity of Loch Morlich, and there were others near Carr Bridge, Dornoch and elsewhere.[11]

Some private railways carried passengers. One such was the Bangour Railway, in fact a curious hybrid between private and public railway. It served the asylum at Bangour, West Lothian, and was built at the expense of the Edinburgh District Lunacy Board. The decision to establish this asylum, on the latest 'village hospital' rather than institutional lines, was taken in the 1890s and it, and railway, were authorised by Act of Parliament in 1900. The railway was one and a half miles long, branching northwards from the line now known as the Bathgate branch, west

Horse trams were familiar in Edinburgh streets in 1889, when this engraving first appeared.
(Author's collection)

of Uphall. It was used to bring in materials for the asylum and, when this was complete, supplies and coal; it was also, after inspection by the Board of Trade's inspecting officer, opened for passenger traffic, in 1905. It was then operated by the North British Railway, in return for a handsome subsidy from the board, and the train service appeared in *Bradshaw*. There was an intermediate station at Dechmont, which dealt with public traffic, but the terminus was described as 'Bangour (Private)', and private it was, even to the extent that the flower baskets hanging from the station building were tended by the hospital gardener. The railway came into its own during the First World War, when the asylum's usual inmates were dispersed and it was designated a war hospital: it then cared for war wounded in immense quantity, who arrived at Bangour in long and all-too-frequent ambulance trains direct from Southampton Docks. After the war the pendulum swung to the opposite extreme: road transport had improved sufficiently to meet the asylum's regular needs, and rather than continue paying a subsidy to the NBR, the board took up an option to terminate its agreement and closed its railway in 1921.[12]

Union Street Aberdeen, Looking East.

Electric trams appeared in many Scottish cities during the Edwardian period. This is Aberdeen's Union Street. (Author's collection)

Another little-known privately owned passenger carrier was the Strabathie Light Railway in Aberdeenshire. This 3 ft gauge line was built without parliamentary powers by the Seaton Brick & Tile Co. and completed in 1899: its main purpose was to carry the products of its owner's brickworks at Black Dog for three and a half miles down the coast to its depot at Bridge of Don, whence they could be distributed by cart around Aberdeen. Passengers were also carried, between Bridge of Don, Berryhill and Black Dog: their numbers increased greatly after Murcar golf course was opened adjacent to the line in 1909.[13]

To carry passengers, the Strabathie railway obtained four formerly horsedrawn tramcars from Aberdeen city tramways. Street tramways, horsedrawn, had originated in the USA; adoption of this specialised form of railway in Britain was greatly aided by the Tramways Act 1870, a general act to facilitate laying rails along the public highway, although motive power was restricted to animals.[14] Two years later the first horse trams in Scotland were operating in Glasgow.[15] The system was rapidly extended, and other places followed suit – Edinburgh, Dundee, Aberdeen, Greenock, even Rothesay and Bridge of Allan. R. D. Stephen describes travelling in 1916 between Causewayhead station and Bridge of Allan in an ancient tram pulled by two horses along a track following the edge of the road: the track was old and in poor condition, and derailments frequent – which simply meant hitching the horses onto the other end of the car and pulling it back onto the track by means of ramps.[16]

By then many town tramways had been electrified. The first electric railway, using current generated by a dynamo, had been demonstrated by Werner von Siemens in 1878 in Berlin and in 1881 in London. The first electric railway in Scotland, likewise temporary, ran at the Edinburgh Industrial Exhibition of 1886, held in the Meadows. The line was a quarter of a mile long with current supplied by a third rail; two cars ran every day of the exhibition carrying passengers for a fare of two pence. Its gauge was probably 2 ft 6 in., for the rolling stock seems subsequently to have been sold to the owner of Carstairs House who in 1886 built a one-and-a-half-mile electric line of that gauge to link his residence with the station. Most regrettably, he was electrocuted when he tripped over the live rail; the line was subsequently worked by horses.

In 1890 an even larger exhibition, the Edinburgh Exhibition of the Arts, Sciences & Industries, was held near Craiglockhart on a site adjoining both the Caledonian and North British Railways: both companies provided temporary stations. From the Caledonian station, a half-mile-long standard gauge electric railway carried passengers to the front of the exhibition.[17]

It was however to street tramways, rather than railways, that electric traction in Scotland was first applied. Mechanical power had been permitted on them since 1879 by a further Act of Parliament. It was only in 1898 however that a two-and-a-half-mile length of horse tramway in Glasgow was electrified, using overhead current collection; but this was so successful that the following year it was decided to convert the whole system. With subsequent extensions, Glasgow eventually had an electric tramway network extending to 134 route miles, served by more than 1,200 tramcars. Other cities and towns followed the example, both by electrifying horse tramways and building anew; eventually there were twenty-one electric tramway systems in Scotland.[18]

An alternative means of applying mechanical power to street tramways was an updated version of the cable haulage techniques of the 1820s. In the new version, a cable powered by a central winding engine ran in a conduit between the rails: cars were attached to it by detachable grippers. Edinburgh was the only Scottish (or British) city where this system was widespread.[19] It was, however, also used to power the Glasgow District Subway when this six-and-a-half-mile circular railway of 4 ft gauge was opened beneath the city in 1896. (There was chaos on the opening day, when delighted passengers travelled round and round and refused to leave the cars!) The Subway later became better known as the Glasgow Underground.[20]

In mid-Victorian times it became a point of contention throughout Britain that rural areas that lacked railways were suffering, while railway construction in such areas was discouraged by the expense of promotion by private bill, and of eventual operation to the Board of Trade's safety requirements for main lines. Some attempts were made to exploit the Tramways Act 1870 to alleviate the position. When the Wigtownshire Railway was authorised in 1872, its branch from Millisle to Garlieston was to be built as a tramway. But there were second thoughts; the branch was eventually built as a railway and a further Act obtained.[21]

The position was eventually alleviated by the Light Railways Act of 1896. Under it, light railways could be authorised, and companies to build and run them incorporated, by statutory order – a 'Light Railway Order' – instead of private Act. On such railways, speed was restricted, but safety precautions were relaxed – level crossings might lack gates, signalling was simplified, for instance.[22] The consequence in Scotland was construction – sometimes aided by Treasury grant – of a series of rural light railways over the ensuing decade. In this way, rail transport was brought to Lauder, Wanlockhead, Dornoch, Lybster, St Combs, Gifford and Moniaive, among other places.[23] The usual Scottish light railway was of standard gauge and operated, perhaps owned, by one of the big five companies, to which it became in effect a branch of its system. But there were cost-saving idiosyncrasies. The light railway from Fraserburgh to St Combs, laid out across sandy links, dispensed with the usual lineside fences: its locomotives were fitted with cowcatchers.[24] The light railway from Elvanfoot to Leadhills and Wanlockhead dispensed with raised platforms at stations: its carriages were fitted with steps. Wanlockhead station, at 1,413 ft above sea level, was the highest on the main railway system, its altitude exceeded in Britain only by the Snowdon Mountain Railway.[25]

Quite different was the Campbeltown & Machrihanish Light Railway, isolated from the main railway system but nevertheless, since it provided onward conveyance across Kintyre for passengers arriving at Campbeltown by Clyde steamer, part of the total transport network. It was of narrow gauge – 2 ft 3 in. – and opened in 1906. Much of it dated from the 1870s, as a mineral railway bringing coal from collieries into Campbeltown, which had been rebuilt and extended under a light railway order to carry passengers also.

The Campbeltown & Macrihanish might not

The 2 ft 3 in. gauge Campbeltown & Machrihanish Light Railway was isolated from the main Scottish railway system, but connected with Clyde steamers at Campbeltown to take passengers across Kintyre to the sands of Machrihanish.

(Author's collection)

have remained isolated if proposals considered by the Glasgow & South Western Railway about 1906–10 had come to fruition. As well as a railway on Kintyre the proposals included hotels, golf courses and a new steamer port at Cour Bay on the east coast. The railway would have linked them, running first across to the west coast and then southwards to an intersection with the C & M, and thence onwards to Southend, a route some thirty-five miles long. The gauge, presumably, would have been 2 ft 3 in.[26] But, like many another proposed railway, it was not built, and remains in the realm of fascinating might-have-beens to stretch the imagination.

Light railway proposals were particularly prone to fall by the wayside, for the period following passage of the Light Railways Act was also the period in which the motor car, and other motor vehicles, first came to Scottish roads. The Fraserbugh–St Combs light railway was the only one successfully completed out of at least eight similar schemes proposed within Great North of Scotland territory during the period 1896–1914.[27] In the region served by the Highland Railway the story was similar. Materials were delivered, and some work started, on a light railway to run from Forsinard to Melvich and Portskerra, but the full capital needed proved impossible to raise, and the line was never completed. The Cromarty & Dingwall Light Railway had actually laid six miles of line westwards from Cromarty by 1914, when outbreak of war brought construction to a halt and, in 1917, the rails were lifted, commandeered for use elsewhere. Other unsuccessful proposals for light railways in the north-west were revivals of earlier schemes, part of a long-running saga which might have seen Aultbea, Ullapool, Lochinver and Laxford Bridge added to the railway map – but did not. Proposals for light railways on Skye and Lewis were equally unsuccessful.[28]

On a wider scale the railway proposal that proved over-ambitious – sometimes from opposition in Parliament but probably more often from difficulty in raising funds – is almost as old as the public railway itself: commonplace during the era of railway expansion and not unknown subsequently. Some have already been mentioned and space allows only a few more of the most remarkable to be considered here. As early as 1807–10 Thomas Telford himself surveyed a long-distance waggonway to run from Glasgow via the Monklands coalfield to Peebles, Melrose and Berwick, bringing the benefits of Lanarkshire coal to the Borders.[29] Some of the same territory was to be traversed by the proposed Caledonian Extension Railway of 1846. This was to run from Ayr to Carstairs where there would be a junction with the Caledonian Railway, authorised the previous year, and then via Peebles to Kelso where it would join a branch of the projected Newcastle & Berwick Railway. It would have enabled the Caledonian to tap into the Ayrshire railway's traffic in the West, and the North British in the East: but it went the same way as innumerable other proposals of the railway mania. No through route ever occupied this corridor, although it was eventually served by branch lines in variety.

Of all the railways that were projected but that remained unbuilt, none excites the imagination more than the proposed Glasgow & North Western Railway of 1883.[30] It was one of many attempts, prior to eventual authorisation of the West Highland Railway, to drive a line north-westwards from Glasgow to Fort William and on through the Great Glen to Inverness. The attraction was that at this date the existing route from Glasgow to Inverness, by the Caledonian and Highland Railways via Perth and Forres, was 207 miles long: the G & NW would have reduced that to about 165 miles. It was to diverge from existing railways at Maryhill on the northern edge of Glasgow, and run via Strathblane and Drymen to follow the east shore of Loch Lomond. Northwards from the loch it would go by Crianlarich and Tyndrum to Kingshouse on Rannoch Moor: and thence down through Glencoe almost to Glencoe village. Here it would turn eastwards for a few miles, following the shoreline of Loch Leven until able to cross the loch by a single span of only thirty-seven feet at Dog Ferry, and head for Onich and Fort William. That southern part of the route had been in places winding and steeply graded: ahead now lay the temptingly direct, and for much of its distance dead level, route through the Great Glen to Inverness.

But the G & NWR was promoted by speculators from afar. One is inclined to suspect the hand of the Midland Railway, among others, behind it – the

Glasgow terminus was to be at St Enoch, and a direct route to Highland grouse moors and Inverness itself would have suited the expansive ambitions of the Midland at this period very well indeed. At any rate Parliament, swayed by the combined opposition of existing railways and steamboat operators, and of some (but by no means all) of the landowners, turned it down. A pity. That descent of Glencoe, particularly, would have been spectacular: despite a 1 in 50 down gradient, for much of the way the line would have been carried high above the floor of the glen, along a hillside shelf on the rocky slopes which culminate in the Aonach Eagach Ridge. A tunnel and avalanche shelters were planned: James Brunlees, who had earlier laid out the Mont Cenis Railway and knew much about such things, spoke up in their favour.

Some proposals were even more adventurous. There were thoughts, over many decades, of a railway tunnel beneath the sea between Scotland and Ireland. A proposal of the 1860s would have run from near the Mull of Kintyre to the Antrim coast near Cushendall, with fourteen and three-eighths miles under water. Some 112 miles of new railway would have been needed on the Scottish side to link with existing railways at Helensburgh and the total distance from Glasgow to Belfast was to be 173 miles; this was to be accomplished in four and a half hours, compared with the then current rail/steamer journey time of nine hours. Later ideas put the Scottish entrance near Portpatrick.[31] Around the turn of the century there were thoughts too of rack railways to the tops of Ben Lomond[32] and Ben Nevis[33].

In urban surroundings, perhaps the most remarkable might-have-been is the Caledonian Railway's proposal about 1890 to continue its line beyond Edinburgh Princes Street terminus. It would have passed through

Following takeover of the Union Canal by the Edinburgh & Glasgow Railway, stone block sleepers from the railway were reused to form the coping of the canal bank at Linlithgow. (Author)

a tunnel beneath almost the entire length of Princes Street itself to a station at its eastern end, and then through another tunnel beneath Calton Hill towards Leith. There it would have connected with the CR's other lines in the area, providing a circular route through north Edinburgh to mirror the North British suburban circle to the south, and providing Edinburgh with an underground section comparable with those in Glasgow. To put this proposal into historic perspective, the CR had then recently completed its extension from Greenock to Gourock which had required cut-and-cover tunnelling beneath the streets of Greenock over a greater distance than Princes Street would have needed, while the North British was grappling with the problem of congestion at Waverley with the unpopular proposal to encroach further upon Princes Street Gardens in order to quadruple its line.

At any rate the NBR successfully countered this unlooked-for competition from the CR by the improvement of Waverley and its approaches, and particularly by construction of its short branch to Leith Central at the foot of Leith Walk.

Surprisingly, this terminus seems never to have been used to its full potential; less surprisingly a contemporaneous offer by the NBR to facilitate passenger interchange at Princes Street station by building an underground low-level station – the NBR passed in tunnel beneath the platforms of the CR terminus above – was, in that competitive era, still-born. (Although such a station, if built, would have been of continuing value today to serve that part of the city, irrespective of whether the CR terminus had survived.)

It is worth considering why no extensive mileage of narrow gauge railways was built in Scotland, since the topography of Scotland is not dissimilar to that of Norway and Wales where their practicability was first demonstrated: in Norway in 1861 on the 3 ft 6 in. gauge (by an engineer trained in Britain, Carl Pihl, using British-built equipment) and in Wales in 1863, when steam locomotives were successfully put into service on the Festiniog Railway by Charles Spooner, on a gauge as narrow as 2 ft or thereabouts. Practicability was confirmed by demonstrations in 1870 of Robert Fairlie's patent bogie locomotive hauling immense trains over the Festiniog Railway. This was followed by a wave of enthusiasm for narrow gauge railways in countries as far afield as New Zealand and the USA, and nearer home in Ireland.[34]

The advantages of narrow gauges were low first cost: small locomotives and rolling stock, running over lines with sharp curves which avoided the need for extensive civil engineering works. The disadvantage was the need for passengers to change trains, and goods to be trans-shipped, at break-of-gauge points where a narrow gauge line met one of wider gauge. So far as Scotland is concerned, the answer is probably twofold. Firstly, although it is a land of mountains, it is also a land of glens which offered suitable routes for standard gauge railways. Secondly, by the late 1860s, the standard gauge network was already too extensive.

Narrow gauge lines were indeed considered. The possibility of building from Dingwall to Kyle of Lochalsh on the 3 ft 6 in. gauge was costed and showed substantial savings: but the inconvenience of break-of-gauge at Dingwall was considered to outweigh these, and funds were saved instead by cutting the route back to Strome Ferry. The third Duke of Sutherland inspected both the Festiniog and the Norwegian lines, and became an enthusiastic convert to the narrow gauge cause. After attending the demonstrations on the Festiniog Railway in February 1870, he commented that he wished he had known more of the Festiniog Railway six years earlier: he could have saved one-third of the £200,000 he had spent on promoting and making railways in the North of Scotland.[35] But when construction of the Sutherland & Caithness Railway to 2 ft 6 in. gauge was proposed, the inconvenience of break-of-gauge at Helmsdale was considered once again to outweigh the advantages. In 1872 however the duke did have the opportunity to put theory into practice when he accepted chairmanship of the Isle of Man Railway, to be built to 3 ft gauge in a location where break-of-gauge presented no problem.

It is intriguing to speculate that if narrow gauges

had become practicable a few years earlier, or the standard gauge had reached Inverness a few years later, then Inverness might have become a break-of-gauge point with everything to the north on the 3 ft 6 in. gauge – in which case the system might well have been more extensive than in fact it was, reaching perhaps to Ullapool and Lochinver. How much of it might survive to the present day is another matter.

The whole question of light and narrow gauge railways was brought to the fore again in 1919 by the report of the Rural Transport (Scotland) Committee. In addition to its detailed proposals for improved roads, new road motor services and new steamer and motor boat services, this recommended construction of a total of 382 miles of new railway, of which 226 miles were to be standard gauge and 156 narrow. Standard gauge was to be used where there would be a direct connection with an existing railway – for instance for lines between Ballater and Braemar, and Garve and Ullapool. Narrow gauge was to be used where there was no connection, which meant almost entirely on the islands: a seventy-five-mile system was recommended for Skye, and a forty-mile one for Lewis. A twenty-mile narrow gauge line was recommended on the mainland between Dunoon and Strachur, no doubt to operate in conjunction with steamer services. The preferred narrow gauge would have been 2 ft 6 in., were it not for the large quantity of war surplus 60 cm gauge locomotives and rolling stock available cheaply in France, which would be suitable provided rails of 45 lb/yd were used in place of the War Department's 20 lb/yd which was too light. The committee had despatched a subcommittee to inspect this equipment. Regrettably, considering all the effort which evidently went into preparing it, the report of the committee seems to have had little or

no lasting effect. The possibility of building railways on Lewis, however, got another airing at this period during the well-meaning but ultimately unsuccessful attempts by Lord Leverhulme to improve conditions there. He proposed a 100-mile network of 3 ft gauge electrified lines at a cost of £1½ million, using electricity generated by a hydroelectric plant. Once again there seems to have been no lasting effect.[36]

Let us now turn to the 'vast mass of miscellaneous property … which has come into the possession of modern railway companies', as Acworth put it.[37] He was writing of railway-owned canals, which he considered 'a very small item' in that vast mass which included 'docks, hotels, steamboats and so forth'. It is worth seeing, therefore, how much of this miscellaneous property the five main Scottish railways possessed in 1922, their last year of independent existence. The totals are: canals, 84¼ miles; docks and harbours, 10 with a part interest in 2 more; passenger steamers, 26 with a part interest in 2 more; and hotels, 16. They also by then possessed 38 motor buses and 20 motor vehicles for goods and parcels, in addition to innumerable horse-drawn road vehicles.[38]

Most of these have been well described in detail elsewhere, and only a summary is needed here. The eighty-four and a quarter miles of canals comprised the Union Canal, which as mentioned had been purchased by the Edinburgh & Glasgow Railway in 1848 and had therefore subsequently become the property of the North British; and the Forth & Clyde Canal which, including the Monkland, had been purchased by the Caledonian in 1867 in order to obtain control of an east coast port – namely Grangemouth – for export of Lanarkshire coal.[39] Conveniently, the canal company itself had already built the branch railway from Falkirk to Grangemouth. The railway companies

When the Caledonian-backed Lanarkshire & Dumbartonshire Railway was built in the 1890s it crossed over the Caledonian-owned Forth & Clyde Canal at Bowling. Despite the awkward angle a swing bridge had nonetheless to be provided for the benefit of ships with tall masts such as the one in the background. (National Railway Museum)

accepted their general obligation under the Regulation of Railways Act 1873 to keep their canals open and navigable, but had little incentive to develop them: on their railways, they were carriers as well as providers of track, but on their canals, they provided the track for shipowners and boatowners, with whom they were in competition, to do the carrying. Indeed the North British, acting in concert with the Corporation of Edinburgh, had obtained powers in 1913 to close the Union Canal's Edinburgh terminus, Port Hopetoun, for redevelopment, new quays being provided further out.[40] The Forth & Clyde Canal however had remained busy until 1914, when general closure of the Firth of Forth to civilian shipping during the First World War hit its trade badly.[41]

So far as docks were concerned, the railway companies did have every incentive to develop them. The Caledonian enlarged Grangemouth docks in the late 1870s and again, very much more, between 1898 and 1906. The resulting complex included some sixty miles of railway tracks on or near the quaysides, in addition to a large new marshalling yard at the approaches, with over 3 million tons of freight passing through annually.[42] On the North British, coal shipments through its harbour at Burntisland were more than 2 million tons in 1910.[43] The full tally of railway-owned docks and harbours was: Caledonian: Grangemouth, Bowling and South Alloa; North British: Burntisland, Bo'ness, Methil, Alloa and Silloth (Cumberland); GSWR: Troon and Ayr, and a part-share in Girvan. The Portpatrick & Wigtownshire Joint Railways' undertaking included Stranraer harbour, so

Traffic passed seamlessly between train services and steamer services. This parcels waybill from 1882 is for three parcels to be carried by train from Glasgow Queen Street to Balloch Pier, but their eventual destinations are Luss and Inversnaid – so they will be carried up Loch Lomond by paddle steamers of the Loch Lomond Steamboat Company. Later in the decade the steamboat company was taken over by the railway. (Author's collection)

that in other words the Caledonian and GSWR each had a quarter-share in it. Railway companies did, of course, have access to many other docks and harbours beside those which they owned – including, in some instances, those of other railways over which they had running powers.

Operation of trains in connection with steamers dated back to the Ardrossan-Liverpool steamer service of 1840. This did not outlive completion of an all-rail route to the South, but steamers between Ardrossan and Belfast became a lasting feature. The Glasgow, Paisley & Greenock Railway from its opening in 1841 ran in connection with those Clyde steamer operators who were prepared to cooperate, by connecting with trains at Greenock to carry passengers onwards to Clyde coast towns and resorts, and to the islands, and vice versa. The Caledonian continued the practice.

Many steamer operators preferred to compete, by continuing to go all the way down the river from Glasgow. There were intermittent short-lived attempts by railway companies to run their own steamers on the Clyde, but the first to be successful in the long-term was that of the North British Railway. Following the amalgamations of the 1860s the NBR gained rail access to the north shore of the Firth of Clyde; it had been operating steamers between Silloth and Irish ports since 1862, and in 1866 it placed its own steamers on the Clyde. (The powers of the railway companies to operate steamers were various and restricted: steamers often belonged legally to directors, or subsidiary steam packet companies, but were operated as part of a railway's network.) The NBR Clyde steamers operated initially out of Helensburgh, until a new rail-served pier was opened at Craigendoran in 1882.

Completion of its own route to Greenock in 1869 gave the Glasgow & South Western Railway access to the south shore of the Clyde, and its trains connected with Clyde steamers at Greenock Albert Harbour, later Princes Pier; for the time being, the steamers were independently owned. Passengers arriving at the Caledonian station at Greenock had to walk to the pier, a disadvantage that had been alleviated to some extent by construction of the branch to Wemyss Bay where station and pier did adjoin one another. To regain its full advantage, the Caledonian determined to extend its Greenock line for three and a quarter miles to a new pier at Gourock, an extension which with its 2,100-yd tunnel beneath the streets of Greenock was opened only in 1889. As the opening date approached the CR found that, nevertheless, the steamer operators were showing a marked disinterest in using the new pier: so the railway, employing one of the most enterprising of their number, Captain James Williamson, as marine superintendent, established the Caledonian Steam Packet Company, Ltd (in fact, a syndicate of CR shareholders) to run its own steamers. Railway, pier and steamers came into operation simultaneously. The Glasgow & South Western Railway obtained powers from Parliament in 1891 to operate its own steamers, and its own fleet upon the Clyde.

There ensued, for a quarter of a century until 1914, what O. S. Nock has described as the finest rail and steamer service the world has ever seen. He was writing specifically of the Caledonian service: whether protagonists of the other two railways would have agreed with that is open to doubt, for competition between the three was rife and all three operated their combined train-steamer services very efficiently indeed. There was not merely excursion traffic: there

was much business traffic too, at its peak at summer weekends when Glasgow merchants' families stayed at the seaside during the week and the breadwinner joined them for Saturday to Monday. Competition long antedated the railways' acquisitions of their own steamer fleets, and tales of racing between rival steamers, each heading for the same pier, are well known. Acworth notes that in 1889, between 4.00 p.m. and 4.30 p.m., eleven boat trains left Glasgow by one route or another, and there were thirteen steamers in connection with them. Dunoon, by the fastest service, was sixty-two minutes from Glasgow via Gourock; Rothesay, eighty via Wemyss Bay. By 1910, when things had evidently stabilised, typical fast times were Dunoon, seventy minutes, Rothesay, ninety; and in 2006 the current timetable shows Dunoon, seventy-eight minutes, Rothesay again ninety. Yet there was even more to it than that, for the combined rail/steamer services brought many other communities on the far side of the firth, such as Blairmore, Kilmun and Inellan, into swift direct communication with Glasgow, with but a single change between train and steamer – a change for which sometimes only two minutes were allowed.[44]

Establishment of a steamer service between Stranraer and Larne in 1862 was mentioned in Chapter 4. Although railway-backed, it proved short lived, for traffic – in the continuing absence of a mail contract – was limited and the crossing sometimes stormy; there were other false starts before the Larne & Stranraer Steamboat Company Ltd was formed in 1871, backed by the Portpatrick Railway and by Irish interests. This started operations the following year, and was rewarded by a mail contract from 1874. The service became a lasting feature of travel between Scotland and Ireland, the Portpatrick Railway's share passing in due course to the joint committee. In 1893 a reorganisation brought the Larne & Stranraer Steamship Joint Committee into being, one-fifth share being held respectively by the Caledonian, GSW, LNW, Midland and Belfast & Northern Counties Railways.[45]

The Loch Lomond steamers too became a joint undertaking, of (unusually) North British and Caledonian Railways. The Caledonian & Dumbartonshire Railway, mentioned in Chapter 4, became in due course part of the North British Railway, and in 1888 its associated North British Steam Packet Co. took over the old-established Lochlomond Steamboat Company. But at this period the Caledonian was expanding, building a line from Glasgow outwards along the north shore of the Clyde where previously the NBR had held a monopoly, and the CR proposed to extend this line to Loch Lomond and to place its own fleet of steamers on the loch. The North British seems to have accepted joint ownership of the line from Dumbarton to Balloch, and of the loch steamers, as a lesser evil. So the Dumbarton & Balloch Joint Line came into being in 1896. Curiously, on land the joint line owned the track, but the two companies operated their own trains over it; but on the water, the 'track' was the public navigable loch, but the vessels were owned jointly. Here as elsewhere the railway-owned steamers provided passengers with a service comparable to that of a railway branch line, with through bookings between piers and railway stations, and parcels and livestock carried too.[46]

The North British was, with its predecessors, the only railway to operate steamers on the East Coast. The ferries which crossed the Firths of Tay and Forth before the bridges were built have already been mentioned. In 1867 the company also acquired the ancient ferry over the Forth between South and North

The very close links between a railway company's railways and its hotels and steamers are confirmed by this pair of advertisements from the back pages of the North British publication *The Epistles of Peggy*. (David Stirling collection)

Queensferry. When the Forth Bridge was opened in 1890 this was not closed, but rather leased out; the NBR resumed operating it itself in 1919. The Granton–Burntisland ferry also survived opening of the Forth Bridge; in 1922 the company had one vessel on each of these crossings.[47]

Ownership of the passenger steamer fleets at the beginning of 1922 was made up as follows: Caledonian,

6 ships; GSWR, 6; North British, 8; Dumbarton & Balloch Joint line, 6; Portpatrick & Wigtownshire Joint Railways, 2. The totals would have been higher but for losses on war service, unreplaced; they did increase during the course of the year when the Caledonian took over steamers on Loch Tay and Loch Awe. The Highland Railway had tried owning and operating steamships in the 1870s, found it did not pay, and subsequently preferred to run in connection with independently operated shipping routes.[48] The location of the Great North, alone among the principal Scottish railways, made shipowning irrelevant.

Coach services, before there were railways, were based around coaching inns, and the Garnkirk & Glasgow Railway followed this precedent in 1832 when it opened an inn at Gartsherrie, its eastern extremity, principally for the benefit of excursion parties.[49] It does not seem to have remained in business for long and when, later on, hotels were opened for railway travellers they were at first independent of the railway companies. Thus Inverness had a Station Hotel from 1856, the year after the line itself was opened, Dumfries had one from about 1865, and Aberdeen from 1870. In the 1860s there were proposals for a hotel at Perth to be owned jointly by the railway companies that owned the station, and for a Caledonian Railway hotel in Edinburgh, but financial difficulties meant that these lapsed for the time being. At Achnasheen on the Dingwall & Skye line a house was purchased by the railway in 1870 to become a hotel, its operation leased out to tenants.

So the first hotels in Scotland to be owned and operated by railway companies themselves appear in the late 1870s: in 1877 when the North British took over the hotel adjoining Queen Street station, Glasgow, and the following year when the Highland

Railway bought the Station Hotel at Inverness. The first hotel to be built specifically as a railway hotel was opened in 1879 at the Glasgow & South Western Railway's grand new terminus at Glasgow St Enoch, where inter alia it provided a suitably imposing street frontage. The example was followed by the Caledonian at Glasgow Central (hotel opened 1885), by the GSWR at Ayr in 1886, and by the Caledonian, North British and Highland Railways acting jointly at Perth, where the Station Hotel was belatedly opened in 1890.

In the same year the Great North of Scotland railway acquired the Palace Hotel, Aberdeen. This led to a remarkable dispute, for the hotel's 'boots' was regularly sent to the joint station's platform to tout for custom. Two other hotels complained about this and got the backing of the North British Railway, one of the station's other users. It was 1896 before the dispute was settled with agreement that all hotels' boots should be allowed on the platforms equally.

The Highland Railway bought a house at Kyle of Lochalsh for conversion to a hotel in 1896, and the GSWR, having bought and rebuilt the Station Hotel at Dumfries, reopened it in 1897. In Aberdeen the GNSR acquired a second hotel, the Station, in 1910 in preparation for the proposed reconstruction of the station itself.

Edinburgh gained fine railway hotels worthy of a capital city early in the 1900s: the North British Hotel was opened above and adjacent to Waverley station in 1902, and the Caledonian Hotel was opened at Princes Street station in 1903, each by the eponymous railway. These hotels continue – although no longer in railway ownership – to provide landmark buildings at the east and west ends of Princes Street. The North British Hotel had been building since 1894 as part of the Waverley station reconstruction. The subcommittee charged with overseeing it obtained advice on architect's remuneration from the North Eastern, Caledonian and Glasgow & South Western Railways (an interesting example of how competing railway companies could cooperate when it suited them) but were turned away by the owners of the Metropole Hotel at Brighton who feared even at that distance that concepts might be copied. When the North British Hotel was opened the manager was paid £1,000 a year and the head chef £364; the head hall porter was on £1 a week but presumably had more opportunities than the chef to enhance his remuneration by tips.

All these hotels catered primarily for travellers, although no doubt some, such as those in Edinburgh, were used also by visiting tourists. In 1899 the Great North of Scotland Railway opened a hotel which was itself in the nature of a resort, aimed squarely at the tourist market. Having opened in 1896 a branch line from Ellon, on the Buchan line, to Boddam on the coast, it then opened at Cruden Bay a large hotel complete with golf course, bowling green, tennis courts, croquet lawns and two miles of sandy beaches. A 3 ft 6 in. gauge electric tramway connected it with the station, a third of a mile away. In the long term this venture would prove a failure, but initially it was a great success: patrons included Sir William Burrell, and members of the McEwan and Crawford families (brewers and biscuit manufacturers respectively).

The initial success of the Great North's Cruden Bay Hotel was observed closely by other railway companies, with particular reference to the golf course. The Highland Railway opened a large hotel at Dornoch, overlooking the golf course, in 1904; the Glasgow & South Western a larger one at Turnberry, with two golf courses of its own, in 1906. Both of these were associated with newly built light railways, the Dornoch Light Railway of 1902 and the Maidens & Dunure Light Railway, opened simultaneously with the hotel; it is against this background that the GSWR's proposals at this period for hotels, golf courses and a narrow gauge line on Kintyre should be considered. At Turnberry, the main entrance to the hotel led off the railway station; but the hotel also had accommodation for guests' motor cars, and for their chauffeurs.

The Highland Railway continued the trend by building the Highland Hotel at Strathpeffer Spa, opened in 1911. The 'Strathpeffer Express', put on at the same time and bypassing Inverness, has already been mentioned in Chapter 5. Tourist tickets to Strathpeffer, on sale as far away as Liverpool, included seven days' accommodation at the hotel.

This trend reached its zenith at Gleneagles. Here a luxury hotel with two first-class golf courses was planned from 1909 by the Caledonian Railway. Construction started in 1913 only to be suspended during the First World War. After the war the golf courses were completed first and were an immediate success. Construction of the hotel recommenced in 1922, aided by a siding leading to the site from the Crieff branch, and reuse of stones from Jerviston viaduct, near Motherwell, which was being demolished. And that was the stage reached at the time of the grouping.[50]

The thirty-eight motor buses owned by Scottish railways in 1922 all belonged to the Great North of Scotland Railway which had been a pioneer of this type of transport. Motor buses had originated around the turn of the century – one early route which started in 1898 was in Edinburgh between the Post Office and Haymarket. Certain English railway companies started motor bus services in 1903, and the Great North was the first to do so in Scotland, in May 1904. The first route was between Braemar and Ballater,

Scotland.

Seaside & Golfing Resort, CRUDEN BAY

Thirty Miles by rail from Aberdeen.

Splendid Beach over Two Miles long. Sea Bathing, Boating, Fishing.
HEALTHY CLIMATE. BRACING AIR.

THE GOLF COURSE OF 18 HOLES,

laid out by the Railway Company, is one of the best in the Kingdom.

LADIES' COURSE of 9 HOLES.
Putting Green and Putting Course.

CRUDEN BAY HOTEL

OWNED BY

THE GREAT NORTH OF SCOTLAND RAILWAY COMPANY.
Occupies a charming site overlooking the Bay.
LIGHTED BY ELECTRICITY. LIFT. LOUNGE. GARAGE.
Special Accommodation and Convenience for Golfers.
Bowling Greens. Tennis Courts. Croquet Lawns.
Electric Tramway for Visitors between Cruden Bay Station and Hotel.
Address Inquiries to The MANAGER, Cruden Bay Hotel, Port Erroll, N.B.

The Palace Hotel, Aberdeen, and Station Hotel, Aberdeen, also owned by
the Great North of Scotland Railway Company.

The Cruden Bay Hotel, opened by the Great North of Scotland Railway in 1899, was the first of the resort hotels established in open country by the railway companies, and was the model for later ventures such as Turnberry and Gleneagles. The electric tram that connected it with the station can be seen in front of the main entrance. (Author's collection)

where the buses connected with the trains to and from Aberdeen; at Braemar the company established a booking office complete with an official in familiar railway uniform. From 1906 the company's bus services rapidly expanded; they ran in connection with the company's trains (although certain routes ran direct to and from Aberdeen) and were generally considered as a preliminary to construction of railways, at least in the early days. The Caledonian and the North British Railways also both tried operating rural motor bus services during the first decade of the twentieth century.

All this must be considered in relation to the very rapid expansion of independently owned bus services at this period: according to Hunter, in 1909 there were 584 motor vehicles licensed for passenger services in Scotland, and by around 1913 motor bus services could be found throughout Scotland. Some of these did connect with trains, most notably the heavy motor wagons of the Sutherland Motor Traffic Company which since 1905 had been carrying passengers, mails and goods for forty or sixty miles from railheads on the Highland Railway to places in the far north-west. Indeed the inadequacies of the roads for such vehicles were cause for concern to the 1919 rural transport committee. But alone among the Scottish railway companies the Great North seems to have appreciated the potential for motor bus services in evenly populated rural areas, and the desirability of keeping them if possible in its own hands. By outbreak of war in 1914 it was operating 336 route miles of railway and 150 miles of bus routes. The war saw seasonal routes discontinued for the duration, and in the difficult times which followed there was a slight contraction in the total route mileage, but at the time of the grouping it was still substantial.[51]

Change initially came slowly, after the grouping. The Highland Railway's Loch class no. 122 *Loch Moy* had become no. 14382 of the LMS before she set out from Perth with this local for Blair Atholl. (National Railway Museum)

FROM GROUPING TO NATIONALISATION

When the author was a small child, the presence of the Big Four railway companies – London Midland & Scottish, London & North Eastern, Great Western and Southern – was all-pervading in railway matters such as the important Hornby Train catalogue: they seemed as solid as the hills, as ancient and as long-lasting. Such is the childish perception. In fact, the collective life of the Big Four was to be short, from the beginning of 1923 until the end of 1947, and for most of those twenty-five years they were to be in trouble, one way or another. But this was not initially evident. The grouping was, in general, popular.[1] Politicians on the Left saw it as a step towards nationalisation. Politicians on the Right saw it as a profitable consolidation of businesses.[2] Railwaymen saw it as a breaking down of the old watertight compartments, with North British drivers from Edinburgh Haymarket for instance learning the road to Newcastle.[3] Enthusiasts noted the posters on stations announcing 'our new name' and looked forward to what the future might bring, particularly in the way of new liveries for locomotives and coaches.[4]

Decisions on the names for the two companies into which Scottish railways were grouped had not been reached without some heart-searching among the directors. There might have been a London, Midland & Northern Railway[5] in the West, and a Great North Railway[6] in the East: but the names eventually chosen were those given above, and the initials LMS and LNER soon became familiar.

The effect on joint lines and on running powers of course varied according to the effect of the grouping on the companies concerned. The first joint line of all, between Glasgow and Paisley, became solely owned by the LMS. So, more remarkably, did the Portpatrick & Wigtownshire Joint Railways, for all four owning companies – London & North Western, Midland, Caledonian and Glasgow & South Western – had been grouped together. The same even applied to the shipping service between Stranraer and Larne, for the Belfast & Northern Counties Railway – formerly the fifth of the joint owners – had some years earlier been absorbed by the Midland Railway. But elsewhere, joint lines continued. The Dumbarton & Balloch Joint Line, and with it the Loch Lomond steamers, was now owned jointly by LNER and LMS. The LMS too retained a quarter-share in the Forth Bridge Railway Company, inherited from the Midland, even though for practical purposes the Forth Bridge had become part of the LNER system. As for running powers, the LNER continued to reach Aberdeen – and its own lines further north – by running powers over the LMS from Kinnaber; while LMS trains from Edinburgh to Stirling and Oban exercised running powers over part of the

LNER main line between Edinburgh and Glasgow.

Properly speaking, the new companies were formed from 'constituent companies', which were amalgamated together, and 'subsidiary companies', which were then absorbed. So the eight constituents of the LMS included the Caledonian, Glasgow & South Western and Highland Railways (the principal English constituents were the London & North Western and the Midland Railways); among the subsidiary companies were numbered the Callander & Oban, and Killin Railways, and others which had hitherto retained nominal independence in one form or another.[7] Amalgamations and absorptions were achieved by issue of shares in the LMS in exchange for those of the companies absorbed. In most cases this had been done amicably in time for the target date of 1 January 1923. In at least one case it was not. Famously, the board of the Caledonian held out for better terms than those at first offered and took its case to the tribunal; it was July before it was settled and the CR became part of the LMS.[8]

At this date, in terms of paid-up capital, the LMS was the largest railway company in the world.[9] Its first board was formed from directors of the constituent companies: numbering initially twenty-four, it included one director each from the GSWR and the Highland, to which were belatedly added three from the Caledonian.[10] It had been meeting during the latter part of 1922, and that December decided that 'a Scottish Local Committee be appointed for the management of the railways in the Scottish Division', to be formed of four directors and ten other shareholders domiciled in Scotland. The work of the Scottish Division – soon, apparently, renamed the Northern Division[11] – was to be performed by divisional officers reporting to the deputy general manager for Scotland.

But the work of both committee and officers (who were drawn from the constituent companies) was very much circumscribed. The committee was to report on Scottish matters to the main board; it had some commercial responsibility, but all matters of policy in which other sections of the company were concerned would be decided by the board, and these decisions would be binding on the Scottish Committee. The divisional officers were responsible in departmental matters to the chief officers of the company.[12]

With its routes extending to around 7,500 miles, the LMS was the largest of the Big Four. Contained within it were companies that had been in competition, in rivalry, with each other since the beginning of railways: Caledonian and Glasgow & South Western in Scotland, Midland and London & North Western even more so in England. So vast an undertaking, composed of so many disparate parts, needed an exceptional form of organisation, and an exceptional man to run it. He was found in Josiah Charles Stamp. Stamp had entered the Inland Revenue in 1896 as a sixteen-year-old clerk. Combining a brilliant intelligence, colossal energy, encyclopaedic memory, a strong liking for statistics and a sense of humour, he had risen rapidly through the Civil Service and then moved to big business, in which he was strongly influenced by American methods.[13] LMS chairman Sir Guy Granet, formerly of the Midland, seems to have brought him (by then he had become Sir Josiah Stamp) quietly into the LMS early in 1926 to be President of the Executive, whatever that might mean. 'I say that we do not want any ... president of the executive. He is a very able man, but it is economy we want' emphasised Col. Hilder, shareholder, at the annual meeting in February.[14] What it did mean became evident during the ensuing year. As senior officials

The lettering on the brake van is 'LMS', but otherwise this scene of a mixed train preparing to depart from Strathpeffer is little changed from Highland Railway days.
(Author's collection)

retired, their positions went with them. The post of deputy general manager for Scotland was abolished on retirement of its first and last incumbent, Donald Matheson, former general manager of the Caledonian. In their place appeared an American-style executive committee of the president and four vice-presidents, each of the four being responsible for a particular segment of the company's activities.[15] Within another year Granet had stepped down as chairman, and Stamp had been elected in his place.[16] This highly centralised form of direction proved effective. But it and its originator were not necessarily popular with railwaymen, particularly in Scotland where, since it contained some of the least remunerative parts of the company's system, there was greatest scope for the economies that soon became necessary.[17]

The constituents of the London & North Eastern Railway also had difficulties in reaching agreement on terms, but when the dust had settled its board of twenty-six directors included four from the North British and one from the Great North of Scotland. Chairman was William Whitelaw of the North British, his reputation enhanced by his successful battle with the Ministry of Transport over post-war compensation.[18]

The LNER's administrative system was decentralised, almost federal in nature, and was based on establishment of three geographical areas corresponding to the pre-grouping companies. The North British and the Great North of Scotland Railways together formed the LNER's Scottish Area, presided over by a general manager (Scotland) to whom the departmental officers were responsible. South of the border were the North Eastern Area and the Southern Area, and

The LNER was already in existence in the summer of 1923 when R.D. Stephen propped his bike against the footbridge at Causewayhead and dashed over it to get this photograph of North British 4-4-0T no. 1404 leaving with a local train from Stirling to Alloa and the Devon Valley. The locomotive dated from 1880 and would be withdrawn the following year. (National Railway Museum)

in London, headquarters was presided over by a chief general manager, and held the whole edifice together with marked success.[19] A Scottish Area local board of directors provided a conduit for two-way passage of information between the main board on the one hand and area staff and public on the other.[20]

On the ground, the most obvious immediate effects of all of this were both increasing change and increasing uniformity. LNER railwaymen from London to Lossiemouth were now being issued with identical uniforms to a new pattern. Locomotives started to appear in new liveries: on the LNER, the apple-green of the former Great Northern Railway, and on the LMS a red similar to that of the Midland Railway. Goods locomotives of both companies were black.

New initials appeared on tenders and cabsides; new numbers, too, and very much higher ones than were familiar, for the new companies, as they renumbered their locomotives into a single series, tended to fit those from Scottish companies in at the end. On the LMS constituents, where two- or three- digit numbers had been usual, five digits now became the norm. On passenger coaches, the effect was similar. LMS coaches started to appear in Midland maroon; the LNER chose varnished teak, and repainted NBR and GNS coaches in brown to match. The new liveries for coaches had both been seen in Scotland before, on through trains from the Midland and the East Coast Routes respectively.

All this happened quickly, but not instantaneously. R.D. Stephen noted two locomotives still in

Caledonian blue at Stirling shed in June 1926.[21] On 3 August of that year, Hamilton Ellis recorded the composition of the 1.30 a.m. from Perth to Inverness – perhaps emulating Foxwell & Farrer's description of 1888 – and not just the composition but also its rainbow combination of colours. The pilot engine was in red, the train engine still in green; the thirteen coaches had originated variously with the Caledonian, LNW, Highland, Midland and Lancashire & Yorkshire Railways, their colours a mixture of green, red, white and brown.[22] In this case however the mixture of original owners was probably due in part to an increasing practice of drafting in coaches from the South to replace elderly coaches in Scottish railways' own stock, particularly those of the Highland Railway. As late as 1938 the Wick-Thurso local train was observed to comprise a Highland locomotive with three coaches from respectively the LNW, Midland and Furness Railways.[23]

On the water, the Caledonian Steam Packet Co. became a subsidiary of the LMS, but retained its name. There were now but two railway steamer fleets on the Clyde, for the steamers of the Glasgow & South Western Railway were absorbed into the Caledonian SP Co.'s fleet.[24]

Of the benefits which the grouping might bring in terms of enlarged resources, there was an interesting demonstration in January 1924. For rugby internationals at Murrayfield, the Caledonian Railway regularly provided an all-Pullman excursion for supporters from Glasgow. The North British had few dining cars to match this, but now the entire resources of the LNER could be brought into play: not only were the usual two dining cars on the evening express from Waverley to Queen Street doubled to four, but Aberdeen supporters were provided with a train of no less than eleven dining cars, drawn not only from North British stock but also from as far afield as the North Eastern Railway, the Great Northern Railway and even the Great Central Railway. As the northbound special accelerated through Haymarket that evening it emitted, according to R. D. Stephen, a delightful odour of bacon and eggs.[25]

There were other signs that the companies were looking ahead. In 1923 the LMS, building on a tradition of fine poster design among its constituents, commissioned a series of paintings by Royal Academicians for a new range. One of the first depicted *The Scottish Highlands*. The following year it completed and opened Gleneagles Hotel, where in addition to the golf courses there were indoor swimming pool, tennis courts, bowling green, croquet lawn, ballroom for 200 couples and 12 miles of 27 in. wide carpet down the corridors. All this cost the guest 12s. 6d. a night for a single room, or £1. 5s. 0d. with bath en suite.[26]

Both companies carried out comparative trials of locomotives from their constituent railways. The LNER pitted 4-4-2 locomotives from its three East Coast main-line constituents – Great Northern, North Eastern and North British – against one another between Newcastle and Edinburgh in August 1923.[27] The LMS carried out trials between Leeds and Carlisle during 1923–4, and between Preston and Carlisle, which included the climb over Shap, in 1925–6. Express locomotives, of both 4-4-0 and 4-6-0 types, were involved from the Caledonian, Midland, London & North Western and Lancashire & Yorkshire Railways. Train loads were of the order of 350 tons. The results showed clearly that the best performances were provided by compound[28] 4-4-0s of Midland Railway type. At first, the LMS had continued to build locomotives to pre-

LNER **WESTERN HIGHLANDS** LMS

IT'S QUICKER BY RAIL

FULL INFORMATION FROM L·N·E·R AND LMS OFFICES AND AGENCIES

With innumerable opportunities for display on stations from one end of Britain to the other, railway poster art reached its zenith between the wars. In this example the LNER and the LMS are jointly encouraging rail travel to the Western Highlands. What was then a delightful contemporary scene has become with the passage of time a period piece: steam train, open-wire telegraphs, haycocks protected from the weather by tarpaulins weighed down by boulders, girl in cloche hat, boy in long shorts. Whoever bothered to fiddle around doing up *both* braces buttons at the back, specially when you were in a hurry to run down the hayfield to wave to the train? (NRM - Pictorial Collection / Science & Society Picture Library)

grouping designs for use in the relevant area. Now, under Chief Mechanical Engineer Sir Henry Fowler, himself a Midland man, it started to build Midland Compounds in quantity. In Scotland, they proved popular with enginemen on both Caledonian and Glasgow & South Western sections.[29]

There was more to come. The Midland had had a policy of standardising locomotive design, of building large numbers of locomotives to a limited number of designs. The LMS, on the other hand, had inherited at the grouping no less than 10,316 locomotives, of 393 different classes. Some classes were old, some

The new order: LMS Royal Scot class no. 6130 was brand new, not as yet given a name, and probably running in when photographed near Slateford in 1928 with an express from Edinburgh Princes Street to Glasgow Central. It will take the direct line via Shotts, as indicated by the Caledonian-style semaphore indicator mounted above the front buffer beam. The train includes a Pullman dining car. (National Railway Museum)

new, some very small in number. Maintaining stocks of spares, particularly boilers, for so many classes was expensive: better, when heavy overhaul was needed by a locomotive which was old, or of a small class, to withdraw it and replace it by a new locomotive of standard design. Such a policy, initiated by Fowler, appealed greatly to the Stamp regime. By the end of 1936 the total number of locomotives was reduced to 7,691 and of classes to 173,[30] and the process continued.

This policy bore hard on locomotives of GSWR origin. Of the 528 locomotives that company brought to the LMS at the grouping, 419 had been withdrawn by 1932. Comparative figures for the Caledonian were 1,077 and 137. O. S. Nock attributed this to the robust design of the Caledonian locomotives.[31] Others, more darkly, noted the prevalence of Caledonian men among the senior officers of the Northern Division. Many of the GSWR locomotives had been replaced by Midland-type 2P 4-4-0s which, though old-fashioned and by

One of the features of pre-grouping photographs is how small the locomotives often seem in relation to the length of train. The practice continued into the 1920s, as this North British pug had been renumbered into the LNER series when photographed with this remarkably long train at Craigentinny, Edinburgh (National Railway Museum)

no means over-powered, were cheap to maintain.[32]

On the LNER the course of events was different. As its chief mechanical engineer the LNER had inherited from the Great Northern Railway one of the ablest steam locomotive designers the world has ever seen: H. N. Gresley. Even before the grouping, Gresley had built for the GNR two large Pacific – 4-6-2 – locomotives to haul its express trains. One of these, on trial in 1922, hauled a 610-ton, 20-coach train from King's Cross to Grantham, 105.5 miles, in 122 minutes, including 27 miles at an average of over 70 mph. This, clearly, was the way ahead for the East Coast main line, and the GNR started to build another ten such locomotives. The first of these, completed the following year by

the LNER, was no. 1472, later renumbered 4472, *Flying Scotsman*.[33] The LNER almost immediately decided to have forty more, of which twenty were built in Glasgow by the North British Locomotive Co. Five of these were delivered to Edinburgh Haymarket shed in mid-1924, and set to work on the main line to Newcastle.[34]

The 10.00 a.m. train from King's Cross to Scotland had by then been known as the 'Flying Scotsman' for many years, and naming the locomotive thus gave the name a degree of official recognition. Early in 1925 the LNER published a publicity booklet entitled *The Flying Scotsman – The World's Most Famous Train*, and it seems that it was soon after this that the name started to appear in public timetables, and that the destination boards on the carriages started to give the name of the train, as well as its destination (at this date Edinburgh, Glasgow, Aberdeen and Perth).[35] Nevertheless giving both a locomotive and a train the same name produced a degree of confusion in the public mind which has persisted ever since, particularly since a locomotive's name is specific to that locomotive, irrespective of the train it is hauling, while a train's name is specific to that train service in the timetable, irrespective of the locomotive and rolling stock which form it on any particular day.

By 1925 it must have been becoming clear to the LMS hierarchy that 4-4-0s hauling light trains were all very well, but that many expresses on the West Coast main line were heavy enough to require double-heading, while the presence of high-powered locomotives hauling heavy trains on the East Coast route provided a challenge it must meet, and urgently. In 1926 the decision was taken to have fifty large 4-6-0 locomotives built; the design was no development of earlier work by any LMS constituent, but was derived from locomotives recently put into service by the Southern Railway, nor were the locomotives built in any of the company's own works, but by North British Locomotive Co. in Glasgow. The first, no. 6100 *Royal Scot*, was delivered in July 1927;[36] the company's own long-established 10.00 a.m. express from Euston to Glasgow and Edinburgh was given the name 'Royal Scot' at about the same time. At the annual meeting in February 1928 Sir Josiah Stamp happily informed shareholders that by using these powerful and economical locomotives, and changing engines only at Carlisle, the up and down Glasgow trains were being worked by three locomotives in place of the eight used formerly.

Until the previous September, the train had been double-headed, with engines changed at Carnforth. The run to Carlisle, non-stop, was for reasons of economic working, Stamp pointed out. That it was the world's record daily non-stop run was only incidental.[37] Maybe, but the LMS publicity people seem to have made sure that everyone had heard of it. The LNER determined to do better. There was no question of accelerating the trains: the agreement that London to Edinburgh, whether by East Coast or West, should take eight and a quarter hours still held. The LNER determined that from the start of its summer timetable, the 'Flying Scotsman' would run non-stop from King's Cross to Waverley, 392.9 miles; some of Gresley's Pacifics were equipped with tenders fitted with corridors to link footplate with train, so that engine crews could change over mid-way.[38]

To this the LMS had no long-term answer, for the down 'Royal Scot' called at Symington to be divided, one part going to Glasgow, the other to Edinburgh. But on 27 April, four days before the 'Flying Scotsman' was due to start its regular non-stop run, the LMS grabbed the limelight: for that day only, the down 'Royal Scot' was run in two parts throughout. Royal Scot class no. 6113 took one part non-stop to Glasgow, 401.4 miles; and, perhaps even more remarkable, the six coaches of the Edinburgh portion were taken to Edinburgh Princes Street, 399.7 miles, non-stop by a compound 4-4-0. Cecil J. Allen, noted pundit on locomotive performance, described this event as 'sly humour' on the part of the LMS – but then, he was himself an LNER man![39]

The LNER's non-stop journey was indeed lengthy. Since it was no quicker than the journey by stopping train, one may speculate why it was introduced at all. Perhaps, since it would scarcely have been practicable before the grouping, it may have been viewed as a convincing demonstration of the fact of amalgamation, of operation of the route by a single company throughout. At any rate to minimise possible tedium, new and luxurious restaurant cars were provided, decorated in Louis Quatorze style; a travelling newsboy offered papers and magazines, and in subsequent years a hairdresser and a cocktail bar were added.[40]

On the North British Railway, trains were equipped with destination boards mounted on the front of the locomotive, their shape curved to match the upper part of the smokebox. For the locomotive of the first non-stop train to London, Haymarket shed provided such a board, but lettered it 'Flying Scotsman'. The idea was quickly copied by King's Cross. It was soon used for other named trains also. Thus originated headboards for named trains, of the type which became familiar throughout Britain[41] and indeed outlasted steam itself into the diesel era, by which time of course the curved shape had become irrelevant.

The late 1920s were the period when names which would soon become familiar were given to many expresses. In 1927 the long-established 'Corridor' became the 'Mid-day Scot', and the overnight LMS express for Aberdeen and Inverness became the 'Royal Highlander'; the daytime trains from St Pancras to Edinburgh and Glasgow became the 'Thames–Forth Express' and the 'Thames–Clyde Express' respectively. On the LNER the overnight train from King's Cross to Aberdeen became the 'Aberdonian' in 1927; it included portions for Perth, Inverness and Fort William. In 1928 the 'Queen of Scots' was established as an all-Pullman daytime train from King's Cross via Leeds and Harrogate to Edinburgh and Glasgow.[42]

Since 1923 one of sleeping cars in the Aberdeen

portion of the overnight train from King's Cross had been worked forward over the former GNSR to Craigellachie, Elgin and Lossiemouth: the LNER's most northerly extremity. This was a service which would continue until 1939.[43] Until 1928, sleeping cars were for first-class passengers only; in September of that year, third-class sleeping cars were introduced simultaneously by the three railways out of the Big Four that operated sleeping cars – LMS, LNER and Great Western. They were then included in trains between London and Scotland; the internal Scottish sleeping car service, between Glasgow and Inverness, had to wait until 1932. There were four berths in each compartment, and rugs and pillows only were provided, rather than full bedding: but overnight third-class passengers could at last lie down.[44]

Sunday trains gradually appeared, or reappeared, on the former Highland and GNS systems. The LNER started to run restaurant cars, and year-round sleeping cars, over the West Highland line in 1929. The LMS had initially expanded operation of Pullman dining cars in Scotland, but in 1934 on expiry of the contract it bought them and ran them itself.[45] They continued to be a feature of travel in Scotland for many years: some survived into the British Railways era, when their interiors brought a touch of fading opulence to travel on the Far North line.[46]

The 1920s saw construction of one of the most extensive narrow gauge industrial railways in Scotland, the British Aluminium Co. Ltd's Lochaber Narrow Gauge Railway. By 1920 the company's works at Foyers and Kinlochleven were unable to meet increased demand for aluminium, and a new and larger works was planned at Fort William, with its own hydroelectric plant. This required a fifteen-mile tunnel to bring water from Loch Treig. To aid construction, two connected 3 ft gauge temporary railways were built. One, the Pier Railway, ran for about one and three-quarter miles from a pier on Loch Linnhe to the base camp, close to which the factory was built. The other, the Upper Works Railway, ran inland following approximately the intended course of the tunnel with its eleven intermediate access points – headings or shafts – from which it was to be driven. Both railways were lightly built, but here at last some of the war surplus equipment, which had so impressed the Rural Transport Committee, was put to good use. Contractor Balfour Beatty purchased six of the 4-6-0 tank locomotives, which had been built by Hunslet Engine Co.: they went back to the maker for conversion to 3 ft gauge.

These railways carried the materials, men and supplies essential for construction of the aluminium works and its associated hydroelectric scheme; aluminium was first produced in 1929. The Pier Railway was then replaced by a permanent line, substantially built but still of 3 ft gauge, steam worked. It carried materials between pier and factory. Inland, after a period of indecision, it was decided to retain the Upper Works Railway, despite its light construction and several miles of 1 in 30 gradient, for access when tunnel maintenance was needed. Motive power was internal combustion locomotives, and 'speeders', or motor trolleys. The total length of the permanent railway was about twenty-one miles, plus branches.[47]

First World War light railway technology was also used in the 1920s to give access to grouse moors – this was long before the days of four-wheel drive motor vehicles. One such line, on Dalmunzie estate, Glenshee, was of 2 ft 6 in. gauge; another, the Duchal Moor or Hardridge Grouse Railway, near Kilmacolm, was of 2 ft gauge. Both used 'Simplex' internal combustion

locomotives of the type developed for First World War light railways.[48] The Dalmunzie line continued in use for many years after the 'big house' became a hotel; a remarkable outbuilding combined the functions of garage, game larder and engine shed.

Cable haulage on the Glasgow District Subway was eventually replaced by electric traction in 1935, although the original cars, suitably modified, were retained.[49] The same year saw the construction of Kerr's Miniature Railway, which would become an enduring feature of West Links Park, Arbroath, adjoining – and contrasting with – the East Coast main line. Originally of 7¼ in. gauge, it was rebuilt to 10¼ in. gauge in 1938.[50]

So far, all this sounds very positive. But, particularly on the main railway system of Scotland, it was being achieved against a background of great and unprecedented problems. It is debatable for a start whether the grouping, both in principle and in the actual arrangements, was really capable of achieving its objectives of regulated regional monopolies allied to the economies of scale. It was one thing for management and men of competing independent companies to work together, under government direction, at a time of national emergency. It was quite another to expect them to bed down together in an amalgamated concern where one or other of the constituents must eventually predominate, or at least appear to do so. But in any case in Scotland it was only on those routes formerly served by both Caledonian and Glasgow & South Western Railways that this situation actually arose: and that meant between Glasgow and the Clyde Coast, and between Glasgow and Carlisle. Elsewhere two companies – now the LMS and the LNER – both continued to have two routes each between Edinburgh and Glasgow, and throughout the Central Belt there continued to be a mesh of competing lines. The route between Aberdeen and Inverness continued to be divided between two companies. Indeed new problems arose: the route between Edinburgh and London St Pancras continued to be divided between two companies, but these were no longer natural allies: they now competed for traffic between Edinburgh and London over routes which they owned throughout.

One cannot help but wonder what the effect would have been if the principle of amalgamating Scottish companies end-on with English ones had been accepted early in the legislative process which led up to the grouping, rather than at the last minute when it was grafted onto a pattern of amalgamation for English companies which was already accepted. The overall pattern might then have been very different. It is possible to visualise the Midland staying independent of the London & North Western, but amalgamating with both the Glasgow & South Western and the North British (over which the amalgamated Great Northern and North Eastern companies would have inherited the North Eastern's running powers to Edinburgh), while the LNWR could have amalgamated with the Caledonian, the Highland and the Great North as well. But rewriting history can lead to unlimited speculation!

As for regulation of rates and fares, it is a truism that the straitjacket of regulation, appropriate to monopoly, was imposed on the railway companies just at the moment when that monopoly was ceasing to exist, with the rapid rise of other forms of transport.[51] But for the LMS and the LNER, there appeared at first to be greater difficulty: after a brief post-war boom came the general depression of trade. Coal traffic was scarcely affected by road competition, but throughout the LNER for example the tonnage of coal carried, 102

million tons in 1923, was down to 87 million tons in 1925 and the trend continued.[52]

The position was exacerbated by the General Strike of 1926. This was called by the Trades Union Congress in support of coal miners who were facing cuts in wages and losses of jobs. There was no specific railway issue; but most railwaymen responded. The strike started on 4 May and normal train services ceased. Through the efforts of volunteers, ranging from university undergraduates to retired railwaymen, and those railwaymen who continued to work, a very limited train service replaced them, only two passenger trains each way daily between Edinburgh and Dundee for instance. But the service was steadily increased, day by day. Stones were thrown at strike-breaking engine crews, and in Northumberland an Edinburgh–London train was derailed by striking miners, but in general on the railways the strike was not violent, and after ten days a settlement was reached.[53]

The railways' troubles were far from over, however, for the miners' strike continued for many months more. Not only was the usual coal traffic missing, but imported soft coal proved less than adequate as locomotive fuel; some locomotives were converted to burn oil. Train services were still dislocated in the autumn.[54]

On the LNER at this period there were cuts in staff, locomotives placed in reserve, wagons left unrepaired. In 1928 all staff from directors down took a temporary cut of 2½ per cent in salaries and wages, which was to persist for two years.[55] On the LMS Sir Josiah Stamp told shareholders at the annual meeting in March 1929 that the reasons for loss of freight train revenue were bad trade and road competition, with the emphasis on the former. In 1932 he illustrated the position vividly by pointing out that of the 241 blast furnaces on the

LMS system (and it may be taken that Scotland was the location for a substantial proportion of these) only 41 were then at work. The following year the figures were down to 216 and 32.[56]

None of the Big Four railway companies had come near to achieving its intended standard revenue. As Stamp remarked in 1929, the economies arising from amalgamation were being offset by reduced rates and charges, and by loss of traffic.[57] The LMS and the LNER, serving the heavy industries of Scotland and the north of England, came off worst. In 1934 the shortfall from standard revenue on the LMS was 42.07 per cent; on the LNER, as much as 44.97 per cent.[58]

Then, at last, trade started to recover. But there was another threat. While the railway companies had been preoccupied by reorganisation, new regimes for wages and charges, and the Depression, motor road transport had been establishing itself. The total of motor vehicles in use throughout Britain increased from 229,428 in 1918 to 845,799 in 1921, 2,181,832 in 1929 and 3,084,896 in 1938.[59] Roads were improved. Many country roads were surfaced with tarmacadam for the first time. During the 1920s motor roads were built between Edinburgh and Glasgow, and over Rannoch Moor on the route from Glasgow to Fort William; the road between Perth and Inverness was reconstructed. Less was done during the 1930s, but in 1936 the Ministry of Transport became the highway authority with direct responsibility for through trunk routes, of which there were 1,948 miles in Scotland.[60]

Before the First World War, motoring had been the province of the wealthy. In the 1920s mass-produced motor cars brought motoring to the middle classes. They embraced it enthusiastically.[61] When R.D. Stephen's father, a minister, took the family on holiday to Strathpeffer in 1925, they went, for the first time, by car: notwithstanding, much of the holiday seems to have been spent observing railway operations around Strathpeffer and Dingwall![62]

The rapid growth after the First World War of motor road transport for freight continued into the 1920s. Not only were road hauliers' costs low, but whereas railway rates were based largely on the value of the commodity concerned (a practice derived originally from the manner in which turnpike road tolls were levied), road hauliers charged according to the service provided. This gave road transport an additional edge with valuable goods. It was also more flexible in terms of points of collection and delivery, without trans-shipment. This made it particularly attractive to agriculture. Road transport was unregulated: railways were obliged to carry whatever goods were offered, and not to discriminate unduly between customers. Railways responded to the challenge of the road by lowering rates, and by taking over some of the largest road hauliers such as Pickfords, which was acquired jointly by the Big Four railways. But road transport was in general the province of the small firm, and of businesses operating their own delivery vehicles.[63] Railways also started to mechanise their own cartage services for collection and delivery of goods and parcels to and from stations. The old-established Scottish cartage contractor Wordie & Co. Ltd became half-owned by the LMS.

Motor-bus services expanded greatly during the 1920s. For short journeys, urban and rural alike, they offered flexibility and convenience that the railway could not match. Nor, in many cases, could electric tramways, with their services confined to expensive-to-maintain tracks. Many small tramway systems closed between the wars; only the largest city systems remained.

To combat road competition in the 1930s, use of road-rail containers was greatly increased. Here punnets of raspberries are being loaded into an insulated container. It is already mounted on a flat wagon but doubtless at the end of its rail journey will be transferred to a road vehicle for onward carriage to fruit market. The wagon is fitted with continuous brakes so can travel at passenger train speeds. Outside the soft fruit season containers of this type were used for frozen and chilled meat. (National Archives of Scotland, BR/LMS/5/128 – Science and Society Picture Library)

In 1928 the railway companies obtained, by Act of Parliament, general powers to operate passenger, parcels and merchandise services by road. It was in the aftermath of this, in 1933, that they acquired road hauliers as mentioned above. More extensively, they acquired shareholdings in bus operators throughout Britain, but never more than a 50 per cent holding. In 1929 the LMS and the LNER each acquired a 25 per cent shareholding in Scottish Motor Traction Co. Ltd which had built up a network of subsidiaries operating bus services throughout much of Scotland south of Inverness. Bus services in the north-east, which the LNER had inherited from the Great North of Scotland Railway and had recently expanded, were handed over to SMT subsidiary W. Alexander & Sons Ltd in 1930–1.[64] In 1930 the LMS acquired a 50 per cent interest in Highland Transport Co. Ltd., operating buses north of Inverness; it had already in 1928 acquired a similar interest in David MacBrayne Ltd, the noted west-coast shipping line which had since 1906 been building up, on land, a network of bus routes in the area it served. So, except in the largest cities where there were municipal bus services, bus transport throughout Scotland came very much under the influence of the railway companies, but not under their control.[65]

Under the Road Traffic Act 1930, bus services were regulated: they were required to have road service licences to which existing operators, road or rail, could object.[66] The Road & Rail Traffic Act 1933 applied similar regulation to road haulage of freight. Owners of vehicles needed carriers' licences, which distinguished between vehicles used for carrying the owner's own goods ('C' licences), and those used for hire and reward ('A' licences – there was also an intermediate 'B' licence). 'A' licences were issued only where existing transport facilities appeared inadequate.[67]

This was all very well from the railways' point of view, but it left unaltered the road hauliers' ability to undercut railways' regulated rates and charges. There were occasional moves towards regulation of road rates, but in 1938, their freight traffic rapidly ebbing away, the railway companies went on to the opposite tack. In a memorandum to the Minister of Transport, the Railway Companies' Association submitted that

(A) The existing statutory regulation of the charges for the conveyance of merchandise traffic by railway, together with the requirements attached thereto, including such matters as classification, publication and undue preference, should be repealed.

(B) The railways, exactly like other forms of transport, should be permitted to decide the charges and conditions for the conveyance of merchandise which they are required to carry.

Future regulation should be applied to all forms of transport, it added; the railways were not asking for preferential treatment or protection.[68]

This was the railways' campaign for 'A Square Deal'. Such a fundamental change attracted much public interest, not least from road haulage, which pilloried the railways' action as the 'Square Wheel' campaign. By mid-1939, however, the principle had been accepted by the government. Then came the Second World War, and the opportunity for legislation was lost.[69]

Meanwhile, for car owners who nevertheless were unenthusiastic about very long journeys, the railway companies offered special rates for carrying motor cars in covered trucks by passenger train, provided one first-class or two third-class passengers were making the same journey. The rate in 1937 was 3d. per mile for an outward journey, 1½d. a mile for the return, 50 miles minimum. From London, Scotland was a popular destination.[70] Such services had been known in special circumstances for years. The Caledonian Railway had carried cars by rail over Connel Ferry bridge in the 1900s before converting the bridge for rail/road use.[71] On the Highland Railway, and latterly the LMS, cars could be carried by rail to Kyle of Lochalsh from Strathcarron or even Garve.[72] At that period Kyle could otherwise be approached by road only by means of ferries at Strome or Dornie.

Though the coming of the internal combustion engine had rejuvenated road transport and turned it into a formidable competitor, it had also produced a competitor of a different sort: the aeroplane. The landing of Louis Blériot at Dover in 1909, having flown from Calais, suggested that the aeroplane was a machine of great potential as a means of transport,

The railway companies were pioneers of air transport and formed Railway Air Services to operate flights on their behalf. Here preparations are made for an RAS flight to Scotland at Croydon aerodrome on 29 November 1934. Passengers could buy tickets at railway stations and send heavy luggage in advance by train. (National Railway Museum)

rather than a mere novelty. Certainly there was a great deal of interest in aircraft: when an international aviation meeting was held at Lanark racecourse in 1910, 200,000 people attended and the Caledonian Railway had to double its single-track branch to Lanark in order to cope.[73] During the 1920s there were many attempts to start commercial air routes both internationally and within Britain, but none as yet was wholly successful. Aircraft were still small, unreliable, and slow, and navigation was in its infancy. Pilots navigated by following features on the ground, such as railway lines – which could lead to the embarrassing situation that, when an aeroplane was battling into a strong head wind, it might be overtaken by the trains below.[74] The railway companies, however, took these pioneering efforts seriously enough to obtain powers, in 1929, to operate air services themselves.

A curious diversion from the true path of progress was the Bennie Railplane, a suspended monorail car powered by propellers driven by electric motors. Inventor George Bennie of Glasgow sought to combine aircraft and rail technology, by building a network of monorails above existing railways and roads to provide high-speed, comfortable passenger travel unaffected by weather conditions. He described his railplane as a guided airship. There were other comparable proposals, but Bennie's was the only one to take physical form, with a railplane running

LUXURIOUS NEW STEAMER
"JEANIE DEANS"

SAILINGS ON WEEK DAYS

7-36 a.m. Craigendoran to Dunoon.

8-15 a.m. Dunoon to Kirn, Kilcreggan and Craigendoran.

*10-10 a.m. Craigendoran to Dunoon, Kirn, Blairmore, Lochgoilhead and Arrochar.

*2-10 p.m. Arrochar to Lochgoilhead, Blairmore, Kilcreggan and Craigendoran.

4-35 p.m. Craigendoran to (Kilcreggan Sats. only), Kirn, Dunoon, Innellan, Craigmore and Rothesay.

6-20 p.m. Rothesay to Craigmore, Innellan, Dunoon, Kirn, Kilcreggan and Craigendoran.

* FAMOUS THREE LOCHS TOUR
(Loch Goil, Loch Long and Loch Lomond)

Passengers on this tour travel between Craigendoran and Arrochar or Arrochar and Craigendoran by the Steamer " Jeanie Deans."

FAST CONNECTING TRAINS WITH THE ABOVE SERVICES
From and to Edinburgh (Wav. and H'mkt), Linlithgow and Falkirk (High)

SPECIAL SUNDAY CRUISES
FROM CRAIGENDORAN
TO

12th July, 30th August. **BRODICK BAY, ARRAN,** via Kyles of Bute and back via Garroch Head.

19th July, 23rd August. **TARBERT, LOCH FYNE,** via Kyles of Bute in both directions.

26th July. **CATACOL BAY, ARRAN,** via Kyles of Bute and back via Garroch Head.

2nd August. **LOCHGOILHEAD.**

9th August. **ROUND BUTE AND CUMBRAES,** via Largs Channel and back via Kyles of Bute.

16th August. **LADY ISLE (TROON),** returning via Largs Channel.

6th September. **ARROCHAR.**

13th September. **LOCH STRIVEN, ORMIDALE AND ROUND BUTE.**

TRAIN AND STEAMER TIMES AND RETURN FARES			
	LEAVE a.m.	ARRIVE BACK p.m. p.m.	FARE s. D.
EDINBURGH (Waverley) ...	7 40	10†31 or 10 47	11 0
LINLITHGOW	8 5	10† 8	9 6
FALKIRK (High)	8 17	9†57 or 10 17	8 6

† One hour earlier from 26th July.

For Conditions of Issue of Tickets, see over.

LONDON & NORTH EASTERN RAILWAY

July 1931.   (10-M)   (S.C. 21501)

Hugh Paton & Sons, Ltd., Printers, Edinburgh.

Railway steamers continued to be popular in the 1930s, for both business travel and pleasure cruises. (Robert Forsythe Collection)

on, or rather beneath, a test track carried on a girder construction over sidings near the LNER's Milngavie station. The car was built by William Beardmore & Co. Ltd of Dalmuir, whose other products included locomotives and airships. The test line was completed in 1930, attracting much attention, and for several months the public rode in the car, up and down its short line. Sadly Bennie was unable to attract sufficient commercial interest for a full-scale line to be built and eventually went bankrupt; the eye-catching Milngavie trial line remained in existence until the mid-1950s.[75]

In any event, Bennie had been working on his proposals since the early 1920s, but by the 1930s aircraft technology had advanced far enough for commercial airlines to become a practical reality. Although not perhaps a fully economic one: passenger aircraft were still small, and companies to operate them mushroomed only to face constant reorganisation or failure. The first scheduled air services in Scotland started in 1933. Against this background, the Big Four railway companies jointly, and with Imperial Airways as a fifth partner, formed Railway Air Services Ltd in 1934. It was to operate air services on behalf of the railway company of the relevant area, and at its financial responsibility.[76]

Aircraft speeds were such that a worthwhile saving in journey times, compared with surface transport, could be shown only where a sea crossing was involved. The LNER considered an air service over the route London–Norwich–Hull–Newcastle–Edinburgh–Aberdeen, but decided against; alone of the Big Four, it then took no further direct part in developing air services. So the first Railway Air Services route to serve Scotland was established on behalf of the LMS, and the actual route was Glasgow–Belfast–Manchester–Birmingham–London: or, to be precise in terms of airfields, Renfrew–

Aldergrove–Barton–Castle Bromwich–Croydon.[77] Then as now, access to airfields, inevitably out-of-town, was a problem. The service, once every weekday in each direction, carried passengers and mails: inland airmail services were started experimentally at this time. The following year RAS took delivery of the first of its de Havilland Dragon Rapide aircraft with which it was to be closely associated.

As well as establishing Railway Air Services, the railway companies followed a policy similar to their policy towards road transport, that is, by investing substantially in other operators. The LMS in particular took a 40 per cent stake in Scottish Airways Ltd, which was formed in 1937 from two earlier Scottish airlines and operated to the Western and Northern Isles and elsewhere.[78] Routes continued to fluctuate frequently, both those of an individual operator, and between operators severally. But, as a poster reminded potential air travellers, the railway-associated airlines offered not only 'multi-engined aircraft' and the 'latest two-way radio' but also 'Air-Rail-Steamer ticket interavailability; Luggage in advance by Rail at low rates; Railway Bulk Travel Vouchers accepted; Seat Reservations may be made and Air Tickets obtained at any Railway Station or Agency'.[79] 'Passenger's Luggage in Advance' was the scheme, familiar to rail travellers, by which heavy luggage (such as school trunks, in the author's recollection) could be sent on ahead; 'Bulk Travel Vouchers' were available to commercial firms so that their representatives, who travelled widely, could do so at cheap rates. Taken all in all those last four inducements seem indeed to provide food for thought to those concerned with integration of transport at the present day.

Back on the ground, the inevitable consequence of the growth of bus services was closure of rural railways and stations. Railway closures were not new. For instance the Solway Viaduct, defective and no longer needed for iron ore traffic, had been closed in 1921.[80] The Campbeltown & Machrihanish Railway lost its coal traffic with the closure of the colliery in 1929, and contemporaneously lost most of its passenger traffic to buses: it closed in 1931.[81] By then the LMS, confident that its newly established interests in the bus industry gave it the power to coordinate bus and train, had already started on a programme of wholesale closures of branch lines.[82] Among those in Scotland closed to passengers in 1930 were branches to Denny, Bonnybridge, Kilbirnie, Newhouse, Hopeman and Fochabers:[83] none of them long, but a foretaste of the future. On the LNER, the branch lines to Old Meldrum, Boddam and Fort Augustus were closed to passengers in 1931, 1932 and 1933 respectively.[84]

Another option open to the railways in these difficult times was to reduce working expenses. To this end the LNER had purchased some eighty-five self-propelled steam railcars during 1925–8; some of these came to Scotland where they were used on the Aberfoyle branch and on the Aberdeen suburban services. There, regrettably, they were insufficient to forestall withdrawal of these services in 1937. The LMS used similar steam railcars on some branch lines in Scotland, such as that to Wanlockhead.

Of more lasting significance the LMS, seeking to reduce the costs of shunting in marshalling yards in the early 1930s, hit on the possibilities of diesel-electric and diesel-hydraulic shunting locomotives. Trials confirmed the economies likely to arise from locomotives that required a crew of one man instead of two and demanded little time for servicing: from this originated the first large-scale use of diesel locomotives in Britain.[85] Meanwhile that railway's programme of standardisation of steam locomotives was proceeding apace, and given a substantial boost by the arrival in 1932 of William Stanier as chief mechanical engineer. He came from the Great Western Railway, which had had a stud of powerful standard locomotives for decades, with a mission to equip the LMS similarly.[86] He was to succeed handsomely. A minor piece of standardisation, which was nevertheless readily apparent, was his adoption as standard of the deep-toned locomotive whistle of the Caledonian, which in due course came to be heard throughout the LMS system from Thurso to Bournemouth.

A 'Chief Officer for Scotland' was appointed by the LMS in 1932 as a stage in the devolution (sic) of commercial management in order to obtain close local contact with the public.[87] The Scottish Local Committee continued to function.

Measures were taken to retain freight traffic and to recover it from the roads. On both LMS and LNER, more and more wagons were being fitted with continuous brakes, which enabled goods trains to be accelerated.[88] Shock-absorbing wagons were built to carry fragile goods.[89] The 'Green Arrow' service introduced in 1928 enabled consignments to be registered and tracked.[90] Freight containers, dismountable bodies which could be transferred between road vehicle and rail wagon for door-to-door transit, had been known since the earliest days of steam railways; now they were introduced in quantity, increasing from 350 to 15,500, throughout Britain, between 1928 and 1938.[91]

On the water, the LMS in 1928 acquired a half-share in David MacBrayne Ltd, as mentioned in connection with that company's bus services. The other partner was Coast Lines Ltd. Two Clyde shipping operators were taken over by the LMS in 1935 – Williamson–Buchanan Steamers Ltd and Turbine Steamers Ltd;

the latter's two ships were transferred to MacBrayne.[92] The 1930s were a great period for excursions by train, in which the steamer services played their part. A 'day excursion' from Euston to Staffa and Iona in 1935 meant that excursionists travelled overnight to Oban, spent the day on their sea voyage and returned south the following night. Earlier, in 1932, the LMS had offered a midsummer overnight excursion from Glasgow to Wick and Thurso, which included restaurant and sleeping cars, and special buses to John o' Groats. There were many less ambitious Sunday excursions from Glasgow and Edinburgh. The first Sunday excursionists to arrive in Fort William were nonetheless greeted by closed shops and houses with drawn blinds.[93]

The ultimate excursion train however was the 'Northern Belle', the luxury touring train of the LNER, which made its first journey over eight days in summer 1933. Originating at King's Cross, its 4,000-mile itinerary included Edinburgh, Aberdeen, Glasgow, Mallaig and Edinburgh–Newcastle via the Waverley Route and Riccarton Junction. The train's fifteen vehicles included restaurant cars and sleeping cars; over the West Highland line it was divided into day and night portions. Tourists' itinerary included cruises on Loch Lomond and the Firth of Clyde. On the return from Mallaig the train halted for ten minutes on Glenfinnan Viaduct for tourists to enjoy the view and, if a photograph which appeared in an illustrated paper is to be believed, they were able to descend from the train and walk about on the track. The tour was a great success and was repeated about three times a year until the Second World War.[94]

In 1932, at last, came relaxation of the long-standing agreement that the journey time between London and Edinburgh should take at least eight and

"THE CORONATION"
DESIGNED BY SIR NIGEL GRESLEY CHIEF MECHANICAL ENGINEER L·N·E·R IN HONOUR OF THE CORONATION OF KING GEORGE VI 1937
KING'S CROSS - EDINBURGH IN 6 HOURS
LONDON AND NORTH EASTERN RAILWAY

The LNER publicises 'The Coronation' express. The six-hour schedule allowed for the first time a late afternoon departure from London with arrival in Edinburgh the same night. For a train which bystanders saw rushing towards them out of the dusk, the muted colours of the poster seem wholly appropriate.
(NRM – Pictorial Collection / Science & Society Picture Library)

Publicity brochure for 'The Coronation' express of 1937, King's Cross to Edinburgh. Despite the claim, it was not Britain's first streamlined train – the wording has perhaps been transferred unaltered from publicity material for the 'Silver Jubilee' of two years before.
(McEwan Collection, East Dunbartonshire Information & Archives)

a quarter hours. There followed, over the next five or six years, a series of successive accelerations by each route, East Coast and West, which resulted not only in a marked reduction of the journey time, but also in the world speed record for steam trains. But this was not the uncontrolled 'racing' of the late Victorian era:

the LNER and the LMS kept each other informed of plans.

When the non-stop 'Flying Scotsman' reappeared that summer, its schedule had come down from eight and a quarter hours to seven and a half hours, and further accelerations followed.[95] The next big step was made south of the Border. It was evident to the LNER that a high-speed train from Newcastle to London in the morning, and back again in the evening, would meet a demand from businessmen to be able do a day's work in London without spending a night away from home. The train took shape in 1935 as the 'Silver Jubilee' express, named to mark the celebrations for the jubilee of King George V. Gresley provided his latest Pacific locomotives of the A4 class, streamlined with the wedge-shaped front which would become famous: it was of value in reducing wind resistance, but its publicity value was probably greater, particularly when the entire train, specially built, was coloured silver too. On trial the train ran at 100 mph or more for thirty miles on end; once put into service it proved extremely popular with a four-hour schedule between Newcastle and London – which meant running at over 90 mph on a daily basis.[96]

Even at these speeds, there was no prospect of a day return service between Edinburgh and London. What might be done, however, was an evening train service between the two cities, offering businessmen departures much later in the day than anything known hitherto. This was achieved in 1937: the train, named 'Coronation' as part of celebrations for the coronation of King George VI, again comprised a streamlined A4 locomotive and specially built coaches, and when it went into service that July it reduced the journey time, so recently standing at eight and a quarter hours, to no more than six. Departure times were 4.30 p.m. from Waverley, 4.00 p.m. from King's Cross.[97]

It was with a set of coaches from the 'Coronation' that in 1938 the A4 *Mallard* which incorporated all the refinements resulting from sixteen years of development work – and ostensibly during trials of

quick-acting brakes – achieved the world speed record for steam traction, unbroken and now unlikely to be broken, of 126 mph.[98]

Meanwhile, what had been happening on the LMS? In 1933 Stanier provided it with its first Pacific locomotives – two only, initially, *The Princess Royal* and *Princess Elizabeth* – with their design owing much to the Great Western's latest express locomotives, the King class. But those were 4-6-0s; on Stanier's 4-6-2s the wheel arrangement allowed a longer boiler and a wider firebox which meant in turn they had the capacity to produce steam, without clogging their grates with ash, to enable them to run the entire 401-mile journey from Euston to Glasgow on a regular basis[99] – the first locomotives to be able to do so. At the annual meeting of the LMS in February 1934 the chairman proudly told shareholders that the two locomotives, between them, were hauling the up and down 'Royal Scot' trains every day: work which had required three locomotives of the Royal Scot class.[100] A further batch of Pacifics, with improvements, was built in 1935, and the original pair were improved too. In November 1936 *Princess Elizabeth* took a 225-ton test train from Euston to Glasgow in less than six hours, averaging 68.2 mph. On the return journey the following day she averaged over 70 mph. In between there had been engineering heroics through the night at St Rollox Works to make good a defect that had appeared during the down journey.[101]

A high-speed train service between Euston and Glasgow materialised the following summer as the 'Coronation Scot'. Pacific locomotives of the Princess Coronation, or Duchess, class, were provided – streamlined, but to a rather more bulbous outline than the A4s – and new coaches to match. On a demonstration run 114 mph was achieved, which

The up 'Coronation Scot' of the LMS approaches Beattock summit behind no. 6222 *Queen Mary*. Maybe photographer M. W. Earley underestimated its speed and intended to arrive in time for a closer shot; whether he did or not, he has left us a fine view of the train hurrying through the countryside, just as it appeared to every lineside picnicker and ploughboy. The date is 24 July 1939: within a few weeks the Second World War will break out, and the brief but glorious era of high-speed streamlined steam trains will come to an end. (National Railway Museum)

remained a record until trounced by the LNER a year later.[102] A late-afternoon departure time was considered, but found to cause too much dislocation to existing train services, and the traditional early-afternoon departure was retained.[103] The 'Coronation Scot' was scheduled to depart at 1.30 p.m. and take six and a half hours for its journey.

The 'Coronation Scot' and the 'Coronation' both started to run on the same day, 5 July 1937. Both trains were painted blue. The 'Coronation Scot' was in Prussian blue; silver stripes rose in curves from a point low down on the front of the locomotive, to run in parallel back along the sides of entire train. The eight coaches included two kitchen cars to serve both first- and third-class passengers at their seats; interior decoration was 1930s-modern, and all passenger coaches had forced ventilation. The 'Coronation' must have

been even more striking: locomotive in Garter blue, coaches in Garter blue below, paler blue above. Here too were two kitchens and meals at seats. The coaches were air-conditioned. At the rear in summer was the observation car, with flattened 'beaver tail' to match the locomotive; in winter, when most of the journey was after dark, it was omitted. Internally, the style was no longer derivative: gone was Louis Quatorze, and in its place Art Deco flourished.[104] A contemporary account described the train as 'luxurious as a super-cinema, efficient as a Dreadnought'.[105]

The late 1930s saw many other train services improved. Trains between the North of England and Scotland were accelerated. Within Scotland, the LMS in 1937 accelerated its best trains between Glasgow and Aberdeen to take no more than 3 hours for the 153 miles.[106] Railways were still essential for distribution of mails. The 'West Coast Postal' from London to Scotland was celebrated by W.H. Auden in his noted poem 'Night Mail', written for the General Post Office documentary film of the same name which was made in 1936. To this author, the poem has the most banal of opening couplets: 'This is the Night Mail crossing the border/Bringing the cheque and the postal order' – but the poet redeems himself a few lines later when he describes the locomotive 'Shovelling white steam over her shoulder'. What more apt description could there be of successive exhaust beats from a steam locomotive at speed?[107]

In all this, the streamlined trains of the late 1930s seem to symbolise a railway system emerging from grimy depression into shining optimism. Regrettably, on a wider scale, no such optimism was justified: on 3 September 1939 the Second World War broke out.

It came as no surprise. Railways had been making their preparations, and so had the government. Two days before the actual outbreak of war the government took control of the railway companies, as in the First World War. To run them, a new Railway Executive Committee appeared; revenues were to be pooled, and distributed in pre-war proportions. There were later modifications.[108] The first test of the new arrangements came straight away: aerial bombardment of cities was thought to be imminent, so children, teachers and expectant mothers were evacuated. In Scotland alone, over the three days 1–3 September, trains carried 178,543 evacuees.[109]

A few days later came drastic deterioration in passenger train frequencies and speeds, with withdrawal of restaurant cars and reduction in sleeping cars. Some of these restrictions were relaxed, during what appeared to be a phoney war, only to be reimposed when things became truly serious. The high-speed Anglo-Scottish trains were withdrawn, and passenger trains generally were much decelerated. The schedule for the 'Flying Scotsman' train, King's Cross to Waverley, was drawn out to 8 hrs 55 minutes.[110]

Train loads, on the other hand, were much increased. So flexible was the steam locomotive that A4 class Pacifics, designed to haul light trains at high speeds, proved themselves equally well able to haul huge loads: for example on 5 April 1940 when no. 2509 *Silver Link*, built five years before for the 'Silver Jubilee', left King's Cross on the 1.00 p.m. for Edinburgh with no fewer than twenty-five coaches.[111] On the West Coast route, according to Cecil J. Allen, one of the features of travel at this period was the queue of passengers that formed every morning at Glasgow Central for the 'Royal Scot': from the platform barrier it reached out of the front of the station, round the corner and for a hundred yards or so down Union Street.[112] Overnight, to carry all the passengers who needed to travel between Euston and Glasgow, three trains were provided, one of them reserved for service personnel. On the East Coast route, on the other hand, through coaches to and from stations on the former Highland Railway were withdrawn.

Through trains for naval personnel reappeared between Euston and Thurso.[113] When the Admiralty asked the LMS to provide catering on the leave trains between Perth and Thurso, the railway company brought out some of its Pullman cars from the sidings in which no doubt they had been languishing: but since no crews were available, it was arranged for them to be staffed by the Salvation Army. Buffet cars on military leave trains between Stranraer and London were staffed by the NAAFI.[114]

For mails, bag exchange apparatus was taken out of use, and from September 1940 no sorting was done on TPOs: the Euston–Aberdeen 'West Coast Postal' continued to run as a train of stowage vans.[115] On the freight side, LMS plans for high-speed freight trains between London and Glasgow had to be shelved.[116] But with the outbreak of war, private-owners' wagons were requisitioned – and there were about 577,000 of them, throughout Britain, belonging to some 4,000 different owners (historically, they represented a direct link with pre-steam railways regarded as public highways). They were pooled with railways' own wagons and an Inter-Company Freight Rolling Stock Control was established in 1941, with marked improvement in wagon utilisation. Private-owners' coal wagons, for instance, were returned to colliery districts loaded with goods.[117]

Domestic air services initially stopped on outbreak of war and aircraft were requisitioned, but in 1940, following agreement between the government and seven airline companies, which included Railway Air Services Ltd and Scottish Airways Ltd, the Associated Airways Joint Committee was set up. Routes considered to be of national importance restarted; all incorporated sea crossings.[118]

The St Enoch Hotel in Glasgow, where pre-war patrons had included the Duke of Windsor, Enrico Caruso and Jack Buchanan, was requisitioned by the Navy to become HMS *Spartiate*.[119] The Cruden Bay Hotel became an Army hospital. It did not reopen after the war, and was demolished.[120] Railway-owned ships were requisitioned too. The *Princess Maud* – its peacetime run was between Stranraer and Larne – was shelled during the Dunkirk evacuation, but was still able to bring troops home. Railway workshops were busy producing the needs of war; railwaymen struggled on despite the blackout.

So far as bomb damage was concerned, Scottish railways seem to have got off relatively lightly, at least compared with railways further south, although Greenock suffered. Lord Stamp, as Sir Josiah had become, was sadly killed by a direct hit on his home in 1941. Railwaymen joined the Home Guard, and sometimes found themselves on guard duty one night in six in addition to normal work. At least two Scottish Home Guard units had their own armoured – and armed – trains. One at Inverurie was built around a camouflaged 2-4-2 tank locomotive of Great Eastern Railway origin and a large Caledonian Railway double-bogie tender. There was another in the Edinburgh area.[121]

Even before the war, plans had been made for construction of two new ports, primarily for use in the event that Glasgow and/or Liverpool became crippled by bomb damage. These took shape as the military ports of Faslane, on the Gareloch with a rail connection to the West Highland line, and Cairnryan on Loch Ryan, served by a new branch line from Stranraer, nearly seven miles long and operated by the War Department. Cairnryan saw much use after the USA entered the war: ships bringing military equipment from America discharged their cargoes there as the invasion of Europe approached.[122] American service personnel were brought across the Atlantic on the *Queen Mary* and the *Queen Elizabeth*, and landed at Greenock. That meant that when one of these liners arrived, as many as thirty-six special trains were needed to carry its occupants further on their journey.[123]

Other special trains were provided for military commanders such as Montgomery and Eisenhower, often under conditions of extreme secrecy. McKillop records his experiences of them, as driver. On one occasion, secrecy was so good that as he approached a wayside station with a special bearing the Supreme

Commander of Allied Forces in Europe, he observed that the signalman, who evidently expected the daily pick-up goods, had the road set and signalled for the coal siding. He decided that this was the one occasion when he must ignore the standard instruction to obey all signals regardless, and drifted up to the station with the whistle blowing loud and long. Eventually the signalman got the message and took action: McKillop heard the slam of the points being reversed from a hundred yards away, and saw the signals jerked off more quickly than he had ever known.[124]

In general, railways were exceptionally busy during the Second World War. A few branch lines were closed nonetheless, during the war and its immediate aftermath: Dumfries to Moniaive to passengers in 1943, Wick to Lybster completely in 1944, Ellon to Boddam in 1945, Spean Bridge to Fort Augustus in 1946. Overall, the experience of railways during the Second World War was, as during the First, that of being overworked and under-maintained.[125]

Yet the war also provided an opportunity for people to take stock, to consider what sort of Britain was wanted at the war's end. Government thinking inclined towards close overall control of transport – the principles of the Square Deal campaign were no longer acceptable – perhaps even nationalisation, for which Labour ministers in the wartime coalition cabinet were pressing.[126] The railway companies marshalled their own varying ideas on the subject and in 1943 presented a memorandum to the Minister of War Transport *Post War Transport Proposals*. They urged that post-war changes should be directed solely to securing the most efficient and economical use of all forms of transport; to this end, so far as ownership was concerned, they favoured the status quo, with increased coordination with other forms of transport. They also made known

various proposals for developments within the railway industry, of which one in particular, in the present context, is worth quoting:

Consideration is being given to the possibility of formulating a scheme under which the whole of the railways in Scotland would be worked on a unified basis. Such an arrangement would probably be desirable for geographical and operating reasons …[127]

By the middle of 1945 attention was also being focused on the inequality of track costs borne by rail and road transport: notably that rail had not only to pay for track maintenance but also to pay interest on capital cost, while road transport, although it contributed to maintenance through licences and taxes, did not contribute towards capital cost of roads.

But to modern eyes the most striking of all proposals made by the railway companies at this period are those for air transport. These emerged in a memorandum to the government which they put forward in 1944. This revealed a comprehensive plan by the railway companies to set up, in conjunction with shipping companies, a new airline company which would serve not only the British Isles but also the Continent. Daily flights to destinations as far afield as Moscow, Istanbul, Lisbon and Iceland were envisaged; only the latter, however, seems likely to have had a direct flight from Scotland – a flight from London was to call at Glasgow and Stornoway en route. London was to become the great point of interchange for most other foreign destinations.[128]

Maybe other direct flights from Scotland would have followed, had these plans come to fruition. But these and other railway company proposals of the period – and they were many – were stillborn. With the war ending, the general election of July 1945 produced a Labour government with a landslide majority, and nationalisation of railway companies, among much else, became inevitable. Firm proposals 'to bring transport services ... under public ownership and control' were announced on 19 November.

There were as yet no details of the form that public ownership might take, while government control of the railways, through the Railway Executive Committee, continued and would continue until nationalisation became a fact a little over two years later.[129] Meanwhile, with the threat of change hanging over them, the railway companies were attempting to overcome the backlog of maintenance. In this they were not helped by continuing shortages of materials and men, while traffic remained heavy. The poor state of the track demanded innumerable speed restrictions, only gradually relieved. Restaurant cars started to reappear in the autumn of 1945 – between Glasgow and Aberdeen, for instance. So did travelling post offices. The streamlined expresses of the late 1930s did not, and it would be many years before train speeds in general recovered fully.

In the air, Railway Air Services resumed direct flights linking Glasgow and London in the summer of 1945 – the northern airport, at first Prestwick, was later Renfrew, and the southern, Croydon. The following summer, Douglas Dakota aircraft came into use, twenty-seaters with stewardesses to serve refreshments; by then there were four services daily between Glasgow and Belfast. But the air services were the first part of the railways' undertakings to be affected by nationalisation. The Civil Aviation Act 1946 established British European Airways as a state-owned corporation. At first, however, internal flights were provided by existing companies on behalf of BEA, and that November Railway Air Services and Scottish Airways started a jointly operated service from London Northolt to Glasgow and Aberdeen on this basis.

It was on 19 December 1946 that a Railway Air Services Dakota was involved in a most remarkable accident: taking off from Northolt for Renfrew during a heavy snowstorm, it failed to gain height despite every attempt, clipped the roofs of several houses and finally came to rest balanced on the damaged roof of a house in a suburban street, looking for all the world like a hen on her nest. The crew, however, and the sole passenger, were unhurt: they were able to lower themselves into what remained of the roof space of the house, walk down the stairs and out of the front door. The house was eventually repaired by its owner and renamed 'Dakota's Rest'.

In February 1947 the services, aircraft and staff of Railway Air Services and Scottish Airways were absorbed fully into BEA.[130] From that date on, administration and development of air services – within Scotland, within Britain, and to and from other countries – which might have gone forward in coordination with railways and other surface transport, became almost wholly divorced from them. It is a situation which is still far from being rectified. That is why so much space has been given to the subject here.

Nationalisation proposals for railways eventually gelled in the Transport Bill, introduced in November 1946. The simple option, that the government should acquire all the shares in the railway companies, or majority holdings, was evidently ignored: there seems to have been minimal contact between those drafting the bill and those with experience of running railways. The bill envisaged creation of a British Transport Commission with immense responsibilities: it was (in the words of Act as eventually passed) 'to provide, or secure or promote the provision of, an efficient, adequate, economical and properly integrated system of public inland transport within Great Britain for passengers and goods'. It would take over the railway and canal companies and private-owners' wagons (tank wagons for oil etc. were the sole exception[131]), acquire in due course long-distance road haulage companies, and exercise wide influence over passenger road transport, harbours and coastal shipping. To assist it in its task there were to be a series of 'executives', themselves public authorities; initially there were to be five, responsible respectively for railways, docks and inland waterways, road haulage, London Transport and hotels. The possibility of dividing the responsibilities of the executives by geographical area, that is, by transport need rather than transport mode, was apparently considered but (outside London) discarded. We are living with the consequences yet.

Publication of this radical and far-reaching measure seems to have galvanised the railway companies into an active campaign of opposition, in which they suddenly found themselves at one with the Road Haulage Association. The LNER, financially the least strong of the Big Four, put forward as an alternative a plan which it had formulated earlier, a 'halfway house' which would involve the railways in selling land, track, structures, stations etc. to the State, and leasing them back to operate train services. But opposition proved futile, apart perhaps from achieving slightly improved compensation for shareholders.[132]

During the bill's passage through Parliament, Scottish interests strongly urged devolution of authority for transport in Scotland. In this they appear to have achieved some limited success. South of the Border, the Railway Executive in due course divided railways up into regions based upon the old companies, but north of it the systems of both LNER and LMS were merged into a single Scottish Region.[133] Maybe the companies' own ideas on the subject also played some part.

The Transport Act received the Royal Assent in August 1947; vesting day was 1 January 1948.

Unlike the Grouping, the motives for nationalisation were primarily political. 'What if …?' in relation to historical events is seldom a question worthy of much consideration, but at this turning point in railway history it is worth pausing for a moment to consider what might have happened next if political considerations had not imposed nationalisation. The railway companies, acting in their own commercial interests, were already well on the way to transforming themselves into providers of transport by rail, road, water and air, and this multi-modal trend would doubtless have continued. In Scotland, railways would almost certainly have become a single undertaking, owned jointly by LMS and LNER. Their train services, for passengers, parcels and freight, would have been closely coordinated with the bus services, coastal ships, air services and road haulage services of associated companies. There would certainly have been some reduction in railway route mileage, as duplication of routes was reduced, and in some cases alternative modes found to answer better. Overall, travel throughout Scotland would have been easier.

One other thing is clear. The Big Four railway companies, whatever their shortcomings and handicaps, were, when acting together, an immensely influential pro-rail lobby with government. On nationalisation that lobby disappeared overnight, for those running the railways became subservient to the government, depending upon it for funding and for their very appointments. Railways and public are still the worse off for that.

When St Rollox staff and friends went on a works outing to Carlisle in 1899, fourteen special trains were needed, all hauled by Dunalastair 4-4-0 locomotives of the first and second versions. Here are some of them. No. 721 was the original *Dunalastair*, and designer J. F. McIntosh himself stands on the right. (National Railway Museum)

HOW RAILWAY EQUIPMENT HAD DEVELOPED

The previous five chapters have described the development of the railway system, and its train services, between the 1840s and the 1940s. In them something has been said of the development of locomotives, coaches and other railway equipment, but only to the extent that such developments had a direct influence on the development of train services. It is the exceptional that has been mentioned, rather than the typical. Before continuing it is desirable to say something of the typical although, if the chapter heading 'How railway equipment had developed' were posed as a question, the answer would be 'in many respects, surprisingly little'. In its equipment, the railway system that came into national ownership in 1948 had more in common with the railways of a century before than it did with those of the present day.

Locomotives for the early public railways were built, as mentioned in Chapter 2, by established engineering firms such as Murdoch & Aitken, and J. & C. Carmichael. Builders specialising in locomotives and other railway equipment soon appeared; Robert Stephenson & Co. was first in the field, in 1823, and to it the directors of the Garnkirk & Glasgow had turned for their first locomotives. Charles Tayleur & Co. – later better known as the Vulcan Foundry – followed in 1830 and in due course built some of the earliest

locomotives for the Caledonian Railway.

The more general trend continued to be for general engineering firms to turn increasingly to locomotive building. Neilson & Mitchell of Glasgow built their first locomotives in 1843, turned to locomotives exclusively in 1855 (from which date the firm's name became Neilson & Co.), and established a new and larger works at Springburn about 1861. Hawthorns of Leith was established about 1846 by R. & W. Hawthorn of Newcastle, which had been building locomotives since about 1831: the original intention was to erect locomotives brought in parts by sea from Newcastle but locomotives were soon being built in their entirety, and with completion of the rail link to the south the firm became independent of the original business. Andrew Barclay of Kilmarnock, which had been in business as general engineers since 1840, built its first locomotive in 1859, the first of many.

Henry Dübs, who had been Neilson's works manager, set up his own locomotive works in Glasgow in 1864. Sharp Stewart of Manchester, who had been building locomotives since 1834, moved to Glasgow – where they had room to expand – in 1888. In 1903 these two firms joined with Neilson Reid & Co. (successor to Neilson & Co.) to form the North British Locomotive Company. There were many lesser firms, some of them short-lived.

North British Locomotive Co., with more than 7,500 employees, was the largest locomotive building firm outside North America. Locomotive building had become one of Scotland's most important industries; Scottish locomotive builders built locomotives for use in Scotland, in England and all over the world. To tell the story of the industry in full would take far more space than is available here.[1]

However the early locomotive builders soon found that competition had arisen. The early steam railways established workshops to maintain their locomotives, and the tools, equipment and skills needed for heavy overhauls to steam locomotives fall scarcely short of those needed to build new ones. As early as 1834 a new locomotive was built for the Monkland & Kirkintilloch Railway at the Ballochney Railway's Greenside works, where the earlier locomotives were maintained, and more followed.[2]

All the principal pre-grouping railways in Scotland eventually built locomotives in their own workshops, but equally all continued to obtain locomotives from outside builders. First to build its own locomotives was the Edinburgh & Glasgow, which in 1844 built at its Cowlairs works two exceptionally powerful (for the period) 0-6-0 tank locomotives in an attempt, ultimately unsuccessful, to replace cable haulage by locomotives on Cowlairs bank. Other, more conventional, locomotives were built subsequently. The Glasgow, Paisley, Kilmarnock & Ayr Railway's works were at Paisley, and locomotives were built here from 1845 until 1852, when all work was transferred to the GSWR's new works at Kilmarnock. The Glasgow, Paisley & Greenock likewise started to build locomotives at its Greenock works in 1845; after amalgamation in 1847, the Caledonian Railway built locomotives here in substantial numbers until

manufacture was transferred to the new works at St Rollox, Glasgow, in 1854. Locomotives were also built for a decade or so by the Scottish Central Railway at Perth and the Scottish North Eastern Railway at Arbroath.

The North British Railway built locomotives at St Margaret's, Edinburgh, from 1856 until 1869: after the amalgamation with the Edinburgh & Glasgow Railway, Cowlairs became the NBR's principal works. The Highland Railway first built a locomotive, at Lochgorm works, Inverness, in 1869 (although some parts from earlier locomotives were incorporated), and then built many more over the ensuing thirty-seven years. The Great North of Scotland Railway built two locomotives at its cramped Kittybrewster works, Aberdeen, in 1887, and then built no more until as late as 1909, by which date it had opened new and capacious works at Inverurie.[3]

Design of locomotives, and quite often of carriages and wagons too, and their operation, were the responsibility of the locomotive superintendent or his equivalent – actual titles varied. Detailed design work was the responsibility of his draughtsmen, upon which individual superintendents depended to a greater or lesser extent. During the pre-grouping period there was much interplay of ideas and designs for locomotives and other forms of railway equipment, between Scottish and English railways. The Border may have provided, until the grouping, an immutable barrier between the railway companies of Scotland and England, but it presented no barrier at all to locomotive superintendents who often moved freely, during their careers, between Scotland and England and vice versa.

Among the earliest to do so were two protégés of Joseph Locke, Robert Sinclair and Alexander Allan,

Throughout the 1850s, 1860s and 1870s the Caledonian Railway favoured the 0-4-2 type for goods work.
(East Dunbartonshire Information & Archives)

both of Scottish descent. Sinclair became locomotive superintendent of the Glasgow, Paisley and Greenock Railway, and then of the Caledonian Railway in 1849 and in effect also of the Scottish Central until Allan arrived from Crewe in 1853. Both eventually moved south again, Sinclair to be locomotive superintendent of the Great Eastern Railway. Patrick Stirling, a Scot, was briefly locomotive superintendent of the little Caledonian & Dumbartonshire Railway during the early stages of his career, which also included spells with Neilson and with Hawthorn at Newcastle; he became locomotive superintendent of the Glasgow & South Western Railway from 1853 until 1866, when he moved south to the Great Northern Railway to

remain there until he died in harness in 1895 at the age of seventy-five or thereabouts. William Stroudley, born near Oxford, was works manager at Cowlairs in the early 1860s before becoming locomotive superintendent for the Highland Railway at Inverness in 1865. In 1869 however he moved far to the south, to the Brighton works of the London Brighton & South Coast Railway for the definitive part of his career. In the early years he was closely associated with Dugald Drummond, originally from Ardrossan, who worked under him at Cowlairs, Inverness and Brighton before being appointed locomotive superintendent of, successively, the North British Railway (1875–82) and the Caledonian Railway (1882–90); he eventually

Edinburgh & Glasgow
Railway no. 88 was a
2-2-2T built originally
by Neilson for
the Caledonian &
Dumbartonshire Railway
on 'light locomotive'
principles.
(East Dunbartonshire
Information & Archives)

moved to the London & South Western Railway. Later in the pre-grouping period, William Pickersgill came from the Great Eastern Railway to be locomotive superintendent of the Great North of Scotland Railway in 1894, and stayed there for twenty years before moving to the same post on the Caledonian. Some locomotive superintendents did stay within Scotland, such as James Manson, who trained under Patrick Stirling at Kilmarnock, became locomotive superintendent of the Great North of Scotland Railway in 1883, and returned to the Glasgow & South Western in 1891 to occupy the same position. Locomotive superintendents who spent their entire working lives with one company or its successors, such as David Jones, locomotive superintendent of the Highland between 1869 and 1896, and J. F. McIntosh, locomotive superintendent of the Caledonian between 1895 and 1914, were the exception rather than the rule.

McIntosh was also an exception in having spent the early part of his career on the footplate; an engineering apprenticeship was more usual, followed by a variety of posts of steadily increasing responsibility, and sometimes an interval in marine engineering. General character varied widely: Dugald Drummond was a notoriously irascible martinet, James Manson greatly concerned for the welfare of his men. Locomotive engineering was a small world, and some personal links have already been mentioned. There were family links too: Patrick Stirling's brother James was works manager under him at Kilmarnock, and succeeded as locomotive superintendent in 1866, staying until he left for the South Eastern Railway in 1878. Likewise, Dugald Drummond's younger brother Peter joined him first at Brighton, and was works manager under him at St Rollox, before moving as locomotive superintendent to the Highland Railway in 1896, and then the Glasgow & South Western in 1911.[4]

In Chapter 3, locomotive development was left at the stage at which the earliest main lines were equipping themselves with Bury-type 0-4-0s and

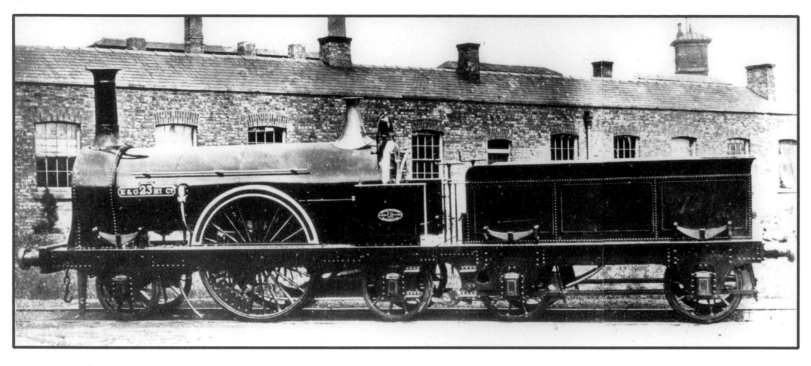

Locomotive design matured in the 1850s, to produce elegant machines such as this, one of a series of 2-2-2s built by Beyer Peacock in Manchester for the Edinburgh & Glasgow Railway in 1856.
(East Dunbartonshire Information & Archives.

Stephenson-type 2-2-2s. Throughout the period of this chapter there was a continuing tendency for steam locomotives of successive types to be larger and more powerful than earlier ones – yet locomotives of small, simple types comparable with some of the earliest survived for a remarkably long time. The 0-4-0 soon became outclassed for main-line work, but continued to be used in specialised situations, such as mineral branches with sharp curves. 'Fower-Wheelers'[5] or 0-4-0s were still being built by the GSWR and the North British in the 1860s and 1870s, and lasted in some instances through to the 1920s. In tank engine form the 0-4-0 became valuable particularly for lines serving docks and harbours, with their sharp curves. When the Great North of Scotland Railway obtained two 0-4-0 tank locomotives in 1855, they were used to bank heavy trains up the steep gradient out of the then Aberdeen terminus at Waterloo Quay, and for

shunting about the quays themselves. The 0-4-0 tank locomotive would last almost as long as there were steam locomotives in general use.

Development of the main railway system of Scotland having come a few years later than that of England, Scottish railways were able to take advantage of technical developments south of the Border. The Glasgow & South Western Railway was equipped initially with 2-2-2s for passenger trains, and 0-4-2s and 2-4-0s primarily for goods; the North British with 2-2-2s, 0-4-2s and some 0-6-0s for the coal traffic from Dalkeith. These were mostly, if not entirely, inside-cylinder locomotives, that is, with the cylinders between the frames. That implied crank axles, which in those days were difficult to manufacture and prone to break in service. One solution was to mount the cylinders outside the frames, which in turn gave rise to difficulties of mounting them securely, while locomotives of this type were inclined to nose from side to side while on the move. Nevertheless in 1847 Robert Sinclair provided the Caledonian Railway with 0-4-2 locomotives of this type for slow-moving goods trains, with evident satisfaction, for they were subsequently much used on the CR and its associated lines, and also on the GSWR.

In the meantime in the south Alexander Allan had been instrumental in originating the distinctive 'Crewe Type' double-framed outside-cylinder locomotive in the early 1840s: the outside frames were supported by leading and trailing wheels, the inside by the driving wheels, and inside and outside frames together formed a massive framework to support the cylinders; these were inclined, slightly but nonetheless conspicuously. Robert Sinclair started to build 2-2-2s of this type at Greenock in 1846 using drawings obtained from Crewe. 'Crewe Type' locomotives then came into common use throughout the Caledonian Railway and the other railways associated with it, and in due course on the Highland Railway too; the Highland and its predecessors consulted Allan over locomotive design after his arrival at Perth.[6] A 2-4-0 variant appeared, and the Crewe Type became familiar from Carlisle to Thurso.

An echo of Allan's influence is also to be seen in the 2-4-0s designed for the opening of the Great North of Scotland Railway by Daniel Kinnear Clark – born a Scot, but by then a consulting engineer in London, who nevertheless had charge of Kittybrewster locomotive works for the first couple of years. Their outside cylinders too were mounted in double framing at the front of the locomotive.

Even more distinctive in appearance than the Crewe Type were locomotives built to the patents of Thomas Russell Crampton. Crampton sought a steady-

Caledonian Railway no. 100 was one of a series of large-wheeled 2-4-0s designed by Benjamin Conner during the 1860s and derived from the Crewe Type. She is seen here at Barnhill, Perth. (Perth Museum and Art Gallery)

riding locomotive, and achieved it in a locomotive of striking appearance by placing the large driving wheels to the rear of the firebox, and so keeping the centre of gravity low by mounting the boiler over the smaller, unpowered carrying wheels. His fertile mind produced many variants of layout, but this was the most common and was adopted by three Scottish railways during the period 1847–50 – the Dundee, Perth & Aberdeen and the North British, which had one each, and the Aberdeen Railway, which had two. Crampton's designs became popular on the Continent, less so in Britain, and had no lasting influence on locomotive design in Scotland – although the North British was proud of its example, as mentioned earlier, and ran it for sixteen years before rebuilding it into more conventional form, which was longer than any other British railway.[7]

The earliest tank locomotives, carrying their supplies of coal and water on the locomotive itself, to be used in Scotland appear to have been two 2-2-2Ts built for the short Paisley & Renfrew Railway in 1837.[8] The concept was slow to catch on: locomotives of any sort were not initially used for shunting, which was still done by horses. These would give way to locomotives only gradually. But tank engines were clearly economical where journeys were short, and during the late 1840s and early 1850s the trend towards larger locomotives was briefly reversed by a fashion for light tank locomotives. These had originated from attempts to make steam railcars combining locomotive and coach on the same underframe, which soon evolved into a separate small tank locomotive hauling a coach: the locomotive being typically a long-wheelbase 2-2-0 with cylinders set to the rear of the front wheels. Such locomotives were tried, with varying degrees of success, by the isolated Morayshire and Caledonian & Dumbartonshire (Bowling–Balloch) Railways.

A noted exponent of the light locomotive was the London locomotive builder George England, whose lightweight, low-centre-of-gravity 2-2-2T *Little England* was an admired exhibit at the 1851 Great Exhibition. It however was regarded as an 'express tank locomotive', and when a locomotive of this type underwent extended trials on the Edinburgh & Glasgow Railway it was found able to haul six first-class coaches at 60 mph. The builder evidently having a liking for locomotive names that were harmonious, indeed punning, this locomotive was called *Wee Scotland*.[9]

When the North British started to build locomotives in 1856, the first two were 2-2-2 tank locomotives for Borders branch lines; they were followed by a series of 0-4-2Ts. For main-line work tender locomotives were preferred and the Edinburgh & Glasgow Railway obtained in the same year a series of inside-cylinder 2-2-2s from the Manchester builder Beyer Peacock to haul its express trains. They were handsome machines with clean lines, compared with the sometimes ungainly layouts of locomotives designed during the previous decade, but more than that they were good performers too – rebuilt, some were still running in the early twentieth century. Locomotive design was maturing.

In 1857 Patrick Stirling designed express 2-2-2s with outside cylinders for the Glasgow & South Western Railway. He would design many more 'single driver' locomotives, and continue to favour them for express trains long after most engineers had, as trains became heavier, adopted coupled wheels: his ideas would reach their zenith with his famous '8 ft singles' built for the Great Northern Railway between 1870 and 1895. Scots returning home would find at King's Cross that their compatriot had provided the 'Flying Scotsman' with a 4-2-2 of striking appearance derived mainly from its 8 ft diameter driving wheels, and its performance would be as good as its looks. It was Stirling who famously likened a locomotive with coupled wheels to 'a laddie runnin' wi' his breeks doun'.[10]

In adopting driving wheels as large as 8 ft diameter he had been anticipated as early as 1859 by Benjamin Conner, who had come from Neilson to succeed Sinclair as Locomotive Superintendent of the Caledonian. In that year Conner introduced a class of 2-2-2s with driving wheels of that diameter; probably Allan had some input into the design: certainly it was derived from the Crewe Type. Stirling too was familiar with it. Despite the single pair of driving wheels, these locomotives successfully hauled West Coast expresses between Carlisle and Glasgow – including Beattock Bank – until the 1880s. Probably having a high proportion of the total weight on the driving wheels was a help.[11] Dugald Drummond added two 2-2-2s of his own design to the North British, former E & G, stud in 1876; design of the noted Caledonian Railway 4-2-2 no. 123 of 1886 owed much to these. This locomotive was mentioned in Chapter 5, as was the general revival in the fortunes of single-driver locomotives following the introduction of powered sanding gear.

The North British Railway had used 0-6-0 tender locomotives for goods traffic from the start, but was at first little imitated, 0-4-2s being preferred elsewhere. But the GSWR started to use 0-6-0s regularly in the 1860s, and the Caledonian in the 1870s. This type then became the staple of goods motive power throughout the Lowlands until well into the twentieth century. Notable examples were the Caledonian Railway's 294 class of 1883, well known as 'Jumbos', and the later 812 class of 1899 which were really mixed-traffic locomotives, often used on passenger trains. In the Highlands, matters evolved differently: the Highland Railway had no 0-6-0s until 1900, and then not very many; the Great North had none at all.

These latter two railways lacked the heavy goods and mineral traffic of railways serving the Central Belt. What they did have increasingly, as lines were constructed economically into ever more unremunerative districts, was plenty of sharp curves. The 1860s were a period when increasing attention was being paid to introducing some lateral flexibility into locomotive wheelbases[12] – until then, long-wheelbase locomotives had often been built without flanges on the central pair of wheels. In North America railways had been lightly laid and sharply curved since the beginning, and the problems that arose had long since been countered by widespread use of locomotives with leading, swivelling bogies – by 4-4-0 locomotives particularly.

It was William Cowan, Locomotive Superintendent of the Great North of Scotland Railway since 1857, who introduced the 4-4-0 tender locomotive to Scotland in 1862. Hitherto the GNSR had relied principally on rigid-wheelbase 2-4-0 locomotives but, for the sharp curves west of Keith, Cowan designed a class of bogie 4-4-0s which were built by Robert Stephenson & Co. Stephenson had earlier built bogie 4-4-0 tank locomotives, and had first built bogie 4-4-0 tender locomotives for British use in 1860 for the Stockton & Darlington Railway's western extension over the Pennines to Tebay.[13]

The 1862 4-4-0s for the GNSR had rigid pivots for the bogies; similar locomotives of a second series, built by Neilson in 1865, had for the first time the important improvement of bogie pivots with lateral movement.[14] The type evidently met the needs of the Great North, for from then on the company acquired no more 2-4-0s, nor did it acquire anything larger than a 4-4-0: until the grouping it relied upon 4-4-0s for passenger and goods trains alike. The early 4-4-0s proved to be long-lasting: *Meldrum Meg*, mentioned in the prologue, was one of them.

The Highland Railway was slow to follow the GNS example, but in 1873 David Jones, observing that rigid-wheelbase 2-4-0s found the sharp curves of the Dingwall & Skye line hard going, rebuilt one with a front bogie in place of the leading pair of wheels. It was followed by another, and then in 1874 by ten new 4-4-0s for the main line, and eventually in 1883 by the 'Skye Bogie' class for the Dingwall & Skye line itself.[15]

By the late nineteenth century the Caledonian had standardised on 0-6-0s for goods work; some locomotives were fitted with continuous brakes and used also on passenger trains, particularly to the Clyde coast. They were long-lived; in this picture one is entering Wemyss Bay with a passenger train in LMS days. The first vehicle is a horse box. (Author's collection)

All retained that conspicuous feature of the Crewe Type, the substantial framework which supported inclined cylinders.

The Callander & Oban line had sharp curves in common with the Dingwall & Skye, and the Caledonian at first worked it with 2-4-2 tank locomotives with radial axleboxes for the leading and trailing wheels – such axleboxes being another contemporary solution to the wheelbase flexibility problem. However successful such locomotives may have been elsewhere, they were unsatisfactory here – possibly because of a design fault – and in 1882 were replaced by new 4-4-0s, the 'Oban Bogies' of proportions comparable to the 'Skye Bogies' and equally successful.[16]

By this date the 4-4-0 type, usually with inside cylinders, was being used widely for main-line passenger trains, and would continue to be for decades to come. First in the field, in Scotland, had been the North British in 1871, followed by the GSWR in 1873. Drummond's famous 4-4-0s of 1877 for the Waverley Route were mentioned in Chapter 5. After moving to the Caledonian, Drummond provided it with equally fine 4-4-0s of similar appearance. J. F. McIntosh built on Drummond's foundations but, drawing no doubt on his own footplate experience, in his famous 'Dunalastair' 4-4-0s of 1896 added much larger boilers and firegrates, to produce seemingly unlimited steam. Over the next eight years the design would be enlarged several times, to produce successively the versions known as Dunalastair I, II, III and IV.[17]

In the early decades of the twentieth century, when larger locomotives had been built for the most important expresses, railways were still building new 4-4-0s for other work which was only a little less important. Notable were the Scott and the Glen classes of the North British (the former being named after characters in Scott's novels, the latter after Highland glens).

Superheating was introduced in Scotland in 1910, the first superheated locomotive being a Dunalastair IV 4-4-0;[18] late examples of the Scotts, and the Glens, were superheated too. Superheating equipment increased the weight at the front of the locomotive: excessively so on 0-6-0s, as McIntosh found after building four superheated 0-6-0s in 1912, and subsequent locomotives, otherwise similar, were built with an additional pair of wheels as 2-6-0s, the first of their type in Scotland. Three years later, and for the same reason, Peter Drummond built some very successful superheated 2-6-0s for the Glasgow & South Western Railway.

In tank engine form, 4-4-0Ts were used for local trains by the North British Railway, the Caledonian and the Highland Railway – the latter, having in 1892 picked up cheaply two 4-4-0 tank locomotives intended for export to Uruguay but left on builder Dübs & Co.'s hands, liked them sufficiently to order more on its own behalf. Much more popular, however, was the 0-4-4T, a more convenient wheel arrangement which allowed the trailing bogie to fit neatly beneath cab and coal bunker. Such locomotives were eventually to be found on all five of the main Scottish railways and were a particularly familiar sight on the Caledonian. Even the fourth Duke of Sutherland acquired one, in 1895, to replace the earlier 2-4-0T. It was named *Dunrobin* like its predecessor, and fitted with an extra large cab to accommodate the duke and his distinguished guests.

Increasing freight traffic over the Highland main line led David Jones to design his noted 'Jones Goods' 4-6-0s. When introduced in 1894 these were the most powerful main-line locomotives in Britain, and the first locomotives of this wheel arrangement to run here. Once again the wheel arrangement had long been familiar in North America, and it is noteworthy that conditions on the Highland main line – a mountainous single-track route resulting in infrequent but heavy trains – probably more nearly resembled American conditions than did those of any other British railway. The class proved useful for passenger trains also, and Peter Drummond followed it in 1900 with 4-6-0s intended specifically for passenger trains, the Castle class.

Use of this wheel arrangement spread to the Caledonian in 1902, when McIntosh built a class of small-wheeled 4-6-0s for the Callander & Oban line. Unlike Jones's 4-6-0s, these and subsequent McIntosh 4-6-0s had inside cylinders. In 1903 he built two large and powerful 4-6-0s for the main line and then, having gained experience with these, introduced in 1906 his very successful 903 class 4-6-0s for express passenger trains. The first of these, no. 903 *Cardean* became the regular engine for 'The Corridor', out from Glasgow to Carlisle and back again every day: one of the best-known locomotives in Britain. Crowds gathered daily to see her off on her evening departure from Carlisle.[19]

By then Manson was building 4-6-0s for the Glasgow & South Western; on both railways the incentive, largely, was the increasing weight of Anglo-Scottish expresses following introduction of corridor coaches and dining cars. The North British Railway took a different route to increased power: its East Coast partners were already using locomotives of the 'Atlantic' or 4-4-2 type and the NB, taking into account the sinuous nature of the Waverley Route, decided to adopt the same type with its short rigid wheelbase. The first appeared in 1906; they were used on the NBR's principal expresses.[20] Their huge, high-pitched boilers gave North British Atlantics an impressive appearance. They were famous locomotives, popular with the public;[21] they were less so with enginemen for they pitched and rolled abominably at speed and a fireman new to them might find it difficult to stand, let alone fire.[22] Nevertheless to be an Atlantic driver was the peak of a NB engineman's career, and his wife would be treated with appropriate respect when visiting the Co-op.[23] Alone among Scottish railways the NBR also adopted the 4-4-2 wheel arrangement for tank locomotives, from 1911 for suburban and branch line passenger trains.

The early-twentieth-century trend towards ever larger passenger locomotives was briefly accompanied, throughout Britain, by an opposite trend – a revival of interest in small and compact motive power for passenger trains where traffic was limited. This again took physical form in production of steam railcars or 'railmotors'. Two Scottish railways tried them in 1904–5: the Great North, which used them on (among other routes) the Lossiemouth branch which had known light locomotives long before, and the Glasgow & South Western. On neither railway did they last for much more than a decade or so, although those on the GSWR do seem to have been economical: one was said to run all day on a couple of barrowfuls of coal.[24] The subsequent further revival of the type, prompted by the need for between-the-wars economies, has already been mentioned in Chapter 8. Steam railcars offered the advantage of being bidirectional; this could be retained, and combined with the flexibility of separate locomotives and coaches, in the auto-train: the push-pull arrangement in which the locomotive remained coupled to one end of a train of one or two coaches, irrespective of direction of travel, and was driven remotely from a driver's cab in the end coach when the locomotive's position was at the rear. This concept was a lasting one: it became familiar on, for instance, the local trains between Craigendoran and Arrochar & Tarbet, which were still being operated in the late 1950s by North British 4-4-2Ts working push-pull with a couple of compartment coaches.[25]

Overall, however, the trend during the early twentieth century was towards increasingly large, and heavy, locomotives. The point was made dramatically when the Highland Railway's powerful new superheated 4-6-0 *River Ness* was found, on delivery to Perth in 1915 by builder Hawthorn Leslie of Newcastle, to be overweight for HR track and structures, and also too large for its loading gauge.[26] The faults were not the builder's, however, but the consequence of errors accumulated between

Final fling: the 4-6-4T locomotives designed by Whitelegg for the GSWR and put into service in 1922 were perhaps the most imposing of all pre-grouping locomotives, their huge size enhanced by boiler cladding of planished steel. (National Railway Museum)

the Highland Railway at Inverness, North British Locomotive Co. which had prepared a design when construction of a new class was first considered, and the North British Railway which eventually prepared the working drawings on the HR's behalf. HR chief engineer Alexander Newlands banned the class from HR metals; HR locomotive superintendent F. G. Smith (who had succeeded Peter Drummond) was offered the alternatives of resignation or dismissal. He chose the former.

The six locomotives of the class went to do sterling work for the Caledonian over the West Coast route. Eventually, in the late 1920s – by which time Newlands was chief civil engineer of the LMS – the track and structures of the Highland main line were strengthened sufficiently to allow them to run over the route for which they had been intended. Nevertheless, it is interesting to find that Newlands in *The British Railways*, published in 1936 after his retirement, remained critical of the cult of the big engine, and pointed out that this meant not only big trains but also strengthened bridges, stronger track, and lengthened platforms and sidings. The thrust of his argument was, however, that railways with ever-longer trains appeared to be moving away from their road competitors who valued frequency of service more highly than unit size.[27]

Earlier, the vogue for larger and larger locomotives had extended to tank engines as well as tender engines. William Pickersgill provided the Caledonian with some handsome and free-running 4-6-2 tank locomotives, built by North British Locomotive Co. in 1917 for the fast trains to the Clyde Coast and known to facetious railwaymen as 'Wemyss Bay Pugs' – a 'pug locomotive' properly being the smallest and most insignificant type of shunting 0-4-0 T.

The trend, however, reached its zenith with the 'Baltic' or 4-6-4 tank locomotives designed by Robert Whitelegg and built for the Glasgow & South Western Railway in 1922.[28] Whitelegg had trained under his father, who had been locomotive superintendent of the London, Tilbury & Southend Railway from 1875 until 1910, when son succeeded father. The weights of LTS trains had been increasing rapidly, and to haul them Whitelegg designed a powerful superheated 4-6-4 tank locomotive; by the time six of these were delivered late in 1912, however, the LTSR had been taken over by the Midland Railway.[29] Whitelegg found employment elsewhere, and then in 1918, moving as it were from a small railway at one extremity of the Midland system to one at the other, he came to be locomotive superintendent of the Glasgow & South Western Railway where Peter Drummond had died in office.

His first priority was to attempt to make good the ravages of wartime over-use upon its stock of locomotives. But the GSWR lines from Glasgow to Ayr and the Clyde Coast had much in common with the London, Tilbury & Southend Railway; before long Whitelegg was designing a large modern 4-6-4T to haul its trains over these lines. Tank locomotives of any sort had been a rarity on the GSWR, although Drummond had provided eighteen useful 0-6-2Ts for goods and mineral trains, and ten more were on order when Whitelegg arrived. At any rate, six 4-6-4T locomotives were built by North British Locomotive Co. and delivered in April 1922 – huge, impressive modern machines. As Philip Atkins has put it, at one bound the GSWR, which had lagged behind its contemporaries, stood in the front rank of British locomotive practice.[30]

It looks as though there may have been an element of jockeying for position in this – over on the Caledonian Pickersgill was attempting to develop a high-powered three-cylinder 4-6-0 – for it was already clear that restructuring of the British railway system was coming. In the event, however, Whitelegg stayed for only three months after the grouping, as LMS divisional mechanical engineer at Kilmarnock. He then left to become general manager and chief engineer of noted locomotive builder Beyer Peacock & Co. Ltd., while his locomotives (though not devoid of problems) were putting up good performances on heavy trains between St Enoch and Ayr, Ardrossan and Kilmarnock. Had Whitelegg had the opportunity to develop the type, a 4-6-6T version might have appeared, with a coal bunker large enough to allow it to be used on the main line to Carlisle.

No locomotive superintendent from any Scottish railway went on, following the grouping, to become chief mechanical engineer on the LMS or the LNER. Responsibility for locomotives and rolling stock for use in Scotland now lay in the south, and purely Scottish lines of development came to an end. That is not to suggest that Scottish needs and conditions were neglected. Locomotives from pre-grouping English companies were sent north, in some cases with great success, and new classes were designed specifically for Scottish use. This was particularly so on the LNER. Additional 4-4-0s were urgently needed on former-NBR lines, and the LNER provided twenty-four new locomotives based not on any North British class, but on the Great Central Railway's Director class. But these 'Scottish Directors' were given names derived, like earlier NBR locomotives, from the works of Sir Walter Scott; they were up to the job, and they soon became popular. For freight traffic, the LNER's J38 class 0-6-0 of 1925 was intended specifically for the coalfields of Lothian and Fife.

Perhaps the most remarkable import was that of B12 class 4-6-0s from the former Great Eastern Railway to the Great North of Scotland. One was tried in 1926 and found suitable, for despite being a six-coupled locomotive its rigid wheelbase was short, and from 1931 they were imported permanently to become the mainstay of the section's motive power. Many were fitted with feed-water heaters, which meant a large and ungainly piece of equipment mounted on top of the boiler between chimney and dome. To a generation newly enthused by the Great Outdoors, a B12 was clearly carrying a rucksack on its back: the locomotives gained the nickname 'Hikers'.[31] More fancifully still, a newly arrived southern visitor travelling on the 7.50 a.m. from Aberdeen to Inverness wondered if he would soon feel as much at home as apparently did the train's former GER 4-6-0 'forging ahead … round what must seem to it like an unending succession of Manningtree curves'.[32] (For those not in the know, Manningtree is where the Harwich branch joins the GER main line by a triangular junction, two sides of which are very sharply curved.)

The arrival of Gresley's Pacific locomotives on the

Gresley Pacific *Prince Palatine* was built in 1924 and lasted until 1966, latterly reduced to hauling goods trains over the Waverley Route. She is seen here a year before withdrawal, at Edinburgh. (Brian Dickson)

East Coast main line in the mid-1920s has already been mentioned in Chapter 8. They came into use on the Waverley Route, too, in 1929: indeed one example of the class, no. 2749 *Flamingo*, is said to have been shedded at Carlisle for this purpose throughout her entire career, from 1929 to 1961.[33] The Waverley Route with its sharp curves and steep gradients could scarcely be more different from the long straight levels of the East Coast main line, yet such superb locomotives were masters of both. These were A3 Pacifics, incorporating improvements (including redesigned valve gear and

Built by the LNER specifically to haul the heaviest trains over the difficult route between Edinburgh and Aberdeen, Gresley's 2-8-2 *Cock o' the North* emerges from the tunnel beneath The Mound in 1937.
(National Railway Museum)

higher boiler pressure) from the originals, which were rebuilt to match.

Gresley was ever willing to incorporate the latest innovations into his designs, usually though not invariably with success. From 1925 he was experimenting in the use of poppet valves for steam distribution, in place of piston or slide valves, fitted to locomotives of several different types. When fifteen new three-cylinder D49 class 4-4-0 locomotives were built in 1927–8 for use in Scotland, one of them was fitted with poppet valves. These locomotives, the Shire class, were named after Scottish counties. R. D. Stephen notes that two were based at Perth, where the

drivers described them as 'grand engines'.[34]

Nevertheless by 1930 double-heading, usually by a 4-4-2 plus a 4-4-0, was common on heavy trains between Edinburgh and Aberdeen – a particularly difficult route where the starts from most of the principal stations are uphill – and it was specifically for this route that Gresley produced his P2 class 2-8-2 in 1934. The first two were *Cock o' the North* (with poppet valves) and *Earl Marischal* (with piston valves for comparison); four others followed. This class might have been Gresley's masterpiece: locomotives able to haul 550-ton overnight trains including heavy sleeping cars, owing much in their design to recent work by

André Chapelon, the noted French locomotive engineer, and the only express passenger 2-8-2s ever to run in Britain. Yet they were, rather, Gresley's 'near miss': many minor problems accumulated to become a major one, and his successor eventually rebuilt them as Pacifics in 1943.[35] Gresley's masterpiece was, instead, the A4 class, and although the LNER built many more Pacifics subsequently, none surpassed the A4s.

Turning to the LMS, one Scottish locomotive design which did exert some continuing influence on post-grouping motive power was a powerful 2-6-0 which Pickersgill had prepared and was ready to build for the Caledonian: with detail alterations, this formed the basis of the design for the LMS 2-6-0s which, from their ungainly inclined outside cylinders and valve gear, gained the nickname 'Crabs'.[36] They were nonetheless popular and successful locomotives, particularly over the Highland main line.

That was in the earliest days of the LMS. The policy of standardisation, which soon emerged, and with it the arrival in Scotland of many 4-4-0s of Midland Railway type, has already been mentioned. For freight, the Midland Railway 4F 0-6-0 was adopted: twenty-five were built by Andrew Barclay at Kilmarnock in 1927 and many more followed. In addition to powering freight trains, these locomotives were invaluable, when fitted with a large snowplough, for clearing snow blocks – and were employed for this purpose until the end of steam. For shunting, Midland Railway-type 0-6-0Ts appeared in quantity.

The arrival of William Stanier as chief mechanical engineer of the LMS, his development of Pacific locomotives and the consequent marked accelerations to London–Glasgow expresses, have been mentioned in Chapter 8. Less spectacular but of even greater importance, because the effects were so much more

Stanier provided streamlined Pacifics of the Princess Coronation or Duchess Class for the 'Coronation Scot' of 1937; later examples of the class were not streamlined, and two final ones were built by his successor H. G. Ivatt in 1947 with detail improvements including roller bearings. One of these was named *Sir William Stanier FRS* and is seen in Edinburgh in 1964. (Brian Dickson)

widespread, was his development of the class 5 mixed-traffic 4-6-0. The LMS (and, later, British Railways) classified locomotives according to power, through eight gradations from 0 to 7 with the letter 'P' or 'F' generally added to indicate passenger or freight locomotives (unlike the LNER, which classified locomotive classes by letter according to their wheel arrangement, 'A' for 4-6-2, etc.) That locomotives of different types were needed for passenger and freight work was the received wisdom: yet the Great Western Railway already had a general purpose, or 'mixed

LMS class 5 4-6-0s were introduced in 1934, and then built at intervals until nationalisation and indeed subsequently. No. 44998 (BR numbering) was built by the LMS in 1947. She is seen here at Aberdeen in 1965, and when withdrawn two years later had become one of the last steam locomotives in service in Scotland. A diesel shunting locomotive appears in the background. (Brian Dickson)

traffic', 4-6-0 in its Hall class, and Stanier had had a hand in its design. From this he developed for the LMS his class 5, with 6 ft diameter driving wheels, two large cylinders and all the modern improvements (rather than innovations) of the day: a locomotive well able to haul any sort of train other than the heaviest mineral trains and the fastest expresses.

The first line over which class 5 4-6-0s went into regular service, in 1934, was the Highland main line where they were an instant success, displacing Castles, Rivers and Crabs alike. Before many years were out, class 5s or 'Black Fives'(for they were painted in freight locomotive black rather than passenger locomotive red), were ubiquitous throughout the LMS lines in the Highlands. When traffic was heavy, they were used double-headed: better to do this, on lines where heavy traffic was a seasonal phenomenon, than to use larger locomotives which for much of the time would be under-employed – as was happening to the P2s between Edinburgh and Aberdeen. In all, 842 Black Fives were built (the final 100 after nationalisation) – the largest total for any class of tender locomotive to run in Britain.[37]

For heavy goods trains, Stanier introduced his 8F 2-8-0s in 1935: not at first built in great quantity, for the need was not so great as for the class 5s, they became a familiar sight only after adoption during the Second World War as a standard locomotive for use throughout Britain and overseas.

In the early 1930s the North British Glen 4-4-0s then working the West Highland line were supplemented by some K2 2-6-0s, which Gresley had designed originally two decades before for the Great Northern Railway. Then in 1937 he provided the first of his K4 class, designed specifically for the West Highland, a powerful three-cylinder 2-6-0 with light axle loading: maximum train load, 180 tons with a Glen, increased to 300 tons with a K4.[38]

Gresley's most important mixed traffic locomotive, however, was the V2 three-cylinder 2-6-2 introduced in 1936, in many respects the equal of a Pacific and used in Scotland, particularly between Edinburgh

During the Second World War 2-8-0 goods locomotives to a standard 'Austerity' design were built for the Ministry of Supply and operated by railway companies throughout Britain; many were bought by British Railways in 1948 after nationalisation. One of these is passing through Coatbridge Sunnyside with a freight train on 4 November 1960. Overhead wiring is in place for the electric passenger trains, which were due to start running a few days later. (Don Martin)

and Aberdeen. The first of the class was named *Green Arrow*, associating it with fast freight service; as many as 184 V2s were built. There might well have been more but for Gresley's death from a heart attack in 1941.

It is not unduly cynical to comment that with Stanier LMS shareholders got standardisation and a dividend, but with Gresley LNER shareholders had to make do with technical innovation and a world speed record. There were of course many other factors, but under Gresley's successor Edward Thompson, who seems to have had an aversion both to Gresley's methods and to Gresley the man, the emphasis immediately turned towards simplicity of design and ease of maintenance.

It was Thompson who had the P2s rebuilt as Pacifics, in the process reducing their adhesive weight so much that they became notorious for slipping and became so unpopular in Scotland that they had to be transferred south.[39] Much more constructively, by the end of 1942 Thompson had produced the first of the B1 class two-cylinder mixed-traffic 4-6-0s, providing the LNER with a locomotive equivalent to the LMS class 5, and a class which would eventually be seen all over its system.

To assist with the immensely increased freight traffic of wartime, there worked in Scotland two classes of 2-8-0 neither of which had originated with a British railway company. The Austerity 2-8-0s were built for the Ministry of Supply from 1943 onwards;

This Edinburgh & Glasgow Railway carriage of c.1860 is still primitive compared with later vehicles, but to third-class passengers of the period accommodation which was enclosed, and glazed, was a welcome improvement on what had gone before. Guard rails still enabled luggage to be carried on the roof.
(East Dunbartonshire Information & Archives)

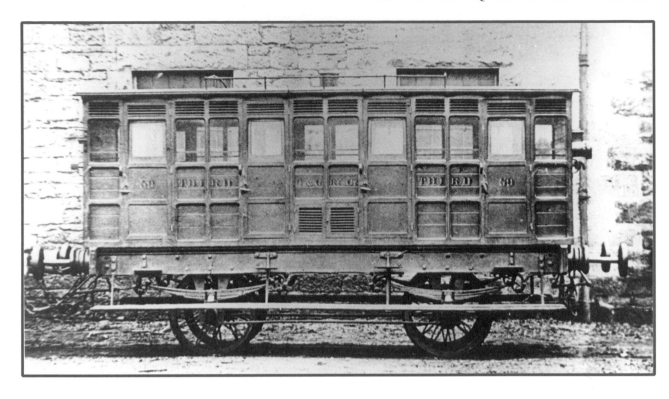

eventually a large quantity passed into British Railways ownership. The others were, so to speak, birds of passage: the United States Army's American-built S160 class locomotives, which were set to work in Britain pending their onward transfer to the Continent after the invasion.

By the 1940s railway electric traction had been fully practicable for many decades, and diesel traction was making great strides. But this was in other countries, not Scotland. Of electric traction on the LMS and the LNER in Scotland there was none, although both companies used it to a limited extent in the South. Diesel traction seems to have been found, to any great extent, only in the diesel-electric shunting locomotives of the LMS. There was, however, one curious application of the internal combustion engine. In 1930–1 the LMS experimented, in the South,

with a motor bus equipped not only with ordinary pneumatic-tyred road wheels but also with rail wheels and an arrangement for quick (five minutes or less) conversion between them. It did not catch on, but in 1934 the LNER adopted the principle for a convertible road/rail lorry for permanent way maintenance on the West Highland line.[40] Convertible road/rail vehicles – Land Rovers and larger – continue to be a feature of West Highland line maintenance, and incongruously are encountered by the author from time to time at a local garage which is eleven miles by road from the nearest point on the railway.

By 1947 the LNER had plans to obtain twenty-five 1,600 hp diesel units for trials between London and Edinburgh, plans upon which British Railways did not act.[41] The LMS had plans too, and in conjunction with English Electric did design and build two prototype 1,600 hp diesel-electric locomotives, which could be operated in multiple on express trains.[42] One of these was completed just before nationalisation, the other just afterwards. Together they were often to be found, early in 1950, hauling the 'Royal Scot' between Glasgow and London.[43]

The continuing development of passenger coaches interacted with development of train services, throughout the period from the 1840s until the 1940s. To that extent much has already been written of it, but it is worth looking briefly at the successive stages through which such development passed.

To take a railway representative of the main lines of the late 1840s, the North British when opened from Berwick to Edinburgh possessed – of 'coaching stock' – 111 coaches, 20 luggage vans, 15 horseboxes and 15 carriage trucks. All ran on four wheels. First-class coaches had three compartments, upholstered, curtained and lit by oil lamps; second class were less luxurious; third class, in accordance with Gladstone's Act of 1844, had roofs. All were still equipped to carry luggage, and guards, on the roof, but the presence of luggage vans is suggestive of the transitional period when both were brought, so to speak, down to earth.[44] The principal materials from which these vehicles were constructed were timber, leather and iron – that is, wrought iron, cast iron and, for springs, steel. Bodies were protected by innumerable coats of paint and varnish. The crafts of coachbuilding, for road vehicles, were well established and transferred readily to the new means of transport. So, presumably, did the term 'livery' for the colour scheme of a railway vehicle.

During the next couple of decades progress was slow. Coaches became longer, four or five compartments, and it became more evident that a coach comprised a single body divided into compartments rather than the three separate bodies mounted together of the early days; in third and second-class coaches partitions seldom extended above seatback height. By around 1870 more and more coaches were being carried on six wheels. Guards' brake vans carried luggage, and included a dog box for canine passengers such as A. M. Harbord's 'wise retriever in the van': only lapdogs travelled in passenger coaches.[45] The introduction of long coaches carried on bogies into general British practice in the late 1870s has been mentioned in chapters 4 and 5,[46] as has the contemporaneous introduction of Pullman cars and sleeping cars. With the introduction of bogies, railway coaches started to take on the proportions which remain familiar. It would be many decades, however, before four- and six-wheeled passenger coaches disappeared from regular use. The Caledonian Railway was building new four-wheeled coaches for Edinburgh suburban services as late as 1922.

Brakes, in the early days, could be applied only by drivers and guards – sometimes several of the latter, positioned at intervals down a long train, who responded to whistle signals from the driver. Continuous brakes, actuated by the driver but operating on many or all of the vehicles in a train, were an evident need for both speed and safety. Many ingenious methods of achieving this end were tried: most were found wanting. Two forms proved lasting: Westinghouse brakes, applied through the medium of compressed air generated by the locomotive, and vacuum brakes, applied through the medium of atmospheric pressure applied to a piston on the opposite side of which was a partial vacuum, generated by the locomotive. A pipe the length of the train, with hose connections between vehicles, contained either compressed air or partial vacuum; both types of brake were eventually arranged

Two Caledonian Railway coaches are preserved in running order by the Scottish Railway Preservation Society. Running on bogies, and with compartments, side corridors and corridor connections they are typical of the best practice of a century ago. (Author)

to be 'automatic', that is to say that in the event of a train breaking in two, presence of air at atmospheric pressure in the train pipe would actuate the brakes on both parts. It was in this form that continuous brakes were made compulsory in 1889 on passenger trains.

Of the five main pre-grouping Scottish railways, the Caledonian, North British and Great North of Scotland Railways chose to use Westinghouse brakes, the Highland used vacuum brakes, and the Glasgow & South Western tried Westinghouse and then settled for vacuum. In this it followed the example of its southern partner, the Midland Railway; of other English railways included in Anglo-Scottish routes, the London & North Western and the Great Northern used vacuum, the North Eastern Westinghouse.[47] All this meant that, wherever adjoining railways had standardised on different forms of brakes, rolling stock intended to work through had to be 'dual fitted' with brakes of both types. This affected through trains between for instance Euston and Glasgow, or Inverness and Aberdeen. Locomotives which might from time to time be called upon to haul rolling stock of another company were also dual fitted. Eventually LMS and LNER standardised on vacuum brakes.

Gas lighting for coaches came in in the 1880s, and electric lighting not much later; the latter eventually largely superseded the former, particularly after disastrous fires such as that at Quintinshill. Steam heating of coaches also came in in the mid-1880s – the Caledonian was a pioneer – and lasted for a century.

In 1881–2 the Great Northern Railway built, and put into East Coast Joint Stock service, a coach with

197

a side corridor throughout its length. The corridor gave access from the compartments to lavatories at each end: there was as yet no connection to adjoining coaches. When that innovation came in with dining cars in the 1890s, the classic layout for a British railway coach had arrived. But dining cars, so far as Scotland is concerned, first appeared in the joint stock of the three Anglo-Scottish routes: since few of them came into use on internal Scottish train services before the second decade of the twentieth century, many corridor coaches built in the intervening period (by, for instance, GSWR and Highland Railways) still lacked corridor connections.

Coaches with end coupé compartments, in which passengers sat facing end windows, had been known in the earliest days of main lines, and were perpetuated on the Highland Railway and the Callander & Oban line, where there were fine views from the ends of trains. The arrangement reached its peak with the *Maid of Morven* observation car. For the opening of the West Highland line, the North British acted otherwise: it built bogie coaches in which the central part formed a large saloon with wide windows from which the views on either side could be admired.

Not all passengers were so fortunate. Both the North British and the Caledonian had prison carriages, from which the outlook was evidently limited. Entrances to the compartments, or cells, were from side corridors: in the Caledonian example at least these led, on opposite sides of the carriage, out of a central compartment in which warders could sit so as to see along either corridor.

At the other extreme was a luxurious saloon coach built at the turn of the century by the Great North of Scotland Railway for use by royalty and others – the only vehicle of this type built for a Scottish railway.

For royal journeys over the West Coast Route to and from Ballater, the noted London & North Western royal train of 1903 was preferred.

One of Gresley's first acts, after being appointed locomotive, carriage and wagon superintendent of the Great Northern Railway, had been to build, in 1906, for East Coast Joint Stock, a bogie luggage van with a steel underframe and a teak body. It became the prototype for many main-line coaches built for the GNR and the LNER over the next thirty-five years.[48] By 1914 use of steel for coach components had been increasing steadily over the years, particularly for bogies and underframes, and also for body panelling. In that year, however, the North British Railway specified all-steel construction for some 'dining carriages': delayed by the war, they entered service only in 1919.[49] The LMS started to put all-steel coaches into service in 1926, in quantity. Departing from the usual British practice these were open coaches, with seats arranged two by two facing each other across a table, and on either side of a central gangway.[50] The LNER put coaches of the same layout into service the following year; these had steel exterior panelling.[51] From 1931 the LNER was building corridor coaches with end doors only, rather than exterior doors to each compartment: this enabled wide windows to be fitted. The third-class sleeping cars of 1928, and the special stock built for the streamlined expresses of the late 1930s, have been mentioned in Chapter 8.

Turning to goods rolling stock, typically the Glasgow & South Western Railway possessed, on its formation by amalgamation in 1850, 1,523 mineral wagons, 304 pig iron wagons, 109 cattle wagons and 399 goods wagons. Goods brake vans came into use during the ensuing decade.[52]

Wagons at this period ran on four wheels and were

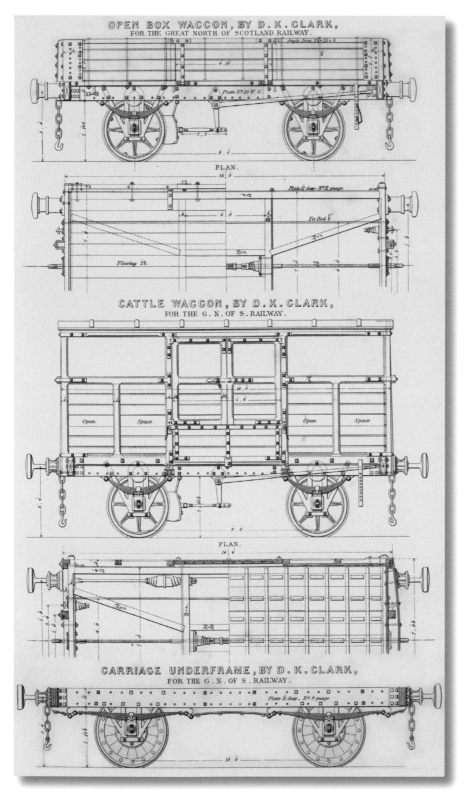

OPEN BOX WAGGON, BY D. K. CLARK,
FOR THE GREAT NORTH OF SCOTLAND RAILWAY.

PLAN.

CATTLE WAGGON, BY D. K. CLARK,
FOR THE G. N. OF S. RAILWAY.

PLAN.

CARRIAGE UNDERFRAME, BY D. K. CLARK,
FOR THE G. N. OF S. RAILWAY.

built of timber with iron fittings. Mineral, or coal, wagons carried a load of six tons, later increased to eight tons. Most of these probably had dumb buffers – that is to say, the timber solebars, or longitudinal frame members, were extended beyond the ends of the body to form buffers, unsprung. Sprung buffers came into use gradually, but dumb buffers lasted a long time – their use was eventually discontinued at the end of 1913.[53]

That long life was probably due at least in part to the conservative approach of owners of private-owners' wagons; so was the continuing small average capacity of wagons in Britain compared with other countries. Traders typically had sharply curved private sidings suitable only for short-wheelbase wagons. In 1887 the railway companies of Britain jointly drew up a standard specification for ten-ton capacity private-owners' wagons; by the early part of the twentieth century specifications had been issued for wagons of much higher capacities, up to thirty tons, yet ten-ton and fifteen-ton capacities remained the most popular. The specifications included sprung buffers and allowed for use of timber, steel and iron in both frames and bodies.[54]

Continuous brakes had not been made compulsory on goods trains, although many goods vehicles were eventually fitted, particularly those for perishable traffic where speed was important. This in turn produced problems. On the Caledonian Railway's branch to

D.K. Clark designed rolling stock for the opening of the Great North of Scotland Railway in 1854, and illustrated it in his book *Railway Machinery*. His cattle wagon repays comparison with the cattle trucks shown in the next picture, and indeed with the one coupled to the Austerity 2-8-0 in 1960, which was illustrated earlier in this chapter.
(Trustees of the National Library of Scotland)

199

There is a fine but not untypical mixture of rolling stock in this goods train on the NBR at Inverkeithing in late pre-grouping days: cattle trucks, closed vans of various sizes, high- and low-sided open wagons, open wagons covered with tarpaulins – on trains like this, the commerce of Scotland depended. (National Railway Museum)

Blairgowrie for instance a dual-fitted locomotive had to be provided, but only during the fruit-picking season, to be compatible with any vacuum-fitted fruit vans which English railways might send there.[55] Goods trains that included unfitted wagons were still running on British Rail in the 1980s: they disappeared only with the disappearance of the traffics they latterly carried, such as coal to rural stations.

The pre-grouping railway companies themselves were keen to use large wagons: in the early twentieth century both North British and Glasgow & South Western had sixteen-ton capacity mineral wagons, and the Caledonian had a fleet of thirty-ton bogie wagons fitted with Westinghouse brakes. Yet in 1921 it was reported that average wagon loadings were, in the USA, 23.5 tons; in Prussia, 8.8 tons; and in Britain, 5.4 tons.[56]

In addition to open wagons and closed vans, there was by then enormous variety in the types of wagons in use. Specialised wagons and vans were provided for fish, meat, milk, cattle, sheep, timber, salt and gunpowder. Tank wagons, with either rectangular or cylindrical tanks, carried oil, tar and other fluids. Covered carriage trucks were seeing less use than formerly, with the coming of the motor car; they were still being used for theatre scenery and furniture vans, and it was suggested in 1912 that bogie carriage trucks might in future be very useful for carrying aeroplane parts.[57] In the 1930s flat wagons for containers appeared, goods wagons were increasingly fitted with continuous brakes, capacities were increased and numbers reduced.

On the track, by the 1850s, stone blocks were giving way to wooden sleepers; rail of double-head section was supported on these by cast iron chairs into which it was wedged by wooden keys. Extra-wide chairs held the ends of rails in alignment at joints. Double-head rail eventually gave way to bullhead; joint chairs to rail-ends clamped together by bolted fishplates, with hot-weather expansion gaps between the rails. Iron rails, later in the nineteenth century, gave way to steel.[58]

On the North British Railway, when it was opened in 1846, two signals were provided at the junction of the Hawick branch with the main line; these were positioned fifty yards either side of the pointsman's box, in front of which were the point levers. An enterprising pointsman, Robert Skeldon, soon became weary of walking to and from the signals many times a day, and rigged up an arrangement of wires and weights to work them from his box, out of the rain. So originated the signal box. But there was more. Authority approved, and added a further signal, 250 yards away towards Edinburgh and likewise worked by wires, to give advance warning of danger: the first distant signal.[59]

These were rotating board signals, which in effect disappeared when turned edge-on to indicate the absence of known danger. But they and other types were eventually replaced by semaphore signals. Initially, when trains were separated by intervals of time, the function of signals was to indicate known dangers; later, when the time interval system gave way to the block system and trains were separated by intervals of space, they indicated whether the line was clear. The progress of the block system depended upon progress with installation of the electric telegraph between signal boxes, to enable adjacent signalmen to confirm, one with the other, whether the lines between were clear or blocked. Block working by telegraph was brought into use between Glasgow and Paisley, to give an early example, in 1865.[60]

The need for instant communication to control trains had become apparent earlier than this on lines built with a single track and passing loops. Much of the Monklands system was laid out like this, and after horsedrawn trains were discontinued in 1848 trains were supposed to run according to timetable. Head-on collisions did occur from time to time, but these, according to Don Martin, were 'generally of a very gentle nature'. The electric telegraph was eventually installed in the 1860s.[61] Meanwhile the first part of the Great North of Scotland Railway had been opened in 1854, single line with passing loops: the electric telegraph was installed from the start, and the progress of trains was regulated by crossing orders telegraphed by an official from a central point.[62] Extensions to the railway were operated similarly. So were the lines that formed the Highland Railway, and so were the Portpatrick & Wigtownshire Railways.

Eventually this system attracted adverse attention from the Board of Trade, which preferred the electric tablet system developed at the suggestion of a Caledonian Railway official by Edward Tyer, and patented by him in 1878. A stock of metal discs, or 'tablets', engraved with the name of a single-line section was held in instruments at each end of it: the instruments were connected electrically so that only one tablet might be extracted at a time, and no more until it was replaced in one or other of them. The tablet was handed to the driver of a train as authority to enter the section.[63] The lines just mentioned were converted to operation by electric tablet during the 1880s and 1890s.

This in turn produced a problem of getting the tablets, in their pouches with hoops attached, onto and off locomotives at places where trains were not scheduled to stop, without risk of injury to enginemen or signalman, or slowing the train down excessively. This was solved by James Manson of the GNSR, who, after experimenting with adapted mail bag exchange apparatus, designed his tablet exchange apparatus specifically to exchange tablets at speed. A public-spirited man, Manson refused to patent it and it was adopted widely.[64]

Enlargement of city stations in the last years of the nineteenth century and early years of the twentieth resulted in some very extensive signalling installations, and mechanical power – electric and pneumatic – was brought to the aid of signalmen whose muscles alone had earlier provided the power to operate points and signals. An extensive electro-pneumatic installation at Glasgow Central, completed in 1908, enabled the whole of this very large station to be worked from a single signal box with 374 miniature levers. It remained in use for more than fifty years. When Edinburgh Waverley was resignalled in the late 1930s, an all-electric installation was provided: colour light signals replaced semaphores, and points were worked by

Signalman at Madgiscroft, on the Caledonian main line south of Cumbernauld, proudly displays the interior of his signalbox with lever frame, block instruments and telephone. (East Dunbartonshire Information & Archives)

Mr Sandy Beveridge, station master at Campsie Glen on the NBR Campsie branch north of Kirkintilloch, demonstrates exchanging the electric tablet with the engine crew.
(East Dunbartonshire Information & Archives)

electric motors. Track circuiting enabled the locations of trains to be shown on illuminated diagrams in the signal boxes, of which there were two, East and West, replacing seven earlier boxes.[65] Meanwhile, since the 1920s, lower quadrant semaphore arms were being gradually replaced by upper quadrant, on both LMS and LNER.

Centralised control of traffic and trains originated on the Midland Railway in the late 1900s. Control office staff, who were in touch with one another by telephone, monitored the operation of the railway continuously, with noted improvements in performance. In Scotland, this system was taken up by the Midland Railway's ally, the North British Railway, as early as 1913.[66] After the grouping it became general throughout LMS and LNER.

The BR standard class 5 4-6-0 was derived from the LMS class 5, but some examples were fitted with Caprotti rotary-cam poppet valve gear to improve efficiency, by enabling timings of inlet and exhaust valves to be independent of one another and reducing the amount of power absorbed by the valve gear itself. One of them was no. 73512, seen at Dundee in 1965. (Brian Dickson)

THE NATIONALISED RAILWAY

British Railways came into being on 1 January 1948. The name was not new: it had been used for some years in advertising material produced jointly by the Big Four, but it was the title now adopted for the nationalised railway system owned by the British Transport Commission and managed by the Railway Executive. Canals and docks formerly owned by railway companies passed to the Docks and Inland Waterways Executive, and railway hotels to the Hotels Executive. However railway-owned ships in Scotland became the responsibility of the Railway Executive. The commission inherited from the railway companies their shareholdings in other concerns such as bus companies. In some of these it later achieved full control by buying the rest of the shares, notably Scottish Motor Traction in 1949 and Highland Transport Co. Ltd. in 1951, but it was to interfere little with their management. MacBraynes, however, was owned half by the BTC, as successor to the LMS, and half by Coast Lines: half nationalised, half private.

So far as railways in Scotland were concerned, the BTC was almost all-embracing but not quite. The Glasgow Subway continued to be owned by Glasgow Council. The Strabathie Light Railway had, remarkably, been bought by Murcar Golf Club in 1924 when its original owner's brickworks closed: it

continued to carry golfers for a few years after 1948. Ownership of electric tramways on city streets was unaffected. The Pullman Car Company had not been nationalised, but was purchased by the BTC in 1954. Industrial railways such as the Lochaber Narrow Gauge Railway continued to serve their owners' needs. The extensive railways owned by colliery companies, however, were nationalised as part of the coal industry and passed to the National Coal Board.

All the businesses of the British Transport Commission were to form one undertaking, and it had a statutory duty to pay its way, taking one year with another.[1] It was to be financed by issue of loan stock – subject to approval of the Treasury, which would guarantee the interest.[2]

The commission's first chairman was Sir Cyril Hurcomb, former permanent secretary at the Ministry of Transport. To help him were four other members including Sir William Wood, former president of the executive of the LMS, and John Benstead, former general secretary of the National Union of Railwaymen. A Scottish element appeared with the appointment as a part-time member of Glasgow accountant Sir Ian Bolton, a former director of the LMS.

On the Railway Executive, most members were former senior officers of the railway companies. As it turned out, Commission and Executive would

J. McIntosh Patrick painted 'The Tay Bridge from my Studio Window' in 1948. No trains can be seen, but three graceful smoke trails from steam locomotives can, and in the present context it is these that deserve attention. Only an artist who had observed the behaviour of such things closely, day by day – but particularly when gales blew down the firth – could have caught them with such precision, and so well. Each is different. Hidden by the branches of the big tree, a locomotive is working hard up the grade onto the main bridge – the smoke is thrown well clear of the chimney before the gale catches it, and it is black because the fireman made the fire up before leaving Dundee and it has not yet burned through. In the distance is the exhaust from another locomotive – white, so mostly steam, and scattered by the wind: the train is running easily towards us, hard work over for the moment and a stop at Dundee coming soon. From the cutting nearer at hand come advancing puffs of white smoke from a third locomotive – not working hard, perhaps shunting. It is a marvellous record of a scene impossible now to re-create, yet so familiar at the time that not one of the people in the painting pays any attention at all to the trains, or the bridge. (McManus Galleries and Museum, Dundee)

frequently be at odds with each other over their respective responsibilities and what these should be. Notoriously, relations eventually deteriorated to the point at which the Executive, required to supply the Commission with copies of the minutes of its meetings but not wanting to give too much away, prepared sets of minutes, which were supplied, and also 'Memoranda of Decisions …', which were not. These were known to staff, from the colour of their paper, as the White Minutes and the Green Minutes respectively.[3]

One of the few things upon which all do seem to have been agreed was the establishment of the Scottish Region of British Railways. This however was primarily an administrative unit, not an economic one. It was presided over by a chief regional officer, who had previously been the LNER divisional general manager (Scotland) – the BTC considered that the Railway Executive itself filled the role of general manager for the entire railway system.[4] But the regions' limited autonomy did extend to selection of a 'house colour' for each: Scottish Region chose a light blue, reminiscent of Caledonian locomotives, which soon became familiar on timetable covers and station nameboards.[5] Indeed railwaymen in general still tended to look back to the period before the grouping. There were still many pre-grouping locomotives in service, and when in 1948 O. S. Nock enquired of a series of Scottish railwaymen which company they had worked for, they answered to a man in pre-grouping terms.[6]

BR's Scottish Region had 3,625 miles of route in 1948, with 1,322 stations of which 302 were for freight only.[7] The new regional administration was put on its mettle on 12–13 August of that year when disastrous storms blocked all former LNER routes to the Border at numerous points, by washouts and landslips: the East Coast main line was affected worst of all. With the assistance of the Royal Engineers, many temporary bridges were installed to enable it to be reopened at the end of October.

The Waverley Route, and the branch from it at St Boswells to the East Coast main line at Tweedmouth, had been repaired much more quickly, and East Coast trains were temporarily diverted to this route, nearly sixteen miles longer than the main line. These included the 'Flying Scotsman' which had just reverted to the pre-war practice of running non-stop between London and Edinburgh; with the diversion, however, it was permitted to stop for water en route at St Boswells or Galashiels. That in turn was treated as a challenge by the skilled enginemen concerned, who on twenty-three occasions managed to complete the 408½-mile journey without stopping: a record which almost certainly still stands.[8] Train services were still recovering gradually from the war: for instance the 'Queen of Scots' Pullman train was reinstated in 1948.

For fuel in 1948, Scottish Region motive power used 2,286,000 tons of coal, 30,000 gallons of diesel oil and no units of electricity at all.[9] Serious proposals for substantial electrification belatedly made their appearance in 1951 in the report made by the Glasgow and District Transport Committee to the BTC – the Inglis Report, so-called after committee chairman Sir Robert Inglis. This envisaged electrification of suburban services at a cost of over £10 million (at 1951 prices). It also envisaged construction of a new fourteen-platform north station which would become the terminus for train services then using both Buchanan Street and Queen Street, with a grand entrance approximately where there are now the concert hall and adjoining shopping centre. Queen Street High Level Station would have become a bus station. That these latter proposals came to nothing is to be regretted; most of the proposed electrification has been achieved, over time. Glasgow's electric tramcars, in accordance with the report, ran for the last time in 1962, the last of any town or city in Scotland.[10]

A fruitful source of discord between British Transport Commission and Railway Executive lay in choice of the type of motive power to be built. The Commission wished both electric and diesel traction for main lines to be investigated fully; the Executive, notwithstanding that both forms of traction were now well established in other countries, preferred to stick with steam. This policy was personified in R. A. Riddles, the Executive's member responsible for mechanical engineering, who considered that main-line electrification was the proper successor to steam, but unlikely to be achieved during that period of post-war national austerity with its restrictions on capital investment. In the meantime steam locomotives, which, although of low thermal efficiency, were cheap to build, appeared preferable to diesels, which though more efficient, were comparatively expensive to build.[11] And steam locomotives used home-produced fuel, but fuel for diesels, in those days before North Sea oil, had to be imported.

The consequence, as well as interim construction of many locomotives to pre-nationalisation designs, was design and construction of a range of standard steam locomotives in twelve classes,[12] of which 999 locomotives in total were built between 1951 and 1960. The range covered locomotives in all power grades, from those for branch line locals to heavy main-line freight and express passenger trains. Of particular value in Scotland were the class 5 4-6-0s and the class 4 2-6-4Ts, both of which had close similarities to

earlier LMS classes, and the Clan class light Pacifics, which had no direct predecessor but which could put in good work between, for instance, Carlisle and Stranraer, although in the end only ten were built. They were named after Scottish clans. All classes were good locomotives, straightforward, easy to maintain and available for most routes even where weight or loading gauge were restricted, but built when the day of the steam locomotive, for general use, had already reached its gloaming.

Production of standard coaches,[13] also under Riddles's direction, was more satisfactory and such coaches would in many cases have very much longer

BR standard classes included small locomotives as well as large: class 2 2-6-0 no. 78054 waits to leave Tillynaught with the two-coach branch train for Banff in 1963. (Brian Dickson)

lives than the locomotives built contemporaneously. Notable features included all-steel construction, light and airy interiors and buckeye couplings. These coupled automatically, and little slack between them meant few jerks for passengers. Only the bogies eventually gave trouble, when they became worn. Twelve types of corridor coach were introduced

BR standard light Pacific no. 72008 *Clan Macleod* attains Beattock summit, heading for Glasgow. (Brian Dickson)

in 1951, including both compartment and open saloon coaches, and others types including sleeping cars followed later. In the meantime sleeping cars which were built in 1952 followed in general pre-nationalisation designs but incorporated for the first time third-class compartments with only two berths, one above the other, which were provided with full bedding.[14]

Standard wagons too were produced, notably the all-metal sixteen-ton mineral wagon of which over 200,000 were eventually built, largely replacing the private-owners' mineral wagons inherited at nationalisation. Nevertheless these were short-wheelbase wagons, seldom fitted with automatic brakes and never, in regular service, with automatic couplings. BR was hamstrung in attempts to modernise goods wagons comprehensively as long as there was a requirement for them to enter innumerable sharply curved private sidings, and while wagons remained small they had to be easily coupled and uncoupled for shunting. Many specialised types of wagon had also to be built.[15]

While this was happening, the public was turning increasingly away from rail transport. Many people had bad memories of wartime travel in delayed and overcrowded trains. Passenger travel by bus and coach was increasing rapidly during the late 1940s – usage of the London–Edinburgh coaches of Scottish Omnibuses doubled between 1947 and 1951 for instance.[16] This BR did eventually manage to counter to some extent in 1953 with its 'Starlight Special' overnight trains between London and Edinburgh, and London and Glasgow. Fares were low and trains included an all-night buffet car; Edinburgh trains remarkably started their journey from London Marylebone.[17]

Whitegates level crossing was on the Monkland & Kirkintilloch Railway as it approached Kirkintilloch basin. By 1960 coal was no longer going out by canal, but there was a coal merchant to be supplied and a foundry needing raw materials, so the line was still open for freight. Locomotive no. 68352 (J88 class) was a North British design of more than fifty years earlier, but the first two wagons in the train are BR all-steel mineral wagons of which an enormous quantity were built in the 1950s. (Don Martin)

In the meantime petrol rationing, which had continued since the war, at last came to an end in 1950. Mass-produced cars were becoming available in increasing quantities, and before long it would become clear that the true competition lay not between rail and road, but between public transport and private. On the freight side, the BTC had absorbed the largest road hauliers, and was gradually taking over the smaller ones. The reaction of businesses was to turn increasingly to operating their own C-licence vehicles, notwithstanding motor lorries were still limited to a maximum speed of 20 mph; it would eventually be increased to 30 mph in 1957.[18] Despite intentions, actual examples of integration of the BTC's rail and road freight services were few.

In 1951 however the Conservatives returned to power with Churchill as prime minister. The consequence was the Transport Act 1953. There were two main provisions. Firstly, most of the BTC's road haulage interests were to be sold off: in the carriage of freight, the free market was to replace integration. As it turned out, peacetime railway freight traffic (throughout Britain) peaked in 1951; in terms of ton-miles carried per year, road transport in due course overtook rail in

In the early days of British Railways there were still odd byways to be found. The Gartverrie branch of the Monkland & Kirkintilloch passed beneath the Caledonian main line by a dip in which flood water accumulated, and the bridge was so low that locomotives with cut-down boiler mountings were needed. J 36 class no. 65287 in this condition cautiously approaches the location on 11 August 1961. (D. Martin)

A wet day at Kyle of Lochalsh in 1960. There was still enough freight traffic to require a shunting locomotive. (Author's collection)

1955.[19] Secondly, the Railway Executive was abolished, in the interest of decentralisation it was said. Area boards were established – after an interval during which an interim organisation sufficed – for each region, and chief regional managers were appointed with responsibility for day-to-day operation. Hurcomb retired and was replaced as BTC chairman by General Sir Brian Robertson, a distinguished ex-soldier with a strong record in administration, who probably strengthened central direction, at the expense of the area boards, more than had been intended originally.[20] The 1953 Act also required the membership of the BTC to be increased, with two members having a special responsibility for Scottish affairs. The additional Scottish member was Lt-Col Donald Cameron of Lochiel, appointed in 1954.

As an aside to these momentous events, it is worth noting that when Cameron of Lochiel, as clan chief, hosted a great gathering of Clan Cameron at Achnacarry in 1956, a special train carried members of the clan from Queen Street to Spean Bridge. The locomotive was no. 72001 *Clan Cameron* (visiting the West Highland line specially for the occasion); driver, fireman and guard were Camerons to a man, and held in reserve at Crianlarich, in case of need, was K4 class no. 61995 *Cameron of Lochiel*.[21]

British Railways as a whole was profitable until 1955; after that expenditure exceeded receipts, and the gap started to widen dramatically. But Scottish Region, regrettably, was worse than this: the only years in which its receipts exceeded or equalled expenditure were 1948 and 1951. Then the shortfall increased year by year (with one exception) until 1962, when working expenses of £58.9 million produced a gross revenue of £44.5 million.[22]

By the mid-1950s passenger trains, so recently

overcrowded, were running half-empty or worse. To look at the Scottish Region summer timetable for 1954 is to be struck not only by how extensive the system still was, but also by how limited were the train services provided over so much of it. Round the Edinburgh Suburban & South Side Junction line clockwise, for instance, there were but six trains a day, plus two more between Duddingston and Waverley. Between Aberdeen and Ballater there were three, with one more during July. Between Ladybank and Perth there were only two, between Crieff and Comrie but one. Between Edinburgh and Galashiels via Peebles there were three: I recall seeing these go by on the last stage of their journey and thinking how empty they were. Such limited services do not seem likely to attract passengers, while making little contribution to meeting fixed costs: but the list could go on and on. In all these cases the train service was much reduced compared with earlier times: the inference must be that railway management was responding to reduced traffic by withdrawing trains, and that this was a vicious circle. Certainly in 1956 Scottish Region management went on record with the opinion that it would be unrealistic to contemplate wholesale closure of branch lines, as railways had a social obligation to the communities served.[23]

Nevertheless there were closures of stations and branch lines at this period: Haddington, for instance, lost its passenger trains in 1949, Aberfoyle in 1951 (and goods trains too in 1959). Comrie to Balquhidder was closed to all traffic in 1951 also, but was retained and reused a few years later for construction traffic for a hydroelectric scheme.[24] The Ladybank–Perth route was closed to passengers in 1955, Edinburgh Waverley to Airdrie via Bathgate, and Polmont to Bo'ness, in 1956. The Border Counties line from Hexham

Inducements to passenger travel in the 1950s included 'holiday runabout tickets' allowing unlimited travel for a week in a specific area.
(R. Forsythe Collection, courtesy British Railways Board (Residuary) Ltd.)

In the 1950s, as prosperity started to return, people turned away from railways. By 1951 for instance the Aberfoyle branch train was reduced to a single coach, which seems lost in the emptiness of its terminus.
(East Dunbartonshire Information & Archives)

to Riccarton Junction was closed to passengers in October of that year: locomotives carried wreaths upon their smokeboxes.[25] The ancient station at Garnkirk was closed to passengers in 1960; the light railway to Dornoch closed to all traffic the same year. This list is by no means exhaustive.

The BTC in its new guise was still large and cumbersome, slow to respond to the need for change – Gourvish calls it a 'creaking dinosaur'.[26] It did however take over and develop a scheme prepared by the Railway Executive in its last days, for reducing costs and increasing traffic on branch lines by introducing lightweight two-car diesel trains – diesel multiple units or DMUs. Technically such things had

been feasible for twenty years or so, but BR put its first DMUs into regular service in 1954, in Yorkshire and other English locations.[27] The first to run in Scotland came on extended trial from the Eastern Region during the summer of 1956.[28]

By then, far more extensive change was in the air. Early in 1955, after twelve months' consideration, the British Transport Commission had published its plan for 'modernisation and re-equipment of British Railways'. The only possible course, it stated, if the railways were to continue in being, was to bring them properly up to date. To this end it envisaged expenditure of £1,200 million over fifteen years. The West Coast main line would be electrified from London as far

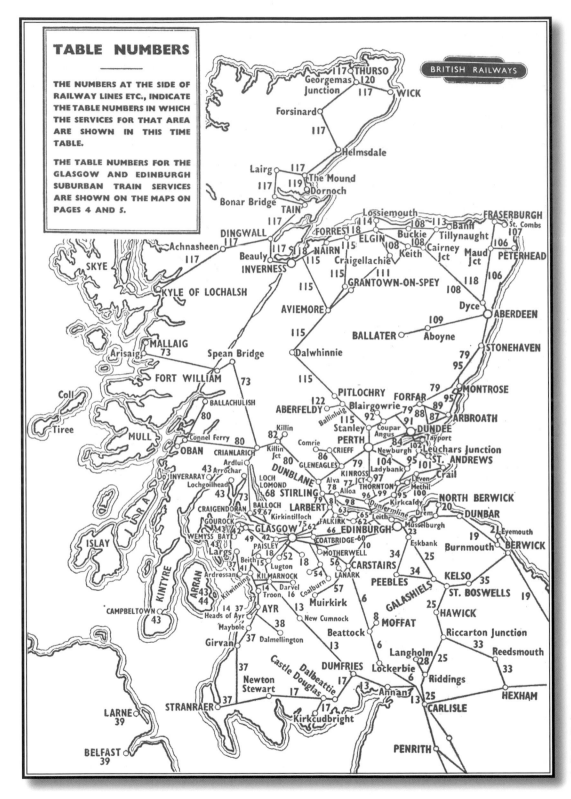

Although some branch lines had already closed by 1954, when this map appeared in Scottish Region's timetable, the railway system was still very much more extensive than at the present day. (BRB (Residuary) Ltd.)

BRITISH RAILWAYS

WITHDRAWAL OF
PASSENGER TRAIN
SERVICE
FROM
RATHO
STATION

ON AND FROM
MONDAY, 18th JUNE, 1951

The Passenger Train Service will be withdrawn from Ratho station.

Passengers for Ratho will be booked to Edinburgh from which place a bus service operates.

Passenger train parcels and miscellaneous traffic will continue to be dealt with at Ratho Station and a collection and delivery service will be given by motor vehicle connecting with the passenger train service.

Freight train traffic will continue to be dealt with at Ratho Station. A collection and delivery service will be given by motor vehicle for freight train traffic in less than truck loads.

Ratho station, on the Edinburgh & Glasgow line, was closed to passengers in 1951. Closure notices such as this would become an all too familiar sight over the next couple of decades. (East Dunbartonshire Information & Archives)

north as Crewe (and thence the lines to Liverpool and Manchester); the East Coast as far as Doncaster, or perhaps York. Lesser electrification schemes included 190 route miles of Glasgow suburban lines. Where lines were not electrified, diesel locomotives and diesel multiple units would be introduced, in quantity. Loss-making steam passenger trains on branch lines would be replaced – by DMUs where these might stimulate

additional traffic, or else by road services.

Steam locomotive construction would cease; the changeover from steam to electric or diesel power would be progressive, area by area. Since many of the 19,000 steam locomotives then in use were modern – and built for a forty-year working life – steam locomotives would be withdrawn selectively.

There would be improvements to track and signalling to allow speeds of 100 mph on main routes. Freight services would be accelerated by fitting all wagons with continuous brakes, and by construction of modern marshalling yards. From all of this, a return of £85 million a year was anticipated; BR's annual turnover was then approaching £500 million.[29]

That was the plan, belated but in several respects revolutionary. Just how belated was emphasised (perhaps unconsciously) by *The Railway Magazine* which reported, on the page opposite its article announcing the BR modernisation plan, introduction of a through train service between Paris and Syracuse (Sicily), 1,450 miles, which except for an interval on a train ferry was to be electrically hauled throughout.

The late start did provide one benefit: it was possible to adopt the newest techniques for electrification, lately introduced on the Continent. Instead of electrifying at 1,500 volts d.c. as originally planned, the BTC decided in 1956 that future electrification should be at 25 kV a.c., 50 cycles. A lighter conductor wire meant that lighter overhead structures could be built, and the cost of power supply equipment would be reduced as would current consumption. The disadvantage was that greater clearances around the overhead wiring were required; where these could not be obtained, the line voltage could be reduced to (it was in due course decided) 6.25 kV. Overall, electrification at 25 kV rather than at 1,500 volts would be cheaper in both

Lightweight diesel multiple units first appeared in regular service in Scotland in 1958, on lines around Edinburgh. An illustrated BR brochure announced their arrival. To contemporary train passengers the interiors were quite unfamiliar, owing as much to road vehicle design as to rail. (R. Forsythe Collection, courtesy British Railways Board (Residuary) Ltd.)

Blue trains came to Glasgow Central suburban services in 1962. (R. Forsythe Collection, courtesy British Railways Board (Residuary) Ltd.)

first cost and in operating cost.[30] It continues to be the system employed.

The first stage of the Glasgow suburban electrification scheme was authorised later in 1956, and was therefore designed for the 25 kV a.c. system. Two separate routes were electrified, north and south of the Clyde. The former was from Airdrie through Queen Street Low Level to Helensburgh, via both Drumchapel and Clydebank, and including the branches to Springburn, Bridgeton Central, Milngavie and Balloch. The latter was from Glasgow Central High Level to Motherwell

and Neilston High, with the Cathcart Circle. The total route mileage was 71. The task was huge. It included raising overbridges, and lowering track in tunnels, to obtain the necessary clearances despite use of 6.25 kV on the inner suburban area. It also included erecting the overhead equipment and providing power supplies, resignalling with colour-lights and much relaying of track.[31]

Ninety-one three-car electric multiple unit trains were built to BR designs by the Pressed Steel Co. Ltd at Linwood, near Paisley. Their bogies, to the

An express service of diesel trains between two cities was a new concept in the Britain of 1957. Before such a service was introduced between Edinburgh and Glasgow, the public were encouraged to have a look at what was coming their way. (East Dunbartonshire Information & Archives)

British Railways drew on the talents of the well-known railway artist Terence Cuneo to publicise Glasgow electrification. As his painting makes clear, electrification meant not only smart clean modern trains, but also installation of overhead electric wiring and new signalling – all this in sudden contrast to an older, grimier world where steam still persisted, both on rails (on the left) and on the river (on the right). (NRM – Cuneo Fine Arts / Science & Society Picture Library)

delight of enthusiasts, were recognisably derived from those developed by Gresley for the Great Northern Railway four decades before. There was nothing else old-fashioned about them. Electrical equipment was innovative. Wrap-round front windows gave them an attractive appearance. Sliding doors gave access to airy open-saloon interiors. Externally they were painted in the regional colour, Caledonian blue: the Blue Trains.[32]

The north side route, though longer, was ready first – the scheme for the south side route included resignalling Glasgow Central. On the north side, the service of electric trains started on 7 November 1960, trains which were faster, more frequent and above all cleaner than the trains they replaced.[33]

It was a false start. On 13 December on a train near

Renton a transformer exploded, injuring the guard and seven passengers. There were other incidents, less serious but similar. The entire fleet of Blue Trains was withdrawn, pending an exhaustive enquiry into the cause, and subsequent modifications; a temporary service of steam trains replaced them. The Blue Trains eventually reappeared in October 1961. Passengers flocked to use them; bus traffic fell away. The south side route followed in 1962.[34]

In their modified form, the Blue Trains evidently were satisfactory: as class 303, and repainted in successive liveries, they were familiar over many decades. All have now been withdrawn, but I recall my own surprise, when waiting for a West Highland train at Dumbarton Central as recently as November 2002, at the sudden appearance among the succession of more modern trains of a six-car train comprising two class 303 units, Gresley bogies and all.

By the time the Blue Trains were fully operational, diesel multiple units were running in many other parts of Scotland. When the first DMUs to run in Scotland on a regular basis were introduced in January 1957, however, they were no branch-line vehicles but six-car intercity trains, built at BR's Swindon works, and later known as class 126. They provided an express service between Edinburgh Waverley and Glasgow Queen Street.[35] These were the first such trains to run anywhere in Britain, and in concept the true ancestors of all the main-line DMUs operating throughout Britain today. Similar trains were put into service between Glasgow, Ayr and Stranraer in 1959, and intercity DMUs with buffets provided an accelerated service between Aberdeen and Inverness from 1960.

On Scottish branch lines and local services, DMUs first came into regular service in 1958, and soon became widespread. Lines included suburban routes from

The practice of banking trains up Cowlairs incline continued even after dieselisation. In 1960 an English Electric type 4 diesel is getting a helping hand from a steam locomotive. (Don Martin)

Edinburgh Waverley, the Deeside line, Arbroath–Dundee–Perth, Aberdeen to Fraserburgh and indeed the light railway thence to St Combs. Introduction of DMUs was often accompanied by an increased frequency in train service (or perhaps decreased infrequency would be nearer the mark!). Sadly, all too often, although additional traffic was generated, it was insufficient to ensure long-term survival of the line concerned. For instance, despite dieselisation the circular service over the Edinburgh Suburban & South Side Junction line was withdrawn in 1962 and the stations were closed.

Main-line diesel locomotives were originally classified as types 1 to 4 in ascending order of power; towards the end of the 1960s, types were subdivided into classes. The BTC's initial intention was to obtain prototype locomotives in limited quantities from many manufacturers – to a total of 174 locomotives – followed by a three-year test period. This was overtaken by a rapidly worsening financial position, leading to a

Steam age paraphernalia are still conspicuous as BR Sulzer type 4 diesel arrives at Edinburgh Waverley in 1965 with a train from the Waverley Route: water crane on the left, even oil lamps positioned on the front of the locomotive to indicate the type of train. (Brian Dickson)

need to realise economies from dieselisation as early as possible, and in turn to bulk orders of locomotives of types which had not been fully tested. They were put into service from 1957 onwards. Some were better than others. Performance of type 2 diesels built by North British Locomotive Co. was notoriously bad: when they were tried on Glasgow–Aberdeen trains, steam locomotives had to be reintroduced.[36] Such locomotives did not last long. Others did: type 3 locomotives of class 37 built by English Electric appeared in 1961: their last regular passenger duty in Scotland, hauling the Fort William sleeper, came to an

end only a couple of months before this was written.

In Scotland, diesel locomotives first made an impact in the Highlands: they were at work on lines of the former Highland Railway by 1958, on the Great North of Scotland by 1959, and on the West Highland and Callander & Oban lines from 1962.[37] After that, steam workings anywhere in the Highlands were a rarity, although the Killin branch was steam-worked until closure in 1965.

Introduction of diesel locomotives north of Inverness enabled the time for the journey from Inverness to Wick to be reduced from over six hours to four hours by the fastest train in 1962. This process was aided, however, by closure to passengers of twenty wayside stations (out of a total of forty) in 1960. Thirteen of these were between Inverness and Bonar Bridge: the A9 ran parallel, and the buses of BTC-owned Highland Omnibuses had taken their traffic.[38] Multiple closures of stations had happened before, notably in 1956 when thirty were closed to passengers between Glasgow, Perth, Aberdeen and Dundee.[39]

Other aspects of the 1955 modernisation plan proved less effective than the introduction of diesel and electric traction. The programme for fitting vacuum brakes to all wagons proved impracticable, and was formally abandoned in 1960; with it went the prospect of fitting goods wagons with automatic couplings.[40] The programme for new marshalling yards produced, in relation to Scotland, new yards at Thornton, Perth, Carlisle and Millerhill (Edinburgh), completed in the late 1950s and early '60s. Generally such new large yards were attractive in their ability to replace several smaller ones; the project for Thornton, in the Fife coalfield, dated back to the late 1940s. But changes in freight traffic, in the amount and in the manner in which it was handled, meant that they were

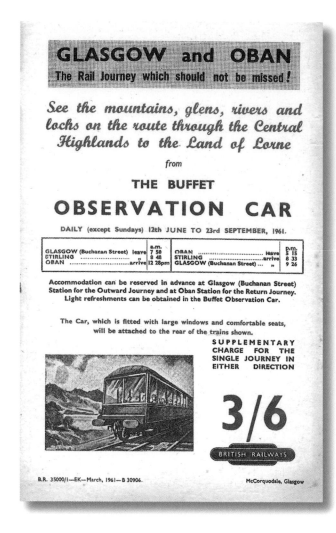

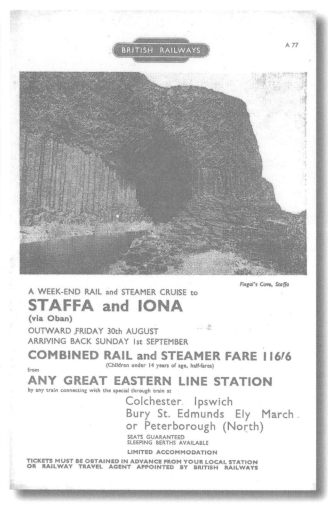

left: Observation car which had formerly run on the Pullman 'Devon Belle' train was attached to trains between Glasgow Buchanan Street and Oban.
(R. Forsythe Collection, courtesy British Railways Board (Residuary) Ltd.)

right: Long distance excursions were a feature of BR in the 1960s. A handbill publicises a weekend excursion, with sleeping cars, from East Anglia to Oban for a cruise to Staffa and Iona.
(R. Forsythe Collection, courtesy British Railways Board (Residuary) Ltd.)

seldom if ever used to full capacity.[41]

While the modernisation plan was being put into practice there were other developments. By September 1956, after an interval of seventeen years, track condition had recovered sufficiently for a late-afternoon departure from King's Cross for Edinburgh to be reintroduced: the 4.00 p.m. 'Talisman'. It was allowed 6 hr 40 min. to Edinburgh, however, compared with the six hours of the 'Coronation'. The West Coast responded the following June with a late-afternoon (4.15 p.m.) departure from Euston for Glasgow, for the first time ever: the 'Caledonian'. which, moreover, with a schedule of 6 hr 40 min. was allowed only ten minutes more than the 'Coronation Scot' had been.[42] As before, A4 and Duchess Pacifics were used; the latter had lost their streamlined casings for ease of wartime maintenance.

The 'Talisman' included some of the coaches that had been built for the 'Coronation'. It did not include the observation cars but these, enterprisingly, were being used on scenic lines in the Highlands: between Fort William and Mallaig from 1956, and between

left: Navy day at Rosyth in 1959 merited an excursion train from Edinburgh direct into the dockyard.
(R. Forsythe Collection, courtesy British Railways Board (Residuary) Ltd.)

right: Combined rail and sea excursions were offered from Scottish stations to Northern Ireland.
(R. Forsythe Collection, courtesy British Railways Board (Residuary) Ltd.)

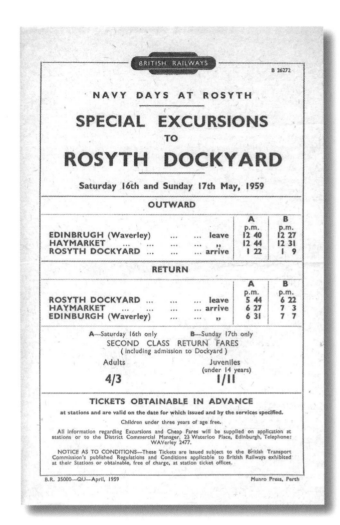

Glasgow and Oban the following year. In 1961 they were joined in Scotland by two observation cars from the 'Devon Belle', a short-lived post-war Pullman train; these were used between Glasgow and Oban, and between Inverness and Kyle of Lochalsh.[43] These observation car services lasted for about a decade.

In 1956, abolition of second class from Continental boat trains, latterly the only trains on which it had been provided, enabled third class, throughout BR, to be redesignated second class. The long-established sleeping-car service between Glasgow and Inverness

was matched from 1959 by an equivalent from Edinburgh. Long-distance excursions reappeared, for instance a combined rail and steamer excursion in 1961 from East Anglia and Lincolnshire to Oban, and thence to Staffa and Iona.

The North of Scotland Hydro-Electric Board was at this period at the height of its programme for building hydroelectric power stations; it also had a statutory duty to aid economic development in the Highlands. It was from the board that the proposal came for battery-electric railcars, to be met at first with a distinct lack of enthusiasm on the part of BR which did not want its technical staff distracted from other aspects of modernisation. The subject reached Parliament. The proposal eventually gelled in conversion at Cowlairs, in 1958, of a 1956-built two-car DMU to battery propulsion; the hydroelectric board paid for traction and control equipment of proven design, from Germany, and provided charging equipment at Aberdeen and Ballater. The battery-electric multiple unit went into service on the Deeside line in the same year, enabling the daily train service to be doubled from three trains each way daily to six. The train ran for four years giving apparent satisfaction; it was then moved to the BR Research Unit, but the type was not perpetuated.[44]

A further attempt to operate branch lines economically was introduction of four-wheeled railbuses. The author recalls, from his time as a National Serviceman in Germany during 1954–5, how commonplace such vehicles already were in that country: but it was 1957 before BR belatedly placed orders, by way of trial, with five different builders for twenty-two railbuses. Nine of these, later increased to thirteen, were allocated to Scottish Region. From 1958 onwards they were used between Gleneagles, Crieff and Comrie, on the former GNSR Strathspey line, between Craigendoran and Arrochar, and in many other places. Initiative was shown: new halts were opened for railbuses, and on Speyside the service was extended in one direction beyond Boat of Garten to Aviemore, and in the other, by reversal at Craigellachie, as a through service to Elgin. But the whole programme, regrettably, was too little and too late, and once again the railbuses lasted for a few years only.[45]

Far more successful was another motive power initiative of the period. None of the early diesel locomotives in the BR modernisation plan was to be of more than 2,300 hp, but late in 1955 English Electric built speculatively a prototype diesel-electric locomotive of no less than 3,300 hp, the *Deltic*. The name was derived from the layout of its 18-cylinder engine, which was in cross-section triangular, like the Greek letter delta (Δ) inverted, with the crankshafts at the angles of the triangle and opposed pistons working in cylinder blocks between; it had been developed as a compact power unit for minesweepers.[46] The prototype ran extensive trials on the London Midland Region which decided against it, perhaps because electrification was going ahead. Electrification of the Eastern Region out of King's Cross had evidently been pigeon-holed, for twenty-two Deltics were eventually ordered for the East Coast main line, of which eight were allocated to Scottish Region. When put into service in 1961 they proved worthy successors to A4s and A3s; the twenty-two Deltics could do the work of fifty-five steam locomotives and enabled the 'Flying Scotsman' and two other trains daily to be accelerated to a six-hour schedule, London–Edinburgh – just in time for the centenary of the 'Flying Scotsman' in 1962.[47]

Hand in hand with improvements to motive power and rolling stock went improvements to track. In place of bullhead rail in chairs, British Railways standardised on heavy flat-bottomed[48] rail on baseplates. By using substantial fastenings with closely spaced sleepers, and pre-tensioning rails to compensate for heat expansion, it was found possible to weld rails together over long distances. By 1961 every region had its own rail-welding plant.[49] BR had also obtained powers to install half-barrier level crossings, operated automatically by trains rather than by crossing keepers; the first in

as that of the railways. With increasing traffic, the drive from London to Scotland became increasingly tedious; it meant, in any case, a night in a hotel en route, perhaps two nights in hotels if the northern Highlands were the goal. To tap into this market BR introduced in 1955 an overnight car-carrier train (later branded as 'Motorail') between King's Cross and Perth. Drivers, their passengers and cars all travelled on the same train, people in sleeping cars or compartment coaches, cars in end-loading vans. The service quickly became popular and further routes were added – York–Inverness in 1956, West Midlands (Sutton Coldfield)–Stirling and Glasgow St Enoch–Eastbourne (for the Channel ports) in 1958; a daytime car-carrier between London and Edinburgh appeared in 1960.[51]

In Scotland itself, road traffic increased by 67 per cent between 1954 and 1961.[52] Responsibility at government level for trunk roads and bridges in Scotland was transferred in 1956 from the Ministry of Transport & Civil Aviation in London to the Scottish Office in Edinburgh;[53] responsibility for railways in Scotland remained almost entirely in Whitehall, which can have done little to help the cause of coordination. And modernisation of the railways, after 1955, was being put into effect against a background of modernisation, equally belated, of the road network. The first seventy-two miles of the M1 motorway, heading north from London, were opened in 1959. The first motorways in Scotland, short sections of what became the M8 and the M74, were completed in 1964 and 1966, and more motorway followed; many trunk roads were made dual carriageway at the same period. Suddenly, on such roads, car drivers could cruise at twice the speed to which they were accustomed.

In such circumstances there was a brief but vociferous campaign to the effect that railways were finished:

Scotland appeared in the mid-1960s. Open crossings protected only by flashing lights followed on lightly used lines.

There were other technical innovations. In 1957 there appeared the headline 'B. T. C. to Use Electronic Computer'. The task of the 'electronic computer', named *Leo*, was to recalculate the distances – around 50 million of them – between all stations and goods depots as an aid to accurate charging of freight traffic.[50]

In the late 1940s and early 1950s, improvement of the main road network had been neglected as much they should be closed forthwith and converted into roads.[54] In practice, few closed railways in Scotland were converted into roads although, of those few, Edinburgh's West Approach Road, occupying the site of the approach tracks to Princes Street Station, is a notable example, and the location of the A6091 past Melrose has already been mentioned.

The improvements to the road system were if anything even more important in relation to freight traffic than passenger. Maximum gross weights permitted for lorries were increased to twenty-four tons in 1955, thirty-two tons (for articulated lorries) in 1964 and thirty-eight tonnes in 1983. Their maximum permitted speeds were again increased, to 40 mph in 1967 and to 60 mph on motorways in 1971.[55] Slowness, delays, loss and damage became associated with rail transport and encouraged use of road transport instead.[56] Such problems could be reduced by use of containers with guaranteed delivery dates: the successful 'Condor' service, introduced in 1959, offered overnight transits for containers between the London area and the Glasgow area, using diesel-hauled trains of twenty-seven fully-braked container wagons between Hendon and Gushetfaulds.[57] The long-established arrangements for 'To be called for' parcels were promoted as the Red Star scheme from 1963.

Air traffic, both between Scotland and England, and to and from Scottish islands, was also increasing rapidly. The Post Office started an airmail service between London and Glasgow and Edinburgh in 1961. Bus traffic, alone among competitors to rail, was showing a decline. This was attributed to the spread of both private motoring and television, which latter encouraged people to stay at home in the evenings rather than go out.

As BR needed increasingly to economise, so increases in railwaymens' rates of pay started to lag behind those of other industries. There were leapfrogging claims by the trade unions, and increasing industrial unrest. When ASLEF members came out on strike for seventeen days in 1955 it was the first national strike in the industry since 1926, and problems continued to escalate. Fares, on the other hand, were repeatedly increased.

The rapidly declining fortunes of the BTC, despite the modernisation plan and other measures to restore them, were occupying an increasing amount of Parliamentary time. By 1959 Harold Macmillan, former director of the Great Western Railway, was prime minister, and Ernest Marples, founder of road construction firm Marples, Ridgeway & Partners, was his minister of transport. In March 1960 Macmillan told the House of Commons that 'the railway system must be remodelled to meet current needs, and the modernisation plan must be adapted to this new shape.'[58] Marples appointed a special advisory group to consider the commission's future. Known as the Stedeford Advisory Group after its chairman Sir Ivan Stedeford, it comprised four prominent businessmen, plus two senior civil servants with a watching brief. One of the four businessmen was technical director of ICI, Dr Richard Beeching.[59]

The advisory group proved unable to agree upon the best structure for nationalised transport,[60] but much of its members' thinking eventually appeared in the White Paper *Reorganisation of the Nationalised Transport Undertakings,* which appeared in December 1960. The heart of the problem, it stated, lay in the railways which, although a vital basic industry, were by then short by about £60 million a year of meeting even their running costs; on top of that were interest charges of some £75 million a year. The railways had capital liabilities totalling some £1,600 million. Of this, £400 million related to accumulated losses financed by Exchequer advances: these would be written off (the sum was eventually increased to £475 million). A further £800 million would be placed in a suspense account subject to neither interest nor repayment. This would relieve the railways of over £40 million annual interest. Reorganised, the railways were then to break even within five years and pay the balance of interest remaining. In the interim, the Treasury would fund deficits; it would also take over responsibility for British Transport Stock.

These provisions took statutory form in the Transport Act 1962. Reorganisation under the Act took the form of establishment of the British Railways Board, three other boards and a holding company, between which the various undertakings of the British Transport Commission were to be distributed. Railways, hotels and the Caledonian Steam Packet Co. went to BRB; canals went to the British Waterways Board, docks to the British Transport Docks Board, London Transport to London Transport Board; just about everything else (including bus interests, the half-share in David MacBrayne Ltd, and the rump of British Road Services) went to the Transport Holding Company. The new boards were in future to act independently of one another. Financial imperatives had made division of transport according to mode almost complete; integration and coordination were largely cast aside.

The Act contained further important provisions. It at last relieved the railways of their common carrier obligations, and in effect gave the BRB freedom to decide whether to carry or not, and at what charges:[61] the commercial freedom that the Big Four companies had sought with their 'Square Deal' campaign so long before. It also restated the functions of Transport Users' Consultative Committees, which had been established as advisory bodies under the 1947 Act. They were now given the important additional and specific task of receiving objections to proposed closures of railways by BRB, and reporting to the minister on the hardship which might be caused.[62] The minister might then give his consent, or he might not.

There was another, and dubious, effect of the Act. Henceforward the Treasury would become the sole source of long-term capital for the nationalised railway system. Investment in it would be either feast or famine, according to changing economic circumstances and government policies.[63]

The British Railways Board, the members of which would be appointed by the minister of transport, was to act through regional boards – of which one was to be the Scottish Railway Board – the members of which it would appoint after consultation with the minister. But long before the Transport Act passed into law, Dr Beeching had been appointed chairman of the BTC in June 1961 (Robertson retired) and chairman designate of BRB. He had disagreed with Stedeford, but had evidently impressed Marples: he had identified that there was a need to establish just what railways should be trying to do, as well as how best to do it. Intensive studies were started on traffic flows, volumes, costs, and suitability to rail, and how to modify freight carrying to attract more freight.[64] Nothing so searching and widespread had ever been attempted before. Something of what was emerging was made public from time to time, notably the specific of the 7.56 p.m. train from Berwick to Edinburgh which was said to cost £164 a day to run, for an average daily revenue of ten shillings.[65] More

A DMU is ready to leave Kirkintilloch for Glasgow Queen Street in 1961. Dieselisation would eventually be insufficient to save the service. (Don Martin)

dramatic, if less sensational, was the discovery that freight traffic to the extent of some 90 million tons a year, then on road, was suitable for rail.[66]

All this came to a climax with the publication in 1963 of *The Reshaping of British Railways* or, as it became familiarly known, the Beeching Plan or the Beeching Report. The thought underlying this, as expressed in its 'Summary', was that railways should be used to meet that part of the total transport requirement of the country for which they offered the best available means, and that they should cease to do things for which they were ill-suited.[67] The railways' advantage was the low cost per unit moved when traffic was carried in dense flows of well-loaded through trains; their disadvantage was the high cost of their specialised routes, while most of the system was still laid out as it had been a century before, with stations spaced closely enough for local distribution of traffic

by horsedrawn vehicles. Results of the traffic studies were included. Three branch lines, two in England and one in Scotland, were picked out for censure as being particularly uneconomic. The Scottish example was Gleneagles–Crieff–Comrie where, it was said, the train service was ten diesel railbuses a day, each of which carried on average five passengers at any one time; the income from them was only one-tenth of the cost of running the service.[68] Of course it is possible to pick holes in this (as in much else of the detail in the plan): notably, that the service between Crieff and Comrie was only three railbuses a day, which scarcely seems enough of an increase from one steam train a day to recover much lost traffic, while the main-line junction at Gleneagles is not really in the direction that people from Crieff want to go. But here as elsewhere in the plan the overall conclusion seems inescapable. In this case it was withdrawal. What was needed

Closed under the Beeching Plan, the line between Kirkintilloch and the main line junction at Lenzie is being dismantled near Back o'Loch halt in October 1968.
(East Dunbartonshire Information & Archives)

simultaneously, of course, was a rail-link station-to-station bus service Stirling–Crieff–Perth with guaranteed train connections at each end, through tickets and a commitment to continued operation indefinitely. But the governmental climate in Britain has seldom favoured that sort of thing.

The proposals in the Beeching Plan were these:

- discontinuance of many stopping passenger train services, and transfer of displaced DMUs to continuing services which were still steam;
- closure of a great many small stations to passengers;
- selective improvement of intercity passenger services with rationalisation of routes;
- damping down seasonal peaks of passenger traffic, enabling coaches to be withdrawn;
- coordination of suburban train and bus services in collaboration with municipal authorities;
- coordination of parcels services with the Post Office;
- increase in 'block'(i. e., bulk) train movement of coal between collieries and distributors;
- reducing uneconomic freight traffic by closing small stations, while retaining potentially good railway traffic;
- attracting more siding-to-siding traffic suitable for through-train (i. e., trainload) movement;
- development of 'Liner Trains'(i. e., carrying freight containers) where there were traffic flows which, though dense, comprised consignments too small for through trains;
- concentration of parcels traffic on 100 main depots;
- rapid withdrawal of freight wagons;
- continued replacement of steam by diesel locomotives for main lines;
- rationalisation of the railways road cartage fleet (i.e. motor vehicles used for collection and delivery of parcels).

If the whole were implemented with vigour, said the plan, much of the deficit might be eliminated over seven years.[69]

The Beeching Plan, with its many positive proposals, was at first well received: *The Railway Magazine* commented that it was 'only six or seven years overdue'.[70] Much of the subsequent development of rail in Britain rests on foundations to be found in it. But the devil lay in the detail, in the specific proposals for passenger train services to be withdrawn and passenger stations to be closed. Bad news gets more prominence than good: the press started to write about the 'Beeching Axe'.

Change, when delayed, is eventually all the more severe in its effect. In Scotland the plan proposed that no fewer than 52 passenger train services should be withdrawn, and 425 stations and halts closed to passengers. According to the maps accompanying it, there would be no passenger trains north and west of Inverness, nor south of Ayr and west of Dumfries, nor in the Borders between East and West Coast main lines (which would themselves lose their local trains), nor in the north-east except for the main line between Aberdeen and Inverness.

The closure processes started almost as soon as the report was published. Unsurprisingly, Gleneagles–Crieff–Comrie and the local service between Edinburgh and Berwick were in the first batch of closures. Lossiemouth, Banff, Rumbling Bridge, Crook of Devon, Dalmellington, Aberfeldy, Craigellachie and Kirkintilloch were among the seemingly innumerable places which lost their passenger trains over the next couple of years. So, surprisingly, was Glasgow Central Low Level, when the service from Coatbridge to Dumbarton through its smoke-filled tunnels was withdrawn.

The procedure was that closure proposals for passenger stations were initiated by Scottish Region, passed to BRB, and referred to the Scottish TUCC which held a public inquiry if, as was almost invariably the case, there were objections. The TUCC considered the hardship involved and made its recommendations to the Minister. Effective restriction, of the aspects which the TUCC could consider, to 'hardship' led to great resentment and the formation of campaigning groups who wished to see the debate widened to include, for instance, the economic circumstances of a proposed closure. As part of this movement the Scottish Railway Development Association (later the Scottish Association for Public Transport) had been formed in 1962, taking the line that the optimum level of closures had almost been reached already: the emphasis should be on continued improvements.[71]

Yet Marples was insistent that, before he took a decision on a closure proposal, everything relevant – buses, roads, commuting needs, holiday travel and more – was considered at ministry level.[72] Certainly most of his consents were conditional in some respect or another, often introduction of improved bus services – but there seems to have been no mechanism to ensure that these would continue indefinitely. And although the majority of closure proposals went through, closure was no foregone conclusion. Never was this more strikingly demonstrated than in 1964 when he refused consent to proposed closure of the lines from Inverness to Wick, Thurso and Kyle of Lochalsh: closure of a few of the wayside stations only was allowed. Nor did he consent to closure between Ayr and Stranraer, and although he consented to withdrawal of trains between Stranraer and Dumfries via the Portpatrick & Wigtownshire line, the overnight trains between Stranraer and London were to continue, diverted via Ayr and Mauchline.[73]

Closure of branch lines and wayside stations to passengers was often, but not invariably, accompanied by their closure to freight, which BR could do without formality.

What of positive developments? Construction of diesel locomotives continued apace. Type 4 diesel-electric locomotives of 2,750 hp were introduced at the end of 1962 and built in quantity – later they became familiar as Class 47.[74] Passengers on the down 'Talisman' in the summer of 1964 found it consisted of newly designed 'Project XP 64' coaches with wide entrance doors, wide windows, seat shells

By no means all stations listed for closure under the Beeching Plan were in fact closed. Bishopbriggs was proposed for closure at the same time as Kirkintilloch, but survived and is seen here in 1976. With a first-generation DMU with yellow warning front, an economy square-box station building, and passengers in flared trousers, the scene is BR of the 1970s in a nutshell. (East Dunbartonshire Information & Archives)

moulded in glass-fibre reinforced plastic, fluorescent lighting, pressure heating and ventilation, light and airy interiors, and litter bins. (These last were a real innovation: accumulated litter under the seats, for want of anywhere better to put it, had been a regular feature of British trains for years.) The coaches were the prototypes of the BR Mark 2 standard coach; they ran on improved bogies, and the production version had an integral body shell.[75] Meanwhile passengers on the 'Night Limited' all-first-class sleeping-car train between Glasgow and London found a pleasant

novelty in the form of the 'Nightcap Bar', a former Pullman car. BRB started to market itself by the shortened title 'British Rail' in 1965, and at the same time adopted the double-arrow symbol which in due course replaced earlier devices of heraldic origin, and remains familiar today as a symbol of railway presence, having outlived its originator.[76]

In February 1965 BRB published *The development of the major railway trunk routes*, a comprehensive plan for the next twenty years. But this second stage of Beeching's reshaping proved still-born. A general election in October 1964 had returned the Labour Party to power; at the end of May 1965 Dr Beeching, after four turbulent years with British Transport Commission and British Railways Board, returned at his own request to ICI.[77]

Anyone who thought that these events might bring an end to closures was in for a shock. Although the former Caledonian main line between Glasgow and Edinburgh via Shotts was reprieved, on account of the hardship which would have been suffered by a great many commuters from the longer journey times by road, this was an exception. The closure Juggernaut rolled on. Notable closures to passengers during 1965 included Edinburgh Princes Street (with trains diverted to Waverley) and Dunblane–Callander–Crianlarich; in 1966, Aberdeen–Ballater, Glasgow Buchanan Street, Glasgow St Enoch (with 250 trains a day diverted to Central) and in 1967 the original West Coast main line between Stanley and Kinnaber Junction, with Glasgow–Aberdeen trains diverted via Dundee. In the latter case the line remained open for freight from Stanley to Forfar, and for a short distance at its eastern end. With Glasgow Buchanan Street closed, trains from Larbert and the North ran to Queen Street; from Cumbernauld, an alternative train service ran to Springburn to connect with Glasgow north electric trains.

Against this background, steam locomotives were being withdrawn very much more quickly than had been anticipated originally. In 1962 alone BR's stock of 11,700 steam locomotives was reduced by a quarter.[78] There was a swan song. Between 1963 and 1966, A4 Pacifics were rostered to work the three-hour expresses between Glasgow Buchanan Street and Aberdeen via Perth and Forfar. In these their last days, their feats of acceleration and high speed became famous. Speeds were sometimes far in excess of the official 75 mph line speed limit: O. S. Nock, reporting one particularly fine run in *The Railway Magazine*, thought it wise to mention neither the date nor the name of locomotive. On that occasion the *average* speed for the 22.4 miles from Stanley Junction to Kirriemuir Junction, pass to pass, was 85.6 mph; maximum speeds in the high 80s were a regular occurrence, and 90 mph was known.[79] Diesels eventually took over in the autumn of 1966.

Yet even that was not the end. For 25 March 1967, Easter Saturday, Scottish Region organised a Grand Scottish Railtour. The route, to be accomplished in the day, was from Edinburgh over the Waverley Route to Carlisle, thence by the West Coast main line to Aberdeen, by the Great North to Craigellachie and Aviemore, and back via Perth to Edinburgh. Much of this lay over lines soon to be closed, and most of it was diesel-hauled. When it became known that the Perth–Aberdeen stage would be steam, by then a rarity, interest boomed and as many as eighteen coaches had to be provided. The locomotives were class 5 4-6-0 no. 44997 and A4 60009 *Union of South Africa*: the latter had just been purchased for preservation in working order, as will be mentioned in the next chapter. These two, with their quarter-mile-long train, reached 75 mph between Coupar Angus and Forfar and 80 mph near Bridge of Dun, and then reached 80 mph again in the dip through Stonehaven station.[80]

In 1965 in Scotland there were still about 300 passenger trains a day rostered for steam haulage. The busiest route was Glasgow to Gourock and Wemyss Bay, with about thirty-nine trains a day worked by steam, pending electrification.[81] But steam traction was disappearing fast. Just when it may be said to have disappeared completely from regular use in Scottish Region is surprisingly difficult to establish: reports

Although the 'end of steam' on British Rail in Scotland came in 1967, commercial use of steam locomotives in industry survived for more than a decade afterwards. This was Bedlay Colliery on the very last day of all, 11 December 1981.
(East Dunbartonshire Information & Archives)

conflict, and in any event it seems clear that even when steam locomotives were no longer based in Scotland, steam-hauled trains were still entering the country from north-west England. But the date, evidently, is some time in 1967. At the end of February there were still six steam trains daily on the Glasgow–Gourock line, and in early summer there was still steam to be seen around Perth, Dundee and Stirling. The last working steam locomotives allocated to a Scottish depot appear to have been J36 class 0-6-0s nos. 65288 and 65345, which were withdrawn from Dunfermline and Thornton respectively on 4 June. But as late as November a few steam-hauled freight trains were still arriving at Mossend yard, north of Motherwell, from Carlisle behind class 5 4-6-0s and 9F 2-10-0s.[82] That is the latest report I have so far found. By April 1968 it was news that there was still a standard 2-6-4T at Cowlairs, being used to steam-heat carriages.[83] The end of steam on BR came that August,[84] with the last trains running in north-west England; after that, steam locomotives were banned, even those which had been bought for preservation.

The disappearance of the steam locomotive was so sudden, so comprehensive and so complete as to defy analogy. Its effect is that people now aged under about fifty can have no clear recollection of steam locomotives in everyday use on BR, but those aged sixty or more grew up in an era when the steam locomotive was as much part of the everyday scene as the motor car.

In any case, after 1967, steam locomotives were still being used on industrial railways, particularly those of the National Coal Board. This continued through the 1970s, although on a declining scale. The last fully commercial working of all by steam in Scotland was on 11 December 1981, at Bedlay Colliery – not far from the Monkland & Kirkintilloch Railway where it had started 150 years before.[85]

Along with the reduction in BR's miles of route and numbers of locomotives went a reduced demand for maintenance facilities. Closures of old-established workshops were another feature of the 1960s: they included Cowlairs, Inverurie and Inverness.

Locomotive no. 27037 shunts timber wagons at Crianlarich Lower in 1979, before setting off for Corpach with another trainload of pulpwood. (Author)

On the positive side, Glasgow electric Blue Trains reached Gourock and Wemyss Bay in 1967; on this thirty-seven-mile route, thirty-eight signal boxes were replaced by three.[86] Following a twenty-two-year agreement made in 1963, a new paper mill at Corpach, Fort William, had been laid out for rail transport and, a couple of years later, regular block trains started to supply it with timber from a loading point established at Crianlarich Lower which was retained for the purpose. Many other block trains appeared: goods carried included petroleum products, fertiliser, cement, even motor cars en route from manufacturer to distributor. Air-braked wagons enabled such trains to run at 60 mph or more. Many such trains were 'company trains' for specific customers; in them the private-owner wagon reappeared, often of specialised

type. This relieved BR of the capital investment, but restricted them to charging for haulage only.

The block-train concept was developed further into the 'merry-go-round' train for carrying coal from collieries to electricity generating stations: permanently coupled trains of air-braked high-capacity wagons would be on the move continuously, being loaded while passing slowly beneath bunkers and unloaded while passing slowly over hoppers. Their first application in Scotland, and one of the first in Britain, was to supply the then new power station at Cockenzie from about 1966. Two trains of twenty-eight wagons each were able to do the work which under the old system, where wagons were used for short-term storage as well as transport, would have required 1,500 wagons. By 1972, two-thirds of the tonnage of freight carried on

BR was being carried by the trainload.[87]

Dr Beeching, addressing the Institute of Directors in October 1962,[88] had promised 'liner trains' carrying containers, and they reappeared in the Beeching Plan. The concept of the container, interchangeable between rail and road, was not new. What was then novel was the fully intermodal stackable freight container for rail, road, sea and, from the late 1960s, ocean transport. The International Standards Organisation standardised on containers eight feet wide and eight feet high. These could, just, be accommodated within the British loading gauge by building wagons with small wheels and low decks. The liner train concept envisaged combining the best features of rail and road, using permanently coupled trains of container-carrying bogie wagons to run at scheduled times direct from terminal to terminal, avoiding marshalling yards. Detention of wagons for loading and unloading would equally be avoided, for the containers would be transferred at the terminals to and from road vehicles which would collect them from consignors and deliver them to consignees. Damage and pilferage would be reduced, speed and all-weather reliability increased. It was, arguably, the most revolutionary proposal in the Beeching Plan: it was to be the future for less-than-trainload traffic. Much of this traffic, manufactured goods and the like, had already been lost to road but could in this way be recovered; where it was still carried by rail by traditional means, it was uneconomic.[89]

Few existing British Rail road vehicles were suitable for carrying the containers. Many of those belonging to British Road Services, C-licence operators and private hauliers were. In any case, much of the hoped-for traffic was already in the hands of private hauliers. For the concept to work, the terminals had to be open to all. It was on this point, particularly the private hauliers,

that the NUR dug in its feet, concerned among much else about redundancies among its members. The Transport and General Workers' Union was initially hesitant too, on behalf of its members in road haulage. All aspects can be justified, depending on your point of view. The consequence was that, just when urgent action was most needed, negotiations dragged on, and on. It was more than three years after the concept was first announced before the first commercial liner train service ran, on 15 November 1965, between London and Gushetfaulds, Glasgow. Even then, to meet NUR objections, all the associated road carriage was being done by BR and British Road Services. But it got a helpful send-off when an early cold snap blocked the road over Shap and stranded vehicles in the snow, while the 'Freightliners' got through on time. It was the following spring before agreement was reached with the railway unions that private hauliers might enter Freightliner terminals.[90] Subsequently the service expanded rapidly and Aberdeen, Edinburgh, Dundee and Coatbridge were added to the Freightliner terminals in Scotland.

In 1968 Freightliner trains started to run between Scotland and East Anglia (Harwich and Felixstowe) for the Continent: a prediction in the Beeching Plan, that liner train services to ports would be especially attractive, would be proved correct. But the internal services never seemed quite to match their early promise, while wagonload traffic rapidly declined. *Railway Magazine*s of the period regularly contained a litany of stations from which 'freight facilities' were being withdrawn.[91] It was at this period that passenger traffic, rather than freight, became the dominant business for BR. Indeed it can be said that after Dr Beeching left BR, although the policies which originated with the Beeching Plan continued, the negative ones were taken too far, and the positive ones not far enough. I do not recollect, for instance, that there was ever any attempt to coordinate parcels traffic between the railways and the Post Office.

Proposed coordination of suburban train and bus services did get a boost, however, from perhaps an unexpected direction. Late in 1965 Barbara Castle was appointed Minister of Transport, and transport policy was steered onto a new course. In mid-1966 a white paper[92] made public new proposals for the future role of existing public transport systems, in a world where the motor vehicle was now dominant – particularly the private motor vehicle with all its advantages (such as individual mobility and convenience) and disadvantages (such as congested cities and roads). These proposals took shape in the Transport Act 1968. It provided for integration of public passenger transport in conurbations, by establishment of passenger transport authorities and passenger transport executives. A PTA, composed mainly of representatives of local authorities in an area designated, was to make the policy for a PTE, a corporate body, to carry out. Greater Glasgow PTA and PTE were established under this Act in 1972; in due course the name 'Strathclyde' replaced 'Greater Glasgow'. The initials SPT became familiar. PTEs were given powers both to carry passengers, and to subsidise BR: in specifying train services in its area, and funding BR, and later ScotRail, to run them, SPT was to prove extremely effective.[93]

There were other important provisions in the Act. The National Freight Corporation was established to integrate the merchandise-carrying activities of the Transport Holding Co. and the BRB, which had been competing against one another. So the BRB's 'sundries' business – that is to say, carriage of miscellaneous less-than-wagonload goods by freight train, as distinct

from 'parcels' which were carried by passenger train at higher rates – was incorporated as National Carriers Ltd and transferred to the NFC. Included was BR's entire fleet of road vehicles used for collection and delivery, and a 51 per cent interest in the Freightliner business. BR subsequently hired back such road vehicles as it needed for collection and delivery of parcels and wagonload traffic. The new corporation was given a duty to ensure that goods were carried by rail whenever efficient and economic, but later became road-orientated.[94]

Road haulage in general ceased to be regulated by carriers' licences, A, B and C: the Act instead introduced a system of operators' licences, concerned primarily with safety.[95]

The Act further established the Scottish Transport Group, and required the transfer to it from British Railways Board of the Caledonian Steam Packet Co., and from the Transport Holding Co. (which was being dissolved) of its bus interests and the former LMS half-share in David MacBrayne Ltd. The new group purchased the other half-share in 1969 and its shipping line, now wholly nationalised, became in due course Caledonian MacBrayne, 'CalMac'. Scottish local authorities were empowered to grant-aid bus services and ferries, and to recover half the expenditure (for buses) or all of it (for ferries) from the secretary of state. The new group was given a duty to cooperate with BRB.[96] Nevertheless the era of the roll-on, roll-off ferry for road vehicles had arrived, and within a few years CalMac was, at government behest, concentrating on such services, by the shortest possible sea crossings. Although some passenger interchange with trains continued, the extent of services was much reduced: no longer did steamer services down the Clyde act as extensions of railway lines on land.

The sun shone on BR in its heyday! The morning train from Mallaig to Glasgow over the West Highland line approaches Tyndrum in June 1979. Second coach is the buffet car.
(Author)

Perhaps the most important aspect of this Act, however, from the railway point of view, was that it gave statutory recognition to the concept that some railway services, although uneconomic, were necessary on social grounds. As early as 1959 there had been ideas at ministry level that financial aid should be provided for railways of this sort, such as those of the Scottish Highlands. The BTC had been unhappy about this, fearing perceptively that government assistance would give the ministry control over its operations.[97] In any case, in the aftermath of the Beeching Plan, BR in general was being supported financially by the government pending the hoped-for improvement in its financial position, which only partially materialised. But now the PTEs were to be able to fund socially necessary commuter services, which were uneconomic in themselves, but of which the closure would nonetheless add to road-congestion. As for other socially necessary but uneconomic railways, such as those in remote areas for which there was no reasonable alternative, the Minister – with the consent of the Treasury – was authorised to make grants for them to BRB, but only for three years at a time.[98] Additionally, local authorities in Scotland were – with the consent of the secretary of state for Scotland – authorised to provide financial assistance for railway passenger services.[99]

These provisions were no panacea. Passenger-train services were withdrawn between Dunfermline, Alloa and Stirling in October 1968, and between Leuchars Junction and St Andrews in January 1969. Astonishingly in retrospect, although less so in the confused circumstances of the period, this left St Andrews without any rail service, despite the opening there a few months earlier by BRB-owned British Transport Hotels of the eighty-bedroom Old Course Hotel, the only new hotel that the undertaking ever built.[100]

And so to the most extensive, and probably the most controversial, closure of all: the Waverley Route from Edinburgh via Galashiels and Hawick to Carlisle. This was no rural branch, but part of a main line which linked capital cities. John Buchan once sent his heroes, hurrying to London, on a 'furious motor race' to catch the Midland express at Hawick.[101] Yet the Waverley Route's fortunes were ever uncertain. The North British Railway could presumably earn more from carrying an Edinburgh–London passenger for 98¼ miles to Carlisle, rather than 57½ miles to Berwick, and perhaps promoted the route over-enthusiastically. The LNER, on the other hand, could earn a lot more by carrying such a passenger all the way

by the East Coast route rather than by handing over to the LMS at Carlisle. And the LMS would no doubt have preferred to take the passenger all the way by the West Coast route, rather than only from Carlisle to St Pancras. After the First World War, train services between Edinburgh and London St Pancras never recovered pre-war speed and frequency, and after the Second World War they were worse still. There were intermittent attempts at improvement, but in any event the Waverley–Midland Route could scarcely have been competitive, for Edinburgh–London travel, once the LMS and the LNER had agreed in 1932 to be bound no longer by the eight-and-a-quarter-hour schedule by East and West Coast routes. It remained important for traffic to and from intermediate places. Latterly part of the problem lay in speed restrictions over colliery workings between Nottingham and Leeds.[102] The apparently obvious alternative, open to BR, of running a Waverley Route express south from Carlisle by the West Coast route to Euston, seems never to have been considered – or, if it was, it was not made public. Or through coaches that way – perhaps combined at Carlisle with a daytime express from Stranraer to Euston (another absentee from latter-day timetables): that would have done much to attract passengers to both lines. One may dream.

On a Friday evening in October 1968 I travelled from Edinburgh to Galashiels. The train was full of young people heading home for the weekend. There was the familiar musty smell of Mark 1 stock when the steam heating came on in autumn. At Galashiels up-to-date colour light signals blazed through the darkness. There was nothing to suggest anything wrong. But the hill country of the Borders is rugged enough to present real problems, steep gradients and sharp curves, to trains on a railway. It scarcely does so to motor vehicles on roads. Proposed closure of the Waverley Route had been announced two years before, in the summer of 1966. The cost of keeping it open with grant-aid under the Transport Act, soon to become law, was considered and found excessive: 11d. a mile for each passenger, compared with the 3d. a mile paid by passengers themselves, it was said.

The Waverley route was closed early in 1969. The last through train was the sleeper to St Pancras, on the night of 5–6 January. Feelings ran high. Famously, the inhabitants of Newcastleton, reluctant to see their last train go, held the level crossing gates closed against it for over an hour in the middle of a snowy night. The parish minister was arrested. Coal trains continued to run south as far as Hawick for a few weeks, until a contract with the local coal merchant expired, and then closure was complete. Some 30,000 people in the Galashiels and Hawick areas were left 40 miles or so from the nearest station.[103]

The closure of the Waverley route had been a long-drawn-out process, much in the public eye. The closure of another main line radiating from Edinburgh, the direct route to Perth through Glenfarg, was by contrast carried out quietly and quickly: yet its effect on the long-term viability of the surviving railway system has probably been greater. As late as 1967 this was classified as a route for development. But when BR applied for grant-aid for it in 1968, the Ministry of Transport's response was that rerouting Edinburgh–Inverness trains via Stirling would be better value. BR therefore proposed closure from Cowdenbeath to Bridge of Earn. The Scottish TUCC, surprisingly, found little evidence of hardship; the Scottish Development Department, the Scottish Economic Planning Board and the Scottish Economic Planning Council found no reason to demur and, despite strong objections

from the Scottish Railway Development Association, consent for closure was given in October 1969 and the line was closed early in 1970. Not long afterwards, the M90 motorway was built over its course through Glenfarg, saving possibly as much as £500,000 in construction costs. It is difficult to believe this did not have a bearing on the closure decision.[104]

BR, however was left with taking passengers between Edinburgh and Perth, and all points north, round by Stirling, sixty-nine and a half miles compared with forty-eight by the direct route, with all that that implied in increased journey times and costs: fares were not to be altered.[105] The position was alleviated partially in 1975 when the goods line from Ladybank to Bridge of Earn with its continuation to Hilton Junction was reopened to passenger traffic, providing a fifty-seven-mile route between Edinburgh and Perth. Subsequently most passenger trains have gone that way; but the road distance from Edinburgh to Perth had become forty-three miles, most of it motorway or dual carriageway, and the railway system continues to operate under this handicap. Indeed the handicap is the greater because at the time of writing the rail speed limit between Ladybank and Hilton Junction is only 55 mph, although there is a proposal to raise it.[106]

A side effect of the introduction of fast trains with good acceleration in the 1960s was less need for mailbag exchange apparatus. Trains conveying TPOs could now wait longer than before at main stations, with local collection and distribution of mails by motor vehicles over wide areas. As late as 1967 there were still fifteen places (nine of them north of the border) at which the 'West Coast Postal' used bag exchange apparatus, but it was used for the last time in Scotland early in 1971, at Stonehaven and Laurencekirk, and for the last time of all at Penrith that October.[107]

Maybe the civil servants responsible for closure of the direct Edinburgh–Perth line supposed that the whole railway system was in terminal decline. There were signs, however, that the climate of opinion was changing, and that the nadir had been reached. While ministerial consent was being given for closure through Glenfarg, it was also being withheld for closure of the branch line to North Berwick – by then the sole surviving passenger branch in south-east Scotland – although train services were to be restricted to times to suit commuters to and from Edinburgh.[108] Far more significant was the survival of the Kyle line. In December 1971 ministerial consent was given for closure, to be deferred for two years pending improved bus services. But it was then deferred again, and the line was finally reprieved in the summer of 1974.[109] Ideas at this time of closing the Fort William and Oban lines were shelved.[110]

Grants for specific socially necessary services – and there had been many in Scotland – were replaced under the Transport Act 1974 by a block grant to BRB for passenger train services, which became known as Public Service Obligation grant. Freight would become self-supporting, but this same Act offered a measure of encouragement in the form of grants to freight customers, planning to switch from road to rail, for capital expenditure on rail terminals.[111] The ministry responsible for railways had become the Department of the Environment in 1970, and would become the Department of Transport in 1976.

By 1974 the route mileage of British Rail in Scotland was down to a little under 2,000 miles.[112] There were still a few closures to come, notably the Paisley Canal line with the branch to Kilmacolm, stump of the GSWR line to Greenock, in 1983,[113] and the line from Balloch Central to Balloch Pier in 1986.[114]

Both closures followed uncharacteristic withdrawal of subsidy by Strathclyde Region, paid through Strathclyde PTE; the latter closure cut off direct rail access to Loch Lomond, one of Scotland's principal tourist attractions. There were other closures for freight, which will be mentioned below. There were also straws in the wind suggestive of revival. As early as 1967 the closed stations at Stewarton and Dunlop, between Glasgow and Kilmarnock, were reopened for commuters. An energetic campaign for reopening of Kingsnowe station, in suburban Edinburgh on the line to Glasgow via Shotts but closed since 1964, was successful in 1971. On the Far North line, Alness station was reopened in 1973, and Muir of Ord in 1976.[115] And although local trains between Ayr and Kilmarnock were withdrawn in 1969 – between Barassie and Kilmarnock they had followed, more or less, the route of the Kilmarnock & Troon Railway – the line remained open for freight and about this time the overnight Stranraer–London train was diverted onto it. A daytime Stranraer–Carlisle boat train joined it in 1977, and later that year a Glasgow–Kilmarnock–Ayr commuter train appeared: 'stealthy resumption' of passenger trains, *The Railway Magazine* called it.[116]

The intercity DMUs between Edinburgh and Glasgow, good though they were, were replaced in 1971 by trains comprising six Mark 2A coaches sandwiched between a pair of class 27 diesel locomotives, the whole wired for multiple unit control. The result was trains every half-hour covering the 47¾ miles between the two cities in 43–45 minutes, quicker than today.[117]

The greatest improvement of the early 1970s, however, was electrification of the northern part of the West Coast main line from Weaver Junction north of Crewe (to which point electrification already extended from Euston) to Glasgow, 235 route miles.

With associated track improvements, resignalling (four power signalboxes plus the existing one at Glasgow replaced 265 manual ones) and construction of thirty-six class 87 locomotives able to haul passenger trains at 110 mph, the work was completed in 1974. From that May there were eight trains a day each way between Glasgow and Euston instead of five; with six of them the previous schedule of 5 hr 55 min. was cut to 5 hr 10 min., and with the seventh, the 'Royal Scot', to five hours exactly.

The eighth daily train between Glasgow and Euston was diesel-hauled over the Glasgow & South Western line to serve Kilmarnock and Dumfries, and had the benefit of electrification from Carlisle to Euston.[118] One can only regret all over again that the Waverley Route did not survive to benefit similarly: two or three hours could have been knocked off the journey times by through trains between the Border towns and London, which might well have made all the difference. But in 1970–1 while the West Coast main line was being electrified the Waverley Route was being dismantled. Another line which did benefit, however, from West Coast electrification was the Highland: the opportunity was taken to introduce a through daytime train service between Inverness and Euston, named 'The Clansman'. The up train, leaving Inverness at 10.30 and running (of course) direct from Stirling to Motherwell via Coatbridge, but further south via Birmingham for the benefit of travellers to south-west England, was into Euston by 21.04. The morning train from Kyle of Lochalsh was soon retimed to connect into it at Inverness.[119]

Associated with West Coast main line electrification was electrification of the branch to Lanark and the loop to Hamilton, completed at the same time. By then, plans had already been made for a further important scheme, to rebuild, electrify and reopen the line through Glasgow Central Low Level between Rutherglen and Partick, and so to provide for the first time an electrified link between the electrified lines north and south of the Clyde.[120] The work was 75 per cent grant-aided by the secretary of state for Scotland; once complete, it was to be operated by BR on behalf of Greater Glasgow PTE. Related to this was refurbishment of the Glasgow Underground which had been transferred from Glasgow Corporation to the PTE in 1973, with provision of new trains. The BR scheme included a new station in tunnel at Argyle Street – the route was named the Argyle Line – and a new station at Partick with escalator interchange with the Underground; the whole was completed in 1979–80.[121] From, presumably, a combination of bright orange PTE livery, diminutive size and rounded shape, the new Underground trains – or perhaps the entire circular railway – quickly gained the nickname 'The Clockwork Orange'. The film *A Clockwork Orange* was popular at the time.

At this period a noticeable improvement in the condition of station buildings became apparent. Modernisation schemes of the 1950s and 1960s had been characterised by a tendency, so far as station buildings were concerned, to demolish and build anew. In 1976 Sir Peter Parker was appointed chairman of BRB, and he in turn appointed Bernard Kaukas as his director-environment. With these appointments came the awareness that cleaning decades of steam-locomotive induced grime off the fabric of stations, with sympathetic restoration of the structures, not only revealed distinguished Victorian and Edwardian buildings but was also far cheaper than rebuilding and just as effective in demonstrating to the public that the railway meant to stay in business. Stations

large and small benefited, notably Glasgow Central.[122] Many stations, and other railway structures, are in any event listed buildings.[123]

Research by BR in the 1960s into wheel and rail dynamics, and vehicle suspensions, had led to improved understanding of these subjects, and so of the characteristics needed for rail vehicles travelling at very high speeds. This in turn led to a programme to develop an 'Advanced Passenger Train' which would tilt on curves, and so be able to run on main lines on their existing alignments at speeds up to 155 mph – as an alternative to building entirely new railways for very high speeds as was already the case in Japan and would subsequently be in France and elsewhere. But development of the APT proved prolonged, and

a second programme was started, to develop a 'High Speed Train', of comparatively conventional type but nonetheless able to travel at 125 mph. It was intended, initially, as a stop-gap. The HST eventually comprised a train of Mark 3 coaches, with air-conditioned bodies 75 ft 4 in. long compared with the Mark 2's 66 ft, and carried on bogies of improved design, sandwiched between two locomotives each of which contained a 2,250 hp diesel engine. By the time it reached production, the locomotives had been reclassified as power cars and the train as a DMU.[124]

After lengthy testing of a prototype, HSTs were branded 'Inter-City 125' and introduced first on the Western Region in 1976; one of them was used on a charter train from King's Cross to Edinburgh and back on 23 July 1977, reaching its maximum speed of 125 mph en route. Then, in 1978, deliveries of HSTs started to Scottish and Eastern Regions, for use on the East Coast main line. Initially they went into service on existing schedules, with the intention that an accelerated train service would be introduced in May 1979.[125]

This was thwarted by the collapse of Penmanshiel tunnel, south of Cockburnspath, on 17 March. At the time the bore was being enlarged so that Freightliner trains could carry 8 ft 6 in. high freight containers through it. Sadly two men working inside were buried beneath a huge rockfall and killed, nor could their bodies be recovered: clearing the tunnel was too hazardous. The decision was taken to seal it, and divert the railway to the west, through a cutting. This meant also diverting the Pease Burn and the A1 main road. The rail diversion is some 1,100 yd long; with much cooperation and hard work by all concerned – BR, consultants, planning authority, contractors – the work was completed six weeks ahead of schedule on 20 August.[126]

On that date the full service of HSTs started between King's Cross, Edinburgh and Aberdeen. The fastest train, the 'Flying Scotsman', reached Edinburgh from London in 4 hr 37 min. In 1954, prior to the modernisation plan of the following year, the 'Flying Scotsman' had taken 7 hr 27 min. It is in accelerations such as this – and they were widespread – that the true measure is to be found of the benefits derived from the modernisation plans and the Beeching report. In the author's view they ensured the survival of large parts of the railway system and are as important as, and probably outweigh, the better-remembered harm done by closures.

In 1982 some East Coast HSTs started to run through from Edinburgh to Glasgow Queen Street and Perth, and in 1984 the 'Highland Chieftain' HST started to run between King's Cross and Inverness via Edinburgh and Stirling.[127] HSTs had started to run on the cross-country service between Edinburgh, Birmingham and Plymouth in 1981.[128]

The Advanced Passenger Train meanwhile had reached the stage of trials of a gas-turbine powered prototype, followed by construction of three electrically powered prototype trains for use between London Euston and Glasgow. But repeated attempts to bring them into service from 1978 onwards were unsuccessful and the project was eventually abandoned in 1986.[129] Although the speed of the prototypes was impressive, the tilt performance was not – at least in any desirable way. This is said to have been a consequence of design by engineers trained in the aircraft industry, who incorporated aircraft-type hydraulically-activated tilt mechanisms. These were unable to react quickly enough to the frequent changes of cant experienced by a train, and were constantly correcting for a change which had been overtaken by three or four later ones. Passengers, apparently, felt sick.[130]

Mark 3 coaches were built also for ordinary locomotive-hauled expresses, and at the end of the 1970s the design was adapted for sleeping cars. The first Mark 3 sleeping cars went into service between King's Cross and Aberdeen in January 1982, and they were running in all the other sleeper trains serving Scotland by the end of 1983.[131]

By the end of the 1960s it was clear that wagonload freight traffic was declining more quickly than Freightliners and block trains could recover it. This led to the introduction of fast scheduled freight trains for wagonload traffic using newly built long-wheelbase wagons fitted with air brakes; the first trains

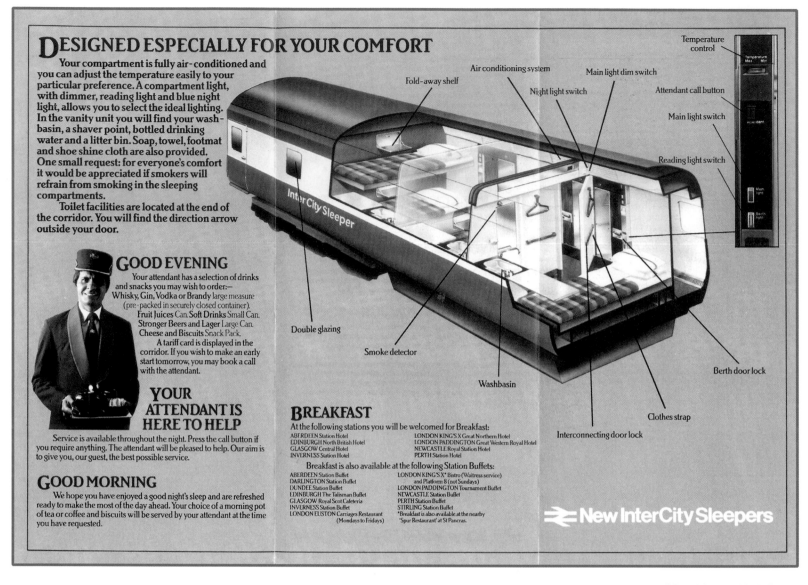

DESIGNED ESPECIALLY FOR YOUR COMFORT

Your compartment is fully air-conditioned and you can adjust the temperature easily to your particular preference. A compartment light, with dimmer, reading light and blue night light, allows you to select the ideal lighting. In the vanity unit you will find your wash-basin, a shaver point, bottled drinking water and a litter bin. Soap, towel, footmat and shoe shine cloth are also provided. One small request: for everyone's comfort it would be appreciated if smokers will refrain from smoking in the sleeping compartments.

Toilet facilities are located at the end of the corridor. You will find the direction arrow outside your door.

GOOD EVENING

Your attendant has a selection of drinks and snacks you may wish to order:—
Whisky, Gin, Vodka or Brandy large measure (pre-packed in securely closed container).
Fruit Juices Can. Soft Drinks Small Can.
Stronger Beers and Lager Large Can.
Cheese and Biscuits Snack Pack.
A tariff card is displayed in the corridor. If you wish to make an early start tomorrow, you may book a call with the attendant.

YOUR ATTENDANT IS HERE TO HELP

Service is available throughout the night. Press the call button if you require anything. The attendant will be pleased to help. Our aim is to give you, our guest, the best possible service.

GOOD MORNING

We hope you have enjoyed a good night's sleep and are refreshed ready to make the most of the day ahead. Your choice of a morning pot of tea or coffee and biscuits will be served by your attendant at the time you have requested.

BREAKFAST

At the following stations you will be welcomed for Breakfast:

ABERDEEN Station Hotel
EDINBURGH North British Hotel
GLASGOW Central Hotel
INVERNESS Station Hotel

LONDON KING'S X Great Northern Hotel
LONDON PADDINGTON Great Western Royal Hotel
NEWCASTLE Royal Station Hotel
PERTH Station Hotel

Breakfast is also available at the following Station Buffets:

ABERDEEN Station Buffet
DARLINGTON Station Buffet
DUNDEE Station Buffet
EDINBURGH The Talisman Buffet
GLASGOW Royal Scot Cafeteria
INVERNESS Station Buffet
LONDON EUSTON Carriages Restaurant (Mondays to Fridays)

LONDON KING'S X* Bistro (Waitress service) and Platform 8 (not Sundays)
LONDON PADDINGTON Tournament Buffet
NEWCASTLE Station Buffet
PERTH Station Buffet
STIRLING Station Buffet
*Breakfast is also available at the nearby 'Spur Restaurant' at St Pancras.

New InterCity Sleepers

Labels: Temperature control, Air conditioning system, Main light dim switch, Attendant call button, Main light switch, Night light switch, Reading light switch, Fold-away shelf, Double glazing, Smoke detector, Washbasin, Berth door lock, Clothes strap, Interconnecting door lock, Inter City Sleeper

BR publicises Mark 3 sleeping cars, introduced in 1982 and still in service.
(R. Forsythe Collection, courtesy British Railways Board (Residuary) Ltd.)

ran in 1972 between Glasgow and Bristol, and the service was later marketed as Speedlink. It was much aided in reliability and economy by development of the computerised Total Operations Processing System (TOPS) to monitor and control freight movements, which was fully operational from 1975.[132]

For the few remaining railways not forming part of the national network, the 1970s were a time of decline.

The Dalmunzie Hotel Railway, for instance, was last used in 1976, and the Lochaber Narrow Gauge Railway in 1977. By contrast there was a detailed proposal at the end of the 1970s for construction of a Swiss-style electric rack railway from Strathpeffer to the summit plateau of Ben Wyvis. This reached the stage of local authority support and a favourable feasibility study by consultant engineers in 1983, but nevertheless seems to

A familiar sight through the 1960s, 1970s and 1980s, a class 303 EMU waits to leave Milngavie. (Author)

closures, and replacement of trains by buses.[134] But it had little effect, apart perhaps from prompting the formation of groups to defend rail, such as the Friends of the West Highland Line.

With sectorisation as it developed, the sectors in effect specified the train services and marketed them, providing rolling stock and infrastructure; and the regions ran the railway. Sectors initially were five in number: Inter-City Passenger, Freight and Parcels, which three were expected to function on a commercial basis; and the social, subsidised railway, London & South East and Provincial passenger services.[135] They were to go through many confusing reorganisations and subdivisions. The sub-sector of Provincial that was concerned with Scotland was combined with Scottish Region, which thus had both operational and, in part, marketing responsibility.[136]

have gone no further.

Establishing the best administrative structure for the nationalised railway was ever a problem. The natural boundaries of the markets served seldom equated with those of the network of railway routes, a consequence of attempting to combine railways built in competition with one another into a single system (although the problem was greater south of the border than in Scotland). What was probably the best solution to be attempted was establishment of a series of business sectors, superimposed upon the regions. This structure emerged in 1982 and was subsequently developed. Nor was it derailed by publication in 1983 of the report of the Serpell Committee. This committee, named after its chairman Sir David Serpell who had served on the Stedeford group and latterly on British Railways Board, had considered the future long and carefully. It suggested the possibility of widespread

Scottish Region was then going through a transformation, consequent on the arrival of Chris Green as chief operating manager in 1979, followed by rapid promotion to general manager in 1984. Green started by focusing on improving care of customers, and care of staff. Both had been neglected, for investment in them showed no quantifiable return. Green not only determined to use up on worthwhile projects his own region's annual allocation of funds in its entirety, but also persuaded BRB to reallocate to him unspent funds from other regions' annual allocations. Much went on refurbishing stations: not just Glasgow Central, but Queen Street, and Edinburgh Waverley and Haymarket were transformed. Other stations followed: Stirling, Aberdeen, Dundee and smaller stations such as Linlithgow. And not just the passenger accommodation, but neglected staff accommodation too, for it is in the nature of railway operation that staff cannot be fully employed continuously, and need somewhere to go when they are not. The better this is, the more likely they are to be on the spot when next needed. Much else followed. As a symbol of resurgence, in 1984 or thereabouts Scottish Region received the brand name 'ScotRail'.[137]

This was indeed a time of resurgence in opening and reopening stations. According to *A–Z of Rail Reopenings*, some thirty-eight new or reopened passenger stations were opened in Scotland during the period 1971–91. Many were reopened following financial support from Strathclyde PTE or, outside the PTE area, the appropriate local authority. The process was much aided in 1981 by passage of a private member's bill through Parliament which enabled stations to be reopened experimentally on the basis that, if it were subsequently decided to close them again, this could be done simply, without going through the full statutory process.[138]

So new passenger stations opened during the 1980s and early 1990s included Livingston South, South Gyle, Wester Hailes, Airbles, Greenfaulds and Loch Eil Outward Bound. Stations were reopened at – among other places – Dyce, Loch Awe, Bridge of Allan, Ardrossan Town, Sanquhar, Stepps and Gretna Green. When Gretna Green was reopened on 20 September 1993 after an interval of twenty-eight years, the first train brought a wedding party, complete with the bride in white.[139]

These stations were all on lines already served by passenger trains. Far more significant was the reopening to passengers in March 1986 of the goods-only line to Bathgate, with improvements to track and signalling, new stations at Uphall, Livingston North and Bathgate itself, and an hourly train service to and from Edinburgh. This, according to Gourvish, was the first time a goods line, outside PTE areas, had

been reopened for passengers since the closures of the Beeching era. Six agencies contributed towards the cost of about £1.5 million: ScotRail, West Lothian District, Lothian Region, Livingston Development Corporation, the Scottish Development Agency and the European Economic Community. Two years later the branch made an operating profit of £224,000.[140]

In June 1986 a station was opened at Meadowbank Stadium, Edinburgh, for use during the Commonwealth Games and other important events; it was located on the Abbeyhill loop, which had earlier lost its local passenger train service.[141]

Extension of the Glasgow North electric train service from Airdrie to Drumgelloch in 1989 required reconstruction of one and a half miles of railway along the trackbed of the line between Airdrie and Bathgate, which had been closed to all traffic in 1982.[142]

Construction of the Cowlairs chord line in 1992 meant building a new railway over a route where previously there had been none, which needed powers from Parliament. The chord enabled trains from Queen Street to run direct, without reversal, to Springburn and Cumbernauld.[143] Several other lines and many other stations were reopened to passengers at this period. Notably, a train service was reintroduced in 1990 between Glasgow Central and Paisley Canal, over the line closed amid contention only seven years before.

With the opening and reopening of lines and stations came new diesel trains – particularly class 156 (Super Sprinters) and class 158 – at the end of the 1980s, to replace first-generation DMUs and locomotive-hauled trains of Mark 1 and Mark 2 coaches. Journey times were reduced, train frequencies increased.

Electrification from Paisley to Ayr and Ardrossan South Beach, with associated construction of new

One of many stations opened during the 1980s was Stepps, on the original Garnkirk & Glasgow line. This is the official opening on 16 May 1989. (East Dunbartonshire Information & Archives)

trains, resignalling, and track improvements to raise the line speed from 75 mph to 90mph, was authorised late in 1982;[144] the branches to Largs and Ardrossan Harbour were subsequently incorporated into the scheme. The whole was completed ahead of schedule: electric trains were introduced between Glasgow and Ayr, Ardrossan and Largs by stages over the winter of 1986–7.[145] Meanwhile electrification of the East Coast main line, often proposed and as often postponed, was eventually authorised by the government in 1984. This was a big project: from Hitchin, to which point electrification already reached from King's Cross, to Leeds and Edinburgh. It would take time to complete.[146]

Sleeping-car passengers benefited from the introduction of comfortable lounge cars, with a service of drinks and light meals, into overnight trains in 1987–88. They were an instant success. But overall, travel by night trains was now in decline – the victim of competition not only from airlines and motorways, but also from accelerated daytime trains. Motorail services were in decline for similar reasons. The InterCity sector was not subsidised, and the network of sleeper trains started to contract, notwithstanding that this aroused the ire of MPs who were regular users. From May 1988 all Anglo-Scottish overnight trains were concentrated on Euston as their London terminal and no longer served East Coast route stations on the way. The overnight train between Stranraer and London (nicknamed, as a link with Ireland, 'The Paddy') was withdrawn two years later. Two years after that, in 1992, it was followed by the overnight train service from Glasgow and Edinburgh to Southampton, Bournemouth and Poole and vice versa.[147]

Class 156 Super Sprinter two-car DMUs reached the West Highland line in 1989. Two of them are seen coupled together in multiple at Bridge of Orchy. (Author)

Meanwhile sleepers on Saturday nights/Sunday mornings, between London and Scotland, seem quietly to have disappeared from the winter 1991/2 timetable, reappeared for the summer only for a few years, and then disappeared for good. Publicity, if any, for this withdrawal was minimal, to the great inconvenience of anyone who wished to spend Saturday in the South and Sunday in Scotland.

Another strange move was withdrawal of seating coaches from all Anglo-Scottish night trains in 1992.

In this case the recently established bus company Stagecoach then arranged with InterCity to hire seating coaches which were attached to the sleeper between Aberdeen, Edinburgh and London, and marketed the service as Stagecoach Rail, with bus connections to and from Perth and Inverness. An odd way of doing things, it seems, but by then political pressures were closing in on BR, as will be described shortly. In any event, the service did not last long.[148]

One part of BR's operations involving overnight

travel which did flourish in the early 1990s was luxury 'land cruise' trains organised by InterCity Charter. Destinations of trains, which originated in London, included Oban, Mallaig and Georgemas for Orkney.[149] In this case BR had probably been shown the way by the privately owned 'Royal Scotsman' luxury touring train, established in 1985 and using, initially, vintage coaches as well as modern rolling stock including sleeping cars for its widespread travels.[150] It is mentioned again in the next chapter.

While passenger traffic was therefore – apart from overnight trains – developing positively during the 1980s, the position with freight, unsubsidised, was less satisfactory. Wagonload traffic, despite introduction of Speedlink, declined, and the number of stations handling it did so dramatically. Magazines of the period contain further lists of stations from which 'freight facilities' were being withdrawn, reminiscent of the passenger closures of two decades before. In 1983 alone at least twenty-nine stations in Scotland were closed for freight, and as well as wayside stations there were some substantial towns on the list, which included not only Alness, Ballinluig, West Calder and Garve, but also Arbroath, Cupar, Dunbar, Pitlochry and Dingwall.[151] After that August there was no freight on the Kyle line. Lines which had so far survived closure to passengers went too. One of them was the line from Stanley to Forfar: once part of the West Coast main line, but latterly reduced to a thrice-weekly goods train. The Angus Railway Group organised passenger specials on the last day (5 June 1982); they travelled at a sedate pace, more reminiscent of the line's 1840s origins than the racing trains of the 1890s or the steam swansong of the 1960s.

Freightliners Ltd was returned to full ownership by BR in 1978, and electrification reached its Coatbridge base from the West Coast main line in 1981. In 1991 direct services from the base included trains to and from Birmingham, Felixstowe, Bristol, London and Southampton. Yet Freightliners Ltd seldom seemed to prosper. In 1978 it had been merged with Speedlink into Railfreight Distribution.[152]

For some small insight into the interconnected reasons for, and effects of, the decline in freight transport by rail, one may turn to R. I. Smith's revealing booklet *Rail Freight in Moray*. Smith in the early 1990s was a road haulier based in Keith and Elgin seeking additional work for his vehicles at times when otherwise they would be idle. The North-East is in principle favourable for rail because of the lengths of hauls to and from the South. So cooperating with BR to encourage rail traffic, much of it in containers, which his firm would distribute locally had evident potential. Whisky, grain, fertiliser and salt were among the traffics available. Yet Smith's booklet is a tale – told with humour and sadness rather than resentment – of incompetencies, inadequacies and frustration. Here is the track machine, parked in the small hours by the engineers so that it obstructed the headshunt at Keith – so that a vital trial consignment of fertiliser is two hours late into the sidings and cannot be unloaded in the day. Smith's firm lost a traffic flow of a mile; BR lost one of 385 miles. Here too is the trainload of salt containers, misdirected to Inverness when they were intended for Keith for unloading in front of the consignor's admiring representative, up for the day from Cheshire. And they will not get to Keith that day, because in the absence of a freight service between Elgin and Keith they will be sent back to Motherwell and out again via Aberdeen arriving two days later. Time and again, in flexibility and speed, rail loses out to road. It is little wonder that the Speedlink service was withdrawn in 1991. By then it accounted for only 2 per cent of BR's total freight traffic, and much of that was redirected into trainloads.[153] But by 1993 there was no freight over the Highland main line.

On the roads, the late 1970s and 1980s saw the gradual evolution of road hauliers into logistics businesses closely integrated with the activities of their clients. They also saw the development of courier services, which by setting up central sorting depots or hubs in the English Midlands could exploit the motorway system to provide reliable overnight transits throughout most of Britain.[154] BR's Red Star service initially benefited from this emphasis on overnight transit,[155] and introduced its own 'Night Star' service for overnight parcels with guaranteed next-day delivery; but the railways' general collection-and-delivery parcels service was discontinued.[156] Newspaper traffic deserted BR during 1986–8.[157]

Trainload freight business was brisk, however. Although closure of the pulp mill at Corpach in 1980 meant loss of the timber trains from Crianlarich, block trains of iron ore started to run between Hunterston and Ravenscraig.[158] By 1989, almost half the wagons on British Rail were privately owned. Coal traffic was lost during the miners' strike of 1984–5, but development of open-cast mining in Ayrshire in the late 1980s led to much increased coal traffic in and from that area, with reconstruction and reopening of several closed lines.[159]

RETB – Radio Electronic Token Block – signalling replaced traditional signalling on the Kyle line in 1984. In this system the 'token', or 'tablet', takes the form of a cab display, issued by radio from a central computer. Semaphore signals and signalboxes are superseded. RETB was subsequently installed on the Far North and West Highland lines.

Computerised ticket-issuing and accounting equipment was provided throughout BR from 1986 onwards: 'APTIS' All-Purpose Ticket Issuing machines, in booking offices and travel centres, and 'PORTIS' Portable Ticket Issuing machines, used by train staff. Within a couple of years Edmondson card tickets, familiar since the earliest days of steam railways, were no longer being issued by BR.[160]

Between 1982 and 1987, ticket barriers at all ScotRail stations were progressively removed and they became 'open stations', with ticket examination done on trains.[161] 'Second class' became 'Standard class' in 1987.[162]

Britain and France ratified the treaty for the Channel Tunnel in 1987. BR and French Railways contracted with Eurotunnel that they would provide rolling stock and plan train services through the tunnel; the Channel Tunnel Act 1987 required BR to plan international through train services 'to various parts of the United Kingdom', to be operated without subsidy. BR then proposed, despite some financial misgivings, through passenger trains between Edinburgh and both Paris and Brussels by day, and sleeper trains between Scotland and the Continent by night. Construction of rolling stock went ahead, as did the tunnel itself.[163]

Industrial relations had been contentious through much of the 1970s and 1980s; new bargaining machinery eventually agreed in 1991 is described by Gourvish as the most fundamental change since 1919–21.[164] Meanwhile in 1990 the NUR had merged with the National Union of Seamen to form the National Union of Rail, Maritime and Transport Workers, 'RMT'.

Electrification of the East Coast route to Edinburgh was working its way north. The possibility of extending it to Glasgow – via Falkirk, via Shotts, or

The Stanley Junction–Forfar section of the West Coast main line, long since reduced to single-track, freight-only status, was closed on 5 June 1982. One of two farewell specials organised by Angus Railway Group is calling at Burrelton. As can be seen from the siding, freight was still passing, but evidently not enough of it. (Author)

via Carstairs – was considered by BR, and turned down as investment unlikely to meet the required rate of return.[165] Then there was a change of heart and it was decided to electrify from Edinburgh to Carstairs. The branch to North Berwick was included in the scheme too – its train service had recovered, from the minimal commuter service when reprieved from closure, to hourly throughout the day. Funds did not, on the other hand, run to electrifying the Abbeyhill loop: rather, in 1988 it was disconnected at the Edinburgh end when the main line was realigned, and the station at Meadowbank Stadium, completed less than two years before, could no longer be used.[166]

The latest development in InterCity motive power appeared: locomotives of class 91, designed to run at 140 mph and haul tilting coaches if required. They could also be used for slower trains – sleepers and parcels trains by night. One end, therefore, was streamlined, the other not; but both were provided with driving cabs. On fast trains they were to remain coupled to the coaches with the streamlined end outwards, hauling the train or propelling it as required and, when propelling, controlled remotely from a driving brake van at the far end. The West Coast main line trains were being converted to a similar means of operation.

With East Coast electrification also appeared Mark 4 coaches, even longer than Mark 3s, and with all the latest design features of the day from push-button operated doors to disabled persons' toilets. A cross-section tapering inwards above the waist gave Mark 4 coaches a distinctive but not unattractive external appearance. It derived from the intention that the same design would be used for the bodyshells for tilting coaches to be built later for the West Coast main line. The first, and as it turned out only, batch of Mark 4 coaches to be built do not tilt, and trains of them alternately hauled and propelled by class 91 locomotives up and down the East Coast main line have become familiar. In the absence of improved signalling the locomotives have been limited to 125 mph in normal service, but evidently have plenty of potential for faster speeds – one such on a pre-introduction press special reached 144 mph, and a test run a few days earlier had reached 161.7 mph.[167]

As it turned out, electrification between Edinburgh and Carstairs was ready first, before the East Coast main line to Edinburgh from the south. Arriving to catch the sleeper from Waverley to Euston on 19 April 1991, I was surprised and delighted to find that it would be electrically hauled throughout: electric working had in fact started on 18 March.[168] The first electrically powered train from King's Cross arrived in Edinburgh on 12 June, and the full electrified service started on 8 July, with the journey usually taking just over four hours.[169] As a demonstration of the new trains' powers, a special made the run non-stop on 21 September in 3 hr 29 min.[170]

Many trains continued beyond Edinburgh to Glasgow Central via Carstairs. This was fine so far as passengers from East Coast stations south of Edinburgh were concerned, although it would have been better still if the direct Caledonian route via Shotts had also been electrified: nearly ten miles shorter and correspondingly quicker. But there was more to it than that. InterCity and ScotRail were intended to become separate businesses, competing against one another for Edinburgh–Glasgow traffic[171] – so far had government thinking come from the early 1970s when the two nationalised carriers of merchandise had been amalgamated to prevent wasteful competition.

What had happened of course was that the Conservatives had been in power since 1979, with Margaret Thatcher as prime minister until 1990. Her antipathy towards railways – or at least her disinterest in them – is well known[172] and is, apparently, unexplained. Growing up in Grantham, where East Coast expresses thundered by every few minutes, she can scarcely have been unaware of railways, or railwaymen. In any event, privatisation of nationalised industries became the policy, particularly after the 1983 election. Not, initially, privatisation of railways themselves – she was too astute for that – rather, during the 1980s profitable, non-core, businesses were sold off. These sales, with sales of surplus railway land, enabled the government to pay reduced subsidies to BR.[173] A cynic might think it asset-stripping.

It started with the hotels: during 1981–4, the railway-owned hotels were sold off. In Scotland that meant the North British and the Caledonian in Edinburgh; the Central and the North British in Glasgow; Gleneagles, Turnberry, the Station Hotels at Perth, Aberdeen and Inverness, and the Lochalsh Hotel at Kyle of Lochalsh:[174] a list which included some of the best-known hotels in the country. The tie which linked them to railways, to their mutual benefit in attracting custom, was broken. Their railway connections, indeed in some cases origins, now tend to be forgotten. It was sad, to say the least, to find in a recent national newspaper article about Gleneagles, once the pride of the LMS, that the answer to 'How do I get there?' was written solely in terms of access by car and ignored the main line trains which continue to call at Gleneagles station;[175] and equally, to read that 'discussions are ongoing' between Network Rail and the present owner of the Balmoral Hotel – formerly the North British Hotel – to reach the agreement necessary before work can start on an improved entrance to Waverley Station from Princes Street.[176]

Other important BR businesses sold at this period were Sealink, its shipping line, in 1984 (the activities of this, however, with the exception of the Stranraer-Larne shipping service, lay south of the Border) and British Rail Engineering Ltd, its manufacturing business, in 1989. Earlier, the National Freight Corporation had been privatised in 1982. The bus industry was deregulated in the 1980s and the companies forming the Scottish Bus Group sold off to the private sector under the Transport Act (Scotland) 1989. The same Act authorised transfer of CalMac to the Secretary of State for Scotland and dissolution of the Scottish Transport Group. A period of confusion in the bus industry after privatisation was followed by emergence of large groups such as Stagecoach and First Group.

During the 1980s the introduction of the private sector into railway operation, and the possible privatisation of BR, in whole or in part, in one form or another, were topics increasingly considered by government, by the press,[177] and by the public. However, it was only after John Major had become prime minister, and the Conservatives had unexpectedly retained power in the 1992 election, that it became a high priority on the government's agenda, something to be achieved in the lifetime of that Parliament.

Railway privatisation seems to the author to be a prime example of the well-known adage that things go wrong when the people who remember what went wrong last time have all retired. As with nationalisation, once again little heed seems to have been paid to those who actually knew how to run a railway, and the simplest option, in this case to divide BR up into regions and bargain with contractors to operate them, was ignored in favour of a vastly more complex structure. Once again the outcome was disastrous, taking many years to put right – in the case of privatisation, the process is not finished yet.

The impetus seems to have come from what Wolmar calls the 'hyperactive privatisation unit' at the Treasury.[178] All the more probable candidates for privatisation had by then been privatised. The structure favoured by the Treasury was to separate responsibility for owning and running the railway from that for operating the trains. Since train operators would compete against one another, this would bring an element of competition into the railway system,

The concept of having a track authority distinct from train operators had emerged in the mid-1980s[179] and was given much impetus by the appearance of European Economic Community Council Directive 91/440/EEC in July 1991. This in turn referred back to two earlier EEC Council Regulations, nos. 1108/70 and 2598/70, both made in 1970.[180] The first of these required that a standard form of accounts should be used for railways, roads and inland waterways, and that it should in each case identify expenditure on the infrastructure. The second supplemented the first by defining the term 'transport infrastructure'. For railways it was to include track, rails, sleepers, points and crossings; and safety, signalling and telecommunications installations. This is all very well, but it overlooks the fact that on a guided transport system such as a railway – and unlike a road or canal – the track not only provides the running surface for the vehicles, but is also an integral part of their steering mechanism. Changing the points for a train is equivalent to turning the steering wheel of a bus. Expenditure on points on a railway is equivalent to expenditure on the steering mechanism of a bus. So is a large proportion of expenditure on rails and track, to the extent that they guide the trains round curves. So the definition appears defective: it can reasonably be argued that the infrastructure of a railway starts below the track. But so long as this defect was confined to the depths of the accounts it probably did not matter too much. Unfortunately it was to emerge into the administrative structure too.

Directive 91/440/EEC incorporates the same definition of infrastructure as the earlier measures, and while Article Six of this directive requires that member states shall ensure that the accounts for business relating to the operating[181] of transport services are kept separate from those for business relating to the management of railway infrastructure, it also directs that member states may provide this separation either by organisation of distinct divisions within a single undertaking, or by management of the infrastructure by a separate entity. The British government, going far beyond what was mandatory, then used this directive as justification for its intended structure for privatised railways.[182]

Just what was intended appeared in the white paper *New Opportunities for the Railways* of July 1992. This had much to say about BR as a 'monopoly', and of the need for competition.[183] Yet a moment's reflection shows that the railways' main problem, over the previous seven decades, was not too little competition, but far too much. As competitors to rail, other forms of public transport got occasional mention in the white paper, the private car and other private transport none at all. To a great extent the white paper addressed a non-issue.

Its proposals were fundamental, nonetheless. The vertical integration of BR was to end. It was to be divided into two units, with separate management and accounts. One of these units, to be called Railtrack, was to own track and infrastructure, and to control day-to-day operations through the signals. It was to remain publicly owned, although it might be privatised in the long term. It was to be responsible for track investment and maintenance, although it would be encouraged to contract out the latter. It would not be subsidised directly – subsidies would be directed at provision of services – although grants might be available for schemes which, while not earning an adequate financial return, offered wider benefits.

Railtrack's revenue would come from charges for access to its tracks. These would be overseen by a government-appointed 'independent Regulator'; another of his functions would be issue of the licences which would be needed by all infrastructure and train service operating companies.

The other part of BR was to continue to operate train services pending their transfer to the private sector. To achieve the latter, operation of passenger trains was to be franchised. The franchises would be awarded by a franchising authority on behalf of the government, and the franchisees would receive grants where necessary. Each franchisee would have a separate contract with Railtrack for use of track and infrastructure; at the start of operations, existing rolling stock would be available for them to rent. Passenger transport executives, as in Strathclyde, would continue

BR introduced class 91 locomotives and Mark 4 coaches for the East Coast main line electrification of the early 1990s. Coach bodies were built to a design suitable for tilting trains, to be built later; and the locomotives could have hauled them or been detached to haul sleepers or parcels trains. But development stopped there, for privatisation intervened; locomotives and coaches have instead become familiar under the GNER banner. (Bill Roberton)

to pay for train services agreed with private operators. There were commitments to a national timetable and to through tickets.

Freight-carrying operations, unsubsidised, were to be privatised outright, by sale. So was carriage of parcels – at that date BR was still carrying 25,000 parcels daily – and carriage of letters for Royal Mail.

Companies wishing to provide new railway services (*sic*, but train services was presumably meant), which could meet operational and safety standards, were to have right of access to the railway network.

For safety, all train operators were to comply with the instructions of Railtrack as the controller of the track and signalling.

The first shadow franchises had been announced early in 1993. They included the East Coast main line and ScotRail. The East Coast included services from King's Cross to Edinburgh, Aberdeen, Inverness and Glasgow Central. There were fears that those north of the Central Belt would be discontinued. For ScotRail, it meant dividing responsibility for track from trains; the track to go to Railtrack, the trains eventually to be franchised. There was talk of a management buy-out.[184]

There was little public demand for privatisation, and much scepticism.[185] When the Conservative government introduced a hugely complex Railways Bill to Parliament early in 1993 it faced not only opposition from Labour, but also strong dissent from its own backbenchers. Much of this was orchestrated by Robert Adley, MP, who probably knew more about the subject than any other MP on either side. It was more than a personal tragedy when he died from a heart attack that April.[186] But dissent eventually achieved little beyond ensuring that senior railcards would continue to be accepted throughout the system.[187] The government proceeded with all the dogged arrogance of an administration determined to push through a defective and unpopular measure.

The Railways Act, 1993, completed its passage through Parliament on 5 November. 'The great rail sale leaves the City underwhelmed' ran the headline in *The Daily Telegraph* the following Monday.[188] Even the Conservatives would eventually admit that, with rail privatisation, they got it wrong.[189]

The structure put into place at privatisation was flawed in two important respects. Both were consequences of the failure to grasp that rail, unlike road and inland waterway, possesses the characteristics of a guided transport system. Our forebears learned this the hard way early in the nineteenth century, and to separate responsibility for trains from track was to turn the clock back 175 years or so. But that is a minor criticism. More to the point, because railway track steers the trains, dividing responsibility for track and trains seems about as sensible as putting two drivers on every bus: one to turn the steering wheel, and the other to work accelerator and brake. Such a system may work, but at best it will be cumbersome, and at worst highly dangerous. This, sadly, was to be the experience of the privatised railway system.

That was the first flaw, and the second is related to it. On a road, a vehicle must stop when signalled to do so – by traffic lights or whatever – but may otherwise go under control of the driver. But on a railway, a train may go only when signalled to do so, and must otherwise stop. As the white paper itself made clear, all train operators would be required 'to comply with the instructions of Railtrack as the controller of the track and signalling'.[190] So the infrastructure manager exercises greater influence over the progress, or otherwise, of a train than does the train operator. The train operator is placed perennially in a false position, offering services to the public which, access contract or no, it lacks the power to deliver. The train operator's performance can never be better than the controller of track and signalling allows. Nor can it be better than the track provided allows. That of course is a familiar problem on roads and inland waterways, but it was not a problem on the vertically integrated railway where track and trains tended to develop in harmony.

That is not to say that privatisation was all bad. On the contrary, for the railways to be funded, so far as possible, from the private sector seems wholly desirable: public sector funding for railways is ever at risk from competing claimants for the taxpayers' money, such as hospital beds and teachers' pay. Over the period of nationalisation, the government steadily increased its financial hold over the railways. At its start, government intervention was limited to the willingness of the Treasury to guarantee the interest on British Transport loan stock. Towards its end, it was setting detailed financial targets not merely for the subsidised sectors of BR, but also for the profitable ones.[191] Nor could BRB carry forward a surplus from a good year to tide it over a bad one: it was covered by the principle of annuality – that, in government, every financial year is treated as a closed period. Nevertheless in the 1980s BR, according to Gourvish, succeeded in turning the rail businesses around: improved financial results and reduced grants led to its becoming the least subsidised railway system in Europe.[192] That is a desirable condition, no doubt, from the taxpayer's point-of-view – yet whether it is compatible with providing the best possible transport system from the user's point-of-view is another question. And the taxpayer and the transport user are but different aspects of the same individual.

In any event it seems to me that the British Railways Board was ever in the uncomfortable position of having responsibility without power. With the board lay the responsibility to run the railways. With its sponsoring ministry and with the Treasury, providers of funds, lay the power to enable the trains to run; and with the trade unions lay the power to bring the trains to a halt.

Amid all this, one regrettable consequence of privatisation was a hiatus in the process of reopening lines and stations. Where the process was already far advanced, it was completed. The train service from Glasgow Queen Street to Maryhill was introduced late in 1993, and stations at Wallyford and Camelon were opened in 1994.[193] But other reopenings which were then being considered, such as from Maryhill to Anniesland, and Hamilton to Larkhall,[194] were delayed by more than a decade. Agreement was reached in 1991 between ScotRail, Central Regional Council and Clackmannan District Council to fund reopening of the line from Stirling to Alloa.[195] But all these authorities, as they then existed, would soon afterwards be swept away, and it is only as I write that the line is being reinstated.

Wylam Dilly with the brothers George Hedley (extreme left) and William Hedley, both in top hats, in 1881, the year before she was moved to Edinburgh. (Science Museum / Science & Society Picture Library)

THE HERITAGE

Even in the latter days of the nationalised railway, a small but flourishing private sector had grown up which might well have contained lessons for those responsible for privatisation had they chosen to look. This was the heritage railway sector, including heritage railways, railway preservation societies and the like.

Heritage railways were vertically integrated, and remain so – they were exempted from the provisions for licensing, access and so on contained in the Railways Act 1993. That does not mean that each is the sole owner of everything to be found upon it. On the contrary, the hard task of raising funds has had the effect that each is usually home to a multitude of pieces of rolling stock and equipment owned by distinct groups as a result of separate fund-raising campaigns. So on a typical heritage railway, although the railway and its train service are operated and marketed by the railway company itself, on any particular train the locomotive is likely to belong to a separate group, and the coaches to a third, while the trackbed may well belong to the local authority acting as ground landlord. Here, therefore, is an example of multiple sources of funds, or investment, without compromising the principle of vertical integration, and one which has been found from experience to work.

Nor is that the only example which might have been studied. Once BR had overcome its initial reluctance,

after the end of steam, to allow steam locomotives back onto its tracks, steam specials hauled by preserved locomotives, and often composed of preserved coaches, became a regular occurrence on BR. Latterly, preserved first-generation diesel locomotives also appeared. So here were complete privately owned and funded trains running over BR. The division of responsibilities was that route and timings, or at least the final decisions on these, were decided by BR, which also provided operating staff – driver, fireman and guard – while marketing of the train and the care of customers on board were the task of the organiser.

But to begin at the beginning. Railway preservation – the concept of retaining historic railway artefacts once their useful working life was over – long preceded the end of steam on BR. It dates from the mid-nineteenth century. We are fortunate that in 1869 the brothers William and George Hedley bought the very early locomotive *Wylam Dilly* when her working days were over, kept her for thirteen years, and then arranged for her transfer in 1882 to the Edinburgh Museum of Science and Arts in Chambers Street, a forerunner of the Royal Museum in which *Wylam Dilly* remains a prized exhibit. The locomotive had been built for their father William Hedley as early as, probably, 1814, one of two built at that time to replace horses on the Wylam waggonway near Newcastle upon

Tyne. Both still exist, and are the two oldest surviving steam locomotives: *Puffing Billy*, probably marginally the older of the two, went to the predecessor of the Science Museum, South Kensington, in 1862.[1]

For the celebrations of the centenary of the Stockton & Darlington Railway in 1925, which included a parade of trains old and new, the LNER restored the GNSR 4-4-0 no. 45A of 1866 to her former magnificence, polished brass dome and all, and ran her with a train of four-wheeled coaches. Afterwards, regrettably, it did not retain her indefinitely but the event, and the LNER's subsequent establishment of its Railway Museum at York, prompted wider interest in preservation of historic equipment. The LMS preserved for their historic interest the first of the Highland Railway Jones Goods 4-6-0s, no. 103, on withdrawal in 1934, and the famous CR 4-2-2 no. 123 in 1935.[2] The LNER, having started to scrap the last two North British Atlantics in 1937, responded to suggestions in the Press that one should be preserved, and reassembled no. 875 *Midlothian* – only to break her up a second time during the Second World War to meet the need for scrap metal.[3]

The right of successive dukes of Sutherland to operate their own locomotive and coaches over the Highland Railway north of Inverness eventually ceased on nationalisation, and locomotive and coaches were put up for sale. The locomotive was the 0-4-4T *Dunrobin* already mentioned; the coaches were two, a bogie saloon built at the Wolverton works of the London & North Western Railway in 1899 and so splendid that it became a prototype for the royal train, and a four-wheeled saloon of 1909 customarily coupled behind the bogie saloon to steady it. The bogie saloon eventually reached the National Railway Museum and remains in it. The locomotive and the small saloon

Glen Douglas, restored to NBR livery, calls at Coatbridge Sunnyside with a special on 30 April 1960. (Don Martin)

passed into the ownership of Capt. J. E. P. Howey, who also owned the 15 in. gauge Romney, Hythe & Dymchurch Railway in Kent. They went south, the locomotive under her own steam for much of the way, and were exhibited at New Romney until 1965 when, after Capt. Howey had died, they were put up for sale again. The new owner shipped them to Canada, and for many years they have been at Fort Steele Heritage Town, British Columbia.[4]

When Highland Railway 4-4-0 *Ben Alder*, the last HR main-line passenger locomotive, was withdrawn in 1953 she was not scrapped but placed in store, being shunted around the system from one locomotive shed to another over the next few years. There was at least one plausible rumour of permanent preservation, but this sadly proved false: although she was still extant as late as 1965, she was subsequently cut up.[5]

Other historic locomotives were treated better. In

Despite showing 'Morningside Stn' as its destination, the sole surviving Edinburgh tram was running beside the Clyde in 1988 on the temporary tramway built within the Glasgow Garden Festival. (Author)

the late 1950s Scottish Region overhauled nos. 123 and 103 and operated them, in their original liveries, on special trains. Two ex-Caledonian Railway corridor bogie coaches were treated likewise, and ran with them. Two other locomotives, still in service but among the last of their type, were also restored to pre-grouping livery: GNSR 4-4-0 no. 49 *Gordon Highlander* and North British 4-4-0 no. 256 *Glen Douglas*. The special trains for which these locomotives and coaches were used travelled widely throughout Scotland, and indeed south of the Border, over the next few years and proved justifiably popular.[6]

During the 1950s and 1960s closures of innumerable

branch lines, and concurrently the rapid decline of steam, prompted widespread interest in preservation of railways as going concerns, and of railway equipment in running order. The first railway to be run by a preservation society was the Talyllyn, in Wales, in 1951; the first closed BR branch line to be acquired and operated by a preservation society was the Bluebell, in Sussex, in 1960. Voluntary groups and individuals were both involved in railway preservation. Ian Fraser, a former pupil of Gresley, already owned a steam road locomotive when in 1958 he bought a withdrawn 2 ft gauge steam locomotive from Dundee Corporation Gasworks. Until that year the retorts had been served

Preserved South African Railways' Garratt, built in 1957 in Springburn by North British Locomotive Co., is displayed at Summerlee Heritage Trust. When in use she hauled 2,000-ton coal trains. Overhead wiring for Summerlee's electric tramway is seen in the background.
(Author)

by a 2 ft gauge railway system to supply coke and remove ash; the locomotives, very small because of limited headroom, had been designed by Dugald Drummond, no less. The gasworks locomotive, named *Bonnie Dundee*, was moved to his house at Arbroath in 1961. Twenty years later Fraser presented the locomotive to the Ravenglass & Eskdale Railway: its diminutive proportions facilitated conversion to the 15 in. gauge.[7]

A new era in railway preservation opened in 1963 with the purchase, on withdrawal from service, of the locomotive *Flying Scotsman* by Alan Pegler, complete with a legal agreement entitling him to run it on BR tracks. The latter point was a mistake BR never made again! All subsequent operation of privately owned locomotives was permissive. During her widespread travels, *Flying Scotsman* has visited Scotland on occasion, and in 2004 passed into ownership of the National Railway Museum. Back in the early 1960s another Gresley-designed locomotive, K4 2-6-0 *The Great Marquess*, was purchased after withdrawal in 1961 by Viscount Garnock, and yet a third in 1964 when D49 4-4-0 *Morayshire* was purchased on withdrawal by Ian Fraser. After cosmetic restoration at Inverurie, he presented her in 1966 to the Royal Scottish Museum.[8]

The Scottish Railway Preservation Society was formed in 1961. It set about methodically building up a collection of relics, first small ones, then large, representative of Scottish railways, and simultaneously

A4 no. 60009, preserved by John B. Cameron, heads through Burntisland in 1990 with a special train run in connection with the centenary celebrations for the Forth Bridge.
(Bill Roberton)

building up, from small beginnings, the support, funds and skills needed to acquire, house, restore, operate and maintain them. Its depot for storage and maintenance was established in a former goods shed at Falkirk, and a landmark event was the arrival there in 1965 of 0-4-4T no. 419, brilliant in Caledonian livery although only later restored to working order. She was joined in 1967 by the North British 0-6-0 *Maude*, named after the First World War general of that surname. A typical pre-grouping passenger tank locomotive and a typical pre-grouping goods locomotive were a sound foundation upon which to build up a collection that would come to include coaches from all the pre-grouping Scottish railways, interesting specimens of traditional goods rolling stock and many more locomotives including

the oldest surviving Scottish-built locomotive, the 0-4-0T *Ellesmere*, built in 1861 by Hawthorns of Leith. In the early 1970s, *Morayshire* arrived on loan.[9]

The concept of a municipal museum of transport for Glasgow arose out of the decision to discontinue the city's tramway system and a desire to preserve a representative selection of tramcars. Part of the former Coplawhill tram depot and works in Albert Drive was selected, and the Museum of Transport opened there in 1964 with exhibits including six tramcars ranging in date from 1894 to 1937, motor cars, horsedrawn vehicles, bicycles and model locomotives. Two years later the museum was much enlarged to enable full-size locomotives to be added. British Railways presented five locomotives, of which four were the restored locomotives that had been hauling special trains – an activity which was doubtless coming to an end anyway with the disappearance of steam from everyday use. The fifth was Glasgow & South Western Railway short wheelbase 0-6-0T no. 9, built for shunting sharply curved harbourside lines in 1917: since being sold by the LMS in 1934 it had been working at a Welsh colliery before being recovered by BR for the museum, the last surviving GSWR locomotive. All five pre-grouping Scottish companies were now represented, and all five locomotives had been built in Glasgow. With space for one more locomotive the museum selected, from several which were offered, a locomotive which differed from those already acquired, yet was typical of pre-grouping motive power – Caledonian Railway 'McIntosh Standard Goods' 0-6-0 no. 828, on loan from the Scottish Locomotive Preservation Trust Fund. No. 828 had been one of only a few locomotives in a large class to be fitted with continuous brakes and used on passenger trains as well as goods. She had therefore been painted in blue rather than black, and to this livery she was restored.[10]

Temporary closure for refurbishment of the Glasgow Underground provided the opportunity in 1979 to add relics of it to the Museum of Transport – not just two of the subway cars, but also a reconstruction of Merkland Street station (which was losing its identity in the construction of an interchange with BR at Partick) in which they could be displayed.[11]

In 1987–8 the Museum of Transport and its exhibits – including tramcars, locomotives and Underground station – were moved to the Kelvin Hall, where more spacious accommodation had become available. In 1988 too an operating tramway reappeared all too briefly in Glasgow, providing transport for visitors through the extensive grounds of that summer's garden

Class 5 no. 5025 leaves Boat of Garten with a train for Aviemore Speyside during the early days of the Strathspey Railway. (Author)

festival. Three former Glasgow cars (one originally from Paisley) were loaned by the National Tramway Museum, Crich, Derbyshire; they were joined by the sole surviving Edinburgh car, loaned by Lothian Region, and an open car from Blackpool.[12]

At the same period a permanent electric tramway was built to carry passengers within the grounds of Summerlee Heritage Park, the open-air industrial museum at Coatbridge. A gap in the Museum of Transport collection – a locomotive built in Glasgow for export, for the export market was always more important for Glasgow locomotive builders than the home trade – was filled by the arrival at Summerlee in 1990 of South African Railways' vast Garratt locomotive no. 4112 which had been built in Springburn thirty-three years earlier.[13]

During the late 1930s the 'Coronation' was regularly hauled by the A4 *Union of South Africa*. This locomotive hauled the up train on what proved to be the train's last run on 31 August 1939. In the 1960s the same locomotive was a regular performer on the Glasgow–Aberdeen three-hour trains. By 1966 she was the best of the A4s then surviving, and on withdrawal by BR was bought by John B. Cameron. Cameron, a Fife farmer in a large way of business, was nephew of Donald Cameron of Lochiel, and would later serve on British Railways Board himself. Briefly, he was able to use the locomotive on BR; the Grand Scottish Railtour of 1967 has been mentioned earlier. Then came the steam ban. Across a farm he had recently bought ran the course of the recently-closed East Fife Central Railway; some of the track remained. Cameron was able to buy the last one and a half miles of it, leading up to its terminus at Lochty. *Union of South Africa*

was moved there, more track was reinstated, and the Lochty Private Railway was inaugurated in June 1967. Later one of the 'Coronation' observation cars arrived, and later still another coach to carry passengers in increasing quantity.

In 1973 at long last the steam ban was relaxed, and *Union of South Africa* returned to BR tracks; on 5 May she hauled the first steam excursion in Scotland after the lifting of the ban. Subsequently she was based at Markinch and steam specials hauled by her became a familiar part of the railway scene in the east of Scotland. For some years the Lochty Private Railway continued to operate too, using other, smaller, locomotives.[14] *Union of South Africa*, after some years in the South, is at the time of writing due to return to Scotland, in company with *The Great Marquess*, purchased by

Part of the motive power of Kerr's Miniature Railway, Arbroath, in the 1980s: Atlantic on the right is a 'pretend engine' driven by an Austin 7 engine in the tender; 0-6-0 *Firefly* on the left is steam.
(Author)

Cameron after the death of her former owner.

It was the ambition of the Scottish Railway Preservation Society to operate its own branch line, and the opportunity appeared to have arrived in 1967 when it learned that the then Highlands & Islands Development Board wished to support reopening of the line from Aviemore to Grantown-on-Spey, a twelve-and-a-half-mile section of the former Highland Railway main line. It had been closed to passengers in 1965, but until 1968 remained in use for freight as far as Boat of Garten to give access to the former GNSR Speyside line. But as negotiations proceeded, it began to seem that not only was Aviemore a long way from the Central Belt, the likely source of most volunteer support, but the proposed financial arrangements might put at risk the collection of locomotives and rolling stock which the society had put its effort into building up. The society pulled out in 1971.[15]

Members still in favour of the scheme then formed the Strathspey Railway Co. Ltd. With funds from sale of shares to supporters (no dividend was envisaged) and financial support from benefactors, from the Strathspey Railway Association and from the HIDB, this was able in 1972 to contract with BR to buy the line, with track still in place, from Aviemore to Boat of Garten. Subsequently it was able to buy the trackbed of the dismantled line from Boat onwards to a point about 2¾ miles short of Grantown. The Strathspey Light Railway Order 1978 authorised BR to transfer the Aviemore–Boat line to the Strathspey company, which was in turn authorised to operate it as a light railway and indeed to build and operate a light railway over the trackbed which it then owned beyond Boat. Later it was able to buy the rest of the trackbed as far as Grantown.

No access to the BR station at Aviemore was

During the 1980s British Rail initiated the Fort William–Mallaig steam train under the name 'West Highlander', using hired-in preserved locomotives. Here class 5 4-6-0 no. 44767 calls at Glenfinnan in 1984. (Author)

The Scottish Railway Preservation Society's North British 0-6-0 *Maude* heads a special train in 1981 to mark the 150th anniversary of the Garnkirk & Glasgow Railway. The viewpoint is that of D. O. Hill's lithograph of the opening celebrations in 1831, reproduced in Chapter 2. (East Dunbartonshire Information & Archives)

The Scottish Railway Preservation Society has been operating railtours, using its own coaches, over the national network since the 1970s. Here a tour from Kirkcaldy to York and Leeds is calling at Inverkeithing in June 2002; locomotive is owned by English, Welsh and Scottish Railway 47746. (Bill Roberton)

allowed at this period, although a track connection was maintained through sidings, and the Strathspey Railway had to build its own station at Aviemore (Speyside) before opening from there to Boat of Garten in 1978. Operation was almost entirely by volunteers; locomotives included an LMS class 5 4-6-0 and two LMS class 2 2-6-0s. They were soon joined by CR 0-6-0 no. 828 which was moved from Glasgow to Strathspey in 1980 and eventually restored to steam in 1993. Just how much hard graft lies behind that last bald statement was well described in Lionel Alexander's article in *The Railway Magazine*.[16]

By 1979 the branch line to Borrowstounness (Bo'ness) – originally an extension of the Slamannan Railway – had grown in importance during the nineteenth century and declined again during the twentieth, to become a freight-only branch from the Edinburgh & Glasgow line at Manuel running as far as a colliery at Kinneil. Beyond, harbour and railway alike were closed, and the site of the once-extensive railway installations was being landscaped by local authorities. Here at last the Scottish Railway Preservation Society found the opportunity to establish an operating line, a new railway to run only approximately on the site of the old, from a new station to be built at Bo'ness for about one and a quarter miles to the end of the line which survived: the Bo'ness & Kinneil Railway. Bo'ness station was complete enough to be opened to the public in 1981, with a shuttle train service operated by stock brought in from Falkirk. The line was opened to Kinneil after a light railway order had been obtained in 1986.

By then, however, the branch from Manuel to Kinneil had closed, in 1980. The SRPS negotiated with BR for its purchase, but could raise funds sufficient only for the trackbed (about three and three-quarters

miles) plus about one and a half miles of the track, most of it at the Kinneil end. The rest was lifted by BR. However, trackbed and remaining track were transferred to the Bo'ness & Kinneil Railway in 1988, which started to reinstate the track that was missing. At this point another problem arose: BR sold the site of the SRPS depot at Falkirk for development and the society had, in a hurry, to evacuate its collection, which was eventually concentrated on Bo'ness where extra sidings and buildings had to be provided. As some recompense BR did then agree to reinstate the junction with the main line.

Sufficient of the line had been rebuilt by early 1989 to enable it to be opened as far as Birkhill, three and a half miles from Bo'ness, and it was subsequently extended to the reinstated junction at Manuel. A new station was opened at Birkhill, adjacent to a former fireclay mine which was being opened to visitors, and this has so far been the terminus for passenger trains. The remainder is used for transfer of rolling stock between national network and heritage railway.[17]

Heritage railways blossomed during the 1980s. Enthusiasts built the 2 ft gauge Alford Valley Railway at Alford, Aberdeenshire, between 1979 and 1984.

The 'Royal Scotsman' luxury tour train heads away from Tyndrum over the West Highland Line in August 1993. (Author)

Volunteers replace sleepers on the Keith & Dufftown Railway, prior to reopening. (Author)

Kerr's Miniature Railway, which had fallen on hard times, was revived through the efforts of Matthew B. Kerr, son of its founder, and a band of volunteers.[18] The 10¼ in. gauge Mull & West Highland Narrow Gauge Railway was opened in 1984: a narrow gauge railway rather than a miniature one, for its equipment is in proportion both to gauge and to passengers, rather than being scaled down from full size. Its function was, and is, to provide a link between Craignure, where the ferries from Oban arrive, and Torosay Castle which is open to the public. The Ayrshire Railway Preservation Group established a steam centre in the early 1980s with working locomotives and brake van rides at the closed Minnivey Colliery. This was formerly served by an extensive industrial system connected to the Dalmellington branch. The centre was subsequently relocated to Dunaskin, a couple of miles away on the same system. Probable closure of the branch line to Brechin prompted formation of the Brechin Railway Preservation Society in 1979; the line was closed in 1981 but successfully reopened in 1993 as a heritage railway, the Caledonian Railway (Brechin) from Brechin to Bridge of Dun. Construction of the Leadhills & Wanlockhead railway started in 1986, a new 2 ft gauge railway on the trackbed of the former standard gauge light railway. Trains run from a new station at Leadhills to Glengonnar, the limit of track, with hopes of extending to Wanlockhead in due course.

A need to speak to the authorities – particularly British Railways – with one voice, and at the same time to promote high standards, had led to formation of the Association of Railway Preservation Societies in

1959. It became a constituent of the Heritage Railway Association, which is today the umbrella body for the heritage railways, railway museums, railway preservation societies and related organisations throughout the British Isles. These organisations are its corporate members, totalling some 246, of which (in 2006) 16 are based in Scotland. To act in their interest on specifically Scottish issues, increasing since devolution, the association formed its Scottish Committee in 2002.

Steam specials returned to the British Rail system in 1973, as mentioned above, and subsequently ranged widely over it. There were, for instance, steam specials in the early 1980s between Inverness and Kyle of Lochalsh, hauled by class 5 no. 5025 based on the Strathspey Railway; and later in the decade *Maude* and other locomotives hauled 'Santa specials' round the Edinburgh South Side & Suburban line – Santa Claus, as is well known, often prefers to desert his reindeer for a steam train.

In the summer of 1984 British Rail itself instituted steam trains between Fort William and Mallaig, hiring in preserved locomotives to haul them. Initially regarded as a series of excursions, they were soon being operated with sufficient regularity to be included in BR's public timetables, and in this respect were, I believe, unique. The operation survived privatisation, passing to the West Coast Railway Co. Ltd of Carnforth, which continues to operate the train daily in summer as 'The Jacobite'. At the end of the season, the opportunity was taken when working locomotives and coaches back to Carnforth to run a public steam excursion over the main West Highland line; from 1999 this practice blossomed out into the Highland Rail Festival, with charter steam trains for photographers and public steam excursions on the

Unique battery electric multiple unit of 1958 was in secure storage at a plant-line depot in 2005, pending its return to the Deeside line by the Royal Deeside Railway Preservation Society. (Author)

Ellesmere, built by Hawthorns of Leith in 1861 and the oldest surviving locomotive built in Scotland, is to be found on Level 4 of the Museum of Scotland, Edinburgh. (Bill Roberton)

Caledonian Railway no. 419 waits to leave Bo'ness. Restored goods wagons in the background include an example with dumb buffers. (Author)

Oban line as well.

Since 1970 the SRPS has arranged special trains over the national network, using its own coaches, usually hauled by a diesel but sometimes by steam. At first the coaches were the historic vehicles in the SRPS collection. In August 1972, for instance, an SRPS special from Falkirk to Mallaig and back included coaches from the North British, Caledonian and Great North of Scotland Railways, as well as coaches of LMS and LNER design.[19] Later a rake of BR Mark 1 coaches was assembled and maintained for railtours which continue to run on occasion through the summer both within Scotland or to and from points south of the Border, often over routes otherwise difficult to accomplish as a day excursion – Carlisle to Oban for instance, and Dunbar to Kyle of Lochalsh.

Railtours in luxury, with participants staying on board but stationary overnight, have been offered

Gresley-designed LNER 4-4-0 *Morayshire* belongs to the National Museums of Scotland, and is seen here at Bo'ness in 2004 following overhaul in the workshops there. (Author)

since 1985 by the 'Royal Scotsman' train. Rolling stock initially included three restored pre-grouping day coaches, and sleeping cars rebuilt from BR Mark I vehicles.[20] New stock was provided in 1990 by converting 1960s Pullman cars as sleeping cars, dining car and observation car. 'State cabins' include one or two beds, writing table, en suite bathroom with shower, and much wooden panelling with inlaid marquetry; with day coaches of similar standard the train provides accommodation to the level of a luxury hotel for thirty-six people.

From 1984 a highly successful series of specials was run under the name 'Northern Belle' between Aberdeen and Dufftown by Grampian Railtours: passengers enjoyed lunch and tea on the train and a distillery visit at the terminus. The line between Keith and Dufftown, although closed to regular passenger trains, had been used for freight until 1982; subsequently almost its only traffic was these specials, sometimes as many as fifty of them during the course of a year. Increased charges brought them to an end in 1991.[21] Inevitably, perhaps, people then sought a means to keep the branch in being. Eventually the Keith & Dufftown Railway Associaton successfully reopened the eleven-mile section from Keith Town to Dufftown as a heritage railway in 2001. Trains are formed of first-generation DMUs, which now have their own nostalgic appeal.

That other remarkable multiple-unit of the same period, the unique battery-electric set which ran on the Deeside line, has been brought back to its home ground by the Royal Deeside Railway Preservation Society. This society, which was founded in 1996, hopes to use it on a two-mile length of the old line,

Preserved first-generation DMU crosses the Keith & Dufftown Railway's viaduct over the River Fiddich. (Author)

In Scotland only the Scottish Railway Preservation Society can assemble a complete train of the pre-grouping period, i.e. pre-1923, and that is only done on important occasions. Caledonian Railway no. 419 heads a train comprising the two CR coaches during the celebrations in 2004 of the silver jubilee of the Bo'ness & Kinneil Railway. (Author)

which it is reinstating between Crathes and Banchory. It has also acquired several GNSR coach bodies requiring restoration in varying degree, and has plans for a workshop and visitor centre at the former Ferryhill depot, Aberdeen.

The opportunity for the Strathspey Railway to enter the main-line station at Aviemore arose in 1997 when Railtrack decided to refurbish the main station building but found that the building on the island platform was surplus to requirements, and so offered the use of it and the east side of the platform to the Strathspey company. The whole station was then

271

Since 1972 the station building of the closed station at Lochee has been home to the Lochee Burns Club. It was built in 1861 on the deviation line, which was opened then to enable trains for the Dundee & Newtyle line to leave Dundee hauled by locomotives rather than by cables up the inclined planes, and its striking and attractive appearance results from architect James Gowans's use of a 2-ft module and a mosaic of multicoloured masonry.
(Royal Commission on the Ancient and Historical Monuments of Scotland, Crown copyright)

repaired and repainted as part of a wider programme to regenerate Aviemore itself; the Railway Heritage Trust (to be mentioned shortly) and Historic Scotland also played a part. The work was completed in 1998, and the Strathspey train service was extended to enter Aviemore over track leased from Railtrack: it is the only station in Scotland used jointly by trains of the national system and a heritage railway. Meanwhile work had been continuing to extend the railway in the opposite direction beyond Boat of Garten, and the next two and three-quarters miles to Broomhill were opened in 2002.[22]

In the same district, but certainly no heritage railway – but nor is it part of the national network – is the Cairngorm Mountain Railway. This cable-operated railway was designed according to the latest Swiss standards for funiculars and opened in December 2001. It ascends 453 metres in a length of 1,950 metres; the top station at Ptarmigan, 1,098 metres above sea level, is evidently the highest railway station in Britain, a few metres higher than Snowdon Summit. The track is laid to a gauge as wide as 2 metres, which aids the stability of the cars in high winds, and for most of the route it is carried on continuous low viaduct so that the snow can blow beneath instead of blocking the line.[23]

The late 1990s saw *Ellesmere*, the oldest-surviving Scottish-built locomotive, depart from Bo'ness for Edinburgh and the Museum of Scotland, to take pride of place on Level 4, *Industry and Empire*. More generally, the SRPS collection continued to expand; indeed it eventually claimed to be the largest collection of railway locomotives, carriages, wagons, equipment and artefacts outside the National Railway Museum.[24] Objects range from Edinburgh & Dalkeith Railway mileposts[25] to a class 303 Glasgow electric train. It proved possible to run this in service, operated push-pull by a diesel locomotive which also provided power for the sliding doors.[26] Equally important is the sole surviving DMU from the pioneering class 126. One of the batch built in 1959, it exemplifies the period of transition from steam to diesel, combining traditional carriage-building techniques and oil-lit tail lamps with diesel engines and multiple unit operation.[27]

To house, display and interpret a large part of its collection, and particularly the wooden vehicles most at risk out of doors, the SRPS opened the Scottish Railway Exhibition – in all but name, a museum of national importance – at Bo'ness in two stages, 1995 and 2002.[28] Some locomotives and pieces of rolling stock move in and out of the exhibition according to whether or not they are in running order, or needed in operation. For the Bo'ness & Kinneil Railway's twenty-fifth anniversary celebrations in 2004, the Caledonian Railway 0-4-4T and the two Caley coaches provided a complete train from a single pre-grouping company, a rarity indeed and one which the public could not merely view but also travel in.

Another exhibit which is expected to move out of the exhibition is NBR 4-4-0 *Glen Douglas*, which has been on loan from the Museum of Transport, Glasgow, and is likely to return to that city to be displayed in a new, enlarged, Museum of Transport forming part of a 'Riverside Museum'.

Largest of all historic railway artefacts – yet sometimes in danger of being forgotten as railway artefacts at all – are the two well-known paddle steamers, PS *Waverley* which was built to the order of the LNER in 1946, and PS *Maid of the Loch* (on Loch Lomond), which was built to the order of the Railway Executive in 1953.

The convincing appearance of Bo'ness station arises from the reconstruction there, over the years, of numerous traditional railway buildings which had become redundant elsewhere. The most notable is the train shed, the overall roof covering platform and adjoining tracks. This formed part of the Edinburgh & Glasgow Railway's original terminus at Haymarket, whence Lord Cockburn set out on his journeys. When the line was extended to Waverley, it was also diverted slightly to the south. But part of the original train shed remained in place until the 1980s, when it was threatened with demolition; instead, it was dismantled, and moved to Bo'ness. Here it adjoins an earlier arrival, the largely timber-built station building from Wormit at the south end of the Tay Bridge. The signal box, of typical Caledonian pattern, came from Garnqueen South junction, where the CR line to the North diverged from the Monkland & Kirkintilloch Railway. It works a fine array of pre-grouping semaphore signals, and leading away from it a line of telegraph poles with cross-arms carries telegraph wires on insulators, a sight still common in the recent past, yet one which has quietly slipped away.

Some of the buildings and structures on the Strathspey Railway have been moved in from elsewhere – the turntable for instance came from Kyle of Lochalsh – but many of the buildings are originals, such as the station buildings at Boat of Garten and, notably, the large locomotive shed at Aviemore. The Ayrshire Railway Preservation Group's shed at Dunaskin, though utilitarian, was purpose-built for steam locomotives as recently as 1964 by the National Coal Board. The Caledonian Railway's terminus at Brechin is a gem, built in 1847–8 and extended in 1894–5. Both the Keith & Dufftown and the Bo'ness & Kinneil Railways include substantial stone arched viaducts, over the Rivers Fiddich and Avon respectively.

BR addressed the problem presented by, particularly, historic stations and viaducts which remained in operational use but which were protected by listing or similar legislative provision,[29] when it established in 1985 the Railway Heritage Trust. This free-standing body, sponsored originally by BRB, is now sponsored by Network Rail and government-owned BRB (Residuary) Ltd; its function is to raise funds, often in conjunction with other bodies such as Historic Scotland and local authorities, for conservation of railway buildings and structures in operational use, and to seek the transfer of those no longer needed operationally to other, sympathetic, bodies. Stations in Scotland which have benefited include Aviemore, as mentioned, Troon and – perhaps the most deserving but least commercially justified – the Edwardian splendour of the rail-steamer interchange at Wemyss Bay.[30]

Distinct from the trust is the Railway Heritage Committee, the statutory body which, post-privatisation, designates artefacts and records that warrant preservation, and supervises their eventual disposal. Designated items of Scottish significance have ranged from a High Speed Train and freight wagons of many different types, to signals of Caledonian and LMS origin at Stirling and the LMS Estates Department's

'Land Books' detailing the golf courses at Gleneagles and Turnberry. The latter items went to St Andrews Golf Museum.[31]

Conversion of the West Highland and Kyle lines to RETB signalling led to withdrawal of staff from most stations – yet sympathetic alternative uses have been found for many of the station buildings. Glenfinnan, in particular, became the Glenfinnan Station Museum with its collection of material relating to the West Highland Railway; Spean Bridge and Plockton have become restaurants, Bridge of Orchy and Tulloch bunkhouses.

Some stations on lines completely closed have likewise escaped demolition when alternative uses have been found for them. Lochearnhead for instance has long been used by Hertfordshire Scouts as a base for hillwalking and sailing. Strathpeffer with its ornate platform canopy became a visitor centre, then the Highland Museum of Childhood. The A-listed station building at Melrose, after fifteen years of dilapidation, was restored as a craft centre in 1987,[32] and now houses an Italian restaurant and a playgroup.

Not far from Melrose is Leaderfoot Viaduct (also known as Drygrange Viaduct), which carried the North British branch from St Boswells to Duns across the Tweed on nineteen masonry arches with a maximum height of 130 ft. So far as BR was concerned, there was at least a market for redundant station buildings, but viaducts and bridges on closed lines were another matter. Unless built of iron or steel and so having a scrap value they had, in the interest of public safety, to be demolished or maintained, both alternatives being expensive; they were also likely to be listed. In 1984 it was reported that BR faced, in Scottish Region alone, a bill of £1.5 million for viaducts, many of them far from the nearest operational railway.

The nineteen arches of Drygrange or Leaderfoot viaduct, built in 1865, still stride across the Tweed – yet this imposing structure was built for no main line, but for a rural byway, the long-closed Berwickshire Railway from St Boswells to Duns. (Author)

In 2006 BRB (Residuary) Ltd is still responsible for maintenance of nineteen bridges and viaducts on closed railways in Scotland, among the 4,000 or so structures for which it is responsible throughout Britain. The Scottish viaducts include grade A listed Leaderfoot: evidently BR's announced intention in 1991 to give it to the nation by transfer to Historic Scotland did not reach fruition.[33]

The great cantilever bridge at Connel, first rail, then rail-and-road, became road-only on closure of the Ballachulish branch in 1966 and was then transferred to the secretary of state for Scotland. It continues to carry the A828; its centenary was celebrated in 2003.[34] In recent years reuse of the routes of many closed railways, rural and urban, for cycle tracks and footpaths has meant that their structures too have come back into use – bridges, viaducts such as the Spey viaduct and even the tunnel in Holyrood Park by which the Innocent Railway approached its terminus at St Leonards.

Older still than this is the Kilmarnock & Troon Railway's four-arch viaduct over the River Irvine at Laigh Milton, disused since 1846 when the line was diverted on being upgraded into a locomotive railway. By the late twentieth century its condition had deteriorated so much that it appeared to be at the point of collapse. Its importance was recognised, and a £1.1 million conservation project in the mid-1990s, headed by Professor Roland Paxton, ensured that it survived for future generations to appreciate this very substantial relic of the first decade of public railways anywhere.[35]

A Virgin Pendolino working between Glasgow and London tilts into the curve near Abington. (Bill Roberton)

THE PRIVATISED RAILWAY

Unlike nationalisation, but not unlike the grouping, privatisation did not take effect overnight. It was, as Gourvish has described it, 'an unprecedented fragmentation of … a highly integrated business'.[1] So first BR had to be divided up. Railtrack became a separate undertaking, and businesses which remained with the British Railways Board werc divided into a great many smaller units which could be either sold or franchised. The new structure was in place by April 1994.[2] Railtrack, which for the moment was to remain in the public sector, owned and ran the railway. But it did not itself maintain it. This was done under contract by British Rail Infrastructure Services, which itself was to be divided in two, one part for continuing maintenance and the other for renewals. Eventually it would be subdivided further, and privatised. Administratively, Railtrack divided itself into zones, the largest of which covered Scotland.[3]

Passenger train operation and marketing was divided between twenty-five passenger train operating companies (TOCs), each with a contract with Railtrack for track access. The operations of TOCs were to be franchised; those serving Scotland were ScotRail, for internal train services, InterCity West Coast, InterCity East Coast and InterCity Cross Country. A campaign for a vertically integrated ScotRail[4] had come to nothing; the only vertically integrated franchise was to be the Island Line in the Isle of Wight, short and physically separate from the main network. Nor were TOCs to own their own rolling stock: they would lease what they needed from rolling stock companies (ROSCOS – rail privatisation was a healthy source of acronyms). Three of these had been established, and BR's fleet of locomotives and passenger rolling stock divided between them. The three ROSCOS were privatised in 1996. In due course they would start to finance new rolling stock, but in the meantime there was an interregnum during which no new rolling stock was ordered – notoriously, it eventually reached 1,064 days,[5] with correspondingly adverse effect on rolling stock manufacturers.

Management of passenger stations was in general franchised to the principal TOC using each station; only the largest, of comparable importance to several TOCs, were to be managed directly by Railtrack. In Scotland that meant Edinburgh Waverley and Glasgow Central.

Freight business was reorganised into five companies, again with access contracts with Railtrack, three of them for freight proper and two for parcels. The intention was not franchising but outright sale. In the event the three freight companies and one of the parcels companies, Rail Express Systems, which carried principally Royal Mail traffic with the benefit of a thirteen-year contract signed in 1993, were sold in 1996 to the Wisconsin Central Transportation Corporation – a go-ahead American undertaking – which named its British operation 'English, Welsh & Scottish Railway',[6] notwithstanding that it would not be a railway, but an operator of trains over Railtrack's railway. Nevertheless, with ownership based in a culture where freight traffic by rail is far more important and prosperous than passenger, EWS immediately showed commendable initiative in developing its business. In Scotland it was building on the enterprise already shown by one of its constituent companies, Transrail, in bringing freight traffic back to Thurso in 1995 after an interval of fifteen years.[7] New services included coal by the trainload from open-cast workings in Ayrshire to Longannet power station on the Forth, and a remarkable precedent was loading of timber onto trains standing on the Far North line, after the last passenger train of the day had passed – and so dispensing with the need for siding or terminal.[8] Perhaps EWS's most distinctive contribution to the railway scene, however, has been the class 66 diesel-electric locomotive, built by General Motors in Canada, and delivered in quantity from 1998. By 2006, EWS was owned mainly by New Zealand, American and Canadian financial interests.

The other parcels company, Red Star, and Freightliner went to management buy-outs in 1995 and 1996 respectively. Freightliner, which initially could only be disposed of by adding the sweetener that the government would pay track access charges for five years, eventually developed into a successful freight business, not only for inter-modal traffic, but also with its 'heavy haul' division distributing, for instance, cement from Oxwellmains (Dunbar) to Ayr, Motherwell, Aberdeen and Inverness.[9]

The numerous contractual relationships between the many parts of the privatised industry were overseen by the Rail Regulator. Another of his responsibilities was sponsorship of the statutory Central Rail Users' Consultative Committee and the associated regional Consultative Committees.

In the process of franchising passenger train services, a vital preliminary was definition of a minimum level of passenger train services, the 'Passenger Service Requirement', for each route. This was done by the Office of Passenger Rail Franchising, headed by the Franchising Director. Generally the requirements seem to have been based around the existing level of service provided by British Rail, but sleeper and Motorail services soon came under the spotlight for their supposed lack of profitability. First, InterCity West Coast decided to withdraw from operating the Anglo-Scottish sleeper services. ScotRail, headed again briefly by Chris Green, offered to take over at least some of them.[10] Then in December the Franchising Director announced that two sleeper services would be omitted from the passenger service requirement: London to Fort William, and Glasgow/Edinburgh to Bristol and Plymouth. Soon afterwards it was announced that Anglo-Scottish Motorail services would also be excluded. Latterly these had been operated by attaching Motorail vans to the sleeper trains. When the 1995 summer timetable came in at the end of May, there were to be but two sleeper trains leaving Euston nightly for Scotland: one with sections for Edinburgh and Glasgow, the other for Aberdeen and Inverness.

These announcements provoked widespread fury, perhaps in part because they appeared as the thin end of a wedge of widespread closures. Much of this fury was focused on withdrawal of the Fort William

The useful overnight sleeper and Motorail train service between Scotland and the West Country was busy during the spring of 1995 but it was discontinued that May in the run-up to privatisation. Nothing adequate replaces it. Here (opened out) is the welcome brochure which travellers found when boarding.
(BRB (Residuary) Ltd.)

On Arrival at Edinburgh

The Night Scot arrives in Edinburgh at 0655. If you are leaving us here it is not necessary to vacate cabins until 0715. Please note that electrical power will not be available to shaver sockets whilst the train is in the station.

Motorail Cars may be collected approximately 45 minutes after arrival.

Should you wish to take breakfast after arrival, the station Food Court is adjacent to the Ticket Office. Alternatively, there are several Hotels within short walking distance.

On Arrival at Bristol Temple Meads

The Night West Countryman arrives in Bristol Temple Meads at 0611. If you are leaving us here cabins need not be vacated until 0635. Please note that electrical power will not be available to shaver sockets whilst the train is in the station.

Motorail cars will be available for collection approximately 30 minutes after arrival.

If you wish to take breakfast after arrival in Bristol, both the Holiday Inn Crowne Plaza Hotel and Hilton Hotel are within 10 minutes walk of the Station approach. Fork right for the Holiday Inn or left for the Hilton.

If you have any comments about this service which is operated by CrossCountry please contact:
Customer Relations Manager
Meridian, 85 Smallbrook Queensway, Birmingham B5 4HX
Telephone: 0121 654 7400 Fax: 0121 654 7487

INTERCITY
CrossCountry

Published by CrossCountry in Birmingham, a division of the British Railways Board. XC/0176/1.95/A30
CrossCountry operate INTERCITY® registered services.

Welcome to

THE NIGHT SCOT
Plymouth to Edinburgh / Glasgow

THE NIGHT WEST COUNTRYMAN
Glasgow / Edinburgh to Plymouth

Every effort will be made to ensure your journey tonight is enjoyable, comfortable and punctual.

Thank you for travelling CrossCountry.

CrossCountry
Sleeper

---

sleeper. There was concern in Parliament, there were campaigns in the newspapers, there were marchers with placards in Fort William. A vigorous campaign by the Friends of the West Highland Lines received strong support from Londoners as well as from inhabitants of the West Highlands. The officially quoted subsidy cost per passenger of £450 was soon discredited when it was found to include a substantial element of fixed costs which, if the train were withdrawn, would not be saved, but simply redistributed among surviving train services.

The manner of operation of the Fort William sleeper at this time was a disturbing example of how what best suits a system as a whole may not suit individual parts of it. Operated by InterCity, it was being run over the West Highland Line, like Anglo-Scottish sleeper services everywhere, as a train carrying solely sleeping car passengers and, perhaps, their motor cars. Passengers, though loyal, could never be numerous. Not many years before, it had been operated, beyond

A Virgin Voyager passes Burntisland on 29 February 2004 with the 08.25 Aberdeen to Birmingham New Street. (Bill Roberton)

Glasgow, by including a sleeping car or two in a train which also carried seated passengers (both local and long-distance), parcels, mails and newspapers in quantity, and probably had a string of fish vans on the back and perhaps a horsebox on the front. Where traffic is inevitably limited, clearly each train must carry as much of as many types as possible. The policy led to a further anomaly: by the 1990s, the latest daily up ScotRail train for ordinary passengers was leaving Fort William about 17.40; although another train was timed to leave over two hours later, this was the sleeper and they were excluded from it.

The eventual saving of the Fort William sleeper was, sadly, not the consequence of reasoned argument, but of legalistic wrangling. In the course of its travels,

the train traversed three short sections of line over which no other passenger trains ran: withdrawal of the sleeper would amount to closure of these sections to passenger traffic. To evade the lengthy statutory closure processes, BR intended instead to run another train over each of them, notably one at 23.58 from Maryhill to Bishopbriggs. Now Highland Regional Council was particularly concerned at withdrawal of the Fort William sleeper, for it had earlier received three successive government assurances that privatisation would result in no deterioration of train services in its region. It took BR to court. At the eleventh hour, an interim interdict was made on 9 May that the Fort William sleeper should not be withdrawn. BR appealed, and lost again.

In the meantime, although not in the public timetable, the Fort William sleeper continued through the summer of 1995: two Fort William cars were added to the London–Aberdeen/Inverness sleeper as far as Edinburgh. Following representations from the Friends of the West Highland Lines, a coach for seated passengers was added to them between Edinburgh and Fort William. Eventually the Fort William sleeper with seated coach was incorporated into the passenger service requirement.[11]

The Scotland-West Country sleeper was withdrawn as planned. On the face of it, it would seem to have had greater traffic potential than London–Fort William; certainly, when using it that spring, the author was assured by staff on board that it was fully booked until the date of withdrawal. Most regrettably, Anglo-Scottish Motorail was lost too; an attempt to revive it in 1999 was not successful. Surviving Anglo-Scottish sleeper services were relaunched by ScotRail as the 'Caledonian Sleepers' in 1996. The wider consequence of the furore over the Fort William sleeper does seem to have been that there were few if any other withdrawals of importance during the privatisation process.[12]

While this fierce local skirmish had been taking place, there had been developments on the wider front. Changing its policy, the Conservative government announced in November 1994 that privatisation of Railtrack was to be brought forward. Motivation appears to have been twofold: to raise funds to reduce the need for taxation during the run-up to a general election; and to make re-nationalisation more difficult.[13] Railtrack was floated as a public limited company in May 1996.

The first franchises for train operating companies were awarded in February 1996, both of them in the South. The first to affect Scotland was that for the East Coast, awarded in April to the Sea Containers' group subsidiary Great North Eastern Railway (another train operator which styled itself a railway). Cross-country was franchised in January 1997 and West Coast in March, both to Virgin Rail, later called Virgin Trains. Although this was a company controlled by Richard Branson, in 1998 Stagecoach acquired a 49 per cent shareholding.[14] In 1999 Chris Green was headhunted to become chief executive.

ScotRail, which had been expected to be one of the first TOCs to be franchised, was eventually the last: Strathclyde PTA, which largely funded ScotRail and was party to the franchise, had been guarding jealously the interests of both passengers and council tax payers.[15] It was eventually franchised to bus group National Express, and the last passenger trains operated by BR ran late in the evening of 31 March 1997 between Edinburgh and Glasgow and vice versa. By the time they arrived at their destinations, after midnight, the franchisee had taken over. Present at Waverley was BR's longest serving employee, John Bowden, who was also the only employee remaining who had started his working life with a pre-nationalisation company, in his case the LNER in June 1947.[16]

Even then the way ahead was not clear, for National Express already operated Scottish CityLink buses throughout much of Scotland. To the author the attractive option seemed to be opening up of buying a through ticket to cover travel from home village (fifteen miles from a station) to London, valid by the once-a-day National Express bus to Edinburgh (with evening arrival), and onward by National Express sleeper. Not a bit of it! National Express Group was referred to the Monopolies and Mergers Commission, by the newly elected Labour government, and in due course had to sell the bus operation.[17]

281

Privatisation of Railtrack had the effect of depriving the government of its principal means of control over the railway system. Despite earlier posturings, the Labour government made no attempt to re-nationalise the railways: just as, long before, the Conservative Party had accepted the fact of nationalisation on its return to power in 1951, so the Labour Party now apparently accepted the fact of privatisation.

The new government did eventually establish the Strategic Rail Authority in 2000;[18] into it were merged the rump of BRB, and the Office of Passenger Rail Franchising.

Devolution, which brought the Scottish Parliament and the Scottish Executive into being in 1999, had initially limited effect on the railway system. The Scottish Parliament was, however, given powers to insist on changes to ScotRail's passenger service requirement – although it must be ready to fund any additional subsidy needed. It was also to provide 'instructions and guidance' to the SRA on Anglo-Scottish services. By late in 2000 the Executive was consulting the public on strategic priorities. In an enlightened manner, integration of train services with other modes of transport figured prominently in its ideas, and received an appropriately enthusiastic response.[19]

As for the newly established organisations operating in the rail industry themselves, the TOCs came together to form the Association of Train Operating Companies, and the Railway Forum was established as an industry-wide strategic think-tank and lobby group.

The Channel Tunnel came into use in 1994; rolling stock for through trains was procured jointly by the national railways of Britain, France and Belgium. The Eurocentral terminal for freight trains between Scotland and the Continent was opened the same year at Mossend, north of Motherwell, and class 92 electric locomotives to haul freight trains between Mossend and Frethun (Calais) were introduced in 1995 (although they were not cleared by Railtrack to work over the West Coast main line until 1998).[20] Railfreight Distribution, the BR sector charged with operating international freight trains, became eventually the last BR subsidiary to be privatised, by sale to EWS in November 1997.

'Eurostar' through passenger train services between London (Waterloo), Paris and Brussels, through the Channel Tunnel, started late in 1994; BRB had established a subsidiary, European Passenger Services Ltd, to operate them jointly with French and Belgian Railways.[21]

Although these services became a lasting feature of the railway scene, through passenger train services between the Continent and Scotland (and anywhere north of London) became instead a sorry tale of promises deferred and broken. The maintenance depot for Eurostar trains was built in west London, and electrification of the North London Line was upgraded to enable them to reach the East Coast main line. For the night trains, construction started of sleeping cars, coaches with reclining seats, and service vehicles which included accommodation for customs and frontier control officials, and a lounge/bar section. Class 92 locomotives were built to haul them. A 'Nightstar' train service between Glasgow, Paris and Brussels was announced, to start running early in 1996. But the cars were complex, and completion delayed; there were changes of plans, and of ownership. The new owner, London & Continental Railways, decided the service would not be viable and that autumn shelved the project. Sufficient Nightstar cars were completed

ScotRail Turbostar enters Perth on 11 April 2002 bound for Aberdeen; beyond it is the daily GNER HST from Inverness to King's Cross, the 'Highland Chieftain'. The picture repays comparison with earlier pictures of Perth in chapters 4 and 5. (Bill Roberton)

for a test train to run as far north as Dunbar on the East Coast main line on at least one occasion in the summer of 1996. Cars complete and incomplete were then stored.[22]

For daytime train services between the Continent and places beyond London, 'Regional Eurostar' trains were built. Pending their introduction to service, European Passenger Services chartered HSTs in 1995 and put on a connecting service between Edinburgh and Waterloo. But the departure time (08.30) was inconvenient, and the journey round London slow: when heading for Eurostar, the normal train service to King's Cross seemed to remain the better option, despite the inconvenience of having to cross London. Furthermore, the connecting trains were restricted, from reasons of policy, to Eurostar passengers

only – no intermediate traffic was allowed. In these circumstances, unsurprisingly, they were little used – with passenger numbers sometimes in single figures – and were discontinued early in 1997.[23]

In August of the same year a Regional Eurostar train was taken to Glasgow Central for clearance tests at platform 10, the platform to be used by trains for the Continent. They were to run via Edinburgh and the East Coast route. At Polmadie depot the equipment for washing Eurostar trains and emptying their toilets was commissioned.[24] The through train service between Scotland and the Continent got that close – but once again it did not materialise.

The Nightstar rolling stock was eventually sold in 2001 for use in Canada. Regional Eurostar trains did for some years operate north of London: on hire to GNER, which used them between the West Riding of Yorkshire and King's Cross. So although Eurostar trains were traversing the route between Leeds and Paris daily, none of them ran through: passengers had to change stations in London.

Once Eurostar trains started to run between London and Paris, what might be called the '100 mph factor' became evident. That was not the speed of the trains: it was the difference between their speeds in Britain and in France. The French, and soon afterwards the Belgians, had ensured that a high-speed line was available to the tunnel. The British government, parsimoniously, had not. Only as I write early in 2007 is the high-speed line between the tunnel and London approaching completion. It is to terminate at St Pancras, hard by King's Cross and within walking distance of Euston, which will at least provide a convenient interchange with trains to and from Scotland. So with that and the accelerations resulting from the high-speed line, the journey between Scotland and the Continent will

On the Far North line, DMU no. 158 715 is at Kildonan on 5 April 2006 as the 15.51 from Wick to Inverness.

(Bill Roberton)

benefit from being quicker and having one change instead of two. But it seems unlikely that there will be through trains unless or until the projected high-speed line north from London is built. In the meantime, Scots are denied the promised opportunity of getting onto the train at Waverley and off at the *Gare du Nord*. Perhaps even more significantly, given the importance of tourism to the Scottish economy, the train-travel-conscious French are likewise denied the opportunity

of getting onto the train at the *Gare du Nord* and off at Waverley.

The whole concept of through trains to and from the Continent seems to have suffered from the fragmentation which was privatisation, the drive which could have been theirs as the flagship services of a national railway system having melted away. This was, however, far from the only thing to suffer. Minor problems escalated, to culminate in three major disasters. All three, mercifully, occurred outside Scotland but are relevant for their consequences upon the railway system as a whole. At two of them, the collisions at Southall in September 1997 and Ladbroke Grove in October 1999, the fragmentation of managerial responsibilities consequent upon the manner of privatisation was a huge contributory factor.[25] At the third, the Hatfield high-speed derailment of October 2000, the immediate cause was inadequate track maintenance, but in that too a large part was played by the fragmentation of responsibilities, between Railtrack and its contractors for maintenance and for replacements.

Railtrack had at first been a high-spending organisation, but by 1999 serious concerns were nevertheless being expressed at the standard of maintenance, and the rapidly deteriorating condition of the railway system under its management.[26] At Hatfield a rail that was known to be defective, but for which replacement had been deferred, shattered under a train passing over it at full speed – no speed restriction had been imposed – which led to the deaths of four passengers.[27] Hatfield is on the East Coast main line: the train was heading for Leeds as it happens, but it might equally well have been heading for Edinburgh.

Bad though the accident was, it is the wider implications of Hatfield that give it its significance. As Wolmar points out, Hatfield and its immediate aftermath demonstrated in the most public way possible that Railtrack lacked the management and skills to carry out its basic functions.[28] Short of engineering expertise (BR's civil engineers had tended to go to the infrastructure maintenance companies on privatisation), its reaction to the accident was to impose speed restrictions, many as low as 20 mph, at any place

where a similar problem was suspected. Initially there were 81 such sites, throughout Britain; a month later, there were 574 speed restrictions in place consequent upon the accident, and the total reached 1,286. The result for punctuality was chaos, with innumerable trains cancelled. In Scotland, so many restrictions were required on the West Coast main line that it was, instead, closed entirely for thirty-six hours until wiser counsels prevailed. Shortly afterwards, matters were made even worse when exceptionally heavy rainfall brought widespread floods. Only gradually, as repairs and replacements were carried out, did matters improve over the ensuing months. Traffic took longer to recover: to give an example, the 113,000 containers moved through Freightliner's Coatbridge terminal in 1999 were down to 55,000 in 2002.[29]

The effect on Railtrack's finances was disastrous. By March 2001 it was stated that compensation to train operators had reached £400 million and that replacing rails over 450 miles of track had cost £180 million.[30] Profits were wiped out: the company sought to be bailed out by the government. The price of its shares – it had earlier been a stock market favourite with the share price showing large rises – fell rapidly.[31] In October 2001 the government placed the company into administration under the terms of the Railways Act 1993[32] – to the vociferous fury of shareholders, or at least a segment of them, who appeared to be going to get nothing but who might, however, have sold earlier when the share price was high. There was no lack of warning that the company was getting into trouble. Shareholders were eventually compensated, with cash – unlike the shareholders in the Big Four railway companies on nationalisation, who were compensated by issue of loan stock.

At the time that Railtrack was put into

administration it was reported that its replacement would be a public trust with day-to-day management and operation in the hands of the train operating companies.[33] The opportunity to restore this degree of vertical integration to the industry was not taken, however, but the replacement body emerged as Network Rail, a company limited by guarantee which would not distribute profits but would re-invest them. Ownership of the railway system was transferred to Network Rail in October 2002: its 'vision' was stated to be 'engineering excellence for Britain's railway' with the corporate objectives, as reported at the time, of improved safety, higher performance, increased system capability, improved relationships with customers and stakeholders, improved financial control, improved stewardship of assets and improved business performance. The geographical administrative structure of Railtrack zones was replaced by a functional structure, to obtain consistency of approach across the whole network – train operators had found a different approach in each zone through which they operated. Day-to-day operation of the system became the responsibility of various 'routes', maintenance and renewals the responsibility of 'territories'. The boundaries of Scotland Route, and Scotland Territory, are in effect those of Scotland itself.[34] During 2003 Network Rail ended maintenance of the system by contractors, and took it back in-house.[35] Renewals, however, continue to be made by contractors. In 2004 incidence of broken rails throughout the system had been reduced to 320, from almost 1,000 five years earlier, and 900 miles of rail were renewed, three times as much as five years earlier: the new owner was tackling the problem.[36]

Network Rail is classified as a private sector organisation. Its sources of funds are now track access charges, revenue grants from the Department for Transport and the Scottish Executive, enhancement funding from the same sources and from outside the industry, and commercial loans backed by a government financial indemnity. As a guarantee company Network Rail has members rather than shareholders, rather more than 100 of them. (This type of corporate body is familiar in the heritage railway sector, although in that case membership is generally more numerous and route mileage substantially less so!) Network Rail's members come in four types. Industry Members include passenger train operating companies, freight companies and rail engineering companies. Public Members (Organisations) and Public Members (Individuals) are selected to represent the wider public interest. The Department for Transport is a member, but as a provider of funds does not exercise its rights. The Scottish Executive was for a time a member, but as a provider of funds withdrew its membership lest there appear to be a conflict of interest. Among the other members is Highland Rail Partnership (HRP is a partnership of rail companies, local authorities and user groups which works effectively for development of rail in its area).[37]

Under the Railways Act 2005 there was substantial additional devolution of railway powers to the Scottish Executive. The Strategic Rail Authority was abolished and the Scottish Ministers were given powers to develop a rail strategy for Scotland, with funding to match. At the same time the Scottish Executive became responsible for overseeing Network Rail's Scottish operations, and acquired sole responsibility for the ScotRail franchise.[38] Transport Scotland was established as an executive agency accountable to the Scottish Ministers to oversee improvement and operation of the rail and trunk road networks – a

Class 334 EMU in SPT livery enters Motherwell on 29 January 2004.
(Bill Roberton)

welcome step towards integration of complementary modes of transport which had for decades been the responsibilities of different government departments located hundreds of miles apart. Nevertheless other related governmental responsibilities were retained by the Scottish Executive's Transport Group. These include ferries, harbours, bus policy, local roads, aviation and, particularly, development of the national transport strategy.[39]

Related to all of this are regional transport strategies, preparation of which is the prime responsibility of Regional Transport Partnerships (i.e., partnerships of local authorities) established under the Transport (Scotland) Act 2005. Strathclyde Passenger Transport's powers to set timetables and fares for rail services in its area were transferred to Transport Scotland in 2005 and SPT, retaining initials and logo, was transformed apparently seamlessly into Strathclyde Partnership for Transport. As, now, a regional transport partnership, SPT continues to have a strong role in developing the rail network in its region; it continues also to operate directly the Glasgow Underground.[40]

At a Great Britain level, the Rail Regulator was replaced in 2004 by the Office of Rail Regulation. Its primary responsibility then was economic regulation of Network Rail and access to the system: to this was added in 2006 regulation of health and safety throughout the railway industry.[41]

Despite Hatfield and its aftermath, freight traffic recovered. This was aided by grants for freight

First ScotRail hires-in locomotives to haul the Caledonian Sleeper trains, as seen here at Inverkeithing. (Bill Roberton)

facilities, that is to say terminals, and for track access: both are made by the Scottish Executive and, for cross-border flows, the Department for Transport, in the interests of reducing road traffic. By 2004–5 rail freight was, throughout Britain, at its highest level since 1977.[42] Although short-distance traffic is economically viable where there are regular flows, rail freight is at its most competitive where the distance is 300 miles or more[43] and much Scottish freight is cross-border. An observer at Carlisle recently noted 'a seemingly endless succession of southbound freights' carrying coal to English power stations from Scottish open-cast workings and deep-water ports.[44] There are regular flows of timber south from Highland forests, and of intermodal traffic in both directions; for the latter, by 2002 speeds up to 90 mph were being

envisaged.[45] Intermodal traffic received a boost from 2000 onwards when old-established construction and logistics undertaking The Malcolm Group Ltd, based at Grangemouth, started to provide combined road/rail transits: inducements to do so included increasing fuel costs, increasing road congestion and the European Union working-time directive, which limited the time lorry drivers could spend in the cab each week.[46] A heritage railway, the Strathspey Railway, uses its link with the main system for through freight trains from time to time: timber and salt have been carried.

The privatised Red Star parcels service was evidently unable to compete with motorway-based courier services: it faded out in 2001. Disruption of train services post-Hatfield was the final straw.[47] Some parcels traffic has continued go by rail, for example

Upgrading of Caledonian Sleeper trains has included refurbishment of the Lounge car interiors. What better way to start the journey south – or north? (First ScotRail)

between Walsall and Inverness, carried for the long haul by EWS on behalf of a courier company.[48] It is difficult to see, however, how a Britain-wide rail-based parcels service could be operated other than by carrying the parcels on passenger trains, which the manner of privatisation seems to preclude, quite apart from the lack of station staff compared with former times. All the same, if a passenger from the 1960s were to reappear, having slept Rip van Winkle-style through the intervening period, I am inclined to the opinion that it would not be the absence of steam locomotives which he or she would find most conspicuous, but the absence of parcels in huge quantities cluttering up the platforms of passenger stations.

The absence of mailbags from passenger stations would be almost as conspicuous. These largely disappeared in 1996 when Royal Mail introduced its Railnet distribution system between nine purpose-built terminals, the principal one being at Willesden and the only one in Scotland adjoining the West Coast main line at Shieldmuir (Motherwell). To work between these terminals, Royal Mail itself had obtained sixteen class 325 electric multiple units to carry containerised mail. These were not sorting carriages: the TPO trains continued to be formed from sorting carriages of BR Mark I design, while the advantages of sorting mail on the move by human sorters at 350 pieces of mail per hour became dubious when compared with electronic sorting equipment which, although stationary, could sort 30,000. In these circumstances the last TPO train to serve Scotland ran in May 2003, and withdrawal of the others was being foreseen. By that date, too, the only passenger station in Scotland still handling mails was Edinburgh Waverley.

In June 2003 beleaguered Royal Mail, squeezed between e-mails on one side and courier services on the other, made the bombshell announcement that it intended, even though the mail contract with EWS ran until 2006, to cease using rail in 2004 and distribute entirely by road and air. But it soon became clear, in the furore which followed, that Royal Mail's issue lay not with use of rail in principle, but rather with EWS, which appears to have been unwilling to scale down the operation to the extent which Royal Mail wished. By the time that the last EWS-operated mail trains ran in June 2004, another freight company, GB Railfreight, was already training its drivers on class 325 EMUS. In time for that year's Christmas rush, Royal Mail arranged for it to operate these trains between Willesden, Warrington and Shieldmuir, on short-term contract. This was in due course changed into a longer-term contract running until March 2006, and then extended again for a further year. In that limited manner, mails are still being carried by rail in Scotland at the time of writing.[49]

A total of 72.9 million passenger journeys by rail originated in Scotland in the financial year 2004–5, an increase of 34 per cent on the figure for ten years earlier. To put that into perspective, however, motorway traffic increased by 42 per cent over the same period although total road traffic increased only 16 per cent, and the number of passengers using Scottish airports was up by 93 per cent; passenger journeys by local buses were down 6 per cent.[50]

One traffic which did not appear to be sharing in this general increase – although it remained steady – was cross-Border passenger traffic by rail.[51] Although Hatfield had a lot to do with this, it is probable that the

With reopening planned, the site of the long-disused station at Larkhall was being cleared of vegetation in March 2004.
(Bill Roberton)

notorious delays in improving the West Coast main line, and in consequence in introducing improved trains, were an important contributory factor. They, and associated cost increases, were also an important contributory factor in the collapse of Railtrack. 'When InterCity handed the line over to Railtrack in the mid-'90s', Chris Green was quoted as saying early in 2003, 'there was only one speed restriction between London and Glasgow. Last summer, there were eighty-eight.'[52] In 1994 Railtrack, newly established, had announced a £1 billion programme to raise train speeds to 150 mph and cut one hour from the London–Glasgow journey time.[53] The intended speed was reduced to 140 mph but by 2002 the cost of the programme had risen to £13 billion: the intended speed was then cut back to 125 mph and the estimated cost to £9.8 billion.[54] According to *The Times* it was the most wasteful, incompetent and scandalously mismanaged project

By August 2005, reconstruction at Larkhall was well advanced. Plant convertible for use on rail or otherwise is in use.

(Bill Roberton)

ever to be undertaken in post-war Britain.[55] In fairness it must be added that increasingly strict Health & Safety requirements had contributed to the escalation of costs.

Meanwhile, in 1997 both Virgin and GNER were planning to introduce tilting trains. By then, tilting trains were running successfully in Italy, Switzerland, Sweden and elsewhere: advances in computer technology enabled the tilt mechanism to be controlled satisfactorily.[56] Although GNER later pulled out, Virgin, which in the absence of the APT was operating its West Coast main line franchise with locomotives and coaches around twenty years old, pressed ahead with plans to replace them entirely by a fleet of tilting trains. These were built by Alstom in partnership with Fiat, based on Fiat's 'Pendolino' ('small pendulum') trains and eventually totalled fifty-three nine-car trains, completed during 2002–4. The West Coast main line

between Glasgow and London with its many curves (although they are at their worst south of the border through Cumbria) is being progressively upgraded for 125 mph running. The maximum permissible cant of the track of 6 degrees (more would be unacceptable for other trains moving comparatively slowly) is supplemented by Pendolinos with up to 8 degrees of tilt: this allows them to run 20 per cent faster through the curves.

The restricted British loading gauge brought problems: it meant that trains could not be allowed to tilt at will, lest they foul structures or other trains. The solution was development of the tilt authorisation and speed supervision system – TASS. 'Balises', or transponders, are installed at intervals of two miles or so on the sleepers and act, it seems, rather like bar codes: lacking moving parts or wires themselves, they are interrogated by a train's on-board computers and authorise it to tilt where it is safe to do so, and also set the maximum speed.

Unlike the APT, the amount of tilt on a Pendolino does not fully compensate for the curvature. On the APT it did, and while passengers' sense of balance conveyed no sensation of tilting, their eyes did do so: this conflict seems to have been a cause of feelings of nausea. On Pendolinos, the sense of balance still conveys a tilting sensation to complement that provided by the eyes. Physically, Pendolino cars are tilted by electric motors. During trials, which were extensive, one Pendolino train reached 146 mph.[57]

Pendolinos entered service gradually from December 2002, working to the existing timetable. By September 2004 sufficient were in service – and West Coast main line improvements far enough advanced – for an accelerated train service to be introduced south of Crewe. This chiefly benefited Manchester–London trains, but nevertheless the best Glasgow–London time was reduced from 5 hrs 6 min. to 4 hrs 41 min. Operation at 125 mph with trains tilting was extended to Scotland, from a point three quarters of a mile south of Carstairs through to Gretna, in time for timetable revisions on 12 December 2005. Since then Pendolinos have operated in tilt mode over this section in daily service, and the journey time from Glasgow to London has been reduced to around 4hrs 25min. The result, over the ensuing year or so, was an increase of 55 per cent in rail travel between Glasgow and London, and a dent in the figures for air travel. By late in 2008 when, it is anticipated, the upgrading of the West Coast main line will be completed, a timing of about 4 hr 8 min. is planned for the northbound journey, and no doubt the southbound timing will be similar; frequency of trains too is likely to be increased. In the meantime, in September 2006 a Pendolino special, operated to raise funds for charity by Virgin Trains, with strong cooperation from Network Rail and other train operators whose scheduled trains were affected, made the southbound run non-stop in 3 hr 55 min. 27 sec., with a maximum speed of 128 mph down Beattock Bank and at other places further south. This time is an all-time record southbound, matched only by the APT's 3 hr 52 min. northbound run in 1982.[58]

For its cross-country franchise, which extended from Aberdeen and Glasgow in the north to Poole and Penzance in the south, with Birmingham as its centre, Virgin inherited from BR a mix of HSTs and locomotive-hauled trains. These also it determined to replace, with a large fleet of four-car class 220 Voyager and five-car class 221 Super Voyager diesel-electric multiple units; both have the capacity to run at 125 mph, the Super Voyagers to tilt also. They were built by Bombardier, in Belgium and Yorkshire. During extensive trials, they even appeared on the Bo'ness & Kinneil Railway for driver training. These trains' eventual introduction to service was initially marred by reports of mechanical failures and overcrowding, but nevertheless they enabled the cross-country train services to be both accelerated and much increased in frequency from 2002. Reliability is now said to be good, and passenger numbers have doubled. Super Voyagers have, like Pendolinos, been operating daily in tilt mode on the main line south of Carstairs since December 2005; they also operate regularly over routes, such as Edinburgh–Aberdeen, where their ability to tilt could be turned to good advantage in reducing journey time if TASS equipment were fitted to the track.[59]

GNER, in contrast to Virgin, inherited at privatisation BR's most modern fleet of long-distance electric trains, and seems to have concentrated to good effect on quality of service, while also refurbishing the HSTs used to provide through train services from Aberdeen and Inverness to London. It is the more to be regretted that at the time of writing the company appears to be in deep trouble, consequent largely, it seems, on difficulties within the American parent company.

In common with all other franchisees obtaining new passenger rolling stock, ScotRail, as a National Express franchise, in due course obtained new multiple unit trains. Pride of the fleet were the Turbostar DMUs (class 170/4) built in 1999–2000. With them it was able to introduce a fifteen-minute interval service between Edinburgh and Glasgow; furthermore, the class 158 DMUs formerly being used between those places could be redeployed to the Far North line with consequent accelerations. At the same time the train service from Glasgow Queen Street to Cumbernauld was extended to Falkirk Grahamston, where there are connections

Local children join Alistair Watson, Chair of SPT and Jack McConnell, First Minister, in opening Larkhall station, 9 December 2005. Some 325,000 passenger journeys were made over the reopened Larkhall line in its first year.

(First ScotRail)

to Edinburgh; Cumbernauld, though located on the original West Coast main line, had lost its local service northwards many years before. New EMUs of class 334 were obtained for Strathclyde PTE in 1999–2001 as replacements for the ageing class 303s. With no locomotives of its own, ScotRail hired in locomotives from EWS to haul the sleeper trains. A particularly welcome development was the general reintroduction in 1999 of seated coaches to these trains, previously restricted to sleepers only. Coaches with reclining seats and buffet service were provided.[60]

Much less welcome was a series of strikes over rates of pay by drivers, members of ASLEF, during the spring of 2002. These were said eventually to have cost National Express £7 million.[61]

Early in 2003 it was announced that a further twenty-two trains for ScotRail would be funded by the Scottish Executive;[62] these appeared as more Turbostars, some to work fast trains between the Central Belt and Aberdeen/Inverness, and some

with higher density seating to work local services out of Edinburgh and Glasgow. Why there was this departure from the principle that trains should be funded by private sector ROSCOs does not seem to have been made clear, unless the cause was that by this date the franchise was already drawing to its end and bids had been invited for a new one. Indeed some of these trains were delivered only after the start of the following franchise period.

Astonishingly, no consideration was given, in the franchising process, to the performance of an existing franchisee, good or bad. Only promises for the future were taken into account. So when ScotRail was voted Rail Operator of the Year in mid-2004, it may perhaps have come as some small consolation to National Express, which had just failed to retain the franchise. This inadequacy in the franchising process was said to have been corrected. [63]

The ScotRail franchise, for which the Scottish Executive had taken on full funding responsibility in April 2004, had been awarded by the executive and the SRA to FirstGroup of Aberdeen which took over in October 2004. This meant that for the first time since the grouping a Scottish company was operating almost all the passenger trains on the national network which started and ended their journeys in Scotland (but not, as was over-enthusiastically reported at the time, 'running the country's railways'). The franchise lasts for seven years, with the option of a three-year extension.[64] This time the franchisee was not obliged to divest itself of bus interests. The franchise was rebranded First ScotRail – corporate identity having presumably taken precedence over the incongruity of giving this name to ScotRail now in its third incarnation!

It is perhaps a little early to view subsequent

Another trainload of coal has been delivered to Longannet, and the empties make their way back alongside the Forth near Culross. (Bill Roberton)

developments objectively, but those which appear significant include:

- First ScotRail taking catering on trains into its own hands – another small step towards vertical integration;
- upgrading of sleeper trains;
- establishment of a customer call centre within Scotland, at Fort William;
- introduction of the 'Adopt a Station' scheme to give community groups a direct involvement in the condition of their local station;
- establishment – with encouragement from Highland Rail Partnership – of the 'Invernet' service for Inverness commuters, so that by the summer of 2006 there were as many as twelve trains a day between Inverness and Dingwall.

Invernet appears in part as a natural extension of the trend over many years towards reopening of stations at the Inverness end of the Far North line, although it embraces too an enhanced train service between Speyside and Inverness.

- improved train services elsewhere, such as departures from the suburban terminus of Milngavie every fifteen minutes instead of every half-hour.

Of Milngavie, more shortly, for the latter two developments are associated with a larger one, the trend towards reopening of stations and reconstruction of closed lines. This reappeared early in the present century, after the hiatus of privatisation, following establishment of a devolved government supportive of rail. Its first results came in 2002 with the establishment of Edinburgh Crossrail. This involved reopening to passengers of one and a quarter miles of line east of Edinburgh, which had latterly been used only for freight but were formerly part of the Waverley Route. Indeed part at least goes back further still, for the Crossrail terminus at Newcraighall is on the route of the Edinburgh & Dalkeith Railway. The Crossrail project was largely funded by the Scottish Executive, and was in due course complemented to the west by the opening of Edinburgh Park station in 2004.[65]

The improved service from Milngavie is associated with the introduction of a service through Glasgow Central Low Level to Hamilton and then onward, following construction of three miles of electrified line over trackbed disused for four decades, to Larkhall. The project was completed in December 2005. Further associated with that was reconstruction of the curve from Maryhill to Anniesland. This enabled Queen Street–Maryhill trains to be extended to the latter place and connect with trains to and from Milngavie and places to the west. About 325,000 passenger journeys were made over the newly rebuilt section of the Larkhall line during its first year.[66]

In the new favourable climate, Clackmannanshire Council resolved in 2002 to submit a private bill to the Scottish Parliament for reconstruction of the Stirling–Alloa line. And not just as far as Alloa – for its continuation to Kincardine also, a total of some thirteen miles. At Kincardine is Longannet power station, its bulk supplies of coal delivered by train from the west of Scotland, which approached Longannet by the Forth Bridge, Dunfermline and the branch line via Culross which was last used by regular passenger trains in 1930s. Stated objectives of the reopening scheme are to provide Alloa with an hourly passenger train service to Stirling and Glasgow, to enable block coal trains to approach Longannet by the short route from the west, relieving congestion on the Forth Bridge, and possibly to provide freight services to other customers along the line and in Fife. The bill was passed in 2004.

West of Alloa, track remained in situ since last used in the mid-1990s, but had to be lifted and replaced by track suitable for heavy coal trains. Between Alloa and Longannet lay the trackbed of a long-dismantled branch line. With support from the Scottish Executive and others, overgrowth was cleared throughout, and structures reconditioned; tracklaying started late in 2006. If progress continues as anticipated, the line will be open before this is published.[67] It is difficult to believe that its completion will not lead to a demand for a passenger train service eastwards from Stirling and Alloa, via Kincardine, Culross and Dunfermline to Edinburgh.

At Edinburgh Waverley itself, the number of trains using the station daily increased by 50 per cent between 1991 and 2006 to reach 576. A very large programme of improvements – probably the largest since that of the North British Railway in the 1890s – was started by Network Rail in 2006, funded by Transport Scotland. Still continuing at the time of writing, this is increasing capacity by improving the track layout and adding more platforms, and will also provide an improved entrance to the station from Princes Street.[68]

Reconstruction of the Waverley Route through the Borders, in whole or in part, seems to have been a live issue almost continuously since it was closed. It is now closer to realisation than at any time previously. Despite inevitable controversy, the bill to rebuild it from Newcraighall to Tweedbank, between Galashiels and Melrose, was passed by the Scottish Parliament in 2006.[69] Further south the Waverley Route Heritage Association is working towards restoration of a section of the line in the vicinity of Whitrope as a heritage railway.[70]

The EdinburghTram (Line One) Act 2006, and a similar Act for Line Two, authorised the re-appearance of electric trams in Edinburgh.

The absence of direct rail links to the airports of Glasgow and Edinburgh has long been both conspicuous and contentious. At the time of writing a bill for a link to Glasgow Airport has just been passed by the Scottish Parliament: it authorises a branch into the airport from Paisley Gilmour Street. Through trains are to run from Glasgow Central.[71] Another bill is before the Parliament for a rail link to Edinburgh Airport. In addition to a line from Edinburgh itself, the link is to provide direct access to the airport from the north and west: the proposal is for a through station, underground, with connections to routes in each of the three directions.[72]

A further bill before the Parliament seeks to reinstate the railway between Airdrie (Drumgelloch) and Bathgate. The bill is promoted by Network Rail, the funding to come from the Scottish Ministers. The whole proposal, including linked improvements, would provide a double track electric railway between Glasgow, Airdrie, Bathgate and Edinburgh: a fifteen-minute interval service is envisaged between Edinburgh and termini west of Glasgow such as Helensburgh and Balloch. The prime purpose of the proposal, however, is to relieve road congestion in the M8/A8 corridor. It will offer an alternative to the motor car for commuters between, on the one hand, West Lothian and the Glasgow area and, on the other, North Lanarkshire and the Edinburgh area.[73] This proposal has arisen out of detailed studies made for

the Scottish Executive in 2000–2 – the same studies are leading to upgrading of the A8 past Coatbridge to motorway standard.[74]

Had the primary intention been to improve communications between Edinburgh and Glasgow, full electrification of the route via Shotts would evidently have been the better option. Only twenty-two out of its forty-seven and a quarter miles remain unelectrified, and unlike Airdrie–Bathgate it is aligned – and was formerly operated – as a main line for express trains. Electrification was being considered in 1990, without result. A proposal to improve it was reported in 2005, with fast limited-stop trains to supplement the present all-stations locals (once described to me by a Livingston resident as 'the milk run'). But it did not extend to electrification.[75]

Looking further ahead, SPT would like to see Glasgow Crossrail. This in effect would mean reopening for passenger traffic the GSWR part of the City of Glasgow Union Railway from Shields Road to Bellgrove, reinstating the link from Gorbals to the main line to Kilmarnock and Carlisle, and building a new curve at High Street to enable trains from the south and west to run through to Queen Street Low Level. The line would also facilitate through trains between the east of Scotland and Ayrshire.[76]

Looking further ahead still, there are thoughts of a third bridge to cross the Firth of Forth, to carry both road and rail.[77] And there are thoughts too of high-speed lines between Glasgow and Edinburgh, and/or between Scotland and London. Such a line would bring the time for the Glasgow–London journey by rail down to three hours or less, competitive with air.[78]

The procedure for authorisation of new and rebuilt railways is likely to be simplified in consequence of

Over newly laid track, more track materials are delivered by rail during reconstruction of the Alloa-Kincardine line. (Bill Roberton)

the Transport and Works (Scotland) Bill, before the Scottish Parliament at the time of writing. If passed, it will replace private bill procedure for this purpose by statutory orders made under its provisions. This will benefit large projects, but will not help small ones, such as heritage railways, which have hitherto been able to use light railway order procedure – this too is to be replaced. However Tavish Scott, Minister for Transport, did give an assurance to the Local Government and Transport Committee that their fees would not be increased.[79]

In *Scotland's National Transport Strategy* the Scottish Executive identifies the key strengths of rail as: supporting urban economic activity by enabling commuting from a wide area; providing quality inter-urban links; providing a critical link in power generation by moving large volumes of coal; and addressing peripherality by providing access to remote communities, for residents and tourists. It foresees that demand for both passenger and freight services will increase by a third over the next twenty years.[80] Network Rail's *Scotland: Route Utilisation Strategy* is written in terms of increasing capacity where needed to relieve congestion (a need which forty, thirty,

Work in progress at Edinburgh Waverley in March 2007 – part of, probably, the most extensive station enlargement scheme seen on Scottish railways for a century. (Bill Roberton)

even twenty years ago would have seemed far from probable). All of which augurs well.

Yet reopenings, and relieving congestion, are all very well, but is it not important also to use the existing rail network to best advantage? There are certainly some remarkable gaps in the train services at present provided. Consider the original West Coast main line northwards from Motherwell by Coatbridge to Stirling. The through service by this route faded out about twenty years ago. Yet in the 1890s the Caledonian Railway's down tourist express would take you direct from Carlisle to Stirling in 125 minutes.[81] Well over a century later, the journey is likely to take you 136 minutes or more, with a change of trains at Haymarket thrown in. The most remarkable gap is perhaps the absence of any through train service between Ayrshire and the capital: you can go by through train from Ayr to Newcastle, but not from Ayr to Edinburgh.

Electrification via Shotts would help to facilitate such a train service, with the trains going in and out of Glasgow Central en route.

Even where a train service is provided, it is sometimes less than adequate. Oban gets but three trains a day from Glasgow (except on summer Saturdays when one extra is provided) and no connection out of the Fort William sleeper at Crianlarich. Yet Oban is more than a town at the end of a long rambling branch line: it is the most important interchange point for shipping services to the Western Isles. Journey times over the West Highland to Fort William are extended, and scarcely competitive, because train speeds are limited – not primarily, I believe, by steep gradients but by sharp curves. Measures to alleviate the problem seem essential.

Gleneagles Station survives, but would doubtless see more use if the train service were less inadequate: a main line station where no trains call for more than five and a half hours (in either direction) in the middle of the day seems unlikely to attract custom. Between Dundee and Arbroath lies a whole string of stations at which but one train each way calls daily. One of them, Golf Street, hit the headlines in 2004 as 'Scotland's least used railway station'.[82] These stations are relics of a local train service that ran every hour or so during the 1970s, but which British Rail later discontinued. No doubt BR continued to run one train each way daily rather than trigger off the statutory closure procedure for the stations, and these two trains then became set in stone in the passenger service requirement. Whether these stations should be closed down, or the train service brought up to something useful, looks like a good question for the new regional transport partnership TACTRAN (Tayside and Central Scotland Transport Partnership).

Remarkable, too, is the lack of reopened stations on the East Coast and West Coast main lines through the Borders, particularly in contrast with the many stations reopened on the Glasgow & South Western line. But ScotRail, in its successive incarnations, has shown much more enthusiasm for reopening stations than have InterCity sector and its successor franchisees. It may well be that the Scottish Executive should have greater input into the cross-border franchising process than it appears to do, both in this connection, and in connection with those routes where cross-border trains serve local and commuter stations equally with ScotRail – such as Edinburgh–Aberdeen.

One of the benefits that seemed likely to emerge from privatisation – although scarcely one intended – was a pan-industry lobby group to push the case for rail with the government. It has to some extent emerged, as the Railway Forum. But worthy and energetic though that concern is, it scarcely seems to carry the clout of the Railway Companies' Association of the 1930s. It may yet have to flex its muscles in Scotland, for although the devolved government has proved very favourable to rail so far, this can scarcely be relied upon to continue indefinitely – particularly if, for instance, one of the schemes for building or rebuilding railways comes to be perceived as costing far more than it should. The Edinburgh Airport link is a worry.

The rail industry has been fortunate that the troubled period since privatisation has been one of increasing travel generally – and, a cynic might add, the passengers have continued to come despite every discouragement. Certainly one of the losses since privatisation is the lack of promotion for rail travel in general. There is nothing to compare with the memorable advertising campaigns put out by the Big

Four companies jointly between the wars, or by British Rail in its 1970s heyday. Who now encourages us to 'See a friend this weekend' or to 'Relax by InterCity'?

The position is aggravated by the extraordinary decision of Network Rail to cease publishing, on paper, the all-line *National Rail Timetable*. This publication is descended from the British Rail all-line timetable, the responsibility for which was, I believe, passed to Railtrack at privatisation. Properly developed, illustrated and with advertising to pay for it, it could have been the industry's principal sales tool: an Argos catalogue for the rail industry, widely available for consultation at stations and also cheap to buy. Only from such a publication, with maps, is it possible for a traveller to establish the full choice of routes and services available, before making the decision which to take and when. Putting it online is no real substitute.

In Scotland, however, the greater need is for a national timetable to cover all modes of public transport. The country's topography, and the history of transport within it, mean that no mode, public or private, has a fully national network. All modes are interdependent. Integration between them is vital. The Scottish national transport strategy's proposals for improved interchanges and through ticketing are welcome.[83] The PlusBus scheme, which enables passengers by rail to buy a ticket which covers also an onward journey by bus, is a good start. But it is important too that timings are coordinated, and connections guaranteed – that is, that if one mode is delayed, others will wait for it, at least for an advertised length of time. Above all, there is a need for a convenient one-stop source of all the information needed to choose the most preferable option for a journey: in other words, a national public transport timetable.

A timetable on paper, that is. The former Highlands & Islands Development Board used to publish an excellent one for its area. This was discontinued not, I believe, from a lack of demand, but in consequence of abolition of the board. Only in a timetable book, with maps, can the full range of options for travel – including routes, modes, operators, times, frequency, fares and catering – easily be made clear.

Computerised timetable pages are tedious, expensive and slow to download and print. The alternative is the computerised travel information service into which the user enters preferred times and dates for travel. Traveline Scotland is a brave attempt at this. Yet it has far to go before becoming fully informative and reliable. It seems to be simultaneously too detailed – based on post codes – and not detailed enough. It appears largely to overlook options for integrating private and public transport, such as travel by car or taxi to a station; and its suggestions for public transport journeys are sometimes eccentric (Edinburgh to Lochearnhead via Glasgow and Crianlarich, to give an example relevant to the author's regular travels). More importantly, such services limit the traveller's freedom of choice. When buying clothes we do not punch our measurements into a computer and take what comes: we study the full range available on the counters – or in the mail-order catalogue – and then choose.

In any event, the railway industry, of all industries, should be wary of discarding traditional techniques prematurely: it is itself an outstanding example of one such which has conspicuously made a comeback.

Privatisation, as I have suggested, addressed a non-issue with a flawed solution. The resulting problems emerged mainly on the engineering side, and these appear mostly to have been rectified by Network Rail.

As for whether railways should be nationalised, or private, or a mixture of both, this appears less important than that they should be properly and consistently funded over a period – a period long enough for substantial investment to be made and to take effect. In this respect Network Rail, with successive funding programmes agreed with government and regulator for five-year periods, ring-fenced,[84] seems in a very much better position than was BR, for ever caught by the principle of annuality.

Yet we are still stuck with administrative separation of rail from wheel, that is, short-term franchises, with separation of steering gear from accelerator and brake. Along with this go a complex regulatory regime and a bureaucratic system for attributing causes of delay. But a return to vertical integration, however desirable in principle, seems unlikely in the immediate future. In any case, things have moved on since privatisation, perhaps not down the best road, but they have moved on. The administrative structure has become familiar; the companies concerned are well established. Running a railway requires teamwork on a grand scale. The best chance that the present structure has of working properly seems to be if all the many parties to it function not, as was intended, in a spirit of competition, but in a culture of partnership towards the greater end of running the railway system.

There are encouraging signs that this is happening. A witness before the freight transport inquiry, held by the Scottish Parliament's Local Government and Transport Committee, commented that the demise of Railtrack appeared to have been a watershed: the collaboration that he was receiving not just from Network Rail, but also from other users of the network, would not previously have been seen. Another witness commented that in Scotland the TOCs and the freight companies worked closely together and cooperated very well.[85] Earlier, Nicol Stephen MSP, when Minister for Transport, had in his foreword to *Scotland's Transport Future* envisaged everyone in Scottish transport working together in partnership.[86]

So in the new era there is room for optimism. Somehow, railways always seem to survive, to continue, somewhere. On a recent visit to Plockton, Wester Ross, it was a delight to find that the quiet of the evening was not disturbed by the distant roar of continuous main-road traffic, as happens over so much of the Highlands, but interrupted only occasionally by the reassuring rhythmical clatter of distant train wheels over fishplated joints.

Another picture. Let us join, at Waverley, the sleeper for London and, having found our cabin and dumped the bags, take our seats in the lounge car. No more rush before morning: we can unwind, dram in hand. The car has an air of what German-speakers would call *Gemütlichkeit*, of relaxed comfort and cosy spaciousness unequalled by any other coach in everyday service. Or any other form of land transport, come to that. The train accelerates gently, sleepers always do (well, nearly always). We pass through the tunnels, then from outside there is a flash of light as we sweep through late-evening Haymarket, illuminated but deserted. The train accelerates away up grade towards Carstairs through the dark. Soon the lights of Ratho are falling away below us to the right, to be followed, more distantly, by Livingston. Time for another dram. All, for the moment, is well.

ADDENDA

The main text of this book was completed in mid-February 2007. During the ensuing six months until mid-August, while it was going through the press, there were several developments which seem likely to be of lasting interest. These are mentioned below.

The Scottish Executive recognised the Scottish Railway Preservation Society's core collection as being a collection of national significance.

In April 2007, the steam railtour 'The Great Britain' covered the length of Britain from Penzance to Kyle of Lochalsh and Thurso. In Scotland the train was hauled in turn by *Duchess Pacific* 6233 *Duchess of Sutherland*, A4 60009 *Union of South Africa*, K2 61994 *The Great Marquess* (for parts of the journey these last two double-headed) and 8F 48151.

Three bills mentioned in the text completed their passage through the Scottish Parliament to become Acts:

- Edinburgh Airport Rail Link Act 2007
- Airdrie–Bathgate Railway and Linked Improvements Act 2007
- Transport and Works (Scotland) Act 2007.

Freight company EWS was bought by Deutsche Bahn, the German State Railway, which also has freight interests in Switzerland and Sweden. Two cross-Border passenger franchises were re-franchised by the Department for Transport: the cross-country franchise, formerly Virgin Trains, to Arriva Trains, and the East Coast franchise, formerly GNER, to National Express.

There has been increasing emphasis on reducing carbon emissions to protect the environment and improve health: *Scotland's National Transport Strategy* devoted an entire chapter to the subject (out of only six chapters in total). For rail transport the aim was to reduce emissions by means of a gradual shift from diesel to electric traction. The Scottish Executive policy document *Scotland's Railways* subsequently identified the following routes for electrification in the medium term (2009–14): Edinburgh–Glasgow via Falkirk, Whifflet, Paisley Canal, East Kilbride and Barrhead/Kilmarnock, Stirling/Dunblane/Alloa, and Cumbernauld. Further details of the Edinburgh–Glasgow proposal were contained in the Scottish Ministers' *High Level Output Specification* made to the Office of Rail Regulation in July 2007, and in Network Rail's Final Report on the proposed electrification (May 2007), both of them to be found on www.transportscotland.gov.uk. The proposal included not only the main line, but also two diversionary routes, via Falkirk Grahamston and via Cumbernauld.

The election in May 2007 brought a Scottish National Party minority government to Scotland. For transport, the SNP manifesto had promised the core principles of full utilisation of the current road and rail network, effective road, rail, sea and air infrastructure, and easier commuting, together with increasingly green, safe and easy journeys year on year. Overall support for rail, it appears from the manifesto, is likely to continue: there are manifesto commitments to, for instance, improvements on the Queen Street–Waverley route, extensive electrification, improved integration of public transport, and support for a fast rail link to London and connection with Europe through the Channel Tunnel rail link. Detail manifesto promises include an 'overland station' at Edinburgh Airport in place of the proposed hub station under the runway, track improvements to cut the Edinburgh–Inverness journey by forty-five minutes, and tilting trains to Aberdeen. Of the wider implications of possible independence for the railway system, however, the manifesto appears to be silent.

APPENDIX

THE ORIGINS OF THE FIRST MONKLAND & KIRKINTILLOCH LOCOMOTIVES, AND THE DODD(S) FAMILY OR FAMILIES

The successful introduction of steam locomotives is so fundamental an event in the history of Scottish railways, and indeed of Scotland itself, that it would be reasonable to suppose that the full facts – the individuals responsible, the course of events – would be certain and well-known. The opposite is the case: they have been clouded in obscurity and uncertainty. I have endeavoured in Chapter 2 to relate what appears to be the story, but it may well be that diligent research will produce further information.

Uncertainty has arisen from two causes. Firstly, there is a surprising dearth of contemporary material about the Monkland & Kirkintilloch Railway in its early days. The National Archives of Scotland appears to hold no collection of material specific to the M & KR among its railway records. An online search of the National Register of Archives produces nothing elsewhere earlier than the mid-1830s. Whishaw's encyclopaedic *Railways of Great Britain and Ireland* of 1842 has no chapter for the M & KR although it includes other early Scottish railways such as the Ballochney, the Garnkirk & Glasgow and the Slamannan.

The Mitchell Library, Glasgow, does however hold a collection of early railway material, accession numbers 53154, 53155, 53156 and 53157, the whole bound together as a single volume of railway pamphlets. Accession number 53156 relates to the Monkland & Kirkintilloch Railway and includes some, but not all, of the early annual reports 'of the committee of management'. These include the important one for the year 1831, which was prepared for the annual meeting on 1 February 1832.

The second cause of uncertainty is Snell's *A Story of Railway Pioneers: being an account of the inventions and work of Isaac Dodds and his son Thomas Weatherburn Dodds*. This was published in 1921; it gives Isaac Dodds the entire credit for design of the first Monkland & Kirkintilloch locomotives, and omits any mention of George Dodds. Judged in isolation, however, it tells a plausible story. Isaac Dodds, son of colliery viewer Thomas Dodds, had been born in 1801 and, having lost his father, was taken on at the early age of eleven or thereabouts by his father's brother Ralph Dodds at Killingworth Colliery as a mining engineer pupil. He was present throughout George Stephenson's early locomotive experiments, and is credited with inventing coupling rods to transmit power from one pair of wheels to the next – and of establishing the practicability of his idea by taking two spinning wheels and coupling them together. (Others, of course, may have thought of the same idea independently.) When George Stephenson and partners opened Robert Stephenson & Co.'s locomotive works in Newcastle upon Tyne in 1823, Isaac Dodds moved thither. By 1825 his apprenticeship was complete, and he opened his own engineering works near Newcastle.

In 1830, according to Snell, Isaac Dodds was engaged as consulting engineer to the Monkland & Kirkintilloch Railway, and Snell then recounts the story of the introduction of locomotives in some detail. Subsequently Isaac Dodds moved in 1832 to the Horseley Company, which at that period was building locomotives, and afterwards had a notable career in engineering. He was consulted, for instance, about the locomotives for the Dublin & Kingstown Railway, and he produced many innovations in locomotive design, including a locomotive valve gear, which provided for varying the cut-off by moving the position of the eccentric around the axle, and which might well have seen widespread adoption had not the Stephenson Link Motion been invented almost simultaneously. The latter is referred to in Warren, pages 366–70.

Snell's was a convincing tale and was accepted by subsequent authors such as E. L. Ahrons in his authoritative *The British Steam Railway Locomotive 1825–1925* and Campbell Highet in *Scottish Locomotive History: 1831–1923* (and indeed by the present author during the 1980s when writing about early railways). But Snell's account is nevertheless flawed, so far as it relates to the Monkland & Kirkintilloch locomotives. Much of this part of his book is derived from Gordon's *A Treatise on Elemental Locomotion …*, of which the relevant part is in turn derived from the M & KR annual report for 1831 with its account of the introduction of locomotives. The original report credits the responsibility for these to 'MR GEORGE DODDS, the Superintendent'. Strangely, in quoting this, Gordon omits the word 'George'; and Snell takes the quotation as referring to Isaac.

Other authors, such as John Thomas in *A Regional History of the Railways of Great Britain, vol. 6, Scotland: The Lowlands and the Borders,* and Don Martin in *The Monkland & Kirkintilloch and Associated Railways,* have referred to George Dodds without reference to Isaac. C. J. A. Robertson in *The Origins of the Scottish Railway System* mentions the locomotives but (perhaps cautiously!) credits no one with their design. The only recent author who has considered the claims of both men seems to be Dendy Marshall in *A History of Locomotives down to the end of the year 1831.* Although he too relied on Gordon's *Treatise* as a source, he ascribes the locomotives to George Dodds, and is somewhat dismissive, not only of Isaac, but also of the locomotives themselves with their 'antediluvian design'.

All this leaves the present author wondering what led Snell to consider that these locomotives were one of Isaac Dodds's achievements, and what led him to consult Gordon's *Treatise.* He was clearly familiar with his subject's obituary in *Minutes of Proceedings of the Institution of Civil Engineers* (vol. 75, 1883–4

part 1, p. 308–14) from which any mention of the Monkland & Kirkintilloch Railway is conspicuous by its absence. He is seldom specific about the other numerous sources he consulted. What is clear however is that he knew family members – Isaac Dodds's granddaughter Miss C.E. Dodds, and also a grandson of his sister – and had access to family papers surviving in about 1910. Is it not likely that somewhere among family traditions and papers there was an indication that Isaac Dodds was indeed consulted about the design of the locomotives, even though he may not formally have been appointed 'consulting engineer'? In 1830 George Dodds had been for several years isolated from the direct line of continuing development of the Stephenson locomotive: he may well have felt that he needed up-to-date advice, and who better turn to than Isaac? Isaac Dodds had been at Robert Stephenson & Co. during at least part of the time when the Stockton & Darlington locomotives were being built, and he was still closely involved with the Stephensons. George Dodds must have known him at Killingworth; possibly they were related. Some of the features of the M & K locomotives – notably the metallic piston rings, a detail innovation of lasting importance – seem more in keeping with what is known of Isaac's character than with George's.

To muddy the waters a bit further still, there has also been uncertainty about the identity of Ralph Dodds. J. G. James in his Newcomen Society paper *Ralph Dodd, The Very Ingenious Schemer* (Transactions of the Newcomen Society vol. 47, pp. 161–78) considered that Ralph Dodds the Killingworth viewer and Ralph Dodd the civil engineer were one and the same. This seems unlikely. Dodd the engineer did have a son called George Dodd, who was much concerned with steamboats on the Clyde and elsewhere from 1815 onwards, but who cannot have had any connection with the Monkland & Kirkintilloch locomotives for he died young in 1827.

NOTES AND SOURCES

A NOTE ABOUT NOTES

Regrettably, it is scarcely practicable to prepare a book such as this entirely from primary sources, however enticing a prospect that might be for a life's work. So although some of this book is drawn from primary sources, most of it is a gathering-together of material from secondary ones. Since these are many and diverse, I have endeavoured to provide copious notes, which I hope may serve to point readers in the direction of further information on particular topics.

PROLOGUE

1. *Scottish Transport Statistics*, chapter 8, para. 2.5.
2. *British Railways Board Facts and Figures*, 33.
3. *Scottish Transport Statistics*, chapter 8, para. 2.1.
4. *Scotland's Transport Future*, 71.
5. *Scottish Transport Statistics*, chapter 8, paras. 2.18, 2.19.
6. *Rail Data Book*, 16, 22. The top stations of the Cairngorm Mountain Railway and the Snowdon Mountain Railway are of course substantially higher than Druimuachdar, but these lines are not connected to the main system.
7. *British Railways Board Facts and Figures*, 33.
8. Mitchell, 194.

1 WAGGONWAYS: THE EARLIEST RAILWAYS IN SCOTLAND

1. Lewis, *Early Wooden Railways*, 103.
2. Mullay, S., 'Did Scotland Lead The Way' in *The Scots Magazine* October 1982, 90.
3. Murray, 65.
4. Nock, *Scottish Railways*, 90.
5. Brown, K., 'The First Railway in Scotland' in *The Railway Magazine* January 1938, 1.
6. Robertson, 7–8.
7. Watters, 2, 14–15; Lewis, *Early Wooden Railways*, 255.
8. Pennant, 566.
9. Broad, 104.
10. Frew, I. D. O., 'The Brora Colliery Tramway' in *The Railway Magazine* January 1960, 55; Simms, 23–4.
11. *NSA*, Clackmannanshire, Alloa, 30.
12. Watters, 15.
13. *NSA*, Clackmannanshire, Alloa, 30.
14. Cameron, 47, 69.
15. Stevenson, ed., 24.
16. Lewis, *Early Wooden Railways*, 147.
17. Stevenson, ed., 23.

2 PUBLIC RAILWAYS AND THE COMING OF STEAM

1. Thomson, G., 'James Watt and the Monkland Canal' in *The Scottish Historical Review* October 1950, 122.
2. 'Old or West Monkland', in Sinclair (ed.), 1793, 533.
3. Leslie, J., 'Blackhill Canal Inclined Plane' in *The Civil Engineer and Architect's Journal*, July 1852, 201. See also Hutton, 42.
4. Robertson, 22.
5. Priestley, 368.
6. Acworth, 6, quoting Aiton, W., *General View of the Agriculture of the County of Ayr*.
7. Lee, C. E., 'The Kilmarnock & Troon Railway' in *The Railway Magazine* January 1939, 63.
8. Robertson, 23.
9. Tomlinson, 114.
10. Marshall, C. F. D., 119.
11. Hunter, J. K., 98–99
12. Robbins, M., 'Sir Walter Scott and Two Early Railway Schemes' in *The Railway Magazine* February 1951, 87.
13. Tomlinson, 58.
14. Stevenson, ed., 139.
15. Stevenson, *Report relative to various lines of railway …*, 26.
16. Tomlinson, 15.
17. Martin, *Monkland & Kirkintilloch*, 8–9.
18. Acworth, 14; Robertson, 70.
19. Robertson, 191.
20. Ransom, P. J. G., 'Miller, John, (1805–83)' in *Oxford Dictionary of National Biography*
21. Robertson, 52.
22. Whishaw, 99.
23. Lythe, S. G. E., 'The Dundee & Newtyle Railway – 1' in *The Railway Magazine* August 1951, 547.

24. Robertson, 65, 362 note 87.

25. Maj. Gen. C. W. Pasley, Inspector-General of Railways, quoted by Lee, C. E. 'The Dundee & Newtyle Railway – 3' in *The Railway Magazine*, December 1951, 848; Robertson, 21.

26. Martin, *Garnkirk & Glasgow,* 9.

27. Martin, *Monkland & Kirkintilloch,* 10–11.

28. Hill & Buchanan, 5; Martin, *Monkland & Kirkintilloch,* 77.

29. Tomlinson, 153–8.

30. e.g., Ransom, *Transport Revolution,* 157–63; Ransom, *Victorian Railway,* 45–53; Rolt, 159–75; Wood, N., 301 *et seq.*

31. Davison, 33; *Mechanics' Magazine,* 31 October 1829, 163; Wood, N., 323, 330.

32. Warren, 207; Wood, N., 323, 330.

33. Martin, *Garnkirk & Glasgow,* 17; Marshall, C. F. Dendy, 190.

34. *Report of the Committee of Management of the Monkland & Kirkintilloch Railway Company* to the general meeting of proprietors on 3 Feb. 1830, contained in Mitchell Library, Glasgow, Railway Pamphlets, accession no. 53156.

35. *Report of the Committee of Management of the Monkland & Kirkintilloch Railway Company* to the general meeting of proprietors on 1 Feb. 1832, contained in Mitchell Library, Glasgow, Railway Pamphlets, accession no. 53156.

36. Smiles, 49.

37. Mountford, C. E., 'The Hetton Railway – Stephenson's original design and its evolution' in Bailey, (ed.), 76–95; with further information kindly provided by C. E. Mountford and by Russell Wear whose genealogical research has confirmed that George Dodds of Hetton and George Dodds of the Monkland & Kirkintilloch are one and the same. See also Ferguson, N., 'Anglo-Scottish Transfer of Railway Technology in the 1830s' in Bailey, (ed.), 179–81.

38. Summerside, 42–3.

39. Skeat, 96–7.

40. *Glasgow Courier,* Saturday 25 September 1830.

41. Gordon, 58.

42. Hill & Buchanan, 5; Wood, N., 333–4.

43. *Report of the Committee of Management of the Monkland & Kirkintilloch Railway Company* to the general meeting of proprietors on 1 Feb. 1832, contained in Mitchell Library, Glasgow, Railway Pamphlets, accession no. 53156.

44. Rolt, George and Robert Stephenson, 163–4.

45. *Report of the Committee of Management of the Monkland & Kirkintilloch Railway Company* to the general meeting of proprietors on 1 Feb. 1832, contained in Mitchell Library, Glasgow, Railway Pamphlets, accession no. 53156.

46. *Report of the Committee of Management of the Ballochney Railway* to the general meeting of proprietors on 7 February 1832, contained in Mitchell Library, Glasgow, Railway Pamphlets, accession no. 53155.

47. Martin, *Garnkirk & Glasgow,* 14.

48. Hill & Buchanan, un-numbered page carrying descriptions of Hill's views.

49. Whishaw, 85; Ahrons, 27.

50. Chambers, 397.

51. Whishaw, 98, 97.

52. *British Transport Commission, Report and Accounts for 1948,* 321.

53. Martin, *Monkland & Kirkintilloch,* 18, 20.

54. *Edinburgh Evening Courant,* 26 August 1839; *Glasgow Herald,* 26 August 1839, 4.

55. Martin, *Monkland & Kirkintilloch,* 45–7.

56. Martin, *Monkland & Kirkintilloch,* 58.

57. Robertson, 73.

58. Robertson, 73.

59. Ransom, *Victorian Railway,* 247–51.

3 THE FIRST MAIN LINES

1. Quoted in *Mechanics' Magazine,* 31 October 1829, 168.

2. Robertson, 101.

3. Ransom, *Victorian Railway,* 66, 69, 94–6.

4. Robertson, 127–8, 152.

5. Webster, 138–43.

6. Robertson, 140–3.

7. Robertson, 194.

8. Robertson, 197.

9. Stephenson Locomotive Society, 5.

10. Stephenson Locomotive Society, 5.

11. Gourvish, *Mark Huish,* 49.

12. Robertson, 194.

13. Handley, 101.

14. Handley, e.g. 109, 132, 134, 164, 248, 267.

15. Robertson, 270–3.

16. Robertson, 275–80; Acworth, 31–3.

17. Stephenson Locomotive Society, 5–6.

18. Broad, 111–2.

19. Stephenson Locomotive Society, 5.

20. Whishaw, 102.

21. Cockburn, 110.

22. Ransom, *Victorian Railway* 166–72 describes locomotive development at this period in more detail.

23. Whishaw, 10, 118.

24. Stephenson Locomotive Society, 24.

25. Ransom, P. J. G. and Woodward, G., 'Davidson, Robert' in Day and McNeil (eds), *Biographical Dictionary of the History of Technology,* 195.

26. Ransom, *Victorian Railway* 198–205 decribes coach development at this period in more detail.

27. Whishaw, 109–10.

28. Acworth, 21.

29. Martin, *Monkland & Kirkintilloch,* 46.

30. Stephenson Locomotive Society, 5.

31. Whishaw, 117–8.

32. Whishaw, 320.

33. Robertson, 241–2.

34. Gourvish, T. R., 'The Railways and Steamboat Competition in Early Victorian Britain' in *Transport History* vol. 4, 1972, 11.

35. *Bradshaw*, 1842, 32.

36. Martin, *Monkland & Kirkintilloch*, 12.

37. Whishaw, 3, 80, 105, 117, 122.

38. Cooke, 15–6.

39. Stephenson Locomotive Society, 55.

40. Robertson, 260–1.

41. Lindsay, 83.

42. Gourvish, T. R., 'The Railways and Steamboat Competition in Early Victorian Britain' in *Transport History* vol. 4, 1972, 2.

43. Stephenson Locomotive Society, 6, 46.

44. Cook, T., 5.

45. Gourvish, *Mark Huish*, 65.

46. Robertson, 237.

47. Whishaw, 1.

48. Robertson, C. J. A., 'Early Scottish railways and the observance of the sabbath' in *The Scottish Historical Review* vol. 57, 1978, 143–167 covers the subject fully.

49. Stephenson Locomotive Society, 2.

50. Whishaw, 1.

4 HOW THE SYSTEM GREW

1. The Parliamentary process is described extensively in Williams vol. I, 71–88 and in Robertson, 176–181.

2. Full title, 'An Act to attach certain Conditions to the construction of future Railways authorised by any Act of the present or succeeding sessions of Parliament; and for other Purposes in relation to Railways'.

3. Reed, M., 'Who Runs The Railways? The relationship between the government and the operators' in *Journal of the Railway & Canal Historical Society* May 2004 525–6; Robertson, 176.

4. Lewin, 103, 130

5. *Blackwood's Edinburgh Magazine* October 1845, 453–66; Thomas, J., *Callander & Oban*, 11–16.

6. Hadfield, *Atmospheric Railways*, 214, 221; Lewin, 228, 209.

7. *The Illustrated London News*, 6 December 1845, 362.

8. Cockburn, 167, 185.

9. Lythe, S. G. E., 'Early Days of the Arbroath & Forfar Railway' in *The Railway Magazine* February 1953, 129.

10. *Minutes of Proceedings of the Institution of Civil Engineers*, vol. 75, 1883–4 part I, 313.

11. Stephenson Locomotive Society, 8.

12. Handley, 254.

13. Tomlinson, 478–9.

14. Bennett, 57–8; Ellis, *North British Railway*, 30–2; Sutherland, J. H., 'Before the Forth Bridge' in *The Railway Magazine* January 1939, 4–5.

15. National Archives of Scotland, BR/EGR/1/10, 11 & 12.

16. Nock, *Caledonian Railway*, 34–40.

17. Robertson, C. J. A., 'Early Scottish railways and the observance of the sabbath' in *The Scottish Historical Review* vol. 57, 1978, 153–6.

18. Lewin, 401.

19. For Crampton locomotives, see Chapter 9; see also Ellis, *North British Railway*, 15–17.

20. Ransom, *Victorian Railway*, 112–6.

21. Wilson, 6–7.

22. Clinker, C. R., 'Excursions Extraordinary' in *Journal of the Railway & Canal Historical Society* May 2004, 567.

23. National Archives/Public Record Office RAIL 727/1.

24. National Archives of Scotland, GD112/48/12, item 8; Ransom, *Loch Lomond…*, 70, 99–101.

25. Handley, 100.

26. Acworth, 118.

27. Fryer, *Portpatrick & Wigtownshire*, 12.

28. Barrie, D. S., 'Portpatrick Today and Yesterday' in *The Railway Magazine*, January 1939, 9–13.

29. Fryer, *Portpatrick & Wigtownshire*, 22–4.

30. Vallance, H. A. 'The Waverley Route' in *The Railway Magazine* January 1952, 4–6; Vallance, H. A. 'The Border Counties Line' in *The Railway Magazine* September 1955, 591–3.

31. Allen, C. J., *Titled Trains …*, 84.

32. Mullay, A. J., *Rails across the Border*, 126–45; *The Railway Magazine* January 1952, 71.

33. Mitchell, 200.

34. The effects of snow and floods on the railways of the Highlands, and the defences against them, are described extensively in Ransom, P. J. G., *Snow, Flood and Tempest*.

35. Vallance, H. A., 'One hundred years at Druimuachdar Summit' in *Railway Magazine* November 1963, 5.

36. National Archives of Scotland, BR/HR/4/100.

37. Acworth, 116.

38. Acworth, 122.

39. Jackson, 57.

40. Vallance, *Great North of Scotland Railway*, 84.

41. Caplan, N., 'Struggle for central Scotland', *Trains Illustrated* no. 50, April/June 1984, 22–5.

42. Acworth, 67–8; Nock, *Caledonian Railway*, 46–7; Marshall, *Scottish Central Railway*, 120.

43. Williams, *Midland Railway*, 153–61.

44. Williams, *Midland Railway*, 160.

45. Stephenson Locomotive Society, 12–14.

46. *MPICE*, 1893 part I, 359–364.

47. Pendleton, 534–6, 556; Vallance, *Highland Railway*, 30–1, illustration of opening ceremony (page un-numbered).

48. *The Railway Magazine*, January 1952, 64.

49. Acworth, 114–5.

50. Robin, G.H., 'The City of Glasgow Union Railway' in *The Railway Magazine* January 1960, 20–6.

51. Stephenson Locomotive Society, 55–6; Ellis, *North British Railway*, 77.

52. Handley, 343–7.

53. Anderson, *Songs of the Rail*.

54. Smith, D.L., 46.

5 THE GOLDEN AGE

1. Birkbeck, J.L.R. 'Demolition of Belah Viaduct' in *The Railway Magazine*, November 1963, 13

2. Accounts of the rise and fall of the first Tay Bridge appear in Rolt, *Red for Danger*, 95–104, Ellis, *The North British Railway* 80–93 and Thomas, *The North British Railway* vol. 1, 217–37. Recent discussion of the causes of the disaster is to be found in: Law, J.N.C., 'Sir Thomas Bouch – a scapegoat?' in *The Railway Magazine* March 1965 160–3; 'In Defence of Sir Thomas' in *The Railway Magazine* September 1965, 537–8; Dow, Bill 'Destined for Disaster' in *The Scots Magazine* December 1989, 275–86; Earnshaw, A., 'Sir Thomas Bouch CE: Hero or Villain' in *Back Track* vol. 5 no. 5, 1991, 232–40.

3. Collapse of the Tay Bridge is described in relation to later accidents caused by gales in Ransom, *Snow, Flood & Tempest,* 156–65.

4. Dow, Bill, reference as note 2 above.

5. Perth & Kinross Archives, PE 19, bundle 59.

6. Construction of the second and surviving Tay Bridge – no small achievement – is described in Ellis *The North British Railway* 116–121.

7. Acworth, 70–1 and 189–91; Ellis, *The North British Railway,* 123–5; Ellis, C. Hamilton, 'The Glasgow Underground Lines: III – The City & District, L.N.E.R.' in *The Railway Magazine* January 1939, 35–9.

8. Lindsay, 97–8.

9. Smith, D.L., 27–8.

10. Stephenson Locomotive Society, 15–18; Acworth, 166–8.

11. Fryer, *Portpatrick & Wigtownshire*, 37–8, 43.

12. Fryer, *Portpatrick & Wigtownshire*, 39–43.

13. Vallance, *Highland Railway*, 68–9.

14. Vallance, *Highland Railway*, 38; Acworth, 74–5.

15. The detailed story has been well documented recently by John McGregor, *The West Highland Railway: Plans, Politics and People*.

16. Handley, 19–20; Sanderson, 12.

17. This sorry tale is related in Ransom, *Loch Lomond and the Trossachs …*, 185–9, 194–7.

18. Thomas, *West Highland Railway*, 108–16.

19. *The Railway Magazine*, October 1956, 719.

20. Acworth, 45–52; Ellis, *North British Railway*, 125–32; Handley, 145–6, 165, 245–7, 329–31 provides interesting details of working conditions; *The Forth Bridge* (British Rail leaflet) provides statistics.

21. Thomas, *Callander & Oban* 126–7, 132.

22. Acworth, 53–6; Vallance, H.A., 'From the Forth Bridge to Perth' in *The Railway Magazine*, January 1958, 3–9.

23. Foxwell & Farrer, preface.

24. Acworth, 63–5.

25. Foxwell & Farrer, 62.

26. Nock, *Railway Race to the North*, 46.

27. Foxwell & Farrer, 16–21, quoting *Pall Mall Gazette*, 6 September 1888.

28. Harvie, C.T., 'Railways at the Edinburgh Exhibitions of 1886 and 1890' in *The Railway Magazine* January 1962, 13–14.

29. Fryer, *Single Wheeler Locomotives*, 56–64.

30. Nock, *Railway Race to the North*, 46.

31. Nock, *Railway Race to the North*, 78–9, 84–6.

32. Nock, *Railway Race to the North*, 88–9.

33. *The Railway Magazine*, January 1952, 63.

34. Nock, *Railway Race to the North*, 100.

35. Nock, *Railway Race to the North*, 111–23.

36. *The Illustrated London News*, 31 August 1895, 260.

37. Semmens, P., 'High Speed Trains: The centenary of the "Railway Race to the North" in *The Railway Magazine*, January 1995, 23.

38. Cooper, B.K., 'The Southerner in Scotland' in *The Railway Magazine* January 1939, 6.

39. Acworth, 146–7.

40. Smout, 101–2.

41. McKillop, 5, 24.

42. Smith, D.L., 46.

43. Dow, 5.

44. Cattanach, D., 'The Great Scotch Railway Strike' in *The Journal of the North British Railway Study Group*, Autumn 2004, 11.

45. Acworth, 109.

46. McKillop, 74.

47. Cattanach, D., 'The Great Scotch Railway Strike' in *The Journal of the North British Railway Study Group*, Autumn 2004, 3–13.

48. Ellis, *British Railway History 1877–1947*, 212–16, 222; Smout, 106.

49. Cattanach, D., 'The Great Scotch Railway Strike' in *The Journal of the North British Railway Study Group*, Autumn 2004, 6.

50. Bagwell, P.S., 'National Union of Railwaymen' in Simmons & Biddle, 1997, 342

51. Gourvish, *British Railways 1948–73*, 121.

52. Ellis, *British Railway History 1877–1947*, 261–2; Bagwell, P.S., 'trade unionism' in Simmons & Biddle, 1997, 534.

53. Ellis, *North British Railway*, 39–40; Thomas, *North British Railway*, vol. 1, 108–11 includes track plan of the station.

54. Foxwell & Farrer, 60.

55. Ellis, *North British Railway*, 80.

56. Thomas, *North British Railway*, vol. 2, 23–4.

57. Thomas, *North British Railway*, vol. 2, 25; Ellis, *North British Railway*, 133–4.

58. Middlemass, 95.

59. Nock, *Caledonian Railway*, 112–16.

60. Vallance, *Great North of Scotland Railway*, 130, 136.

61. Stephenson Locomotive Society, 17.

62. Acworth, 5.

63. Simmons, J., 'Cardwell, Edward, Viscount' and 'commissions and parliamentary committees' in Simmons & Biddle, 1997, 72, 94.

64. Vallance, *Great North of Scotland Railway*, 105–15.

65. Vallance, *Highland Railway*, 74–6.

66. Vallance, *Great North of Scotland Railway*, 134.

67. Radford, 31.

68. Ellis, *Railway Carriages …*, 156–61, gives details of the trains and their rolling stock. Allen, *Titled Trains …*, 126, states that the West Coast 2.00 p.m. train had been introduced in 1889 and had had a first-class dining car since 1891.

69. Simmons, *Railways of Britain*, 147.

70. Ellis, *Railway Carriages …*, 228.

71. Nock, *Caledonian Railway*, 110–11.

72. Dow, 37.

73. Vallance, *Highland Railway*, 94–5.

74. Vallance, *Highland Railway*, 163

75. Cunninghame Graham, 64–77.

76. Rannie, A., 'Anglo-Scottish Expresses of Fifty Years Ago' in *The Railway Magazine*, part 1, October 1959, 670–6, part 2, November 1959, 786–90.

77. Nock, *Caledonian Railway*, 111.

78. Williams, A., 'Hail Caledonian!' in *The Railway Magazine*, August 1983, 309–11.

79. Marshall, P. F., *Scottish Central Railway*, 142; Jackson, 14, 63; Durie, A. J., 'winter sports' in Simmons & Biddle (eds), 564.

80. Ransom, *Loch Lomond and the Trossachs …* 5–12.

81. Ferguson, *The Great North of Scotland Railway …*

82. *Mountain, Moor and Loch …*

83. Wright, W., 'An episode in railway publicity – tinplate advertising models of the Caledonian Railway' in Cossons, Patmore & Shorland–Ball, 1992.

84. Ellis, *The Trains We Loved*, 183, 185–6; Rannie, A., 'Anglo-Scottish Expresses of Fifty Years Ago' in *The Railway Magazine*, October 1959, 671.

85. Ellis, *Trains We Loved*, 74.

86. Acworth, 131, 141–2.

87. Nock, *Caledonian Railway*, 117.

88. Stephenson Locomotive Society, 38.

89. Gourvish, *British Railways 1948–73*, 1.

90. Geikie, 21–2.

91. Thomas, *West Highland Railway*, 120–2.

92. Allen, *London & North Eastern Railway*, 25–6, gives figures: for the summer Highland Express, 7.15 p.m. from St Pancras, the Midland paid the North British £6,097 between 1903 and 1907; for the Edinburgh portion of the 1.30 p.m. from St Pancras, £5,090 for the four years to June 1908.

93. Robin, G. H., 'Railways of Paisley, Renfrew and Barrhead – 2' in *The Railway Magazine*, April 1958, 278–81.

94. Durie, 163–70.

95. Thomas, *West Highland Railway*, 115.

96. *Stirling Observer*, 6 July 1904, 5.

97. Ransom, *Loch Lomond and the Trossachs …*, 191–3. The namesake of car *Mary Hamilton* appears to have been a child murderess.

98. Behrend, 59–60, 97; Ferguson, N., 'Caledonian Railway Pullman Carriages and their LMS Successors' in *Back Track*, March 2005

6 THE FIRST WORLD WAR AND THE GROUPING

1. Dyos and Aldcroft, 277–8; Bonavia, *The Four Great Railways*, 8–9.

2. Bagwell, P. S., 'trade unionism' in Simmons, J. and Biddle G., (eds), 534–5.

3. *The Railway Year Book for* 1922, 11; *Universal Directory of Railway Officials …* 1946–1947, 518–9.

4. *The True Line …* January 2005, 22.

5. Ellis, *North British Railway*, 211.

6. Rolt, *Red for Danger*, 207–13.

7. Dyos & Aldcroft, 283–4.

8. Smith, D. L., 59–61.

9. Stephen, 148, 46.

10. Stephen, 11.

11. Dyos & Aldcroft, 284.

12. Nock, *Caledonian Railway*, 150; Stephenson Locomotive Society, 51.

13. Lavery, 101–5.

14. 'Bartimeus', 1–35.

15. Kemp (ed.), 713.

16. Ross, 156–7.

17. Ross, 121–2.

18. Vallance, *Highland Railway*, 111, 115.

19. Dyos & Aldcroft, 290.

20. Ellis, *British Railway History …*, 304–6.

21. Bagwell, P. S., 'Strikes' in Simmons & Biddle (ed.), 483.

22. Ellis, *British Railway History …*, 309–10; Melrose, M., '1919 Railway Strike' in *Railway Philately* June 2004, 126–39.

23. Bonavia, *Four Great Railways*, 197.

24. Gourvish, *British Railways 1948–73*, 13.

25. Bonavia, *Four Great Railways*, 11.

26. Hibbs, 106.

27. *The Railway Magazine*, May 1920, 343.

28. *The Railway Magazine*, July 1921, 57; Newlands, 45.

29. Lt Col. A. Murray, MP, *Hansard*, House of Commons, 30 May 1921.

30. Sir H. Hope, MP, *Hansard*, House of Commons, 26 May 1921.

31. Lt Col. A. Murray, MP, *Hansard*, House of Commons, 30 May 1921.

32. Sir H. Mackinder, MP, *Hansard*, House of Commons, 26 May 1921.

33. Lt Col. A. Murray, MP, *Hansard*, House of Commons, 30 May 1921.

34. Sir E. Geddes, MP, *Hansard*, House of Commons, 30 May 1921.

35. *The Railway Magazine* August 1921, 131.

36. *The Railway Magazine* October 1921, 276.

37. Bonavia, *Four Great Railways*, 205–9.

38. *The Railway Magazine* September 1921, 201.

39. *The Railway Year Book for* 1922, 37.

40. Ellis, *North British*, 212, 217.

41. Stephen, 25.

42. Stephen, 16, 20, 31.

43. Vallance, *Great North of Scotland*, 138.

44. Allen, *London & North Eastern*, 115.

45. *The Railway Year Book for* 1922, 34–5.

46. Bonavia, *Four Great Railways,* 205.

7 LESSER FRY, MIGHT-HAVE-BEENS, AND THE 'VAST MASS OF MISCELLANEOUS PROPERTY'

1. Broad, 127.

2. Brown, K., 'The First Railway in Scotland', *The Railway Magazine*, January 1938, 1–4.

3. Inglis, 14–22.

4. Simms, 18–24; Ransom *Narrow Gauge Steam*, 116.

5. Sydall, B., 'Steam at Waterside' in *Back Track* March 1998, 126.

6. Alliez, G., 'Broad gauge in Scotland' in *The Railway Magazine* January 1962, 61.

7. 'The Fair Maid of Foyers' in *The Railway Magazine* January 1965, 54.

8. Gill, D., 'An Electric Railway at Kinlochleven' in *The Railway Magazine* January 1957, 57–8.

9. Vickers, A.A., 'The Winchburgh Shale Line' in *The Railway Magazine* September 1958, 612–5.

10. 'Edinburgh Waterworks Railway' in *The Railway Magazine* April 1998, 44.

11. Cox & Krupa, 42, 50–5.

12. Russell, P.B., 'Wee Bangour Express' in *The Railway Magazine* September 1981, 449–51.

13. Thomas & Turnock, 187–8; *Railway Archive*, issue 5, November 2003.

14. Irwin, C.R., 'tramways, street' in Simmons & Biddle (ed.), 537.

15. *100 years of Electrification*, 4.

16. Stephen, 28–9.

17. Harvie, C.T., 'Railways at the Edinburgh Exhibitions of 1886 and 1890' in *The Railway Magazine* January 1962, 13–17.

18. Hunter, D.L.G, *Scottish Electric Tramways*, 3, *100 years of Electrification*, 6.

19. Simmons & Biddle (ed.), 538.

20. Lee, C.E., 'The Glasgow Underground Railway' in *The Railway Magazine*, January 1955, 23–7.

21. Stephenson Locomotive Society, 13–14.

22. Davies, 50–5, 284–95.

23. Gardiner, L., 'Lore of Little Trains' in *The Scotsman*, 19 July 1975, page 1 of *Weekend Scotsman* section.

24. Vallance, *Great North of Scotland Railway* 118–19.

25. Callender, R.M., 'Change for Wanlockhead' in *The Railway Magazine* January 1978, 16–18. Page 17 includes an illustration of the nameboard of Wanlockhead station, *c.* 1929, including the altitude, 1,413 ft above sea level.. Nevertheless, *The Railway Year Book for* 1922, p. 101 gives altitudes of 1,405 ft for Leadhills station and 1,402 ft for Wanlockhead, these figures presumably being derived from Caledonian Railway sources. Dalnaspidal station, highest on the Highland Railway main line, appears from the Ordnance Survey map to have been at about 1,394 ft.

26. Rankin, S, (ed.) 'Proposed Sou'West Railways in Kintyre' in *Sou'West Journal* session 2003–4, 3–10.

27. Vallance, *Great North of Scotland Railway* 117–20.

28. Vallance, *Highland Railway*, 53–64; Ross, 228–32.

29. Robertson, 12, 32–4.

30. Ellis, C.H., 'The Glasgow & North Western Railway' in *The Railway Magazine* January 1956, 47–50; McGregor, 10, 27–32.

31. *Engineering*, 10 July 1868; Macassey & Scott; Acworth, 168.

32. Thomas, *North British Railway*, vol. 11, 210.

33. McGregor, 230.

34. The subject is covered extensively in Ransom, *Narrow Gauge Steam …*

35. Spooner, 70.

36. Nicolson, N., 107, gives further details.

37. Acworth, 13.

38. These figures have been obtained by totalling the figures for the individual railways given in their entries in *The Railway Year Book for* 1922. The figure for steamers would have been higher but for wartime losses. Another hotel, Gleneagles, was being built.

39. Pratt, 128–9.

40. Pratt, 172–3.

41. Pratt, 141.

42. Nock, *Caledonian Railway*, 121, 123.

43. Ellis, *North British Railway*, 186.

44. Clyde steamers and steamer services have an extensive literature of their own. This brief account has drawn upon: Acworth, 83–92; Duckworth and Langmuir, 1–20, 52–60; Nock, *Caledonian Railway*, 70–7; Stephenson Locomotive Society, 46–51.

45. Duckworth & Langmuir, 103–4; Fryer, *Portpatrick & Wigtownshire*, 23–8.

46. I have covered steamer services on Loch Lomond, and their railway connections, in my *Loch Lomond …*, 94–119.

47. Thomas *North British Railway*, vol. 1., 209; Ellis, *North British Railway*, 219; *The Railway Year Book for* 1922, 244.

48. Ross, 76–80.

49. Martin, *Garnkirk & Glasgow*, 35–6.

50. The story of Scottish railway hotels, along with those of the rest of Britain, is to be found in Carter *An Illustrated History of British Railway Hotels*. Other specific references include: GSWR hotels, Stephenson Locomotive Society, 15–6, 20; Gleneagles, *The True Line*, January 2004, 7, and January 2005, 32; GNSR hotels, Vallance, *Great North of Scotland*, 96, 136; Highland Railway hotels, Ross, 107, 224–6; North British Hotel, Edinburgh, Ellis, *North British Railway*, 133–4.

51. Hunter, *Scottish Buses …*, 3–11; Vallance, *Great North of Scotland Railway*, 121–8, 139; Jackson, 54–5.

8 FROM GROUPING TO NATIONALISATION

1. For the railway historian, however, the grouping has the disadvantage that from this point on it becomes much more difficult to distinguish facts, and particularly statistics, relating to railways in Scotland from those for the amalgamated companies in their entirety, and for Britain as a whole.

2. Ellis, *London Midland & Scottish*, 11.

3. McKillop, 64, 70–1.

4. Stephen, 66–7.

5. Ellis, *London Midland & Scottish*, 11.

6. Allen, *London & North Eastern*, 62–4.

7. *The Railway Year Book for* 1922, 44.

8. Ellis, *London Midland & Scottish*, 31–2.

9. Ellis, *London Midland & Scottish*, 10.

10. Ellis, *London Midland & Scottish*, 33–4.

11. Nock, *Caledonian R.*, 151.

12. National Archives of Scotland, BR/ LMS/26/118.

13. Ellis, *London Midland & Scottish*, 38–9, 175–6. The sense of humour comes through in Stamp's conduct of annual meetings when eventually appointed chairman: eg. *Reports … of AGMs of LMS*, 1928, 11, 27.

14. *Reports … of AGMs of LMS*, 1926, 29.

15. *Reports … of AGMs of LMS*, 1927, 12–14.

16. *Reports … of AGMs of LMS*, 1928, 3.

17. Ellis, *London Midland & Scottish*, 50.

18. Allen, *London & North Eastern*, 26–7, 45–9.

19. Allen, *London & North Eastern*, 66–8.

20. Allen, *London & North Eastern*, 67.

21. Stephen, 128.

22. Ellis, *Highland Engines …*, 69–71.

23. *The Railway Magazine*, January 1939, 72.

24. Nock, *Caledonian Railway*, 174.

25. Stephen, 95.

26. Carter, 45, 75, 114.

27. Stephen, 82; McKillop, 194.

28. i.e., laid out so that exhaust steam from a high pressure cylinder is reused in a low-pressure cylinder or cylinders before passing to the exhaust.

29. Nock, *Caledonian Railway*, 177–81; Middlemass, 62.

30. Barrie, 3, 6–9.

31. Nock, *Caledonian Railway*, 175–6. See also Middlemass, 123–4.

32. Nock, *Caledonian Railway*, 175.

33. Allen, *London & North Eastern*, 119; Bellwood & Jenkinson, 14–16.

34. Stephen, 104–5.

35. Stephen, 107.

36. Nicolson, M., 42–4.

37. *Reports … of AGMs of LMS*, 1928, 11.

38. Allen, *Titled Trains …*, 86.

39. Allen, *Titled Trains …*, 170; Ellis, *London Midland & Scottish*, 48–9.

40. Allen, *London & North Eastern*, 184.

41. Stephen, 142.

42. For details of all these train services, see Allen, *Titled Trains of Great Britain*.

43. Vallance, *Great North of Scotland*, 168–9.

44. Vallance, *Highland Railway*, 177; *Railway World*, September 1968, 406.

45. Ferguson, N., 'Caledonian Railway Pullman Carriages and their LMS Successors' in *Back Track* March 2005.

46. Rolt & Whitehouse, 119.

47. Howat, 5, 8–11, 20, 24, 30, 38, 68; Reid Thomas, D.D., and Price, R.E.B., 'The Lochaber Aluminium Works Railway, Fort William' in *The Railway Magazine*, April 1955, 241–5.

48. *The Railway Magazine* September 1955, 612; January 1983, 41.

49. Ellis, *Railway Carriages …*, 252–3.

50. Little, 5, 13.

51. See, for instance, Allen *London & North Eastern*, 70.

52. Allen, *London & North Eastern*, 70.

53. Allen, *London & North Eastern*, 75; Ellis, *London Midland & Scottish*, 42–3; Middlemass, 147; Stephen, 76, 126–8.

54. Allen, *London & North Eastern*, 75–6; Stephen, 77, 128–34.

55. Allen, *London & North Eastern*, 77.

56. *Reports … of AGMs of LMS*, 1929, 4; 1932, 3; 1933, 3.

57. *Reports … of AGMs of LMS*, 1929, 6.

58. Newlands, 45.

59. Dyos & Aldcroft, 336.

60. Development of roads at this period is well covered by Jeffreys.

61. Ellis, *London Midland & Scottish*, 44–5.

62. Stephen, 122.

63. Dyos & Aldcroft, 306–7, 316–17, 342–3, 348; Simmons & Biddle (eds.), 171–2.

64. Dyos & Aldcroft, 313, 339; Hibbs, 185; Vallance, *Great North of Scotland Railway*, 172–4.

65. *Universal Directory of Railway Officials …*, 53–68, 438–40.

66. Dyos & Aldcroft, 356–9.

67. Dyos & Aldcroft, 362–6; Boyes, G., 'The British Road Haulage Industry since 1954' in *Journal of the Railway and Canal Historical Society*, May 2004, 520.

68. Printed memorandum by the Railway Companies' Association to the Minister of Transport, *Railway Charges for Merchandise Traffic*, November 1938, private collection.

69. Ellis, *London Midland & Scottish*, 131; Dyos & Aldcroft, 319.

70. Automobile Association, 514; Harris, M. L., 'motor cars, carriage of' in Simmons and Biddle (eds.), 331.

71. Thomas, *Callander & Oban*, 131.

72. Stephen, 124–5.

73. Gillies & Wood.

74. Mondey, D., 'Aviation' in Georgano (ed.), 232.

75. Hendrie, W. F., 'Ahead of his Time' in *The Scots Magazine* May 2005, 492–5, quoting material derived from Black, W. B., *The Bennie Railplane*, East Dunbartonshire Archives, Kirkintilloch, *c.* 2004; Thwaite, M., 'The George Bennie Railplane and Hugh Fraser Airrail Systems of Transport' in *Transactions of the Newcomen Society*, vol. 75, 2005, 42–5.

76. Stroud, 30.

77. Stroud, 33.

78. Stroud, 64, 109.

79. Stroud, 144.

80. Mullay, *Railways across the Border*, 148.

81. Macmillan, 59, 62.

82. *Reports … of AGMs of LMS*, 1931, 13–15.

83. Ellis, *London Midland & Scottish*, 55–6, gives a list of LMS closures during 1927–30.

84. Vallance, *Great North of Scotland*, 175; Thomas, *West Highland*, 183.

85. Ellis, *London Midland & Scottish*, 105–6.

86. Ellis, *London Midland & Scottish*, 135; Bellwood & Jenkinson, 5–6.

87. *Reports … of AGMs of LMS*, 1933, 7.

88. Allen, *London & North Eastern*, 83; Ellis, *London Midland & Scottish*, 114.

89. Ellis, *London Midland & Scottish*, 117.

90. Boyes, G., 'freight traffic' in Simmons & Biddle, (eds.) 170.

91. Dyos & Aldcroft, 309.

92. Duckworth & Langmuir, 86, 25.

93. Nock, *Scottish Railways*, 34–5; Thomas, *Scottish Railway History …*, 40; Stephen, 91.

94. *The Railway Magazine*, January 1952, 71; Thomas, *West Highland*, 124–5; *The Sphere*, 13 July 1935, 63.

95. Allen, *London & North Eastern*, 199.

96. Allen, *Titled Trains …*, 180–1.

97. Allen, *Titled Trains …*, 62–4.

98. Bellwood & Jenkinson, 67–71.

99. Bellwood & Jenkinson, 20–1.

100. *Reports … of AGMs of LMS*, 1934, 19–20.

101. Ellis, *London Midland & Scottish*, 145–6.

102. Ellis, *London Midland & Scottish*, 146, 149.

103. *Reports … of AGMs of LMS*, 1937, 24.

104. Ellis, *London Midland & Scottish*, 148; Allen, *Titled Trains …*, 63, 66; Nettleton, C., 'The "Coronation" Observation Cars' in *National Railway Museum Review*, Spring 2005, 33–4.

105. Brown, K., 'The First Railway in Scotland', *The Railway Magazine*, January 1938, 1.

106. Allen, *Titled Trains …*, 24–5.

107. Morgan, (ed.), 540–2.

108. *Universal Directory of Railway Officials …*, 10, 495.

109. *Universal Directory of Railway Officials …*, 495. The total for the whole of Great Britain was 1,220,496.

110. Allen, *Titled Trains…*, 88.

111. Allen, *London & North Eastern …*, 167.

112. Allen, *Titled Trains …*, 171.

113. Allen, *Titled Trains …*, 171.

114. *Report on Railway Welfare Facilities for the Forces*, LMS, 1940, 5–6; private collection.

115. *Universal Directory of Railway Officials …*, 496–7.

116. Ellis, *London Midland & Scottish*, 114.

117. *Universal Directory of Railway Officials …*, 518–9.

118. Stroud, 69.

119. Carter, 119.

120. Vallance, *Great North of Scotland …*, 182.

121. I. N. F., 1–4; McKillop, 139–40; *The Railway Magazine*, May 1995, 23.

122. Smith, D. L., 'Rusting Rails by Loch Ryan' in *The Railway Magazine*, January 1971, 15–17.

123. Muir, R. S., 'Fireman's memories 1940s – 1950s' in *Sou'West Journal*, no. 35, 34.

124. McKillop, 135–6.

125. Gourvish, *British Railways 1948–73*, 3–5 summarises the overall position.

126. Gourvish, *British Railways 1948–73*, 16–20; Bonavia, *Four Great Railways*, 195–7.

127. Gourvish, *British Railways 1948–73*, 23; joint memorandum by the four main-line railway companies to the Minister of War Transport, *Post-War Transport Proposals*, 1 September 1943, private collection.

128. Memorandum to His Majesty's Government *The Railways' Plan for Air Transport* Railway Companies' Association, London, October 1944, private collection; Stroud, 99.

129. Gourvish, *British Railways 1948–73*, 6; Bonavia, *Four Great Railways*, 197–8.

130. Stroud, 81–92.

131. Simmons & Biddle (eds.) 171.

132. Bonavia, *Four Great Railways*, 197–201; Gourvish, *British Railways 1948–73*, 24–8; Transport Act, 1967, section 3.

133. *Industry and Employment in Scotland*, 1947, 55.

9 HOW RAILWAY EQUIPMENT HAD DEVELOPED

1. Much of the story can be found in Lowe, Nicolson, Nicolson & O'Neill, and Wear

2. Martin, *Monkland & Kirkintilloch*, 118–9.

3. Lowe, 153, 193, 196, 243, 331, 513, 567, 568.

4. Useful short biographies of some Scottish Locomotive Luperintendents are to be found in Ellis, *Twenty Locomotive Men*, and Nock, *Steam Locomotive*.

5. Smith, D. L. 24–5.

6. Nock, *Caledonian Railway*, 51–6; Vallance, *Highland Railway*, 131; Marshall, P. F., 165–8; Lee, C. E., 'Genesis of the "Crewe" Type Locomotive' in *The Railway Magazine*, May 1951, 303–5; Chaloner, W. H., 'Alexander Allan's Own Claim' in *The Railway Magazine*, June 1951, 416–18.

7. Sharman, 10, 16, 36, 37.

8. Whishaw, 393; Stephenson Locomotive Society, 25.

9. Bennett, A. R., 'Locomotive Building in London' in *The Railway Magazine*, Nov. 1907, 383–5.

10. Ellis, *Twenty Locomotive Men*, 78.

11. Ahrons, 143; Nock, *Caledonian Railway*, 56–8.

12. The subject is considered at greater length in my *Narrow Gauge Steam …*, 38–40 in particular.

13. Vallance, *Great North of Scotland*, 147; Ahrons, 149–50.

14. Vallance, *Great North of Scotland*, 148; Ahrons, 162.

15. Ahrons, 198–9; Vallance, *Highland Railway*, 140–3.

16. Thomas, *Callander & Oban*, 168–72.

17. Nock, *Caledonian Railway*, 126–9.

18. Nock, *Caledonian Railway*, 137. Superheating meant subjecting the steam to further heat after it had left the boiler on its way to the cylinders. This increased its volume, and reduced condensation in the cylinders – one of the most important contributions ever made towards increasing the efficiency of the steam locomotive. See also Highet, *Scottish Locomotive History …*, 205–9.

19. Nock, *Caledonian Railway*, 133–4.

20. Atkins, 4–6.

21. Stephen, 22.

22. McKillop, 33–4, 39–40.

23. Thomas, *Scottish Railway History …*, 64.

24. Highet, C., 'Scottish Steam Railcars' in *The Railway Magazine* December 1969, pp 672–5; Smith, D. L. 28–9.

25. Atkins, 34–7.

26. This extraordinary event and its circumstances have received much attention from historians. See Atkins, P., 'Hawthorn, Leslie and the Highland Railway' in *Back Track* March 1998, 141–4; Highet, *Scottish Locomotive History* 220–2; McKenna, E., 'Highland Locomotive Controversy' in *The Railway Magazine* January 1974, 9–12; Ross, 156–8; Vallance, *Highland Railway*, 156.

27. Newlands, 130.

28. Stephenson Locomotive Society, 42.

29. Atkins, C. P., 'Robert Whitelegg's Masterpieces' part one, in *The Railway Magazine*, March 1973, 124–6.

30. Atkins, C. P., 'Robert Whitelegg's Masterpieces' part two, in *The Railway Magazine*, March 1973, 173–6.

31. Allen, *London & North Eastern …*, 126.

32. Cooper, B. K., 'The Southerner in Scotland' in *The Railway Magazine*, January 1939, 6.

33. Stephen, 144.

34. Stephen, 140–1.

35. Allen, *London & North Eastern*, 131–3;. McKillop, 112–13;. Bellwood & Jenkinson, 29–32.

36. Nock, *Caledonian Railway*, 176.

37. Farr, K., 'Stanier's Highland Warriors' in *The Railway Magazine*, August 2005, 38–42;. Bellwood & Jenkinson, 45–9; Ellis, *London Midland & Scottish*, 158–60 .

38. Thomas, *West Highland Railway*, 147–9.

39. Allen, *London & North Eastern*, 139–41.

40. Ellis, *London Midland & Scottish*, 85–6; Dow, 43.

41. Gourvish, *British Railways 1948–73*, 88.

42. Ellis, *London Midland & Scottish*, 199–200.

43. Allen, *Titled Trains …*, 172; *The Railway Magazine*, January 1952, 40.

44. Ellis, *North British Railway*, 10.

45. Ellis, *Railway Carriages*, 186.

46. See also Ransom, *Narrow Gauge Steam …*, 87–9.

47. Nock, *Scottish Railways*, 180.

48. Bellwood & Jenkinson, 9.

49. Ellis, *Railway Carriages …*, 237.

50. Ellis, *London, Midland & Scottish*, 89.

51. Allen, *London & North Eastern*, 184.

52. Stephenson Locomotive Society, 45.

53. Simmons & Biddle (eds.), 59.

54. Macaulay & Hall (eds.), vol. 5, 185–94.

55. Brenchley, T., 'Gone But Not Forgotten – The Blair Express' in *The True Line* January 2005, 7.

56. *The Railway Magazine*, July 1921, 56.

57. Macaulay & Hall (eds.), vol. 5, 195–207.

58. Ransom, *Victorian Railway …*, 219–25 covers track development at this period in greater detail. Double-head rail was in section like a dumb-bell, turned on edge; bullhead has the upper swelling larger than the lower; fishplates are two strips of iron, later steel, one either side of the rails and bolted together by bolts passing through the rails.

59. Rapier, R. C., 'On the Fixed Signals of Railways' in *Minutes of Proceedings of the Institution of Civil Engineers*, 1873–4; Ellis, *North British Railway*, 15.

60. Stephenson Locomotive Society, 12.

61. Martin, *Monkland & Kirkintilloch*, 81–4.

62. Vallance, *Great North of Scotland*, 23, 94.

63. Lascelles, 19–21.

64. Acworth 163–6; Vallance, *Great North of Scotland*, 158–9.

65. Nock, *Scottish Railways*, 109–13.

66. Ellis, *North British Railway*, 217–18.

10 THE NATIONALISED RAILWAY

1. Transport Act, 1947, part I, section 3 (4).
2. Transport Act, 1947, part VI, sections 88–90.
3. Bonavia, *Organisation of British Railways*, 51–7.
4. Gourvish, *British Railways*, 1948–73, 40–5; *Transport Services in the Highlands and Islands*, 23.
5. Nock, *Caledonian Railway*, 186.
6. Nock, *Caledonian Railway*, 183.
7. *BTC Annual Report*, 1948, 332, 328. These statistics are given on a regional basis only for the end of the year 1948, but comparison of all-system statistics for end-of-year 1948 with end-of-year 1947 suggests minimal difference for any region between the year-ends.
8. *BTC Annual Report*, 1948, 76–7; McKillop, 86–7; Ransom, *Snow, Flood and Tempest*, 6, 112–17.
9. *BTC Annual Report*, 1948, 384–5.
10. *Passenger Transport for Glasgow and District*; *The Railway Magazine*, February 1952, 79–81 and 123; Beharrell, L.V., 'Glasgow's Blue Trains: some implications' in *British Transport Review*, April 1962, 355–7.
11. Gourvish, *British Railways*, 1948–73, 49, 87–8; see also 'Standardisation and Comparative Costs of Motive Power on B.R.' in *The Railway Magazine*, January 1951, 60–1.
12. *The Railway Magazine*, July 1951, 438–45, 449.
13. *The Railway Magazine*, January 1951, 62; May 1951, 326–8.
14. *The Railway Magazine*, February 1952, 85–7.
15. Harris, M.L., 'Wagons' in Simmons & Biddle (eds.), 552–3.
16. Gourvish, *British Railways*, 1948–73, 92, 115.
17. *The Railway Magazine*, June 1953, 361.
18. *BTC Annual Report*, 1948, 26; Boyes, G., 'The British Road Haulage Industry since 1954' in *Journal of the Railway & Canal Historical Society*, no. 188, May 2004, 515.
19. Boyes, G., 'The British Road Haulage Industry since 1954' in *Journal of the Railway & Canal Historical Society*, no. 188, May 2004, 514–15.
20. Gourvish, *British Railways*, 1948–73, 142, 154–6.
21. Thomas, *West Highland Railway*, 151–2; Obituary, 'Sir Donald Cameron of. Lochiel, KT' in *The Daily Telegraph*, 29 May 2004.
22. Gourvish, *British Railways*, 1948–73, 111, 173–8, 618–21.
23. Gourvish, *British Railways*, 1948–73, 206.
24. Hinchcliffe, B., 'Gone but not forgotten' in *The Railway Magazine*, January 1965, 45–6.
25. Robbins, M., 'End of the Border Counties Line' in *The Railway Magazine*, December 1956, describes the last day.
26. Gourvish, *British Railways*, 1948–73, 161–2.
27. *The Railway Magazine*, July 1954, 458–61, 489.
28. *The Railway Magazine*, August. 1956, 564.
29. *The Railway Magazine*, March 1955, 149–54, 171.
30. *The Railway Magazine*, April 1956, 269.
31. *The Railway Magazine*, June 1956, 413; July 1957, 512–13; February 1960, 83–9; see also Blake.
32. *The Railway Magazine*, December 1960, 831–3.
33. *The Railway Magazine*, December 1960, 825–30.
34. *The Railway Magazine*, March 1961, 176–7; December 1961, 867–8; Beharrell, L.V., 'Glasgow's Blue Trains: some implications' in *British Transport Review*, April 1962, 355–63.
35. *The Railway Magazine*, February 1957, 136.
36. Gourvish, *British Railways*, 1948–73, 286–8.
37. Vallance, *Highland Railway*, 180; *Great North of Scotland Railway*, 185; Thomas, *Callander & Oban Railway*, 179.
38. Vallance, *Highland Railway*, 181–2, 203–4; *Transport Services in the Highlands and Islands*, 17.
39. *The Railway Magazine*, April 1956, 206, 271.
40. Gourvish, *British Railways*, 1948–73, 157, 290 2 gives details of this sorry story
41. Gourvish, *British Railways*, 1948–73, 289–90; *The Railway Magazine*, February 1958, 129–33.
42. Allen, *Titled Trains …*, 32–3, 184–6.
43. *The Railway Magazine*, September 1957, 661; August 1961, 585.
44. *The Railway Magazine*, September 1955, 653; June 1958, 419–20; Jackson, 46; Mullay, A., 'Batteries Included!' in *The Railway Magazine* August 2004, 56–8; NAS, BR/RSR/1/18 etc, Minutes of meetings of Scottish Area Board.
45. *The Railway Magazine* July 1957, 510; April 1958, 275–7; July 1958, 499–501; October 1958, 720–2; November 1958, 800–1; Tolson, J.M., 'Too Little, Too Light and Too Late' in *The Railway Magazine*, January 1968, 4–9; Vallance, H.A., 'The Strathspey Line' in *The Railway Magazine*, January 1959, 9, 51.
46. *The Railway Magazine*, December 1955, 861–2.
47. *The Railway Magazine*, September, 1961, 606–11; August 1962, 531–5; Fiennes, 66–7, 87; *British Railways Progress*, 15.
48. Flat-bottomed rail has an inverted T cross-section and originated in the 1830s: it could be spiked directly to sleepers as a cheap alternative to chaired track. It was much used overseas and eventually developed to the point at which heavy flat-bottomed rail was stronger than bullhead.
49. Cope, G.H., 'Track' in Simmons & Biddle, (eds.), 520–1; *BTC Annual Report*, 1961, 28.

50. *The Railway Magazine*, January, 1957, 64.

51. Faulkner, J. N., 'Motorail 1955–82' in *Railway World*, October 1982, 534–41.

52. *Transport Services in the Highlands and Islands*, 17–18.

53. *Industry and Employment in Scotland*, 1954 and 1956.

54. The arguments for conversion are recited in Lloyd, and refuted in Walsh, B. J. D., 'The Railway Conversion Fallacy' in. *The Railway Magazine*, August. 1959, 568–9 & 571.

55. Boyes, G., 'The British Road Haulage Industry since 1954' in *Journal of the Railway and Canal Historical Society* May 2004, 514–24.

56. Gourvish, *British Railways, 1948–73*, 496.

57. *The Railway Magazine*, April 1959, 284.

58. *The Railway Magazine*, May 1960, 358; also quoted in *The Reshaping of British Railways*, 1.

59. Gourvish, *British Railways, 1948–73*, 308–9, 311.

60. Gourvish, *British Railways, 1948–73*, 310–6 gives details of the factions which arose and their respective proposals.

61. *Transport Act, 1962*, section 43.

62. *Transport Act, 1962*, section 56.

63. Gourvish, *British Railways, 1948–73*, 514–5, 520–1.

64. *BTC Annual Report*, 1961, 2–3.

65. *The Times*, 21 November 1961, quoting Marples in the House of Commons; *The Railway Magazine*, January 1962, 1. Reference to Bradshaw for November 1960 (the closest easily available) shows that this was, over the section of the East Coast Main Line between Berwick and Dunbar, one of only two down stopping trains daily.

66. *The Railway Magazine*, December 1962, 809.

67. *The Reshaping of British Railways*, 57.

68. *The Reshaping of British Railways*, 97–8.

69. *The Reshaping of British Railways*, 59–60.

70. *The Railway Magazine*, June 1963, 373–4.

71. Gourvish, *British Railways, 1948–73*, 413, 456; Hart, T., 'Scottish Railway Development Association' in *The Railway Magazine*, February 1963, 136.

72. *The Railway Magazine*, April 1964, 352.

73. *The Railway Magazine*, September 1964, 729–30.

74. *The Railway Magazine*, February 1963, 779–81; July 1964, 549.

75. *The Railway Magazine*, July 1964, 540–4.

76. *The Railway Magazine*, February 1965, 64–7.

77. *The Railway Magazine*, February 1965, 113; June 1965, 357.

78. Gourvish, *British Railways, 1948–73*, 461.

79. Nock, O. S., 'Locomotive Practice and Performance, Caledonian: Glasgow to Aberdeen' in *The Railway Magazine*, November 1965, 636–41.

80. Farr, K., 'The Grand Scottish Railtour of 1967' in *The Railway Magazine*, September 2003, 30–3.

81. *Scottish Steam Passenger Services*.

82. *The Railway Magazine*, May 1967, 298; August 1967, 478–9; January 1968, 57; March 1968, 188.   But the 'Locomotive Notes' section throughout this period repays study. See also Mullay, *Scottish Region …*, 114–16, 181–2; Sanderson, 61.

83. *The Railway Magazine*, July 1968, 437.

84. Excluding, of course, the narrow gauge Vale of Rheidol section and continued operation of *Flying Scotsman* (p. 260).

85. Martin, D., 'The Bedlay Story: 1831–1981' in *The Railway Magazine*, March 1982, 142–3.

86. *The Railway Magazine*, August 1967, 428–30.

87. *The Railway Magazine*, March 1965, 172–3; April 1965, 197; Gourvish, *British Railways, 1948–73*, 489–91; Fiennes, G. F., 'Trains in Circuit' in *British Transport Review*, December 1962, 28–34; Simmons & Biddle (eds.), 171.

88. *The Times*, 1 November 1962.

89. *The Reshaping of British Railways* 142–8; Simmons & Biddle (eds.), 168–9.

90. *The Railway Magazine*, June 1965, 309; January 1966, 50; August 1966, 478; April 1967, 181; Gourvish *British Railways, 1948–73*, 544–7.

91. See, for instance, *The Railway Magazine*, February 1968, 116. In this issue alone there are listed for withdrawal of freight facilities: Cowdenbeath Old, Glasgow College, North Berwick, Corstorphine, Duddingston, Gorgie East, Granton High, Haddington, Leith Citadel, Morningside Road, Prestonpans and Stobcross.

92. *Transport Policy*. Further white papers followed on specific aspects.

93. *Transport Act* 1968, part II; *SPT Statistics & Trends*, 2; www.spt.co.uk consulted February 2007.

94. *Transport Policy*, 21; *Transport Act* 1968, part I; Land, P., 'National Carriers Ltd: The Early History' in *National Railway Museum Review*, winter 2003/4, 22–3; Phillips, T., 'National Carriers Ltd' in *National Railway Museum Review*, summer 2004, 37; Simmons & Biddle (eds.), 169, 171.

95. Boyes, G., 'The British Road Haulage industry since 1954' in *Journal of the Railway and Canal Historical Society* May 2004, 520–1.

96. *Transport Act* 1968, part III.

97. Gourvish, *British Railways, 1948–73*, 212–13.

98. *Transport Policy*, 4; *Transport Act* 1968, parts II and IV; Reed, M., 'Who Runs the Railways?' in *Journal of the Railway and Canal Historical Society* May 2004, 530–1.

99. *Transport Act* 1968, part IV, section 58.

100. *The Railway Magazine* October 1968, 620; Carter, 48.

101. *The Three Hostages* (1924).

102. Allen, *Titled Trains …*, 199–202.

103. *The Railway Magazine* October 1966, 599; September 1968, 507; February 1969, 61, 109; Thomas, *Forgotten Railways …*, 56–8.

104. Gourvish, *British Railways, 1948–73*, 453–4, 456.

105. *The Railway Magazine*, December 1969, 706–7.

106. *Scotland: Route Utilisation Strategy*, 56, 69, 97

107. *The Railway Magazine*, March 1971, 123; December 1971, 648; Allen, *Titled Trains …* 207.

108. *The Railway Magazine*, November 1969, 649; *The Scotsman* 21 November 1970, *Weekend Scotsman* section, 1, 6.

109. Thomas, *The Skye Railway* 153–8; Gourvish, *British Rail 1974–97*, 62.

110. Gourvish, *British Rail 1974–97*, 62, 535.

111. Gourvish, *British Rail 1974–97*, 12–13; Simmons & Biddle (eds.), 171.

112. *Scotland*, 50.

113. Burnett, J., 'Kilmacolm Branch on Borrowed Time' in *The Railway Magazine*, January 1982, 12–13; The *Railway Magazine*, March 1983, 121.

114. Ransom, *Loch Lomond and The Trossachs …*, 115–17.

115. *The Railway Magazine*, September 1967, 537–8; March 1971; July 1974, 326; November 1976, 553.

116. McConnell, D., 'A Scottish Restoration' in *The Railway Magazine*, January 1979, 17–19.

117. *The Railway Magazine* September 1970, 481; December 1972, 625.

118. *The Railway Magazine* May 1974, 211–18.

119. *The Railway Magazine* December 1973, 601; December 1974, 612; contemporary timetables.

120. Easton, J., 'BR going ahead with plan to reopen Glasgow line' in *The Scotsman* 18 November 1972, 9.

121. *The Railway Magazine*, April 1976, 186–7; December 1979, 569; Kingston, P., 'Royal Trans-Clyde' in *The Railway Magazine*, January 1980, 4–6.

122. Correspondence and conversation between Kaukas, B., and the author, 1979–81; Ransom, *Archaeology of Railways*, 20–5.

123. For descriptions of listed railway buildings in Scotland, see Biddle, Hume & Nock, 121–73.

124. Marsden, C. J., '25 Glorious Years' part one in *The Railway Magazine*, December 2001, 18–24.

125. Marsden, C. J., '25 Glorious Years' part two in *The Railway Magazine*, January 2002, 34–9.

126. *The Railway Magazine*, October 1979, 467, 478–9.

127. *The Railway Magazine*, October 1979, 469; July 1982, 327; July 1984, 285.

128. Marsden, C. J., '25 Glorious Years' part three in *The Railway Magazine*, February 2002, 27.

129. Gourvish, *British Rail 1974–97*, 217–8, 221–2.

130. Stewart & Chadwick, 32–3. But see also discussion of Pendolino trains in Chapter 12.

131. *The Railway Magazine*, February 1982, 58; November 1983, 462.

132. Gourvish *British Railways 1948–73*, 502–5; *The Railway Magazine* September 1976, 444–5.

133. Slater, J., 'Climbing Ben Wyvis' in *The Railway Magazine* December 1983, 484–5.

134. Gourvish, *British Rail 1974–97*, 169–81, 201–2.

135. Gourvish, *British Rail 1974–97*, 104–31.

136. Simmons & Biddle, 57; Stewart & Chadwick, 7.

137. Stewart & Chadwick, 40–5; Pigott, N., 'The Best Chairman BR never had?' in *The Railway Magazine*, March 2003, 19–20; *The Railway Magazine* July 1985, 332; Durie, A. J., 'Scotland' in Simmons & Biddle, 436.

138. Gourvish, *British Rail 1974–97*, 199; *The Railway Magazine*, July 1981, 351

139. *Dundee Courier*, 20 and 21 September 1993.

140. Gourvish, *British Rail 1974–97*, 199; *The Railway Magazine*, May 1986, 302; *The Scotsman*, supplement 'The Bathgate Line', 24 March 1986.

141. *The Railway Magazine* August 1986, 518.

142. *The Railway Magazine* July 1989, 423.

143. *The Railway Magazine* November 1988, 690; *A–Z of Rail Reopenings*, 43.

144. *The Railway Magazine* April 1983, 159.

145. *The Railway Magazine* October 1986, 643; March 1987, 182.

146. *The Railway Magazine* September 1984, 369.

147. *The Railway Magazine* November 1987, 690; March 1990, 154; *Sunday Times*, 14 January 1990; *The Railway Magazine*, March 1992, 6.

148. *The Railway Magazine*, March 1992, 6; May 1992, 6; Gourvish, *British Rail 1974–97*, 389.

149. *The Railway Magazine*, February 1991, 116–21.

150. *The Railway Magazine*, June 1985, 280–1.

151. *The Railway Magazine*, July 1983, 292; September 1983, 381.

152. Collins, M. J., 'A Day in the Life of Coatbridge' in *The Railway Magazine*, December 1991, 894–6.

153. Gourvish, *British Rail 1974–97*, 284–5.

154. Boyes, G., 'The British Road Haulage Industry since 1954' in *Journal of the Railway and Canal Historical Society*, May 2004, 523; Phillips, T., 'National Carriers Ltd' in *National Railway Museum Review*, summer 2004, 37.

155. Gourvish, *British Rail 1974–97*, 289–90.

156. Gourvish, *British Rail 1974–97*, 107, 152, 549 note 46.

157. Gourvish, *British Rail 1974–97*, 289.

158. *The Railway Magazine*, September 1980, 440; MacDonald, M., 'Iron Ore from Hunterston' in *The Railway Magazine*, August 1980, 363.

159. Semmens, P. W. B., 'Ayr Branch Revived' in *The Railway Magazine*, June 1988, 386–7; Wooler, N., 'Scottish Coal Revival' in *The Railway Magazine*, November 1990, 780–5.

160. *The Railway Magazine*, January 1987, 48; March 1988, 148; Wootton, P., 'After Edmondson' in *The Railway Magazine*, July 1988, 480–1.

161. *The Railway Magazine*, September 1987, 557.

162. *The Railway Magazine*, June 1987, 386.

163. Gourvish, *British Rail 1974–97*, 319–20, 327–8.

164. Gourvish, *British Rail 1974–97*, 299.

165. *The Railway Magazine*, May 1988, 285.

166. *The Railway Magazine*, June 1988, 352.

167. *The Railway Magazine*, December 1986, 769; *The Railway Magazine*, November 1989, 722–3 and supplement bound in between these pages.

168. *The Railway Magazine*, May 1991, 308.

169. *The Railway Magazine*, August 1991, 570–1; contemporary BR timetable.

170. *The Railway Magazine*, November 1991, 748–9.

171. *The Railway Magazine*, August 1991, 531.

172. Gourvish, *British Rail 1974–97*, 100–1.

173. Reed, M, 'Who Runs the Railways?' in *Journal of the Railway & Canal Historical Society* May 2004, 531; Gourvish, *British Rail 1974–97*, 365.

174. Carter, 120–2, 124.

175. White, K., 'Weekend Pass: The Gleneagles Hotel' in *Scotland on Sunday, Spectrum* section, 27 August 2006, 31.

176. *Edinburgh Waverley Infrastructure Works Newsletter*, summer 2006.

177. e.g. *The Railway Magazine*, April 1983, 133.

178. Wolmar, 61.

179. Gourvish, *British Rail 1974–1997*, 368.

180. 'Directives' are addressed to member states; 'regulations' are addressed to everyone, according to website eur-lex.europa.eu, section 'Process and players', paragraphs 1.3.1–1.3.3, consulted on 4 March 2007.

181. 'operating': the actual wording of the English version of the directive is '… business relating to the provision of transport services …' It is difficult to glean from this precisely what is intended, and indeed elsewhere also the directive shows signs of having lost much in translation. The equivalent wording of the French version is '… *des activités relatives à l'exploitation des services de transport* …' According to the *Lexique Général des Termes Ferroviaires,* (*Union Internationale des Chemins de Fer*, Berne, 1957) the English equivalent of '*exploitation*' is 'operating': it seems clearest to use this word here.

182. Wolmar, 64–5.

183. *New Opportunities for the Railways* 1, 2, 4, 15.

184. *The Herald*, 3 February 1993; *Scotland on Sunday*, 7 February 1993.

185. e.g. Fildes, C., 'If you think BR was a shambles, just wait for the sell-off' in *The Daily Telegraph* 24 May 1993, 18.

186. *The Railway Magazine*, July 1993, 12; *The Daily Telegraph*, 24 May 1993, 4.

187. *The Daily Telegraph*, 26 May 1993, 1.

188. *The Daily Telegraph*, 8 November 1993, 23.

189. *The Daily Telegraph*, 13 December 2003, 1, 10.

190. *New Opportunities for the Railways*, 17.

191. Gourvish, *British Rail 1974–97*, 108, 267.

192. Gourvish, *British Rail 1974–97*, 147.

193. *The Railway Magazine*, February 1994, 16; August 1994, 9; December 1994, 36.

194. *A–Z of Rail Reopenings*, 43–4.

195. *The Scotsman*, 6 March 1991.

11 THE HERITAGE

1. Crompton, J. 'The Hedley Mysteries' in Lewis, M. J. T. (ed.), 149–64.

2. Barrie, 9.

3. Atkins, 6.

4. *The Railway Magazine*, January 1950, 9–10; May 1965, 290–1; November 1965, 672; March, 1967, 157; March 1998, 43.

5. *The Railway Magazine*, January 1956, 62; November 1965, 634–5; Vallance, *Highland Railway*, 178.

6. Information from Glasgow Museums & Art Galleries, 1988; Nock, *Caledonian Railway*, 111; *The Railway Magazine*, June 1963, front cover and plate opposite p. iv; November 1965, 630–5.

7. Fraser, *The Arbroath Affair*; *The Railway Magazine*, February 1982, 96.

8. *The Railway Magazine*, September 1964, 732; August 1966, 486.

9. Ransom, *Scottish Steam Today*, 33–6.

10. Browning, A. S. E, 'Glasgow Museum Extended' in *The Railway Magazine*, March 1967, 124–7; Dunbar, A. G., 'The Caledonian Railways's '812' 0-6-0s' in *Trains Illustrated* July-September 1984, 10–13.

11. *The Railway Magazine*, February 1980, 70–1.

12. *Glasgow Festival of Trams.*

13. Ransom, *Narrow Gauge Steam*, 8–9.

14. *The Railway Magazine*, June 1967, 358; Ransom, *Scottish Steam Today*, 55–8, 73–5; Percival, D., 'A Flaman Mystery' in *The Railway Magazine*, November 2005, 19–21.

15. Ransom, *Scottish Steam Today*, 37.

16. Ransom, *Scottish Steam Today*, 67–72; Alexander, L., 'Pride of the Caledonian' in *The Railway Magazine*, May 1994, 88–90.

17. Ransom, *Scottish Steam Today*, 38–43; Stirling; *The Railway Magazine*, April 1988, 219.

18. Little, 27–33.

19. Kernahan, J., 'Vintage Train to Mallaig' in *The Railway Magazine*, January 1973, 12–13.

20. *The Railway Magazine*, June 1985, 280–1.

21. *The Railway Magazine*, May 1984, 202; May 1991, 314; December 2001, 57–9.

22. Thomas, C., 'Monarch of the glens' in *The Railway Magazine*, April 2003, 56–61.

23. Thomas, C., 'Rails to the summit' in *The Railway Magazine*, June 2003, 24–8.

24. Website www.srps.org.uk consulted December 2005.

25. *Blastpipe*, Spring 2005, 24.

26. *The Railway Magazine*, July 2005, 84.

27. Website www.srps.org.uk consulted December 2005.

28. Thomas, C., 'The Scottish Railway Exhibition' in *The Railway Magazine*, July 2006, 33–6.

29. i. e., by listing as buildings of special architectural or historic interest, by scheduling as ancient monuments, or by inclusion in conservation areas.

30. Information from Railway Heritage Trust, 1998. Clark, 267–87, describes restoration of Wemyss Bay station from the point of view of the resident architect.

31. *Railway Heritage Act*, 1996, sections 3 and 4; www.rhc.gov.uk consulted Dec. 2006.

32. *The Railway Magazine*, January 1987, 52; November 1987, 727.

33. *The Daily Telegraph*, 12 April 1984; 4 February 1991; www.brb.gov.uk, consulted December 2006.

34. *The Oban Times*, 21 August 2003.

35. *The Railway Magazine*, November 1995, 65; Professor R. Paxton, Heriott-Watt University, speaking at the International Early Railways Conference, Durham, September 1998.

12 THE PRIVATISED RAILWAY

1. Gourvish, *British Rail 1974–97*, 366.

2. Pigott, N., 'The Plain Man's Guide to Rail Privatisation' in *The Railway Magazine*, April 1994, 31–4.

3. *The Railway Magazine*, May 1994, 8.

4. *The Herald*, 15 November 1993.

5. Gourvish, *British Rail 1974–97*, 444 (quoting Ford, R., in *Modern Railways*); *The Daily Telegraph*, 6 March 1995.

6. Gourvish, *British Rail 1974–97*, 290, 418–19; *The Railway Magazine*, April 1996, 7; June 1996, 8.

7. *The Railway Magazine*, December 1995, 12, 43.

8. *Scotland on Sunday*, 15 December 1996; *The Railway Magazine*, October 1997, 6.

9. Gourvish, *British Rail 1974–97*, 419, 441; Shannon, P., 'Freightliner – Ten Years in the Private Sector' in *The Railway Magazine*, July 2006, 12–17.

10. *The Railway Magazine*, February 1995, 12.

11. *The Herald*, 23 February 1995; 26 April 1995; 10 May 1995; 14 September 1995; *The Daily Telegraph*, 6 May 1995; *The Scotsman*, 9 June 1995; *The Oban Times*, 16 February 1995.

12. Wolmar, 72.

13. *The Railway Magazine*, January 1995, 6; Gourvish, *British Rail 1974–97*, 440.

14. *The Daily Telegraph*, 23 June 1998.

15. *The Herald*, 11 February 1997, 1, 2.

16. *The Daily Telegraph*, 1 April 1997.

17. *The Railway Magazine*, August 1997, 9; April 1998, 67.

18. *The Railway Magazine*, February 2001, 12.

19. Clark, R., 'Devolution: Will it prove to be a rail revolution?' in *The Railway Magazine*, October 1999, 87–9; *Strategic Priorities for Scotland's Passenger Railway*.

20. Gourvish, *British Rail 1974–97*, 325–6;. *The Railway Magazine*, September 1994, 10.

21. *The Railway Magazine*, January 1995, 9; Gourvish, *British Rail 1974–97*, 320, 326, 382.

22. *The Railway Magazine*, February 1995, 45; May 1995, 12; October 1995, 50; November 1996, 6; June 1998, 6.

23. *The Railway Magazine*, August 1995, 17; September 1995, 68; February 1996, 80; March 1997, 14.

24. *The Railway Magazine*, August 1997, 9.

25. Wolmar, 120–6, 137–54.

26. Whitehouse, A. & Miles, T., 'Out of Line' in *The Railway Magazine*, September 1999, 49–51; *The Railway Magazine*, January 2000, 13; Wolmar, 163–70.

27. Wolmar, 1–2, 155–63; *The Railway Magazine*, December 2000, 6–10.

28. Wolmar, 9.

29. Scottish Parliament, Local Government and Transport Committee Official Report, 7 March 2006, Col 3465.

30. *The Railway Magazine*, March 2001, 8.

31. *The Daily Telegraph*, 16 January 2001; 6 June 2001.

32. *The Railway Magazine*, December 2001, 4–9; Railways Act, 1993, sections 59–65.

33. *The Sunday Telegraph*, 14 October 2001, Business Section, 1.

34. *The Railway Magazine*, September 2002, 4–5; December 2002, 6–7; information from Network Rail.

35. *The Railway Magazine*, December 2003, 4–5.

36. *The Railway Magazine*, June 2005, 6.

37. www.networkrail.co.uk, consulted in August 2004, January 2007; information from Network Rail and HRP.

38. *The Scotsman*, 19 January 2005; *The Railway Magazine*, December 2005, 65.

39. www.transportscotland.gov.uk, consulted in January 2007.

40. www.spt.co.uk, consulted in January 2007.

41. www.rail-reg.gov.uk, consulted in January 2007.

42. *The Railway Magazine*, September 2005, 10.

43. www.transportscotland.gov.uk, consulted in January 2007.

44. Heaton, J., 'A day in Carlisle signalbox'. in *The Railway Magazine*, October 2006, 14.

45. *The Railway Magazine*, October 2002, 8.

46. *Scotland on Sunday*, 3 October 2004; The Scottish Parliament, Local Government and Transport Committee, Official Report 7 March 2006, cols 3475–84.

47. *The Railway Magazine*, May 2000, 103; July 2001, 10.

48. *The Case for Rail in the Highlands and Islands*, 28–9; *The Railway Magazine*, August 2005, 98; July 2006, 78.

49. *The Railway Magazine*, August 2003, 4–7; October 2003, 48–9; February 2004, 14–19; August 2004, 4; December 2004, 4; July 2005, 9; June 2006, 104.

50. *Scottish Transport Statistics* chapter 8, para. 2.1; Scottish Executive News Release announcing publication of *Scottish Transport Statistics: No. 25 – 2006* consulted on www.scottishexecutive.gov.uk, January 2007. The figure for airport passengers is that for 'air terminal passengers'.

51. *Scottish Transport Statistics* chapter 8, paras 2.2, 2.3.

52. *The Railway Magazine*, March 2003, 23.

53. *The Daily Telegraph*, 1 December 1994.

54. *The Railway Magazine*, December 2002, 4–5.

55. Quoted in *The Railway Magazine*, October 2002, 9.

56. Semmens, P., 'Tilting Trains: How do they work?' in *The Railway Magazine* August 1997, 56–61. The 'why and how' of tilting trains is well covered in this article.

57. *The Railway Magazine*, October 2004, bound-in supplement *Full Tilt: The Pendolino Story*, ii–xv.

58. Information from Network Rail and Virgin Trains; *The Railway Magazine*, November 2004, 6–7; November 2006, 64–6; December 2006, 14–19; January 2007, 9, 34.

59. Information from Virgin Trains;. *The Railway Magazine*, August 2001, bound-in supplement *A New Dawn*, ii, xviii–xxvi; December 2002, 68–9; Heaton, J., 'Super Voyager' in *The Railway Magazine*, September 2005, 37–41.

60. *Outlook*, October–November 1999, 7, 12–15; Marsden, C., 'The A–Z Guide to New Generation Multiple Units'. in *The Railway Magazine*, November 2000, 34, 36; December 2000, 43.

61. *The Railway Magazine*, May 2002, 12; November 2002, 12.

62. *The Railway Magazine*, February 2003, 7.

63. *The Railway Magazine*, August 2004, 4; September 2004, 6, 66.

64. *Scotland on Sunday*, 13 June 2004; *The Railway Magazine*, December 2004, 8; www.transportscotland.gov.uk consulted January 2007.

65. *The Railway Magazine*, August 2002, 72; February 2004, 59; *Blastpipe*, spring 2005, 25.

66. *The Railway Magazine*, September 2004, 65; February 2007, 64; *The Herald*, 10 December 2005.

67. *Stirling Alloa Kincardine Route Re-opening*; www.sakrailway.co.uk consulted August 2006, January 2007.

68. *Edinburgh Waverley Infrastructure Works Newsletter*, summer 2006.

69. *The Herald*, 10 May 2006; *The Railway Magazine*, September 2006, 8.

70. www.wrha.org.uk consulted January 2007.

71. www.spt.co.uk consulted January 2007; *The Daily Telegraph*, 17 January 2007.

72. *The Scotsman*, 18 March 2006; *Scotland on Sunday*, 19 March 2006; www.earlproject.com consulted January 2007.

73. Airdrie–Bathgate Railway and Linked Improvements Bill, Promoter's Memorandum, consulted on www.scottish.parliament.uk, September 2006.

74. *Central Scotland Transport Corridor Studies: A8 Corridor: Final Report:The Corridor Plan* prepared by consultants for the Scottish Executive, 2002; consulted on www.cstcs.co.uk, September 2006.

75. *The Railway Magazine*, April 1990, 216; *Scotland on Sunday*, 10 July 2005; *Scotland: Route Utilisation Strategy*, 65, 117.

76. www.spt.co.uk consulted January 2007.

77. *The Railway Magazine*, April 2006, 9.

78. www.fasttracknorth.org.uk consulted January 2007.

79. www.scottish.parliament.uk.consulted July 2006 re. Transport and Works (Scotland) Bill, policy memorandum; October 2006, re. Local Government and Transport Committee Official Report, 3 October 2006.

80. *Scotland's National Transport Strategy*, paras. 99, 100.

81. Nock, *Caledonian Railway*, 111.

82. *Scotland on Sunday*, 22 February 2004.

83. *Scotland's National Transport Strategy*, paras. 213, 213.

84. Information from Network Rail.

85. The Scottish Parliament, Local Government and Transport Committee, Official Report for 7 March 2006, Col. 3462.

86. *Scotland's Transport Future*, 5.

BIBLIOGRAPHY

A–Z of Rail Reopenings Railway Development Society, Great Bookham, 1992

Acworth, W.M., *The Railways of Scotland* John Murray, 1890

Ahrons, E.L. *The British Steam Railway Locomotive 1825–1925* Locomotive Publishing Co. Ltd, 1927

Allen, C.J., *The London & North Eastern Railway* Ian Allan Ltd, 1966

Allen, C.J., *Titled Trains of Great Britain* Ian Allan Ltd, 5th ed., 1967

Anderson, A., *Songs of the Rail* Simpkin Marshall & Co., 2nd ed., 1878

Atkins, P., *The North British Atlantics and 4–4–2Ts (Locomotives Illustrated* no. 62) Ian Allan Ltd, 1988

Automobile Association, *Handbook 1937-8*, 1937

Bailey, M.R. (ed.), *Early Railways 3* Six Martlets Publishing, Sudbury, 2006

Barrie, D.S., *Modern Locomotives of the L.M.S.* Locomotive Publishing Co. Ltd., *c.* 1937

'Bartimeus', *The Long Trick* Cassell and Co. Ltd, 1917

Baxter, B., *Stone Blocks and Iron Rails* David & Charles, Newton Abbot, 1966

Behrend, G., *Pullman in Europe*, Ian Allan Ltd, 1962

Bellwood, J. and Jenkinson, D., *Gresley and Stanier: A Centenary Tribute* HM Stationery Office, 1976

Bennett, G.P., *The Great Road between Forth and Tay* Markinch Printing Co., Markinch, *c.* 1983

Biddle, G., Hume, J.R., Nock, O.S. and others, *The Railway Heritage of Britain* Michael Joseph Ltd, 1983

Blake, G, *Glasgow Electric* British Railways, Glasgow, 1960

Bonavia, M.R., *The Four Great Railways* David & Charles, Newton Abbot, 1980

Bonavia, M.R., *The Organisation of British Railways*, Ian Allan Ltd, Shepperton, 1971

British Railways Board Facts and Figures BRB, 1978

British Railways Progress, British Transport Commission, 1962

British Transport Commission, Report and Accounts for 1948, HMSO, 1949

British Transport Commission, Annual Report and Accounts for 1961, vol. I: Report, HMSO, 1962

Broad, H., *Rails to Ayr* Ayrshire Archaeological and Natural History Society, Ayr, 1981

Buchan, J., *The Three Hostages,* Hodder & Stoughton, 1924.

Caledonian Railway Carriages, Vans & Trucks: diagram book reproduction. Caledonian Railway Association, 2001

Cameron, A.D., *The Caledonian Canal*, 3rd edition, Canongate Academic, Edinburgh, 1994

Carter, O., *An Illustrated History of British Railway Hotels 1838–1983* Silver Link Publishing, St Michaels, 1990

Chambers, Robert, *Select Writings,* W. & R. Chambers, Edinburgh, 1847

Clark, A.J.C., *Caley to the Coast* The Oakwood Press, Usk, 2001

Cockburn, Henry Lord, *Circuit Journeys* Byway Books, Hawick, 1983 (first published 1888)

Conolly, W.P., *British Railways Pre-Grouping Atlas and Gazeteer* Railway Publications Ltd., *c.* 1958

Cook, T., 'Twenty Years on the Rails', appendix to Cook, T., *Cook's Scottish Tourist Official Directory*, W.H. Smith & Son, 1861

Cooke, W.F., *Telegraphic Railways*, Simpkin, Marshall & Co., 1842

Cossons, N., Patmore, A. and Shorland–Ball, R. (eds), *Perspectives on Railway History and Interpretation*, National Railway Museum, York, 1992

Cox, D. and Krupa, C., *The Kerry Tramway and other timber light railways* Plateway Press, Brighton, 1992

Cunninghame Graham, R.B., *Scottish Stories* Duckworth, 1929 (first published 1914).

Davies, W.J.K., *Light Railways: their rise and decline* Ian Allan Ltd, 1964

Davison, C. St C.B., *Steam Road Vehicles: The forerunners of Motor Cars* HMSO, 1953

Day, L and McNeil, I. (eds.), *Biographical Dictionary of the History of Technology* Routledge, 1996

Dow, G., *The Story of the West Highland*, LNER, 1944

Duckworth, C.L.D. and Langmuir, G.E., *Clyde River and other Steamers* Brown, Son & Ferguson, Glasgow, 1972

Durie, A.J., *Scotland for the Holidays: A History of Tourism in Scotland, 1780–1939* Tuckwell Press, East Linton, 2003

Dyos, H. J. and Aldcroft, D. H., *British Transport: An economic survey from the seventeenth century to the twentieth* Leicester University Press, Leicester, 1969

Ellis, C. Hamilton, *British Railway History 1877–1947* George Allen & Unwin Ltd, 1959

Ellis, C. Hamilton, *Highland Engines and their Work* Locomotive Publishing Co., 1930

Ellis, C. Hamilton, *London Midland & Scottish: A Railway in Retrospect* Ian Allan Ltd, 1970

Ellis, C. Hamilton, *Railway Carriages in the British Isles from 1830 to 1914* George Allen & Unwin Ltd, 1965

Ellis, C. Hamilton, *The Midland Railway* Ian Allan Ltd, 2nd edition, 1955

Ellis, C. Hamilton, *The North British Railway* Ian Allan Ltd, 1955

Ellis, C. Hamilton, *The Trains We Loved* George Allen & Unwin Ltd, London, 1947

Ellis, C. Hamilton, *Twenty Locomotive Men* Ian Allan Ltd., 1958

Ferguson, N. *The Dundee and Newtyle Railway* Oakwood Press, Oxford, 1995

Ferguson, W., *The Great North of Scotland Railway: A guide* D. Douglas, Edinburgh, 1881

Fiennes, G. F., *I Tried to Run a Railway* Ian Allan, 1967

Foxwell, E. and Farrer, T. C., *Express Trains English and Foreign: being a statistical account of all the express trains of the world* Smith, Elder & Co., 1889, re-issued in facsimile, Ian Allan, 1964

Fraser, I. N., *The Arbroath Affair* T. Buncle, Arbroath, 1961

Fryer, C. E. J., *Single Wheeler Locomotives* Oxford Publishing Co., Yeovil, 1993

Fryer, C. E. J., *The Girvan & Portpatrick Junction Railway* The Oakwood Press, Oxford, 1994

Fryer, C. E. J., *The Portpatrick & Wigtownshire Railways* The Oakwood Press, Oxford, 1991

Full Tilt for the West Coast Virgin Trains, 2004

Geikie, Sir A., *Scottish Reminiscenses* James Maclehose & Sons, Glasgow

Georgano, G. N. (ed.), *A History of Transport* J. M. Dent & Sons Ltd, 1972

Gillies, J. D. & Wood, J. L., *Aviation in Scotland* Royal Aeronautical Society, Glasgow, 1966

Glasgow Festival of Trams, Dianswell Productions for Glasgow Garden Festival, 1988

Gordon, A., *A Treatise on Elemental Locomotion … 3rd edition*, T. Tegg & Co., 1837

Gourvish, T. R., *British Rail 1974–97*, Oxford University Press, Oxford, 2004

Gourvish, T. R., *British Railways 1948–73*, Cambridge University Press, Cambridge, 1986

Gourvish, T. R., *Mark Huish and the London & North Western Railway* Leicester University Press, Leicester, 1972

Gradients of the British Main-Line Railways The Railway Publishing Co. Ltd. 1947

Hadfield, C., *Atmospheric Railways* Alan Sutton Publishing Ltd, Gloucester, 1985

Hadfield, C., *British Canals: An Illustrated History* David & Charles, Newton Abbot, 1969

Hadfield, C., & Skempton, A. W., *William Jessop, Engineer* David & Charles, Newton Abbot, 1979

Handley, J. E., *The Navvy in Scotland* Cork University Press, Cork, 1970

Haresnape, B., *Pullman – Travelling in Style* Ian Allan Ltd, 1987

Hebert, L., *The Engineer's and Mechanic's Encyclopedia Vol. II*, 1849

Hibbs, J., *The History of British Bus Services* David & Charles, Newton Abbot, 1989

Highet, C., *Scottish Locomotive History: 1831–1923* George Allen & Unwin Ltd, 1970

Highet, C., *The Glasgow & South Western Railway* Oakwood Press, Lingfield, 1965

Hill, D. O. and Buchanan, G., *Views of the Opening of the Glasgow & Garnkirk* [sic] *Railway, also an Account of that and other Railways in Lanarkshire* Alexander Hill, Edinburgh, 1832

Howat, P., *The Lochaber Narrow Gauge Railway* Narrow Gauge Railway Society, Huddersfield, 1980 (special issue of *The Narrow Gauge*)

Hunter, D. L. G., *Scottish Buses before 1929* Turntable Publications, Sheffield, 1978

Hunter, D. L. G., *Scottish Electric Tramways* Turntable Publications, Sheffield, 1981

Hunter, J. K., *The Retrospect of an Artist's Life* Orr, Pollock & Co., Greenock, 1868

Hutton, G., *Monkland: The Canal That Made Money* Stenlake Publishing, Ochiltree, 1993

Industry and Employment in Scotland HMSO for Scottish Home Department, Edinburgh, 1947–56 (published annually)

I. N. F. *'Gordon Highlander': 4th LNER Battalion H. Q. Company Home Guard* privately printed, 1966

Inglis, J. C. & Inglis, F., *The Fordell Railway* The Munro Press Ltd, Perth, 1946

Jackson, Dick, *Royal Deeside's Railway* Great North of Scotland Railway Association, Huntly, 2001

James, L., *A Chronology of the Construction of Britain's Railways: 1778–1855* Ian Allan Ltd, Shepperton, 1983

Jeffreys, R., *The King's Highway* The Batchworth Press, 1949

Johnson, P., *The British Travelling Post Office* Ian Allan Ltd., Shepperton, 1985

Kemp, P. (ed.), *The Oxford Companion to Ships and the Sea*, Oxford University Press, Oxford, 1988

Lascelles, T. S., *'Green for Allright': an outline of development of railway signalling in the United Kingdom*, undated typescript held by National Railway Museum library.

Lavery, B., *Maritime Scotland* B. T. Batsford Ltd/Historic Scotland, 2001

Lewin, H.G., *The Railway Mania and its aftermath* David & Charles, Newton Abbot, 1968

Lewis, M.J.T., *Early Wooden Railways* Routledge & Kegan Paul, 1970

Lewis, M.J.T., (ed.) *Early Railways 2: Papers from the Second International Early Railways Conference* The Newcomen Society, 2003

Lexique Général des Termes Ferroviaires, Union Internationale des Chemins de Fer, Berne, 1957

Lindsay, J., *The Canals of Scotland* David & Charles, Newton Abbot, 1968

Little, L., *Kerr's Miniature Railway: Scotland's Oldest Small-scale Line* Narrow Gauge Railway Society, Peterborough, 2000 (Special issue of magazine *The Narrow Gauge*)

Lizars, W.H. *Lizars' Guide to the Edinburgh, Glasgow, Paisley, Greenock, and Ayr Railways …* Edinburgh, 1842

Lloyd, Brigadier T.I., *Twilight of the Railways: What roads they'll make!* Forster Groom & Co., Ltd, 1958

Lowe, J.W., *British Steam Locomotive Builders* Goose & Son, Cambridge, 1975

McAra, D., *Sir James Gowans: Romantic Rationalist* Paul Harris Publishing, Edinburgh, 1975

Macaulay, J. & Hall, C. (eds), *Modern Railway Working* Gresham Publishing Co., 1912, 8 vols.

McGregor, J., *The West Highland Railway: Plans, Politics and People* John Donald, Edinburgh, 2005

McKillop, N., *Enginemen Elite* Ian Allan Ltd, 1958

Macmillan, N.S.C., *The Campbeltown & Machrihanish Light Railway* Plateway Press, Brighton, 1993

McNaughton, D., *The Elgin or Charlestown Railway 1762–1863* Dunfermline, 1986

Macassey, L.L. & Scott, W., *Report on Proposed Railway Tunnel between Scotland and Ireland* Harrison & Sons, n.d. but National Library of Scotland copy is bound in with pamphlets dating from the 1860s.

Marshall, C.F. Dendy, *A History of Railway Locomotives down to the end of the year 1831* Locomotive Publishing Co. Ltd. 1953

Marshall, J., *Biographical Dictionary of Railway Engineers*, Railway & Canal Historical Society, Oxford, 2003

Marshall, P.F., *The Scottish Central Railway* Oakwood Press, Usk, 1998

Martin, D., *The Garnkirk & Glasgow Railway* Strathkelvin District Libraries and Museums, 1981

Martin, D., *The Monkland & Kirkintilloch and Associated Railways* Strathkelvin District Libraries andMuseums, Kirkintilloch, 1995

Middlemass, T., *Mainly Scottish Steam* David & Charles, Newton Abbot, 1973

Mitchell, J., *Reminiscences of my Life in the Highlands* vol. II, David & Charles (Publishers) Ltd, Newton Abbot, 1971 (first published 1884)

Mountain, Moor and Loch illustrated by pen and pencil on the route of the West Highland Railway, Sir Joseph Causton & Sons, 1894

Morgan, B. (ed.), *The Railway-Lover's Companion* Eyre & Spottiswoode, 1963

Mullay, A.J., *Rail Centres: Edinburgh* Booklaw Publications, Nottingham, 2004

Mullay, A.J., *Rails across the Border* Patrick Stephens Ltd, Wellingborough, 1990

Mullay, A.J., *Scottish Region: A History 1948– 1973* Tempus Publishing Ltd, Stroud, 2006

Murray, D., *The York Buildings Company* Bratton Publishing Ltd, Edinburgh, 1973 (first published 1883)

New Opportunities for the Railways: The Privatisation of British Rail HMSO for The Department of Transport, 1992

New Statistical Account of Scotland Blackwood, Edinburgh, 1842 (*NSA*)

Newlands, Alex., *The British Railways* Longmans Green & Co., 1936

Nicolson, M., *Glasgow: Locomotive Builder to Britain* Glasgow City Libraries and Archives, Glasgow, 1998

Nicolson, M. and O'Neill, M., *Glasgow: Locomotive Builder to the World*, Polygon Books, Edinburgh, 1987

Nicolson, N., *Lord of the Isles* Weidenfeld & Nicolson, 1960

Nock, O.S., *Scottish Railways* Thomas Nelson & Sons Ltd, 1950

Nock, O.S., *Steam Locomotive: A Retrospect of the Work of Eight Great Locomotive Engineers* British Transport Commission, 1958

Nock, O.S., *The Caledonian Railway* Ian Allan Ltd, 1961

Nock, O.S., *The Railway Race to the North* Ian Allan Ltd, 2nd ed., 1962

Oxford Dictionary of National Biography, Oxford University Press, Oxford, 2004

Passenger Transport for Glasgow and District (report of the Glasgow and District Transport Committee or 'The Inglis Report'), British Transport Commission, Edinburgh, 1951

Pendleton, J., *Our Railways: their origin, development, incident and romance* Cassell, 1894

Pennant, T., *A Tour in Scotland … 1772* Birlinn Ltd, Edinburgh, 1998 (first published in 1776)

Pratt, E.A., *Scottish Canals and Waterways …* Selwyn & Blount, 1922

Priestley, J., *Priestley's Navigable Rivers and Canals*, David & Charles, Newton Abbot, 1969 (facsimile of 1831 edition)

Radford, J.B., *The American Pullman Cars of the Midland Railway* Ian Allan Ltd, 1984

Rail Data Book Avon Anglia Publications, Weston-super-Mare, 1980

Railway Heritage Act, 1996

Railways Act, 2005

Ransom, P. J. G., *Loch Lomond and the Trossachs in History and Legend* John Donald, Edinburgh, 2004

Ransom, P. J. G. *Narrow Gauge Steam: its origins and world-wide development* Oxford Publishing Co., Sparkford, 1996

Ransom, P. J. G. *Scottish Steam Today*, Richard Drew Publishing, Glasgow, 1989

Ransom, P. J. G. *Snow, Flood and Tempest: Railways and Natural disasters* Ian Allan Publishing, Hersham, 2001

Ransom, P. J. G. *The Archaeology of Railways* World's Work Ltd, Tadworth, 1981

Ransom, P. J. G. *The Archaeology of the Transport Revolution 1750–1850* World's Work Ltd, Tadworth, 1984

Ransom, P. J. G. *The Mont Cenis Fell Railway* Twelveheads Press, Truro, 1999

Ransom, P. J. G. *The Victorian Railway and How It Evolved* William Heinemann Ltd, 1990

Reorganisation of the Nationalized Transport Undertakings Ministry of Transport/HMSO, 1960

Report of the Rural Transport (Scotland) Committee, 1919

Reports of Proceedings of the Annual General Meetings of the London Midland & Scottish Railway, 1924–37, private collection

Reports of the Committee of Management of the Monkland & Kirkintilloch Railway Company, Mitchell Library, Glasgow, accession no. 53156

Reports of the Committee of Management of the Ballochney Railway, Mitchell Library, Glasgow, accession no. 53155

Robertson, C. J. A., *The Origins of the Scottish Railway System, 1722–1844* John Donald Publishers Ltd, Edinburgh, 1983

Rolt, L. T. C., *George and Robert Stephenson*, Penguin Books, 1978

Rolt, L. T. C., *Red for Danger* Pan Books Ltd, 1971 (first edition, John Lane 1955)

Rolt, L. T. C. and Whitehouse, P. B., *Lines of Character* Constable, 1952

Ross, D., *The Highland Railway* Tempus Publishing Ltd, Stroud, 2005

Ross, J., *The Spey Viaduct*, Great North of Scotland Railway Association, 2006

SPT Statistics & Trends 2005 Strathclyde Passenger Transport Executive, Glasgow, 2005

Sanderson, M. H. B., *The Scottish Railway Story* HMSO for the Scottish Record Office, Edinburgh, 1992

Scotland HMSO for Central Office of Information, 1974

Scotland Route Utilisation Strategy, Network Rail, 2007

Scotland's National Transport Strategy Scottish Executive, Edinburgh, 2006

Scotland's Railways Scottish Executive, Edinburgh, 2006

Scotland's Transport Future: The transport white paper Scottish Executive, Edinburgh, 2004

Scottish Steam Passenger Services Scottish Railfans, Edinburgh 1965

Scottish Transport Statistics: No. 25 –2006 Edition consulted on www.scottishexecutive.gov.uk, January 2007

Second Report of the House of Commons Select Committee on Transport, 1918

Sharman, M., *The Crampton Locomotive* author, Swindon, 1983

Simmons, J., *The Railways of Britain* Routledge & Kegan Paul, 1965

Simmons, J., and Biddle, G. (eds), *The Oxford Companion to British Railway History* Oxford University Press, Oxford, 1997

Simms, W. F., *Railways of Sutherland* author, Rustington, 1998

Sinclair, Sir J. (ed.), *The Statistical Account of Scotland*, 21 vols, Edinburgh, William Creech, 1791–9

Skeat, W. O., *George Stephenson: The Engineer and his Letters* Institution of Mechanical Engineers, 1973

Smiles, S. *Lives of the Engineers with an account of their principal works* vol. III *George and Robert Stephenson*, John Murray, 1862

Smith, D. L., *Tales of the Glasgow and South Western Railway* Ian Allan Ltd, 1962

Smith, R. I., *Rail Freight in Moray* Leopard Magazine Publishing, Aberdeen, 2000

Smout, T. C., *A Century of the Scottish People 1830–1950* Harper-Collins, 1997

Snell, S., *A Story of Railway Pioneers: being an account of the inventions and works of Isaac Dodds and his son, Thomas Weatherburn Dodds* Selwyn & Blount Ltd, 1921

Spooner, C. E., *Narrow Gauge Railways* E. & F. N. Spon, 1879

Stephen, R. D., *Steam Supreme: recollections of Scottish railways in the 1920s* D. Bradford Barton Ltd, Truro, 1980

Stephenson Locomotive Society, *The Glasgow and South Western Railway 1850–1923* SLS, 1950

Stevenson, R. (ed.), 'Essays on Rail-roads, presented to the Highland Society' in *Prize Essays and Transactions of the Highland Society of Scotland*, vol. 6, Edinburgh, 1824

Stevenson, R., *Report relative to various lines of railway, from the coal-field of Mid-lothian to the City of Edinburgh and the port of Leith …* P. Neill, Edinburgh, 1819

Stewart, V. & Chadwick, V., *Changing Trains: Messages for Management from the ScotRail Challenge* David & Charles, Newton Abbot, 1987

Stirling Alloa Kincardine Route Re-opening (leaflet) Babtie Group, Glasgow, 2002

Stirling, D., *The Bo'ness & Kinneil Railway Guide Book*, Scottish Railway Preservation Society, Bo'ness, *c.* 2000

Strategic Priorities for Scotland's Passenger Railway Scottish Executive, Edinburgh, Consultation Paper, 2000; Response to Consultation Paper, 2001

Stroud, J., *Railway Air Services* Ian Allan Ltd, 1987

Summerside, T., *Anecdotes, Reminiscences and Conversations of and with the late George Stephenson …* Bemrose and Sons, 1879

The Case for Rail in the Highlands and Islands, report prepared by Steer Davies Gleave, Edinburgh for Highlands and Islands Enterprise, Inverness, 2004

The development of the major railway trunk routes British Railways Board, 1965

The Forth Bridge (leaflet B.R. 35028) British Rail (Scotland), 1984

The Railway Year Book for 1922 Railway Publishing Co. Ltd., 1922

The Reshaping of British Railways ('The Beeching Report') HMSO for BRB, 1963

Thomas, J., *Forgotten Railways: Scotland* David & Charles, Newton Abbot, 1981

Thomas, J., *Scottish Railway History in Pictures* David & Charles, Newton Abbot,1967

Thomas, J., *The Callander & Oban Railway* David & Charles, Newton Abbot, 1966

Thomas, J., *The North British Railway* David & Charles, Newton Abbot, vol. 1 1969, vol. 2, 1975

Thomas, J., and Turnock, D., *A Regional History of the Railways of Great Britain* vol. 15 *The North of Scotland* David St John Thomas/David & Charles, Newton Abbot, 1989

Thomas, J., revised Farrington, J., *The Skye Railway* David St John Thomas/David & Charles, Newton Abbot, 1990

Thomas, J., revised Paterson, A.J.S., *A Regional History of the Railways of Great Britain* vol. 6 *Scotland: the Lowlands and the Borders* David St John Thomas/David & Charles, Newton Abbot, 1984

Thomas, J., with extra material by Paterson, A.J.S. and Ransom, P.J.G., *The West Highland Railway* fourth edition, House of Lochar, Colonsay, 1998

Tomlinson, W.W., *The North Eastern Railway: its rise and development* Andrew Reid & Co. Ltd, Newcastle upon Tyne, 1914

Transport Act, 1947 (10 & 11 Geo. 6. Ch. 49)

Transport Act, 1962 (10 & 11 Eliz. 2 Ch. 46)

Transport Act, 1968 (1968 Ch. 73)

Transport Act (Scotland), 1989 (1989 c. 23)

Transport Policy HMSO for Ministry of Transport, 1966

Transport (Scotland) Act, 2005

Transport Services in the Highlands and Islands (Report of the Highland Transport Enquiry) HMSO, 1963

Universal Directory of Railway Officials and Year Book 1946–1947 Directory Publishing Co. Ltd., 1946

Vallance, H.A., revised by Great North of Scotland Railway Association, *The Great North of Scotland Railway* David St John Thomas/David & Charles, 1989

Vallance, H.A., revised by Clinker, C.R., *The Highland Railway* Pan Books Ltd., 1972

Warren, J.G.H., *A Century of Locomotive Building by Robert Stephenson & Co. 1823–1923* David & Charles, Newton Abbot, 1970 (facsimile of original 1923 edition)

Watters, B., *Where Iron Runs Like Water!* John Donald Publishers Ltd, Edinburgh, 1998

Wear, R., *Barclay 150* Hunslet–Barclay Ltd, Kilmarnock, 1990

Webster, N.W., *Britain's First Trunk Line: The Grand Junction Railway* Adams & Dart, Bath, 1972

Whishaw, F., *The Railways of Great Britain and Ireland* David & Charles (Publishers) Ltd, Newton Abbot, 1969 (facsimile of original edition of 1842)

Williams, F.S., *The Midland Railway: its rise and progress* author, Nottingham, 5th edition, 1886

Williams, F.S. *Our Iron Roads: Their History, Construction and Administration*, Gresham Books, Woking, 1981 (reproduction of third edition of 1883)

Wilson, H.S., *T.P.O.: A History of the Travelling Post Offices of Great Britain*, part 3, *Scotland and Ireland* Railway Philatelic Group, Leicester, 1977

Wolmar, C., *Broken Rails: How Privatisation Wrecked Britain's Railways* Aurum Press, 2nd edition, November 2001

Wood, J.L., *Building Railways* National Museums of Scotland, Edinburgh, 1996

Wood, N., *A Practical Treatise on Railroads …* Longman, Orme, Brown, Green and Longmans, 3rd ed. 1838

100 Years of Electrification 1898–1998 Strathclyde Passenger Transport, Glasgow, 1998

PERIODICALS ETC.

Back Track

Blackwood's Edinburgh Magazine

Bradshaw's Railway Companion

Bradshaw's Railway Guide

Blastpipe (Scottish Railway Preservation Society)

British Transport Review

Dundee Courier

Edinburgh Evening Courant

Edinburgh Waverley Infrastructure Works Newsletter (Network Rail)

Engineering

Hansard

Glasgow Courier

Glasgow Herald

Journal of the North British Railway Study Group

Journal of the Railway & Canal Historical Society

Mechanics' Magazine

Minutes of Proceedings of the Institution of Civil Engineers

Modern Railways

National Railway Museum Review

Outlook (ScotRail Railways Ltd)

Railway Archive

Railway Philately (Railway Philatelic Group)

Railway World

Scotland on Sunday

Sou'West Journal (Glasgow & South Western Railway Association)

Stirling Observer

Sunday Times

The Civil Engineer and Architect's Journal

The Daily Telegraph

The Herald

The Illustrated London News

The Narrow Gauge (Narrow Gauge Railway
    Society)
The Oban Times
The Railway Magazine
The Scots Magazine
The Scotsman
The Scottish Historical Review
The Sphere
The Times
The True Line (Caledonian Railway Association)
Trains Illustrated
Transactions of the Newcomen Society
Transport History

INDEX

Entries for the principal railway undertakings appear in this index only where there is a specific reference to the history of that undertaking, such as formation, amalgamation, etc. References to other features, such as locomotives, coaches, stations, publicity, railway-owned bus services and so on are indexed according to subject. The undertakings concerned are: Caledonian Railway; North British Railway; Glasgow & South Western Railway; Great North of Scotland Railway; London Midland & Scottish Railway; London & North Eastern Railway; British Railways; Scottish Region; British Rail; Railtrack; Network Rail.